The Age of
Information

The Age of Information

Information

The past development and future significance
of computing and communications.

STEPHEN SAXBY

NEW YORK UNIVERSITY PRESS
Washington Square, New York

Printed in Great Britain

First published in the U.S.A. in 1990 by
NEW YORK UNIVERSITY PRESS
Washington Square, New York, NY 10003

Library of Congress Cataloging-in-Publication Data

Saxby, Stephen.
    The age of information: the past development and future
    significance of computing and communications/Stephen Saxby.
       p.   cm.
    Includes bibliographical references.
    ISBN 0-8147-7922-0
    1. Computers and civilization.   2. Information technology − Social
    aspects.   I. Title
    QA76.9.C66S29 1991
    303.48′34 − cc20   90−19166
                                                        CIP

For Susan
and my parents

Contents

Preface

This book started life as an introduction to computers and communications for law students studying my course in Information Technology Law at Southampton University. Having taught the course for 10 years I was always struck by the fascination the students had about the development of the technology, soon to be overtaken by an overwhelming fear about where to start. For them it was just too forbidding and technical to get into. Once I had reached about 25,000 words I realised that I was probably writing another book and so decided to press on. I was motivated to do so by a further impression gained while being Editor of *The Computer Law and Security Report*, namely, that many of today's IT users seem locked in the here-and-now in their use of technology. Today's user is confronted by a mountain of hype and terminology to deal with as well as a myriad of standards to follow. There seems little opportunity to push away all this and to stand back and reflect upon how IT has entrenched itself in our lives. Even society has gone through a metamorphosis, emerging as the 'Information Society'. For me the fundamental difference about digital information technology, that sets it apart from everything else, is the discovery that data can be represented in a language that can be read by a machine. The further discovery of the means to translate voice, text, data and imagery into the same language, and to transmit that at the speed of light, will produce unstoppable change. Today, the 'supercomputer on a chip' is an acceptable proposition and an integrated digital telecommunications network looms that will soon span the entire globe.

By comparison with all this, anyone who left school in 1975 would have done so just as the first personal computers were developing and at a time when microprocessor technology was in its infancy. Fifteen years later, those same individuals now work in a technological environment that has rapidly moved on. Despite the obvious gap between those people's formal education and current experience, and no doubt others' too, the evidence from surveys continues to point to the low priority being given to IT training in employment and to the lack of awareness at board level of the strategic importance of information technology within an organisation. Given the pace of technological change it has always surprised me that anyone could entrust the critical functions of their business to the care of the technology, yet not fully prepare either management or workforce for its implications.

I hope that this book will provide information that is both instructive and worth knowing, and will be of some help to all those who are intimidated by the technology, and who feel they are on the outside looking in. I have tried to provide the historical background to the subject as well as an account of its modern elements. Throughout I have attempted to explain how the technology works and how it fits together, in a language that the non-technical person, like myself, should understand. I have deliberately avoided any discussion of policy towards regulation, concentrating simply on the development of information technology as I see it unfold. The book is intended to be used an 'information source' and not to be approached as a philosophical treatise. I hope it will appeal as much to the user of information technology as it may the student trying to gain a foothold in the subject. For this reason I have provided extensive references to the sources I used, so that these can be followed up where necessary. Where I have expressed private opinions I believe them to be defensible, even though, as a lawyer, my perspective may not be perfectly in tune with the opinions of the experts in those fields. The book is nothing more, of course, than a snapshot of developments as I perceive them up to mid-1990. Although events will rapidly move on, it is no bad thing to put a marker down at this point – at the start of the decade culminating in the millennium.

Stephen Saxby
Southampton University
July 1990

ix

Acknowledgements

I am grateful to a number of people who supported me during the writing of the book. First of all to my family – my wife Susan and my three children Rosalyn, Matthew and Eleanor – who had to put up with the constant presence of 'the book' until it was finished. Next, there were the people who helped me gather my sources, including my parents, Vera Wilson, Joan Hoyle and Andrew Schulkins. A big 'thankyou' as well to my friend and secretary Daphne McGinley for undertaking the day-to-day management of the project, sorting out the computer files and helping me with the research and correspondence. Then there were the people who commented upon the draft or gave advice, including my students in the 1989/90 IT law course, Rik Kaspersen, Wendy London, David Davies, David Barrett and Gillian Bull. Finally my thanks to The Macmillan Press and particularly to Rosemary Foster and Hugh Jones for the encouragement they gave and for their faith in the project.

CHAPTER 1

The changing value
of information in the
information society

INTRODUCTION

THE INFORMATION REVOLUTION   Information technology, as many com-
mentators have observed, is in the process of evoking fundamental change
in the character of our society.[1] After a short period of uncertainty, during
which it was perceived that a shift was taking place from 'industrial' to
'post-industrial' society, the nature of that change has become apparent.
The point has been grasped that since information is rapidly becoming the
driving force behind the industrial development of nations,[2] the most
appropriate characterisation to depict that process in the community is by
the expression 'information society'. The change that is taking place has
been described in the following terms by a report of the US Congress,
Office of Technology Assessment (OTA), published in 1986:

> 'Like the printing press, the new information technologies also affect society.
> They are changing the way people work and conduct their business; how they
> interact and relate to one another; the way they learn, create and process
> information, and their needs and expectations. In fact, these new technolo-
> gies are altering the way man views himself and his place in the world.
> Together, the development and widespread use of these new technologies
> have helped to usher in what some social observers characterize as . . .
> "information" society. In this society, the creation, use and communication
> of information plays a central role. Not only will the amount of information

1

continue to increase, but people will also rely on it more and more and in different circumstances. The changes brought on by the new technologies will generate new social, economic and cultural opportunities and choices, which will bring with them the need for major policy decisions.'[3]

Throughout the history of mankind the communication of information[4] has provided the raw material for societal development. It is a trite remark, but nevertheless true, that had methods of conveying meaning and imparting information not been developed, society would have stood still. It is easy, therefore, to be misled into believing that the modern information technology 'revolution' is the first to enable information to be stored, processed, transmitted and accessed by technological means. This is not so, although it is the first to achieve this by electronics-based means. Whereas communication in pre-industrial society was predominantly organised by the kinship or similar grouping, in the information society the communication infrastructure operates through a web of new technology.[5] Within that lies a uniqueness and a potential that outstrips all previous technological advances so far as the movement and exploitation of information is concerned,[6] for it is the first of the information technologies to develop a capacity for processing information automatically.[7]

Prior advances in the development of language, writing, printing and electromagnetic communication were of major significance, not only in their immediate impact, but in their contribution to the staging process that led to the digital representation of information capable of being 'read' by a machine. The story behind the evolution of communication has been one of expansion in the range, capacity, speed and value of what is conveyed. Early man communicated basic survival skills by demonstration, or by primitive language or drawings to those proximate to it. Such information was also conveyed by time to succeeding generations via limited forms of record, through drawings or etchings and subsequently by writing. Two thousand years ago information travelled as fast as the caravans of pedlars and tradesmen who brought news of conquest and discovery gathered from their journey and the people they met at the intersections along the way. Information delivered by this method was likely to be inaccurate or incomplete since much of it relied upon transmission by word of mouth. As information began to be disseminated in the written form, offering greater scope for accuracy in the provision of a facility for setting things down in more detail, the keys to knowledge depended upon the power to access the material and to read one of the ancient languages. Later, printing and the development of transport and of common language led to improvements in the distribution of information. Such factors increased the volume of information available, the means of access to it, its currency and its potential value. A further development took place when information began to be communicated by beacon and subsequently by telegraph, telephone, wireless, film and television, for these innovations meant that access to information was no longer dependent upon physical access to the storage medium as such, but rather upon the communication process itself. These methods, however, provided no comprehensive means of obtaining information fixed in a permanent form by persons neither physically in possession of, nor proximate to, the information-carrying medium. The first machines to render this possible, facilitating admittance to large volumes of stored information to individuals remotely connected to it, were computers.

Information Technology Effects Change Fundamental to this discussion is what it is that makes modern information technology so much more important a development than any other in the history of technological evolution. The answer, in simple terms, is its capacity to effect change. It has provided a stimulus that can be seen not just in terms of new products, services, wealth and success for the richer nations, but in the far-reaching implications for business methods, design and manufacturing techniques and the way individuals interact, travel, entertain themselves, obtain information and communicate. It has introduced degrees of automation and precision in design and manufacturing, in the gathering and analysis of data and in the methods deployed in research and development, that have not been possible before. It has also transformed expectations about what man can achieve with technology and has so increased political interest in the development of policies that will later determine how choices are made.

The clue to understanding how this has occurred lies in contemplating the enormous implications of what underpins the entire information technology revolution: the digital representation of numbers and the consequent ability to perform accurate, repeatable manipulations of those numbers to produce and convey meaning.[8] The result has been graphically described thus:

'With digitization all of the media become translatable into each other – computer bits migrate merrily – and they escape from their traditional means of transmission . . . If that's not revolution enough, with digitization the content becomes totally plastic – any message, sound, or image may be edited from anything into anything else.'[9]

The ability to represent and indeed create and convey stored information in this form has freed the message from the carrying medium.[10] Automation of these processes has made access to and distribution of information significantly more effective and precise, as well as introducing the prospect of producing high-grade timely computer-generated information for selected purposes and users. But the mere storage and transmission of information in digital form would not, by itself, have achieved the societal impact already described, for the result would be no more than an improvement in the techniques for accomplishing those tasks that began with the use of language and of record. There is a second feature of the new information technologies that is of supreme importance to an understanding of their phenomenal potential: the ability of machines automatically to read and process data and execute instructions that are in digital form. Computers are capable of manipulating and rearranging any data stored electronically, using the type of arithmetic/logical concepts that a child learns at school: viz., add, compare and shift.

The speed with which state-of-the-art technology carries out these operations and the complex techniques that have been devised to exploit this capacity have produced an extremely powerful and versatile machine, whose function is conditioned by the context in which the above processes take place inside the machine. As a result, the world has seen the expansion of the technology and its penetration into practically every field of economic activity. Indeed the technology is very much a product of its own success, for today it would be unthinkable not to deploy it in research and development in the design of new hardware and software components. The position today compared with the past has been described thus:

> 'whereas in Edison's day invention was one percent inspiration and ninety-nine percent perspiration, today's digital information system inventions are about one half inspiration and the other half perspiration'.[11]

THE ENHANCED VALUE OF INFORMATION   An essential consequence of the development of computer technology has been the change that has occurred in the character of information, which has blurred the dividing line between ideas and expression, embodiment and function. In terms of the use of information, until the discovery that data could be represented in a form that a machine could read and act upon, it was thought that an unimpeachable distinction existed between the description of the data and its implementation. Information describing a procedure or a process could, for example, be recorded as in an instruction manual for car maintenance or a cookery book. To exploit that information, however, would require human intervention through the individual carrying out the repair or following the recipe. Otherwise the information would remain a passive asset, descriptive but not in itself functional until implemented. Alternatively the information might be translated into a physical form that embodied it as part of a machine or mechanism intended to perform some function. The exploitation or implementation of the value of such information occurred when it was acted upon, either within the intrinsic design of a mechanism, as with a cam or spindle, or as part of a physical process such as measurement or control.[12] Modern information technology is arguably breaching that distinction with computers that can both read data and act upon instructions independently of human intervention. The key functional component is the computer program embedded in a silicon chip or other digital medium. The instructions which operate on the data cannot now be distinguished from the latter as both are represented as binary code in digital form. In the words of the 1986 OTA Report:

'Modern technology has created a new class of functional works. They are hybrids of those works of function that physically implement processes and those that describe processes. Computer programs are hybrid functional works insofar as they employ words and symbols to implement and control a process. Although understandable by humans, computer programs also initiate and control processes or procedures by operating electronic switches in a computer. These switches may, in turn, control other machines or devices.'[13]

The Universal Machine   Thus it could be said that society is in the process of developing a 'universal machine', the concept of which was first envisaged by Alan Turing, one of the pioneers of computer theory. A universal machine is one that is capable of replicating the behaviour of all other machines whose functions can be formally specified. This is achieved by translating the 'information content' of the machine, otherwise expressed within its physical embodiment, into a digital form that the computer can use to simulate and thereby effect the operation of the physical system of the other machine. It does so through formalising the procedure or process into a logical sequence which, when implemented in digital form, can be performed by the computer.[14] In reality the 'computer', as such, is to be found within the circuitry of the silicon chip. Thus today, the computer on the chip finds its way into thousands of machines, from flight simulators to

5

microwave ovens and from digital car washes to the engine chips that monitor and control the performance of racing cars in the course of a grand prix. The process has now gone 'full circle' in the sense that electronics designers use information technology to 'simulate' the process of machine design up to the point when the latter, planned on the computer screen, becomes the reality in the finished product.

It is arguable, then, that society is moving from the 'hard' to the 'soft' machine, in which functionality is independent of physical embodiment – at least to the extent that the logical operations performed by cams or cogs are now executed by the ordered activation or closure of electronic switches in a computer. (This distinction was first used to describe the stored-program digital computer in which the program was conceptually separate from the hardware. In the very first computers instructional changes could only be effected by physical rewiring of the circuitry itself; later this was accomplished by computer software without human intervention.) It must be said, of course, that the soft machine – the method whereby a process or procedure is implemented by the orchestration of those electronic switches through machine-readable programmable instructions – could not function unless it was built into or connected to the physical 'hardware' necessary to perform the operations specified by it.[15] This is accepted, but what has changed is the method by which the machine function is implemented and controlled. Those parts of a machine that physically embody its logical operation within the wider physical construct can now be reproduced by activating the digital representation of that operation as set out within the computer program.

A current illustration of this can be seen in the gradual replacement by British Telecom of its ageing electro-mechanical telephone exchanges. 1989 was the 100th anniversary of the Strowger telephone exchange. In 1889 a Kansas City undertaker named Almon Strowger, who discovered that he was losing business because the local telephone operator was married to a competitor, patented his invention for the automatic switching of a telephone call to a particular destination. It involved a selector mechanism containing a wheel with a series of notches, upon which rested a metal finger connected to an armature attached to a shaft. The switch was activated by the operation and release of an electromagnet which would cause the wheel to turn to a particular point, causing connection to be made to a single telephone unit without the intervention of the human operator. The Strowger system was further perfected and became widely used in exchanges throughout the world. Currently, the ageing stock of

Strowger exchanges, built in the UK from 1912 onwards, are being replaced by digital exchanges which do away with the banks of conventional switching equipment and the miles of intricate wiring attached to it. Instead, rows of blue and grey cabinets housing printed circuit boards containing silicon chips, together with computer screens and keyboards for monitoring performance, replace, in a fraction of the space, what used to take up two floors of intensely crowded electro-mechanical equipment. The change lies in the fact that the electro-mechanical technique adopted by Strowger in his device, which in turn replaced the human operator, is now carried out by a programmable chip. But it is not simply a question of introducing a cleaner and more compact method of achieving the same, for the new digital exchanges are more powerful and versatile, offering a range of additional services for the customer.[16] Maintenance is also much simpler, since if a fault occurs, the card controlling that particular line is replaced with another, and the problem card is sent away for repair.

The universality of the soft machine is not, therefore, to be found in the performance of functions, as such, but in the capacity of modern information technology to replicate the underlying logical characteristics of any systems that process information when activated, often providing additional enhancements and improvements along the way.[17] Since the human brain is the prime example of a mechanism that processes information, the challenge is now to see whether it is possible to simulate artificially the physiology and operational processes of the brain that provide the environment for brain function and, therefore, for human intelligence.

NEW TECHNOLOGY HAS SET INFORMATION FREE   One point that that has been touched upon but perhaps not fully articulated is the significance of being able to represent and define information in a variety of forms. Mathematics, for example, has existed since the civilisations of antiquity, as an elegant means of establishing relations between objects and entities. Pythagoras described numbers as the language of nature and it is clear that people have been using numbers since time immemorial. It is thought that the cultures that created the Hanging Gardens of Babylon and the Egyptian pyramids knew and employed many formulae. It is of course the application of binary arithmetic to electronics that has led to the development of computers.

Until the development of permanent forms of record in digital form, information was invariably stored on paper. This has been the case for almost 2000 years. Storage in a form that can be read by a computer has

7

not only introduced the prospect of automated processing of information but has interposed a machine between the individual and access to the information. The concept of document image processing, whereby documents are scanned automatically and stored upon optical disk for subsequent retrieval, begins to offer a potentially cheaper alternative to paper-based storage media.

This change in the character of the medium whereby information can be stored and retrieved was considered, in 1986, by the Scottish Law Commission in a study on computer crime.[18] It concluded that the advent of computerisation has had the effect of transferring to the realm of unembodied or intangible form many things such as files, records, plans or designs which in the past were possessed with a tangible and material existence. (From a legal perspective this is the distinction between corporeal and incorporeal property.) Apart from recognising the necessity for a thorough re-appraisal of the law in the light of this trend, the study also considered that the change raised social, political, moral and social factors as well.

One result of this development is that proving the original content of a document is not as simple a task, when it is held electronically, as when it is written down on a piece of paper. Verifying the truth of the record and checking to ensure no unauthorised alteration has occurred is dependent upon being satisfied that the computer is working properly and that any audit of computer use thereafter produces no discrepancies that might degrade the record.

Whereas in the past, much information held on computer was replicated on paper, today an increasing amount of information is only held in machine-readable form with no back-up paper copy available. To return to the example of the replacement of the Strowger telephone exchange in favour of the new digital alternative, described above, it used to be the case that when a call was made, the meter for the telephone concerned, displayed at the exchange, visibly clocked up the units consumed by the subscriber during the call. When the time came for billing to take place it was a simple matter of reading the number of units displayed by the meter and translating this into a bill for the customer. Now, no meters are retained since the digital exchange will automatically hold this information in computer storage to be called up when required. No other record is maintained. There is, of course, a potential advantage to be gained by this method as it allows for much more accurate information to be given about the calls made and, with proper measures taken, offers a degree of security that surpasses the protection that might be afforded to manual or mechanical records. But it also means, assuming access is gained electronically, that unauthorised amendment to the record, or mistakes or errors otherwise entered, are liable to become harder to detect and correct.

Computer storage of information also raises questions as to who shall have access to information held in this form and what rights shall be enjoyed in it. Information technology can be seen to have complicated the process whereby rights are granted to authors and inventors, introducing new parties into the arena and changing the roles that people involved in the copyright system play. It has also made the copying, transfer and manipulation of information cheaper, quicker and more private, rendering the enforcement of intellectual property rights more difficult to achieve.[19] Technology can now deliver very high-grade and frequently up-to-the-minute information which in the financial markets, for example, could make all the difference between a profitable and a loss-making transaction. Such possibilities therefore raise the stakes concerning access and control over such information.

There are obviously considerable benefits to be gained by fixing as much information in machine-readable form as possible. Costs of processing, storing, retrieving and communicating information will be less, offering increasing scope for effective and efficient decision-making based on the increased volume of information available. Clearly, for example, in the event of an accident it would be advantageous for everyone to carry a card containing personal information within a magnetic stripe that might be of help in the aftermath, viz., name, address, next of kin, blood type, doctor's and employer's name and address, any medical condition or medicines being taken, any allergies, etc. However, looking at the dangers which such a card presents, the information it contains could be extremely valuable, were it to fall into the wrong hands. It is the digital form in which the information is held that makes it more vulnerable, particularly if the information is held centrally, since it could be accessed, read and copied in that form without the knowledge of the card-holder. Computer-stored information, not available in any other format, could also become an instrument of power, as during an industrial dispute where strikers move first to shut down the employer's computer operations.

A measure of the reliance that society places on systems that store and process digital information is to look and see what happens when a malfunction occurs. When the ageing London air traffic control computer at West Drayton broke down on several occasions in 1988–89, this brought

9

chaos to air services throughout Europe. In addition, there have been numerous reported examples of major losses incurred by the banking sector, local authorities and business organisations when operator errors or program malfunctions have caused computer systems to act upon false information or instructions making wrongful payments or incorrect demands or delivering incorrect quantities or types of goods to either the right or the wrong destination. Tragically there have also been instances of death caused by computers acting upon the wrong instructions or malfunctioning during operation. Such incidents have occurred in the case of aircraft programmed to follow an incorrect flight path or medical systems designed to monitor patient recovery and to control the intravenous flow of drugs into the body. In all these instances it has been the imposition of the computer between the individual and the information, capable of interpreting information, acting upon instructions or denying access to the results, that has led to the problem at hand. Equally, it has been the ability to define information in a form that can be read by a machine that has made the advances possible that have collectively advanced society to its present stage of development.

DISCIPLINARY PERSPECTIVES ON INFORMATION

Before moving forward it would be helpful to an understanding of this discussion to focus a little more closely upon the definition of information, which differs in relation to the context in which the term is applied. Most people, if confronted by the question 'how would you define Information?' would offer the kind of answer found in the dictionary, namely by referring to the act of informing or the condition of being informed; communication of knowledge or knowledge derived from study, experience or instruction. In that very general sense, each one of us both gives and receives information many times a day. It is done through the medium of everyday language and symbols transmitted by word of mouth, through the printed or written word or by modern means of communication. (Separating the act of communication from the information being transmitted is difficult, though, for information relies on communication to fulfil its value.)[20]

To accept such a general description of the term remains patently unsatisfactory, however, given that information is the central value upon which the information technology revolution is based. In particular, the

10

distinction between information and data and how it is addressed by the disciplines of philosophy, mathematics, economics and law must be discussed.

The distinction between information and data could be equated with that between a raw material and the manufactured product. Information can be derived from data when those data are interpreted to produce meaning, and therefore the interpreter must possess the skills necessary to undertake that task and the data available must be appropriate to the user's requirements. Information is derived from data when the latter are used as part of a process, where only a proportion of the available data will be processed or converted into information. The remainder is discarded as surplus data and the information obtained transformed by prescribed action into other information. The context here could involve words and mathematical notation; it could be graphic – involving colours, figures, shapes; or audio-visual – sound, motion, words and graphic symbols.[21]

In broad terms, data refers to descriptions of actual states of entities. It could be a set of facts, events, measurements, opinions or value judgements which, as passive descriptive data, comprise the database from which information is derived.[22]

The data may describe the performance, objectively, of a machine, physical process, social group or business or represent the responses to questions concerning attitudes to a particular matter at a given time. Alternatively, they may be measurements of individuals or groups in a defined context.[23]

The extent to which the data become meaningful as information depends on the extent to which the recipient of the data can interpret and apply them. In a general sense, information does not cease to be information because an individual recipient cannot recognise it as such; for example, because he cannot understand the language or does not know the algorithm necessary to unlock the information, such as knowledge of how latitude and longitude work in map reading or what the symbols mean in mathematics. Used in this sense information assumes the character of knowledge. However, it could equally be said that, in the absence of recognition, the data have not been processed and therefore no information has been disclosed. (The building of the first motor vehicle might suggest that the possibility of its being built had always existed. However, it would be foolish to suggest that the information needed to build it existed, say, 2000 years ago.) In a recent study the distinction has been analysed further.[24] Catala notes that to regard data as merely the basis of information is misleading, as data are increasingly the products of information stored in a computer and transformed by the data processing operation. He prefers to see data not simply as antecedent to the processing but also the result of it. In consequence he sees data in relation to information as that of 'the part to the whole, or of the element to the ensemble'.

THE PHILOSOPHICAL VIEW   As has been said, the meaning ascribed to the term 'information' varies according to branch of knowledge in which the expression is used. In philosophy, the concept of information is linked to theories of knowledge, in the philosophical analysis of such questions as 'What can be known?' and 'How can we know what we know?' and 'What is the distinction between knowledge and belief?'. Such questions are at the core of the study of epistemology, and engage philosophers whose interests lie in metaphysics, ethics and the philosophy of science.[25] (Philosophical discussion of the nature of knowledge has practical benefits, for example in enhancing our knowledge about learning and cognition, particularly in babies, young children and those with learning difficulties. Such study looks, in part, at what concepts an individual forms in relation to the information he is exposed to, on the basis, for instance, that concepts derive their meaning from their informational origin.[26])

THE MATHEMATICAL VIEW   'Information theory' in mathematics is concerned with the measurement of the information content of a message. It was developed by communications engineers involved in the transmission of messages from one place to another, whose objective was to devise equipment to reproduce the input signal with as high fidelity as possible at the output device. Thus information theory is the study of the integrity of the content of a signal as it is transported. The theory pays no heed to the semantic content or matter of the message in question but instead concerns itself with perfecting efficient, cost effective and fast transmission systems. Finding a mechanism to measure the 'information' content of a message as opposed to its distortion ('noise') is a necessary requirement of achieving these objectives.[27]

One of the first individuals to work on the development of information theory was Shannon, who published a paper in 1948, entitled 'A Mathematical Theory of Communication'.[28] The substance of his analysis was that the most efficient system for conveying the maximum amount of information, no matter how complex the message, was by its formulation in binary code. It is of course this theory, known as the 'Sender–Receiver' model, and its use of the state of a mechanism to represent information, upon which the concept of the 'universal machine' – the computer – is based, and where information theory and electronics began to interact; the mechanism being the switching device which can exist in two states: either 'on' or 'off'.[29] The focus had shifted from the investigation of the fidelity of transmission of information to the computational means of processing it. Information theory thus broadened out beyond the study of the integrity of the content of a signal, to analysis of the practice of storing and retrieving information. This has become known as the discipline of 'information science'. Observers later perceived the strength of these investigations in the study of human intelligence which, today, has opened up a vast area of further research known as artificial intelligence, aimed to develop mechanised intelligence modelled very crudely on the processes of the human brain.[30]

Within organisations, information performs a vital function and attracts different levels of value according to its nature. It can reduce uncertainty in decision making, indicate deviation from planned performance or operation, provide a means for detailing plans, forecasts, procedures or guidelines, etc., supply historical evidence of transactions, performance levels, outcomes of decisions, etc., and reduce complexity by improving the user's knowledge and understanding of a situation.[31]

Given the recognition of the increasing value of information as a key tactical and strategic resource within an organisation, information is increasingly defined today in the context of an 'information system' which models the means whereby the organisation captures, processes, communicates and converts data to information.[32] There is much to be gained in terms of adding value to information, if the organisation treats it as a strategic resource and takes time to observe and analyse the information systems operating within. This will encourage the most favourable conditions for information to flow into and out of the organisation in a manner best-suited to its own configuration. Within this framework information is defined as 'that part of the total data available which is appropriate to the requirements of a particular user or group of users'.[33] The most effective system would be the one that succeeded in minimising the amount of data passing through the hands of the user without becoming information.

Modern information technology has enhanced the capacity of an organisation to capture and produce high-grade information or add value to its existing information assets. The new technologies have provided the impetus for a fuller exploitation of information resources within the increasingly complex environment in which an organisation must operate today. If used appropriately, they have also provided a means of handling the serious problem of the almost insatiable appetite for more and more information that an organisation, in its complexity, seems inherently to require.

THE ECONOMIC VIEW   The economic approach to 'information' sees it as a commodity that has a value in the market place. That value, of course, will vary according to a number of factors. Foremost among these will be the function of the information in terms of its value to the recipient in achieving different economic outcomes.[34] This is closely equated with knowledge; the measure, in economic terms, being the effect that possession of the information has on making appropriate choices. Possession of information that shop A is selling certain goods cheaper than shop B will be worth the difference between the two prices to the recipient purchaser, but of no personal value to a recipient who has no intent to purchase, unless the information has a sale value to someone else. Another way of putting it would be to say that if information is received, but not acted upon, resulting in no behavioural change, that particular message contained 'noise' not 'communication'. In economic terms then, information is measured by the efficiency of the economic outcomes which can be achieved by its use. This suggests that information, in the abstract, has no value but is a dimension of its use where value is measured by the efficiency of the outcome; for example the saving in price by purchasing at shop A. The economic view, therefore, limits itself only to information that, in its terms, has a value. The economic exercise will thus devote itself to the issue of pricing.[35]

In the information society certain types of information are at a premium. One key result of information technology has been the acceleration in the time taken to deliver information and the potential expansion of access to it. Intrinsically, the most valuable class of information today is that which is delivered to the recipient, as it formulates, in 'real' time. In the financial and banking communities the market responds in seconds to the latest news, whether it be an economic indicator or a particular share-price movement on Wall Street. It is well known, of course, that computers are programmed to trigger the sale of shares if a particular indicator or set of indicators is detected. Part of the blame for the rapid fall in stock market values on 'Black Monday' in October 1987 was attributed to this process, and controls were subsequently introduced in the United States to minimise the prospect of repetition. Apart from any measurement of value based upon its 'real time' characteristics, another factor in the equation is the legal status of the information.

THE LEGAL VIEW

Information as Property   The legal approach to information seeks a definition of the term that will enable any rights and liabilities to be identified and allocated. The starting point must be to enquire whether, and in what form, 'information' gives rise to property rights, either in the aggregate or totality, that can be enforced and enjoyed? Crucial to this exercise will be the concept of 'property' and the classification of 'information' for without further definition, the terminology is too vague to lend itself to the precision of legal analysis.

'Property', as with 'information', suffers from the problem that it is a commonplace English word and also a term in legal usage. At one extreme is the concept of 'absolute ownership' or 'absolute property' which, historically, although arguably mistakenly, was derived from the Roman term *dominium*.[36] This idea of *dominium* was not expanded upon by the Romans but they named it. Its chief characteristic was its indivisibility, which Austin characterised as 'a right indefinite in user, unlimited in duration and alienable by the actual owner from every successor who, in default of alienation by him, might take the right'.[37] It is suggested that the reason why the Romans did not develop the concept was that they regarded it as so original a fact that it was implicit in the nature of things. It therefore could not lend itself to analysis, either as to content or limitations: 'The owner stands in a certain relation to the material thing which he owns; and neither the nature of such relation, nor of the thing toward which it existed, was regarded by the earlier Roman jurists as a matter calling for analysis or explanation.'.[38]

The link between 'property' and *dominium* in English law was apparent in Blackstone's definition of property as: 'that sole and despotic dominion which one man claims and exercises over the external things of the world, in total exclusion of the right of any other individual in the universe'.[39] Elsewhere, however, Blackstone qualified his definition by recognising that property was subject to 'control and diminution . . . by the laws of the land'. This amendment to the original despotism of the dominion of 'property' is closer to the modern juristic view of 'property' as 'a complex which is divisible into many assortments of component rights, rather than as an integer';[40] that is, as against the intact unity of indivisible ownership. In this sense property is seen as divisible, comprising the aggregate of several independent rights; for example to possess, use, produce, waste, dispose, exclude, etc.,[41] rights which may coexist in the same person or be enjoyed by different persons according to the law of the land. In this sense such concepts as 'absolute property' or 'absolute ownership' fall away to no more than a description of the totality of these rights, not phenomena in themselves but an aggregate of independent rights.

This accords very much with the approach of the great jurist Wesley Hohfeld who argued that to talk of ownership is really to assert that the claimant is vested with a complex aggregate of 'rights, privileges, powers and immunities' that relate to the property in question. He included in this non-material property constituted, for example, in patent and copyright interests. The correlative terms of 'duty, no-right, liability and disability' in the Hohfeldian analysis classified the legal burdens corresponding to the legal benefits enjoyed.[42] To him 'property' was a term full of ambiguity and looseness:

> Sometimes it is employed to indicate the physical object to which various legal rights, privileges, etc., relate; then again – with far greater discrimination and accuracy – the word is used to denote the legal interest (or aggregate of legal relations) appertaining to such physical objects. Frequently there is a rapid and fallacious shift from the one meaning to the other. At times, also, the term is used in such a 'blended' sense as to convey no definite meaning whatever.[43]

(Hohfeld favoured treating the concept of 'property' not as physical objects owned, but as 'the subject of property' signifying the rights of the person over the thing to possess, use, enjoy, dispose of, etc., as against the corresponding exclusion of others to do the same.)

In developing some of these ideas in assessing the legal approach towards information, a sensible starting point might be to consider the relationship between information and proprietary rights. The law has never sought to reduce into possession mere ideas or statements as such even when articulated; for to do so would interfere with freedom of choice and the welfare of the human race, where culture and discovery have been built up upon the store of human knowledge available to all.

Instead the law turns its attention to the form in which information exists and allocates rights in respect of its embodiment in something else. In copyright, for example, the law allocates rights to make copies of particular tangible expressions of information. In the case of information which has been used and applied in the development of a functional work – an invention – the law grants for a period exclusive rights to make, use or sell that particular application of an idea or group of ideas.[44] In these examples human effort has been engaged interactively with information, both to use it and add value to it. The law seeks to encourage this process by encouraging reward for the producer of the work and access to the world at large. Recently, however, as already discussed, the development of modern information technology has tended to confuse the distinction between information and form, since expression, that at one moment may be descriptive of information, may be implemented it functionally the next when activated as a computer program. Much of the current debate in intellectual property law focusses upon this issue and the adaptability of the intellectual property system to recent technological change.

Closer to the concept of property rights in information *per se*, is breach of confidence. This is based on the notion that rights exist in the substance of the information rather than in its expression. Breach of confidence is a civil remedy, restricted to certain types of information, that, broadly speaking, represent a thing of value to the holder; for example secret manufacturing processes, business information of certain kinds etc. The relationship may arise in contract or in equity, either express or implied. Although the duration of the right is theoretically perpetual, the confidentiality of the information may lapse if circumstances change; for example, if the information is disclosed by the 'proprietor' without first establishing the confidence. The position has been described thus:

> The owner of a secret process, not patented, has no exclusive right to make, use or vend the article to which it relates, but he has the right to keep his own knowledge to himself, and to protection of same against one who, in violation of a contract or through a breach of trust or confidence, undertakes to apply the secret to his own use or to impart it to others.

Although academics and legal experts will argue as to the proprietary characteristics of confidential information, the pragmatic position is that the answer is not important. The right only exists in limited circumstances in relation to a limited class of information, which has a functional value and has generally been produced at considerable expense by the 'proprietor'. At present the law does not extend the action against all-comers who acquire the information without permission, or foreclose upon the freedom

17

of outsiders to recreate the information by their own efforts. To that extent, therefore, rights in confidential information could not be said yet to have acquired the status of 'absolute ownership', granting full and complete rights in the information *per se*, enforceable against the world at large.

Rights in Information   If intellectual property law does not recognise property rights in information 'as such', but rather in works embodying information and attracting copyright, patent or other such rights, to what extent does the law hold that proprietary rights may arise in information outside the sphere of authorship and invention? To find the answer it is necessary to look at the law governing areas of communication of information for which extensive regulation exists. As Michael has shown,[45] the rules relating to communication of information are closely related to the exercise of power in society. As such, the rules that are created for the regulation of broadcasting and the media and for rights in certain types of official information have become a benchmark in assessing the character and morality of the State. At a national level the issue is perceived as one of developing policies for the retention, censorship or release of information. Among the considerations will be the need to identify the public interest in relation to the treatment of particular categories of information, such as that bearing on national security, the formulation of government policy, or the welfare of the community.

Although not specifically protected within the British Constitution, the right to receive and impart information is recognised by the European Convention on Human Rights.[46] Increasingly governments are finding it necessary to strive for international consensus on policy. The need has been greatly enhanced by the expansion of access to information that information technology has engendered, whether in the public or private domain. One of the first steps taken by the British Government in the regulation of personal data was the enactment of the Data Protection Act 1984, giving rights to data subjects and imposing obligations on data users. The political pressure for the Act was economic rather than civil libertarian in origin (it was recognised that the Act was necessary to establish some form of regulation that would enable the UK data processing industry to claim that it was operating in accordance with international standards as set out in the Council of Europe Convention on personal data), and its effect has been to transform the development of policy towards personal data from a mere domestic matter to one of international consensus.

To sum up it is clear that the law has never been comfortable with the proposition that information can be possessed, with all the consequences that ensue from 'absolute ownership' or *dominium*. It has taken this position in the face of independent rights found to exist in information on grounds of public policy or human rights. These may embrace rights of access and correction as well as rights of non-disclosure and privacy. Different policies will operate according to the circumstances and the character of the information itself. To bundle this up in a single property right would hand over to the proprietor of the information the freedom to deny access or publish all. Those who formulate the law would claim that their function is to maintain the balance between the competing demands upon information. They have done so by recognising the aggregate of rights that may exist at any one time in information that must either co-exist or compete for supremacy as the prevailing interest.[47] In this sense information develops the character of a 'value', in which claims to draw on that value, whether for example by access, use, exploitation, disposal or control of it, are weighed according to the strength of the claim as determined by national law and international agreement.[48]

ORIGINS AND CHALLENGES OF THE NEW INFORMATION TECHNOLOGY

The development of the 'information society' did not take place in a vacuum. It grew from discovery and innovation that began with the ascent of man as he grew to understand the world and the nature of things, for communication has always been the process by which cultures have developed and have been maintained.[49] What were the forces at work in the climate of thought and discovery that led to the development and exploitation of information technology during the latter half of the twentieth century? The next section looks at this question and develops a historical perspective of the information technology 'revolution'. It also relates current research in physics and biology to the problems of defining information and handling claims to intellectual property in the mapping of the structure of life itself.

CULTURAL INFLUENCES ON THOUGHT AND IDEAS The history of ideas and of their application has always been influenced by the prevailing currents of philosophical thought. Man lives today in the scientific age which developed from mathematics, through astronomy and the Age of Reason to the Enlightenment, the Industrial Revolution and ultimately to modern science. The creator of the scientific method was Galileo (1564 – 1642) through his work in astronomy, the discovery of the physical laws governing the vibration of the pendulum, attempts to measure the speed of light and temperature and the first experiments in the production of a vacuum. In 1609, he made the first astronomical telescope and was able to overthrow the accepted doctrine that the Earth was the centre of the Universe. He also established the validity of the theories of Copernicus (1473 – 1543), who had first suggested that the Earth moved round the Sun and not, as had been believed, the other way round. Science ultimately was to triumph over dogma despite the Catholic Inquisition established by Pope Innocent IV in 1248 for the suppression of 'heresy', and which survived in pockets until the nineteenth century. In June 1633 Galileo was brought before his Inquisitors in Rome[50] following publication of his book *Dialogue on the Great World Systems* that asserted these theories. Under threat of torture he recanted his text stating:

'I, Galileo Galilei, son of the late Vincenzo Galilei, Florentine, aged seventy years, arraigned personally before this tribunal, and kneeling before you, most Eminent and Reverend Lord Cardinals, Inquisitors general against heretical depravity throughout the whole Christian Republic, having before my eyes and touching with my hands, the holy Gospels – swear that I have always believed, now do believe, and by God's help will for the future believe, all that is held, preached, and taught by the Holy Catholic and Apostolic Roman Church. But whereas – after an injunction had been judicially intimated to me by this Holy Office, to the effect that I must altogether abandon the false opinion that the sun is the centre of the world and immovable, and that the earth is not the centre of the world, and moves, and that I must not hold, defend, or teach . . . the said doctrine, and after it had been notified to me that the said doctrine was contrary to Holy Scripture – I wrote and printed a book in which I discuss the doctrine already condemned, and adduce arguments of great cogency in its favour, without presenting any solution to these; and for this cause I have been pronounced by the Holy Office to be vehemently suspected of heresy.'

Galileo went on, in his statement, to admit his 'errors and heresies' and to swear not to assert, verbally or in writing, 'anything that might furnish occasion for a similar suspicion regarding me'. He confined himself in his villa for the remaining nine years of his life.[51]

Newton was born in the same year as Galileo's death. He went on to enhance the infant science with his definitions of the laws of gravity and motion and the development of calculus which was relevant in the measurement of speed and electrical current etc., and in the development of mechanics.[52] If the scientific method is based upon the concept of testing propositions and hypotheses, Newton made the exercise more rigorous,[53] by using mathematics in a dynamic sense in the process of defining the laws of nature upon which ultimately the industrial revolution was to capitalise. The latter was indeed the product of the scientific revolution born of the age of the 'Enlightenment' – 'the Age of Reason'. Reason was the path to knowledge and natural law could only be explained through it. The earlier dogma that had brought Galileo to his knees had been replaced by a natural philosophy of discovery and exaltation of ideas which the mathematician d'Alembert described as having 'brought about a lively fermentation of minds, spreading through nature in all directions like a river which has burst its dams'.[54]

TOWARDS A UNIVERSAL THEORY OF MAN, MATTER AND MACHINE   Writing, in 1973, the text of the widely acclaimed thirteen-part BBC television series 'The Ascent of Man', Bronowski observed that the aim of the physical sciences was to provide an exact picture of the material world. In the twentieth century, he said, experience suggested that this aim was unattainable. What the physical sciences have done, rather, is to 'provide the method to knowledge: there is no absolute knowledge and those who claim it, whether they are scientists or dogmatists, open the door to tragedy'.

Bronowski illustrated his point by reference to the whole spectrum of electromagnetic information, posing the question 'how fine and how exact is the detail that we can see with the best instruments in the world?'. In 1867, James Maxwell, Professor of Mathematics at Cambridge, used pure mathematics to forecast most of the laws governing the transmission and reception of electromagnetic waves, the forerunner of radio signals and radar. He identified light as resembling the properties of wave formation and speculated as to the existence of further waves within the spectrum of visible light from red to violet. (Newton was the first to demonstrate that a beam of sunlight, when transmitted through a prism, is broken up into a spectrum.)[55] Subsequently it was discovered that infra-red and ultra-violet rays existed and that wavelengths differed from the long waves of radar to the short waves of ultra-violet light and X-rays. The wavelength of the light determined what could be perceived with that light. Thus, whereas radar could pinpoint only larger objects, ultra-violet microscopes could examine a single cell, and by enlarging it 3,500 times, enable man to identify a single chromosome; the part of a cell which contains the human genes.[56]

Bronowski observed that, despite such scientific progress, no light, of course, could see the human genes themselves. The point he was making was this; that all information is imperfect and potentially unreliable and only valid so long as no hypothesis or theory is put forward such that on the evidence available, and when tested, the subsequent findings suggest a closer approximation to the 'truth' than the former. Bronowski continued with this fundamental observation:

> 'We are here face to face with the crucial paradox of knowledge. Year by year we devise more precise instruments with which to observe nature with more fineness. And when we look at the observations, we are discomforted to see that they are still fuzzy, and we feel that they are as uncertain as ever. We seem to be running after a goal which lurches away from us to infinity every time we come within sight of it.'[57]

This view has been challenged, at least in the context of theoretical physics by Stephen Hawking, Lucasian Professor of Mathematics at Cambridge University. In his Inaugural Lecture in April 1980, he speculated that, perhaps by the end of the century, 'we might have a complete, consistent and unified theory of the physical interactions which would describe all possible observations'.[58] He believed that man had thought that he was on the brink of this twice before; first, in the early part of the twentieth century with the theory of continuum mechanics (the theory, inter alia, that everything about matter could be understood by measuring substances' co-efficients or of elasticity, viscosity, conductivity, etc.); and second with the discovery of atomic structure and quantum mechanics in the 1920s (the basic postulate of which is the Heisenberg 'Uncertainty Principle' which states that certain pairs of quantities, such as the position and momentum of a particle, cannot be measured simultaneously with arbitrary accuracy), which shattered the descriptive claims of the preceding theories. This latter theory grew in an attempt to account for several physical phenomena that could not be explained by classical mechanics. It postulates that energy transferences take place not continuously, but in bursts of discrete amounts. Hawking believes that although, in principle, man has understood the equations that govern, for instance, biology, he has not been able to reduce the study of human behaviour 'to a branch of applied mathematics'. A unifying theory is needed to 'account for the initial conditions of the Universe and the values of the various physical parameters'.

Hawking believes that a unified theory can be developed from the partial theories of particles and interactions that already exist, provided it survives some crucial calculations that will shortly fall within the capacity of computers to undertake. Such is the rate of development in computational method that he expects computers ultimately to take over the analysis in theoretical physics.

It is in these ideas and research methods that the germ exists of a universal theory of man and machine. If a unifying theory of physical systems and their interaction can be identified and if further development of computing and electronics can produce a form of advanced artificial intelligence, based upon the biological mechanisms that underpin human intelligence, then at that stage, society may well have reached the brink of the super-information society in which the fundamental axioms of life, matter, knowledge and nature can only be approached through computers – the results of which can only be interpreted by other computers.

In a curious way the process will then have gone full circle: from the metaphysics of religious dogma that decried the scientific method of Galileo, to the metaphysics of super-information; i.e. the abstract reasoning and speculation of the intelligent machine. In such circumstances man himself would be obliged to accept these 'fundamental laws' because his own concept of reality denies him access to this information unless he resorts to the very technology that defines and confirms their existence.[59] Just as the Inquisition suppressed heresy, so might a universal theory of matter, man and machine, derived from machine intelligence and interpretation, produce a prescription of reality that 'is rooted in a sort of meta-universe of mathematical objects and relationships'[60]. This becomes the supreme interpretation of what exists in the Universe, thereby limiting the power of the individual to dissent unless he does so within the framework of the computed doctrines.

Hawking, no doubt, would challenge this argument on the basis that a mathematically consistent theory would not in itself affect reality or necessarily mean that the frontier of knowledge had been reached exclusively by technology. Mathematics is for him merely a means of hypothesising, and computers can aid that process. Even if a basic set of laws are discovered he argues that 'there will still be in the years ahead the intellectually challenging task of developing better approximation methods, so that we

23

can make useful predictions of the probable outcomes in complicated and realistic situations'. He believes that the discovery of a unified theory would in fact free knowledge from the grasp of a small band of specialists just as today the general theory of relativity, once understood by only two people, is now appreciated by many thousands of graduates.[61] According to this view a complete and consistent unified theory will lead to a better understanding of events and one within which all human beings can participate.

There are two fields where work is currently underway that illustrates the dilemmas discussed above, and which also raises additional philosophical questions that will ultimately require some form of legal response. These are the attempts to obtain the information to write the 'book of matter' and second, the 'book of man' – two of the major unifying theories of mankind. It is curious that in tackling these projects the problem has been to find, as Bronowski suggested, more precise instruments with which to observe the fundamentals of the Universe and of creation. As the objects of study get smaller, so do the instruments that get at the information become more abstract and more reliant upon abstract theories about reality. The paradox of the situation is evident. As the subject matter to be observed gets smaller, so do the instruments and machines required to investigate these phenomena grow, sometimes in size, and certainly in capacity and cost. As the sciences of physics, astronomy and biology grow ever more complex and the costs of recovering scientific information more expensive, the fundamental questions that must be answered narrow to focus more specifically upon a particular source of investigation, whether that be the state of matter during a tiny fragment of time 15,000 million years ago or a miniscule portion of the gene pool. Whereas the 'book of matter' will contain the story of the formation of the Universe and a unifying scheme that will embrace all fundamental particles and forces, the 'book of man' will describe the genetic fingerprint of life itself, by defining the hardware from which a human being is formed and how hereditary characteristics, from disease to musical or sporting ability, might be transmitted or acquired.

The Book of Matter It is nearly 100 years since the 'discovery' that there might be smaller particles than atoms (the discovery by Thomson in 1897 that cathode rays consisted of particles much smaller than atoms, viz., electrons). The understanding of how electrons[62] and subsequently how

24

other particles interact within materials has aided the development of telecommunications, computing, and all branches of science from microbiology to bioengineering[63] – the word 'electronics' is, of course, derivative of 'electron'. Today particle physicists believe they have identified many more subatomic particles within the 'hard ball' of the atom, as it was perceived to be at the turn of the century. Further experiments revealed an inner structure of electrons and a nucleus; and subsequently a nucleus with protons and neutrons. More recently other particles named 'mesons', 'leptons' (which include the 'electron', the 'muon' and the 'tau', together with three kinds of 'neutrino') were claimed. It is proposed that holding these particles together are others called 'bosuns' that interpose between three of the four forces of nature (strong and weak nuclear forces, electromagnetic force and gravitation). Some particles are heavier than others: the so-called 'X-Bosun' having a mass 1000 million times more massive than a proton. Studies have also revealed 'antiparticles'. In 1932,[65] the antithesis of the electron was discovered – 'the positron' – with the same mass and an equal but opposite electric charge. Both would remain stable if kept apart, but would annihilate to produce a gamma ray if merged. According to the developing theory, unlike the electron, some particles will decay and others form in the process of that decay. Others, still, will decay into something else, such as a muon to an electron and a neutrino to an ant-neutrino.[66]

During the past 30 years physicists have been trying to make sense of these phenomena. In order to test these theories physicists have had to face two particular problems. One is the very tiny amounts of time for which some of these particles are believed to exist: for example, the tau is supposed to live for a mere 10^{-13} seconds. The second is the enormous amount of energy that must be produced to observe these particles. Accelerating particles to very high energies and firing them at fixed or moving targets is the only current method of exploring the atom's interior.[67]

After the Second World War, in the striving to achieve higher and higher energies, the United States and Europe invested heavily in particle accelerators in which charged particles – protons and electrons – could be accelerated to high speeds with the aid of electric and magnetic fields.[68] The first were developed at the Cavendish Laboratory, Cambridge, in 1932, generating several hundred thousand volts. Subsequently new generations of accelerators have been developed each one opening up new levels of particle research. In the 1960s, for example, a Proton Synchrotron was built at Cern, near Geneva, with the backing of 12 European States (now 14). The power of the accelerator was 28-GeV. Acceleration of a particle by 10,000 volts would produce a kinetic energy increase of 10,000 eV. 10^6 eV are called MeV, and 10^9 eV are called GeV (Giga eV).[69] To give a measure of the progress in the last 30 years an Electron Positron (LEP) collider is now being constructed in Cern, at the European Particle Physics Laboratory, that will consist of a ring of magnets 27 kilometres in circumference, and set in a tunnel that will run from the laboratory beneath the edge of the French Jura mountains and back again. When this is complete, beams of electrons and positrons will collide at a total energy of 100 GeV[70] allowing, it is believed, investigation of the so-called 'W' and 'Z' particles 'discovered' in 1983 by the Italian physicist Rubbia and his colleagues, which were predicted by the 'electroweak theory'.[71] These particles are believed to have vanished from the Universe one-hundredth of a second after 'big bang'.[72]

The outcome of all this research, which at Cern costs in excess of £250 million per annum is a theory put forward by the American physicist, Murray Gell-Mann, that three families of fundamental units exist in matter each of which contains two categories of particle – quarks and leptons – both formed in pairs. On earth, so the theory goes, all matter encountered consists of particles from the first family, within which the 'up' and 'down' quarks combine to form the atomic nuclei in which neutrons and protons combine with electrons to form atoms. The other two families are thought to comprise much heavier and more active particles not normally formed within the stable earth environment. In the second family the two quarks are called 'charm' and 'strange'. Physicists have also identified 'W' and 'Z' particles which give further supporting evidence of the existence of three families. Only since 1989 have sufficient 'Z' particles been generated to test the theory.

The race is now on to prove, as a match to 'bottom quark', the sixth and most important quark of all – named 'top quark' – which, if identified, together with Higgs Bosun (which the theory suggests gives mass to all other particles) will establish the theoretical credentials of the three families of fundamental particles.[73] A team at Cern and at Fermilab near Chicago are competing to see if they can be the first to produce the particle.[74] The Cern accelerator could identify top quark if it can be formed at energy levels up to 70 GeV. Fermilab can handle acceleration up to 150–200 GeV and must be favourites to discover it if higher energy levels are required and if the theory is accurate.[75] In January 1987 President

Reagan endorsed a Department of Energy proposal to build an even bigger accelerator, the Superconducting Super Collider (SSC), which may cost up to $6 billion dollars to complete by the time it is expected to run in 1996. The SSC will produce a total energy of 40 teraelectronvolts (1 TeV = 1000 GeV) in an underground ring that will encompass 520 square kilometres.[76]

With this technology physicists hope to prove once and for all the accuracy of their theories and to locate the clues locked up in the first moments of time when the relationships between space, time, matter and energy are thought to have been laid; when Einstein's theory of relativity, that suggests that energy and matter are different expressions of the same thing, could have been tested, since particles are created out of pure energy. Chown comments that at this moment 'what was destined to become the entire visible universe, thousands of millions of light years across, was contained in a volume roughly the size of a pea . . . and the temperature of this superdense material was an unimaginable 10^{-28} degrees . . . One hundredth of a second later the Universe had grown to fill a volume roughly the size of the Sun'.[77]

Contingent upon the success of this vast investment of skill and resources is a satisfactory theory with which to interpret the results of these observations. Hawking and others believe that a Grand Unified Theory or 'law of initial conditions' can be produced that will explain the the forces that govern the behaviour of matter in terms of some single 'superforce' formulated within the quantum theory of cosmology. The objective is to confront the very moment of creation and to assert fundamental laws that will remain, in the words of Paul Davies, Professor of theoretical physics at Newcastle University, 'universal, absolute and timeless . . . possessing attributes that formerly were reserved for God.'[78] The concern he has is why it should be that the complexity of the natural world should necessarily be explained at the level of theoretical physics with what he calls 'a few elegantly simple mathematical principles'. He suggests that today there is concern about this issue; where the laws come from, and whether other laws are possible. Indeed, if the laws of physics are defined precisely in mathematical terms then the existence of man himself was inevitable. For many physicists the worry is to be found in the very 'unreasonableness' of the success of mathematics in describing the physical world.

That view is certainly a concern of Professor Roger Penrose, holder of the distinguished Rouse Ball Chair of Mathematics at Oxford. He doubts whether the sum of human knowledge can be reduced to a series of systematic rules known as algorithms and sees a need to link the output of sub-microscopic research to the 'reality' of experience at the level of human consciousness. He believes that there is much to be learnt from science before we can tell whether the structure of the brain must be biological or whether indeed the advocates of artificial intelligence are right in suggesting that the mind could eventually be 'computable' in a new physical structure.[79] At a practical level, however, the pursuit of this research will almost certainly deepen scientific understanding, resulting in further advances in artificial intelligence, in new forms of data processing and storage, and above all in improved knowledge of the working of the human brain. It also has other applications, in medical science, manufacturing and chemistry, for example in the treatment of cancer patients with neutron beams. However, a niggling question still remains: if the laws of physics correctly reflect reality, is it right to assume that those laws have always existed in the natural order, waiting to be discovered and articulated by man? If so, do the people who extract those laws and write them down have any legal rights in them? Alternatively, will the super-information society claim what is found for itself and so shake the basket of rights in favour of sharing with humanity the secrets of matter at the moment of creation. This question may indeed have to be answered in a different context when the 'Book of Man' is written down during the coming twenty years.

The Book of Man   In the mid-nineteenth century Gregor Mendel became the first to recognise that man could inherit traits, when he propounded the first very basic laws of genetics. After eight years of research and experimentation with the garden pea he had guessed correctly that heredity, in the case of the plant, depended upon two particles now called genes.[80] In 1953 Watson and Crick discovered the structure of the nucleic acid DNA that carries the chemical message of inheritance.[81] It was realised that the normal human being carries 23 pairs of chromosomes, which are threadlike structures made up of a very long DNA molecule that has been elaborately wound up. The chemical message it carries in its spine will, for example, tell cells to make particular proteins like the ones for colouring the eyes blue or the hair black. These are the units of inheritance – the genes.

Approximately 100,000 genes are spread throughout the 23 chromosomes of men and women. The chemical message of DNA is written with an alphabet of four chemical letters – A, C, T, and G. End to end, the genome[82] containing the entire set of chromosomes is 3 billion letters long.

28

Geneticists needed a way of locating within the different parts of the genome the thousands of genetic diseases in man as evidenced by discrepancies in that part of the genetic code. In the case of Huntington's chorea the fault was traced to chromosome four. In the case of Down's syndrome the problem lies in chromosome three and in cystic fybrosis it is seven. However the gene abnormality could be in a single chromosome could be millions of letters away from the location being investigated by the geneticist. Unless a considerable amount of luck occurred researchers might take a lifetime to locate the fault, bearing in mind that a laboratory employing traditional methods might take a year to investigate just 100,000 letters.[83]

What was needed was a way of automating the process of mapping the genome, to enable the geneticists to spend their time on evaluating the information that such a project could produce. Just as astronomy had invested in very powerful telescopes and physics in particle accelerators, biology needed the organisation, investment and technology for a major project of its own. The technology would need to handle the enormous amounts of information that reading the genome would produce. New databases would need to be set up linked into this information, so as to provide the geneticist with details of any one of the diseases under investigation. Above all a technology would have to be produced to prepare the DNA for mapping and for ensuring the accuracy of that automated observation. In this latter area of designing tools for automating industrial processes, the Japanese have been strong and in 1981 Hitachi began work to produce an automatic scanner for reading genome sequences.

The initiative to take on the decoding of the 'book of man' by unravelling the human genome occurred in the United States when the Chancellor of the University of California at Santa Cruz, a biologist named Robert Sinsheimer, gathered together 12 of the leading experts in molecular genetics to discuss the idea. The predicted cost of the project was thought to be about $1 per letter, or $3 billion altogether. The magnitude of the project and its cost worried some biologists, and ultimately the National Institutes of Health turned away from the project. It was however picked up by the Department of Energy, which had the finest technical and computing resources available. The idea had the support of sufficient leading figures in the field to persuade the Department to take it on. One of these supporters was Walter Gilbert, Professor of Biology at Harvard University, who in 1980 had won a Nobel prize for his work in developing a technique for DNA sequencing. He believed the actual task of coding the genome was not itself particularly difficult and could be achieved by

29

automation. Technology was just what was needed to perform a repetitive task accurately and efficiently. The real problem would come later in the evaluation and use of the information extracted.

The Human Genome project is now underway, the project having been divided up so that the parts of the genome representing the chapters and pages of the 'book of man' can be studied separately. At the centre is the Department of Energy co-ordinating work through the Institute at Los Alamos, the Lawrence Berkeley Laboratory in San Francisco and elsewhere. Work is expected to be completed on the genome within 15 to 20 years. The task of deciphering the meaning must wait until the 21st century.

One issue which still has to be resolved is the assertion by Gilbert that the information in the genome sequence will be a copyright work when it is mapped out. Gilbert co-founded a biotechnology company called Biogen that is interested in the genome and working in the area. The argument he makes is that the cost and innovation involved in the coding process justifies the granting of a copyright to the authors who deserve the rewards that copyright protection of the genome would bring.

The contrary view is expressed thus; that whereas an individual can obtain a copyright in a map of the river Thames, that does not grant rights in the river itself. The question here is whether there is any difference between the genome sequence itself and its expression. What the project will achieve is the codification and arrangement of what is present in the genome; information that exists both before and after the process of codification has occurred. In these circumstances then, is it right that anyone should obtain proprietary rights in something so basic as the genetic map of the human being: information that will lead to a precise understanding of the defect in the alphabet of the gene code that causes genetic disorder. Should the words of the gene code expressed in the chemical alphabet described above be capable of ownership through copyright? If not, should the investment in getting at the information be rewarded at all, or effectively postponed until the obvious benefits of new treatments and drugs as well as all the other biological applications that can be expected to follow on later, develop out of the research? This is one issue that is facing the intellectual property system at present, and a cause of some controversy.

A second problem that the law must begin to consider is the consequences of mapping the DNA profile of the individual. In due course, every new born child will have such a record held and available on computer. This profile will contain a complete statement of the genetic makeup of the individual and will indicate whether that individual is prone to certain types of illness such as cancer, diabetes or heart disease. In addition information will be available about lifestyle and diet for the maintenance of good health and how to counteract illness and disease. The issue that ought to be in the minds of lawyers today is what measures are going to be required, in due course, to control the use to which this information might be put. It has been suggested for example, that possession of an 'inferior' DNA profile might lead to discrimination against such individuals for jobs and for places in education. Might production of a 'satisfactory' DNA profile be required as a condition of employment or of obtaining insurance? In addition might some attempt be made to predict talent of some kind in the individual, such as sporting or artistic prowess, based on analysis of his genetic fingerprint? Beyond that, what steps should the law take with regard to genetic engineering designed to correct abnormal genetic code, thereby interfering with the gene pool itself? How this information will be managed and used in the future should be under consideration now.

CHARACTERISING FORMER SOCIETIES   Examining the characteristic portrayals of past societies, it is interesting to look at what the conditions were that led to such depictions. This enables comparisons to be drawn between the dominant features of influence and activity in different societies that have defined their persona. Such influences appear to be based upon either great movements – built upon discovery and innovation in the properties and uses of physical prehistoric materials – or in a transformation of the climate of creativity and philosophical thought. In the palaeolithic mesolithic and neolithic periods of the Stone Age[84] the key influence was man's dexterity in the development of stone implements. The Bronze and Iron Ages which followed saw man develop crafts and tools with metal.[85] The Classical period, which embraced the rise of Greece and Rome, marked the beginnings of Western civilisation and was a time distinguished by the creativity of Greek and Roman art, literature, architecture, and philosophy. Elements of Greek civilisation are known to have existed before c.1000 BC in the Aegean region and that of the Romans from c.753 BC with the founding of Rome itself. However, the classical Greek language in which the great works of Plato,[86] Aristotle[87] and other classical Greek scholars were written became a dormant language for more than 1000 years until the revival of learning in the early Middle Ages.[88]

31

The Middle Ages are generally regarded as describing the period in European history between Antiquity and the Renaissance which began in the fourteenth century. It is often more precisely dated from 476 AD when the last Emperor of the Western Roman Empire was deposed, to 1453 AD when Constantinople was conquered by the Turks.[89] The period from 476 AD to the coronation of Charlemagne, the Frankish King, in Rome in 800 AD is described as the period of the Dark Ages. The term is used less specifically to describe the period from the end of Classical civilisation to the revival of 'learning' in the West at c.1000 AD. The period is so-called as being a time that was lacking in culture and development.

The Renaissance, which began in Italy and spread throughout Europe, reached its zenith in the fifteenth and sixteenth centuries. Its origins can be traced to the school of translators at Toledo in Spain, who began in the twelfth century to translate the ancient texts from the forgotten classical Greek language through Arabic and Hebrew into Latin.[90] This period, marked by the development of trade routes and therefore of greater contact between peoples and sharing of knowledge, is attributed with the revival of interest in classical literature and in the study of nature. The Renaissance has been described as a period when scientific interest flourished in a pre-scientific age.[91] This interest in scientific enquiry can be seen particularly in the paintings and sculpture of the great artists of the time such as Leonardo da Vinci, Michelangelo, Duccio, Botticelli, Brunelleschi and others, who broke away from the optical and symbolic techniques[92] of the Greek, Roman and early medieval artists, to introduce life and perspective into painting, sculpture and drawing on the concepts of mathematics and mechanics (subjects which da Vinci and his contemporaries were studying). These painters were interested in understanding the structure of space and the workings of nature, and art itself was regarded as a form of knowledge and a science. Mathematics, with its classical links, was regarded by Renaissance philosophy as the basis upon which the physical world would be explained.

The 'Scientific Revolution' is the movement which grew out of the dramatic developments in natural philosophy described by the French mathematician d'Alembert in 1759 as a 'new method of philosophising'. In the early eighteenth century, it was mathematics which, following on from Renaissance thinking, was regarded as the greatest revolutionising force.[93] However, with the scientific work of Galileo, Newton, Descartes, Kepler and others to draw on, there was much more confidence than before to put the ideas to use. There was also the influence of the new religion which saw the Protestant church emerge from the break with Roman Catholicism. This accelerated the progress of scientific enquiry because the Protestant theology recognised the presence of the Deity in the laws of nature which God had chosen, whereas Catholic theology was still firmly tied to the literal word of the scriptures.

The period in question – the period of the 'new Science' – spans the seventeenth and eighteenth centuries, referred to as the age of Enlightenment.[94] In the latter of the two centuries philosophers believed that the Scientific Revolution was affecting all human activity. The essence of the natural philosophy of the period was 'reason', or the reasoned approach to nature in which experimentation and rational enquiry featured highly. The period saw a great expansion in scientific experiment, and although there is no simple linkage between the intellectual and scientific climate of the period and the ascent of the industrial revolution which followed, it is clear that the components were there 'in solution', ready to be harnessed by the industrial, social and economic forces of the new order.[96]

The Industrial Revolution, the catalyst which led to the development of industrial society, is generally linked to the period c.1750–1850, culminating in the Great Exhibition of 1851 which celebrated the technological achievements of the age. As Ashton has suggested, many historians have attempted to look for particular features of the times to which the Industrial Revolution can be attributed. In his view its proximate causes were economic, in the 'vast increase of natural resources, labour, capital and enterprise – of what the economist calls the factors of production'.[97] Mathias argues that to be given identity, the concept of a revolution at this time must imply 'fundamental change in the structure of an economy; a fundamental redeployment of resources away from agriculture, becoming evident over time'.[98] In his view no single-cause solution suffices, whether it be Britain's favourable natural-resources position, a Protestant theology in accord with capitalism, a rising population, the development of markets, or an outpouring of inventive genius. Certainly the changes in the countryside and in the cities, and in the lives of those who either remained on the land or gravitated towards the factories and the mines, are among the more obvious and observable characteristics of the time.

What does seem clear is that this was the moment when the ideas of the Enlightenment were truly applied to develop the tools of mass production. In particular this required the harnessing of power and of energy. One historian has described the patents granted to Arkwright for his water-frame and Watt for his condensing steam engine, both in 1769, as two of the most important events in world history.[99] The former managed to mechanise the craft of spinning for the first time, while the steam engine played a fundamental part in the development of industrial production and subsequently in the movement of people and goods by rail and sea and ultimately by road vehicle.

One point that is easily overlooked is that the Industrial Revolution in Britain occurred without intervention of planners, economists or politicians.[100] It was a spontaneous event, achieved by consent and prompted perhaps by the desire of much of the populace to reduce poverty; a forlorn hope for many at a time when the law had not yet intervened to protect workers in the factories and mines from poor wages, harsh and dangerous conditions and exploitation. However, for the nation as a whole, the basic industries of the Industrial Revolution[101] secured Britain's economic strength internationally and its position in the world as a great power. By comparison, the twentieth century has witnessed, at various stages along its course, the erosion of this position, as the strong and powerful nations of the world – the United States, the Soviet Union, Japan and collectively within the European Community – have asserted their strength; a development that has become even more apparent since the emergence of information technology and the arrival of the 'Information Society'.

In sharp contrast with the range of possible causes of the take-off of the Industrial Revolution, the transformation from the industrial economy through the post-industrial service economy[102] to the Information Society can be attributed to a single cause: the spectacular technological advances produced following the post-war development of the computer. What start-up conditions were necessary to incubate such development at this time is a different question. However, before looking at the forces at work in shaping the 'information revolution' it should be pointed out that developments in information technology have been taking place throughout man's history and should not be seen solely in the context of what has happened in the last 30 years or so.

NOTES

1. Books on the general topic include: Tom Forester, ed., *The Information Technology Revolution* (1985, Basil Blackwell); Barrie Sherman, *The New Revolution – The Impact of Computers on Society*(1985, John Wiley & Sons); Ian Miles, Howard Rush, Kevin Turner and John Bessant, *Information Horizons – The Long-Term Social Implications of New Information*

Technology (1988, Gower Publishing); David Simpson, Jim Walker and Jim Love,*The Challenge of New Technology* (1987, Westview Press); Marjorie Ferguson, ed., *New Communication Technologies and the Public Interest* (1986, Sage Publications); and Ian Miles, *Home Informatics – Information Technology and the Transformation of Everyday Life* (1988, Pinter Publishers).

2. Comment by C. Jansen Van Rosendaal, Directorate-General for Telecommunications, Information Industries and Innovation. In *Guidelines for Improving the Synergy Between the Public and Private Sectors in the Information Market* (1989, Commission of the European Communities, CD-54-88-126-EN-C) p. 3.

3. US Congress, Office of Technology Assessment, (The OTA Report) *Intellectual Property Rights in an Age of Electronics and Innovation* (OTA-CIT-302, 1986) pp. 32–3, referencing Sherri Turkel, *The Second Self: Computers and the Human Spirit* (1984, Simon & Schuster).

4. References to 'information' in this introduction are used as a sub-set of the term 'data' from which information is derived. The distinction between the two is discussed more specifically later in the chapter.

5. For further discussion, see the OTA Report (1990) op. cit., pp. 29–37.

6. Ibid.

7. Ithiel de Sola Pool in *Technologies of Freedom* (1986) has argued that the panoply of electronic devices has delivered capacities far beyond anything that the printing press could achieve: 'Machines that think, that bring great libraries into anybody's study, that allow discourse among persons a half-world apart, are expanders of human culture.'

8. See Halton, 'Introduction to Information Technology', in Forester, ed, op.cit., p. 3 *et seq.*

9. Stuart Brand in *The Media Lab: Inventing the Future at MIT* (1986). Quoted in US Congress, Office of Technology Assessment, *Critical Connections: Communication for the Future* (1990, OTA-CIT-407, US Government Printing Office) p. 3.

10. This point was first made by Bing, in the seminal paper 'Information Law'?, *Media Law and Practice*, 2 (219), 1981, pp. 219–239.

11. Sprowl, 'Towards a Unified Theory of Proprietary Protection for digital Information Systems: Avoiding Artificial distinctions between Hardware and Software'. In Campbell, ed., *Data Processing and the Law* (1984) p. 236.

12. The OTA Report, op. cit., p. 78. The report comments: 'For example, a cam in a machine is a physical embodiment of the logical operation: "if there is a 360 degree turn, push rod X." It implements this procedure directly when the camshaft is turned 360 degrees. Similarly, a thermostat physically embodies the logical operation: "if the temperature rises above 70 degrees, turn off switch Z." In each case the design of the object embodies information to a surrounding physical system.

13. Ibid., p.78.

14. See Aleksander and Burnett, *Thinking Machines – The Search for Artificial Intelligence* (1987) Ch. 2.

15. For example, the robot arm fixed with the appropriate tool for welding, painting or assembly, etc.

16. For example, a three-way calling-conference facility, where business meetings can be held down the telephone line or call diversion where calls can be forwarded automatically to any other number in the country. Another facility are the 250 or so 'messages' transmitted by the average digital exchange, which might tell what a call has cost or if necessary sends a screech to alert a subscriber that the handset is not in place.

17. Aleksander and Burnett, op. cit., p. 34.

18. Scottish Law Commission Consultative Memorandum No. 68, *Computer Crime* (1986) p.103.

19. The OTA Report, op. cit., pp. 3, 5, 60 and 97. Information technology can be seen to have complicated the process whereby rights are granted to authors and inventors, introducing new parties into the arena and changing the roles that people involved in the copyright system play. It has also made the copying, transfer and manipulation of information cheaper, quicker and more private, rendering the enforcement of intellectual property rights more difficult to achieve.

20. For a full discussion, see ibid.

21. Burns and Martin, *The Economics of Information*, op. cit., p. 158.

22. For a discussion of the distinction between data and information from an 'information systems' perspective, see Eardley, Marshall and Ritchie, *Information Systems in Development and Operation* (1989) pp. 10–19.

23. I am grateful to Andrew Schulkins, Head of User Services at Southampton University Computing Service, for his help in this analysis.

24. Catala, 'Essay at Synthesis'. In *Freedom of Data Flows and EEC Law.* Proceedings of the 2nd CELIM Conference, at p. 39.

25. See generally, Griffiths, ed.,*Knowledge and Belief* (1967) and Ross, *The Appeal to the Given – A Study in Epistemology* (1967).

26. See generally, Dretske, *Knowledge and the Flow of Information* (1981).

27. See generally, Singh, *Great Ideas in Information Theory, Language and Cybernetics* (1966).

28. Shannon, 'A Mathematical Theory of Communication', *Bell Systems and Technology Journal* 1948, p. 379.

29. An excellent study of these trends can be found in Aleksander and Burnett, *Thinking Machines – The Search for Artificial Intelligence* (1987).

30. This is the concept of 'artificial intelligence' which has been researched for more than three decades, although not identified with such a controversial name until more recently. See further p. 240 post.

31. Quoted from Eardley, Marshall and Ritchie, op. cit., p. 15.

32. Ibid., p.19.

33. Ibid., pp. 12–13.

34. Priest, 'The Character of Information: Characteristics and Properties of Information Related to Issues Concerning Intellectual Property', US Department of Commerce, National Technical Information Service, *Intellectual Property Rights in an Age of Electronics and Innovation*, Con-

tractor Documents 1 (2), Document No. PB87 158218 (1986) p. 349.
35. For further reading, see Burns and Martin, *The Economics of Information*, op. cit., p. 145.
36. Noyes, *The Institution of Property* (1936) p. 296.
37. Blackstone, *Commentaries* II, p. 866. Quoted in Noyes, op. cit., p. 297, n.36.
38. Ibid., p. 296.
39. Ibid., p.2. Quoted in Noyes, op. cit., p. 297.
40. Noyes, op. cit., p.303.
41. Hearn, *The Theory of Legal Duties and Rights* (1883) p. 186.Quoted in Noyes, op.cit., p. 304.
42. Walter Wheeler Cook, ed., *Fundamental Legal Conceptions – As Applied in Judicial Reasoning by Wesley Newcomb Hohfeld* (1966) pp. xii, 10 and 78.
43. Ibid., p.28.
44. Op. cit., p. 61. See further Priest, op. cit., p. 353.
44a. Noyes, op. cit., p. 387.
45. Michael, *Information Law, Policy and the Public Interest*, p.102 *et seq*.
46. European Convention on Human Rights (1951), Article 10.
47. Branscomb has identified 10 such rights in relation to information. These are: to know, collect, acquire, withhold, control, receive, protect, destroy, correct or publish information. For discussion of such rights, see Branscomb, 'Property Rights in Information', in Guile, ed., *Information Technologies and Social Transformation* (1985), p. 81.
48. For further discussion, see Prum, *Information, Data and Continental Law*, p.27*et seq*.
49. For a discussion of the role of communication in the production of culture, see the 1990 OTA report, op. cit., Chapter 7.
50. There were 10 judges present: all Cardinals and Dominicians. One was Pope Urban VIII's brother and another a nephew. Quoted in Bronowski, op. cit., p. 211.
51. He did, however, write a book on the 'New Sciences', concerned with physics not the stars. Quoted in Bronowski, op. cit., p. 218.
52. Discussed in Hankins, *Science and Enlightenment* (1985) p. 17 *et seq*.
53. 'Analysis', for Newton, consisted in 'making experiments and observations and in drawing general Conclusions from them by Induction'. Newton *Opticks*, 4th Ed.(1730); rpt. New York (1952) p. 404. Quoted in Hankins, op. cit., p. 20.
54. d'Alembert (1717–83), quoted in Cassirer, *The Philosophy of the Enlightenment*, trans. Koelln and Pettegrove, (1955, Boston) p. 3. See Davies, op. cit., for discussion of the continuing role of theology in Enlightenment thought.
55. Collins, op. cit., p. 237.
56. Today nanotechnology is burgeoning which shapes and uses materials at scales as small as the individual atom. 'Nano' comes from 'nanometer' which is one thousandth of a millionth of a metre. For a discussion of recent advances, see Phillip Campbell, 'One Small Step is a Giant Leap in Vision'

The Times, 10 May 1990.
57. Bronowski, op. cit., p. 356.
58. Stephen W. Hawking, 'Is the end in sight for theoretical physics?' (1980).
59. Discussed by Davies, op. cit., p. 60.
60. Davies, op. cit.
61. Stephen W. Hawking, *A Brief History of Time* (1988, Bantam Press) p. 168.
62. Electrons dictate a material's physical properties, such as its electrical and thermal conductivity. discussed in Watson, 'Exposing electrons – the positron way', *New Scientist*, 29 January 1987, p. 40.
63. Sutton, 'Ninety years around the atom', *New Scientist*, 8 January 1987, p. 49.
64. Hall, 'The billion-dollar search for Higgs Bosun', *New Scientist*, 12 February 1987, p. 26 at p. 27.
65. The antiparticle of the electron – 'the positron' discovered in 1932 during studies on cosmic rays. Quoted in Sutton, op. cit., p. 50.
66. For example the 'muon' is born in the decay of another short lived particle, such as the 'pion'. Discussed in Sutton, op. cit., p. 50.
67. Close, Marten and Sutton, *The Particle Explosion* (1987) p. 14.
68. For the history of particle acceleration development see Ne'eman and Kirsh,*The Particle Hunters*(1983), English translation (1986), p. 87 *et seq.*
69. Ibid., p. 90.
70. Scientists believe that by replacing the magnets with more powerful superconducting magnets, they can double its energy again to 200GeV.See David Fishlock, 'Managing the Mammoth' in 'LEP and Big Physics', *Financial Times* Survey, 13 November 1989, p. 18.
71. Quoted in Hall, 'The billion-dollar search for Higgs bosun',*New Scientist*, 12 February 1987, p. 26. For this he won a Nobel prize.
72. Each 'Z' lasts no more than a few million-million-million-millionths of a second before disintegrating. With a mass measured at 91.1 GeV this explains the need for large particle accelerators and precise measuring instruments. See Clive Cookson, 'The Search for a "Grand Theory of Everything"', *Financial Times*, 13 November 1989.
73. Clive Cookson, 'The Search for a "Grand Theory of Everything"', *Financial Times*, 13 November 1989.
74, 'Equinox', *Race for the Top*, Channel Four Television, first shown September 1989. Further work in this area is being carried out by the Stanford Linear Accelerator Centre (Slac) in California.
75. The Fermilab accelerator is called the CDF which stands for 'Collider Detector at Fermilab'.
76. Quoted in Hall, op. cit., p. 27.
77. Chown, op. cit., p. 2.
78. Davies,'Law and order in the Universe', *New Scientist*, 15 October 1988, p. 58.
79. Professor Roger Penrose, *The Emperor's New Mind* (Oxford University Press, 1990). See Pearce Wright, 'A Brief History of Mind over Matter', *The Times*, 17 May 1990, p. 35.
80. Mendel published his results in the *Journal of the Brno Natural History*

Society. They were not understood and were ignored.

81. DNA stands for deoxyribonucleic acid. Discussed in Bronowski, op. cit., p. 390.
82. The complete haploid (i.e. normal) set of chromosomes. Universal Dictionary, op. cit., p. 638.
83. This point was made in the BBC Horizon programme on the Genome Project in January 1989.
84. The Stone Age contains four periods: Eolithic, the dawn of history; Palaeolithic, the old Stone Age when tools were fashioned by chipping; Mesolithic, a transitional stage; and Neolithic, the new Stone Age, when tools were fashioned by grinding or polishing. See Collins, op. cit., p. 375.
85. In the East the Bronze Age may have begun c.5000 BC, and in the West perhaps c.2000BC, continuing until c.1000 BC. The Iron Age marked the development of a cultural phase. In Europe ironworking became general in the Mediterranean c.1000 BC. See Collins, op.cit., pp.62 and 208.
86. The Greek philosopher (427–347 BC) whose dialogues instituted the study of philosophy.
87. Greek philosopher (384–322 BC) who wrote the *Organon*, the *Politics*, the *Ethics* and the *Poetics*.
88. Discussed by Derry and Williams, *A Short History of Technology* (1960) p. 13 *et seq*.
89. Universal Dictionary, op. cit., p. 976.
90. Discussed by Bronowski, op. cit., p. 177 *et seq*.
91. Butterfield, 'Renaissance Art and Modern Science', *Origins of the Scientific Revolution*, ed. Kearney (1964) p.3.
92. Discussed by Kline, 'Painting and Perspective', in Kearney, ed., op. cit., pp. 18 and 20. An optical system 'attempts to convey the same impression to the eye as would the scene itself'. Symbolic art contained 'settings and subjects intended to illustrate religious themes and induce religious feelings rather than to represent real people in the actual and present world'.
93. See Hankins, op. cit., p. 1 *et seq*.
94. Ibid.The French named the period the *siècle des lumières* – the 'century of light'.
95. For example, eighteenth century physics included medicine and physiology as well as heat and magnetism. Natural history included zoology, botany, geology and meteorology and mixed mathematics included, *inter alia*, astronomy, hydraulics, horology, navigation, surveying and fortification. Discussed in Hankins, op. cit., p.10 *et seq*.
96. Discussed by Mathias,'Who Unbound Prometheus? – Science and Technical change, 1600–1800', in Musson, *Science, Technology and Economic Growth in the Eighteenth Century* (1972) p.69 *et seq*.
97. Ashton, 'Some Statistics of the Industrial Revolution in Britain', in Musson, op. cit., pp. 115–16.
98. Mathias, *The First Industrial Nation – An Economic History of Britain, 1700–1914* (1969) p.2.
99. Cardwell, 'Science and the Steam Engine 1790–1825', in Mathias ed.,

Science and Society 1600–1900 (1972) p. 81.

100. Mathias, op. cit., p.4.
101. Textiles, ship-building, minerals, transport, industrial tools, engineering, etc.
102. Miles and Gershuny, 'The Social Economics of Information Technology', in Ferguson ed., op. cit., argue that the 'Information Society' could be described as a second coming of the 'Post-Industrial' society – the first arising from the shift of emphasis from primary production to the service economy which, prior to the expansion of economic activity concerned with information flow and brought about by the technology, nevertheless produced social forces to justify the expression 'Post-Industrial Society'.

CHAPTER 2

Previous information technology 'revolutions'

THE DEVELOPMENT OF COMMUNICATION AND RECORD

NEW TECHNOLOGIES OF COMMUNICATION The Commander of the Spanish Armada would not have understood, indeed would have thought it presumptous of any society to take upon itself, the mantle of the 'Information Society', for he knew the value of accurate information and the consequences of the lack of it when required. It was a failure of communication between himself and his land forces, lack of local knowledge about tidal movements in the channel and the failure on the part of the designers of the Spanish artillery to obtain information about the time it took to re-load and re-position heavy guns during battle, compared with the performance of the smaller and more responsive artillery of the British forces, that ultimately cost him the campaign.

The technologies of communication and record have been developing since the very earliest times. Man has always sought to communicate his thoughts and ideas, first of all in the primeval world through primitive speech to those nearby and subsequently to the next generation by early forms of stored information. It has been perceptively remarked that language, although devoid of technology is correlative to the tool:[1] the tools and customs of paleolithic man provided the only source of information to subsequent generations about specialised activities such as hunting and preparing shelter, until words were fashioned from the sounds of animals and nature into a crude vocabulary. This probably occurred to an increasing degree towards the end of the Paleolithic period.[2] Later on, man discovered the techniques of storing information through painting. Some

41

of the earliest paintings recorded are those of c.20,000 BC in the caves of Altamira in the Santander province of Spain, such as the recumbent bison or the outline of the hand of man himself.[3] In Lascaux, in France, is a cave painting of a hunter gored by a wounded buffalo, the author no doubt intent upon recording the event.[4]

It is an interesting observation that as communication developed there was an expansion in the amount of detail which could be stored and transmitted. At the same time direct communication through speech, custom or possession of tools, which required proximity in space and time between recipient and communicator, gave way to the passing of information to those who were there, not simultaneously but subsequently, in the following generation perhaps. However, the form of storage contained in simple drawings on cave walls, lacked the scope to record detail (cave paintings have been described as the first 'read only memory' form of data storage)[5]. Another more sophisticated method was needed, and that of course was writing.

Although man most certainly took his inscriptions from the cave walls to other media such as wood, stone or other less durable materials and found ideographic forms of expression[6] to represent experience and ideas, cuneiform writing of wedge-shaped characters did not appear until c.4000 BC. The first surviving example is that of the temple archives of Sumerian Erech, contained on a set of tablets dating from c.3500 BC.[7] Sumer was the southern part of ancient Mesopotamia and the Sumerians who lived there from c.5000 BC are regarded as one of the oldest known civilisations in the world. Apart from cuneiform writing they are thought to have invented the wheel and the plough.[8] Later, in the same region, the Babylonians and subsequently the Hittites and the Egyptians developed the art upon clay. The Egyptians developed more rapid styles of writing[9] just as computer design today looks for better and more efficient methods of data storage than before.

The first indication of linear representation can be seen in the earliest forms of the Greek language in Knossos c.1400 BC. However by then a primitive alphabet was in use possibly as early as c.2000 BC among a Semitic people in communication with Egypt. It is also known that an alphabet, similar in character to the Arabic was used in Ugarit on the north coast of Syria prior to c.1300 BC.[10] The ancestor to the alphabet used today in most Indo-European and Semitic languages is the Phoenician alphabet. That alphabet spread with trade and colonisation as the Phoenician people spread from land between the Lebanon and the Mediterranean and from the cities of Tyre and Sidon to places as far afield as Carthage, Cornwall and the Scilly Isles. Derry and Williams comment that alphabetic writing began in Greece c.850 BC. The link to the present day continues through the Etruscan and Roman alphabets to Latin, first identified in the seventh century BC. In the century before Christ the Latin alphabet comprised 23 letters. Modern English has added only three: v, w, and j.[11]

The alphabet is to language as binary code is to computing. The construction of language and of words proliferated as a result of this powerful and flexible instrument of communication. To spread such writing, however, required a more suitable media than the walls, tablets and clays of earlier times. The first step forward towards the recording of information on paper came with the use of parchment,[12] first made in Pergamum in Asia-Minor c.250 BC. The Dead Sea Scrolls, discovered by a Bedouin in 1947 in a hillside cave near the north end of the Dead Sea, have been dated c.200 BC–100 AD. Parchment was used in Europe first of all in the employ of the Church and later on for public legal documents. Just as the producers of today's information technology face pressures to reduce the cost of data storage in computers, similar concerns existed in relation to parchment. Two hundred pages of parchment – enough to compile a reasonably sized book, required the skins of 12 sheep; the cost of writing in terms of subsistence and rewards for the author was considerably less than the costs associated with the medium which carried the work.[13]

THE INTRODUCTION OF PRINTING   It was not until paper was discovered in the West that any tangible progress could be made in the dissemination of works that was to come eventually with printing. Paper had in fact been manufactured in China centuries earlier while the rest of the world was still using parchment. The Chinese had discovered paper-making at the end of the first century AD.[14] Paper was in general use in China for approximately 500 years until the methods became known to the Moors and Arabs c.751 AD following the capture of Chinese paper-makers. Knowledge of the process gradually spread from Sicily to Spain, and from there to Italy and Germany. In England the first paper mill was established by John Tate at Stevenage, Hertfordshire, in 1489.

The stage was now set for the introduction of mechanisation into the process of recording the writings of authors that was to come in c.1455 with the invention of the printing press. What had happened up to this point was the evolution, first, of a method by which one person could communicate to another through the techniques of language by means of speech and, second, of media that could hold and carry information in ever more detail to a wider and wider audience using pictures, then pictographic symbols and finally the linear signs which ultimately formed an alphabet. In contrast with with the rudimentary forms of sharing and recording information that early man had mastered, a code and a method of communication of that code had emerged, transcending space and time as between the originator and recipient of the information fixed in the work. With the advent of printing, information was about to be made available in such amounts and to such numbers as to be orders of magnitude beyond what had gone before.

It is not surprising that the Chinese, with their early discovery of how to make paper, were also the first to develop a rudimentary form of printing from movable blocks. The precise time when this method came into use is not known but the Romans understood how to imprint designs on plaster and textiles from patterns cut on wooden blocks. It is also known that the block method was used to produce playing cards and religious artefacts. The Mongol empire also printed paper currency described by Marco Polo in the thirteenth century.[15] Whether printing was re-discovered in Europe or copied from the East is not understood for certain, although there is evidence that the existence of printing, as opposed to knowledge of its technique, was known of in Europe prior to the fifteenth century. Certainly, in that century similar prints to those of the East appeared in Venice and in some southern German towns. A problem that had yet to be overcome was finding a suitable ink with which to fix information upon the medium paper. The pigmented water ink used by scribes did not work well with the printing block, and its suitability deteriorated further with the later use of metal blocks. The watery solution would collect in droplets on the paper, which absorbed the liquid and blurred the imprint. Improvements came in the fifteenth century with the use of lamp-black, a grey or black pigment made from the soot of powdered charcoal or other carbonaceous materials, and mixed with a drying oil such as linseed. The latter oil was certainly used by the Flemish painters as a varnish in the early years of the century.

In addition to ink, paper and block, the fourth element required to complete the process of printing was the press itself. The first method used was to rub the back of the paper against the block with a leather pad, but this would of course produce problems with the lack of uniformity in the pressure that was applied. This was resolved by the screw press which worked well with the new ink since the paper would not get damp and move about. However, the printers faced the same problem as the early designers of computers who had to interfere physically with the hardware every time they wanted to amend the instructions to the machine. The print block had the characteristics of a 'read only memory' chip, in that once it was imprinted with the data to be reproduced it could not be changed. What the printers needed was an 'erasable, programmable, read only memory' device, which could be redesigned to print other works once the task was complete. This came with the invention of movable type, in which letters prepared from a mould could be used and used again inter-changeably on the block.[16]

Laurens Coster of Haarlem was probably the inventor of movable type c.1420–30. The first book printed in this way was probably *Speculum Nostrae Salutis*, followed by the 42-line Gutenberg Bible printed in 1455 by a goldsmith Johann Gutenberg of Strasbourg, who established a printing press in Mainz in 1448. It is estimated that composing a single page of the Bible took one man a day to achieve, very slow by modern standards but impressive for the time. The characters which formed the type were probably prepared with a steel punch. A Frenchman, Jenson, inventor of Roman type, was next and began printing at Venice in 1470. In 1475 William Caxton, an Englishman, began printing in Westminster after gaining experience in Bruges.[17]

Up to this point the experience was very similar to that of the birth of computing. There were problems of how to store data in a form in which it could be held safely, and without the risk of loss or decay, for later reproduction. There were also difficulties to overcome with regard to programming the machinery that was to reproduce the information. In the case of print the answer came with movable type; in the case of computers it came with the development of software as a form of instruction to the computer that would operate independently from the hard wiring of the machine – the hardware.

THE COMING OF BOOKS AND NEWSPAPERS In the 50 years following the introduction of printing the output of books was spectacular. The printed word had, in that short time, eclipsed the entire product of the previous thousand years.[18] Calculations based upon the 30,000–35,000 surviving books, representing 10,000–15,000 different texts, printed between 1450 and 1500, suggest that up to 20 million books could have been printed during this period worldwide.[19] This is based on the assumption that the average print run was no greater than 500 at that time.[20] Printers were primarily in the business for profit, so that until the market developed they tended to concentrate upon the established literature that had been in private circulation before.[21] From the decline of the Roman Empire until the twelfth century, the monasteries and other associated institutions held the monopoly of book production. Thereafter the development of learning outside the monastic walls grew, reflected in the founding of the universities.[22] Caxton, for example, drew on the texts of these periods and published translations of Virgil and Boccaccio, stories from Greek mythology, works of edification and English classics from Chaucer, Gower and from the Arthurian cycle.[23] There was general interest in historical accounts, and statutory texts and law books were printed as use required. Science was in its infancy, but medieval compilations were produced such as *Speculum Mundi*, a vast work in four parts, written in the main some two centuries before.

However, the English had entered into printing somewhat late. The centre of the book market was not London but Paris, supplying the universities with books. The political and social consequences of the capacity, potentially, to reach the populace at large was not immediately apparent. Neither was the opportunity seized very quickly. There is a view put forward that printing may have inhibited rather than facilitated the acceptance of new ideas, since the books printed did not challenge popularly-held beliefs and prejudices, but tended instead to re-inforce them.[24] There were further problems in publishing current information through books, in that the populace was not well equipped to use books. Few individuals could read and initially the significance of the mechanisation of print was not understood and was ignored.[25] However, in due course books did become the instrument of political and religious debate. For example, between 1525 and 1547 some 800 separate editions of religious works were printed in English, many of them strongly Protestant in content.[26]

Henry VIII (1509–47) could see the benefits as well as the dangers of this resource, and while using it to promote his own causes against the Roman Catholic Church, he found it necessary to protect his position through censorship. After statutes were passed[27] encouraging the import of books, the position was reversed. Those exempted within the printing trade from the restrictions of the 1484 Act governing the trade of foreigners found the position reversed by Statutes passed in 1523, 1529 and 1534. Thus free trade in books was at an end and the alien printers, bookbinders and sellers were subject to controls.[28] By Royal Proclamation a year later, a list of prohibited books appeared against 'blasphemous and pestiferous Englishe bokes, printed in other regions and sent into this realme', as well as 'the admission and divulgence of the Olde and Newe Testament translated into English'.[29] By a further Royal Proclamation issued through the Privy Council in 1538, control was extended to all books containing 'erroneous and seditious opinions'.[30] From this time on 'no persons or persons in this Realm shall . . . print any book in the English tongue, unless upon examination made by some of his Grace's Privy Council, or other such as his Highness shall appoint, they shall have licence to do so'. Further controls were placed by proclamation in 1551 and 1553.[31] The stage was set for a censorship war. In the words of one commentator:

> the story of the press is largely the story of the efforts of Authority to control it. All the resources of Church and State alike were thrown into this struggle, and for more than two hundred years the press was to enjoy only exceedingly brief and virtually accidental intervals of official liberty, separated by long periods of prohibition and repression'.[32]

The high water mark of the controls imposed upon freedom of expression and of access to information occurred in 1662 with the passage through Parliament by Charles II of the Printing Act – 'An Act for preventing the frequent abuses in printing seditious, treasonable and unlicensed books and pamphlets and for regulating of printing and of printing presses'.[33] The Act provided that no person could print a book or erect a printing press or house the same, without giving notice to the Stationers' Company, which had obtained its Royal Charter from Mary Tudor in 1557. Books in English could not be printed overseas or imported here without a special licence from the Archbishop of Canterbury, Bishop of London or other person empowered to grant licences. Approved texts were granted a license to print and three copies of every text produced had to be deposited for the King, in addition to that held be the Stationers' Company.[34] Persons permitted to have a printing press had to deposit security of £300 to the Stationers not to print unlicensed texts, and powers of search and seizure were provided to enable the Master or Wardens of the 'Licenser' to go with a constable and search premises for unlicensed books, to seize offenders and to demand an inspection of the licence. Others entitled to license texts included, for common law books – the Lord Chancellor; for books of history or affairs of state – the Secretary of State; for books on heraldry – the Earl Marshall of England; and for all others – the Bishop of London.

The Act also sought to restrict the craft by reducing the number of Master Printers to 20, as well as requiring that all replacements for them be Englishmen.

The Act came into force on 10 June 1662. There was some recognition by the powers-that-be of the stringency of the measure, since it contained a renewal provision to be applied after two years. The Act continued in being until 1695, when a Parliamentary committee was unable to agree on reforms following the objections raised to the efficiency of the measure by a largely Whig House. It is interesting to note from today's standpoint that the 1688 Bill of Rights, introduced following the Civil Wars, had nothing to say about the press.[35] Overt censorship, however, was now at an end, and the privileges to print granted by licence during the period of control were to shift subtlety to focus upon certain rights in the copy of the work itself. The change of emphasis was to be officially embraced in the Copyright Act 1709, 'An Act for the Encouragement of Learning by vesting the Copies of printed Books in the Authors or purchasers of such Copies during the Times therein mentioned'.[36]

The result of these measures meant that the full benefits of printing, so far as dissemination of literature and information to a wider audience was concerned, were not free of formal censorship until the beginning of the eighteenth century. There had been many news-sheets and pamphlets published during the seventeenth century, but much of them contained little more than gossip or advertisements. The climate of censorship had eased for the time being, such that it was now possible to produce news-papers legally. Although the potential readership was still small, the economic, demographic and technological conditions were now present to encourage such enterprise. A market, albeit a small one, now existed for news of events, both at home and overseas, although the Government still believed that news itself was not safe in the hands of all the people. What Parliament had realised, however, were the potential revenue implications of a stamp duty tax on papers. Stamp Acts were later introduced for this purpose in 1725 and 1757.

From about 1720 the concept of a weekly newspaper was commonplace. The earliest surviving copy of a provincial newspaper is issue number 91 of the *Bristol Postboy*, dated 12 August 1704, which probably began in 1702. The first provincial paper was the *Norwich Post*, which began in 1700.[37] In London, however, 'an eager news-starved public was ready and waiting'.[38] Printed 'newsbooks' in defiance of the censor, had circulated in London since the 1640s. Many publications were very guilty of flagrant plagiarism and frequently changed their titles from week to week.[39] The Printing Act[40] of 1662 put paid to this activity and an Official Surveyor of the Press was appointed in 1663, with strong powers of search and seizure. However, the Official Surveyor promptly obtained a patent to produce newspapers himself. Ultimately others collaborated to compete with what became known in its 24th issue of 5 February 1666, as the *London Gazette*.[41] In 1704 the paper had a circulation of 6000. There was competition among Master Printers to exploit this ready market by producing newspapers. A shake-out of the industry was inevitable, as too many papers chased too little news, roaming the coffee houses and taverns for gossip and eye-witness accounts from those returning home from war.[42] There were also complaints of invented news.

Thereafter the story is one of growth and development in the newspaper and book trade as the market place developed into more specialist sectors, such as the educational, scientific, religious and leisure markets. An increasing range of material was becoming available and the number of potential readers was increasing in response to population growth, the developing book trade, both at home and overseas, and the increase in literacy within the population at large. Latin, the language of scholarship, was in decline. Whereas one survey has shown that 77% of books printed before 1500 were written in Latin, the language began to lose ground in the sixteenth century and thereafter, although the process was very gradual.[43] Printing had standardised spelling and phrases to meet the requirements of a lay public that wanted text it could understand. This made economic sense as well. Books that could not be sold lost money.

In England, the Reformation movement of the sixteenth century, that sought reform of Western Christianity, was significant in the development of the English language through the translations of scripture and religious works. Further, the encouragement of imports of books prior to the onset of censorship in the 1530s led to translations and their publication in the English language, enriched with Latin, French and Spanish expressions.[44] Books of English grammar began to appear too. These influences, then, which operated through the catalyst of printing, begin to explain how grammar, spelling and vocabulary – the means of communicating information, and using information through books, evolved, producing a national language in which the literature could be written and understood.

In the United States development of inter-personal communication was somewhat different from the European experience. Communication across the Atlantic in the seventeenth and eighteenth centuries was gradually replaced by interaction between the American colonies.[45] Establishing communication networks was further intensified by the political situation that culminated in the Declaration of Independence in 1776. However, population centres in the nineteenth century still tended to be somewhat insular 'island communities'. Developments in printing, the distribution of books and newspapers and cultural exchange centred around particular interests and political groups.

THE INFORMATION SOCIETY – ECHOES FROM THE PAST   In conclusion, the evolution of ideas and of information-flow, through the development of printing, books and newspapers, produces some unexpected analogies with the development of the Information Society in the twentieth century. Indeed, the history of printing and of publishing represents a microcosm of the concerns society faces today with information technology.

First there was the problem of distributing information that could not easily be recorded because parchment, upon which the scribes produced their text, was both expensive to make and not particularly 'user friendly' in terms of its working life and durability. Similar problems occurred with computers. The hardware in the early pioneering days was crude and expensive to set up, and its restricted storage capacity and propensity to malfunction were apparent.

Next there were communication problems, as few individuals could read books or understand the language with which they were written. Moreover, the time it took to produce and to reproduce text was very slow, so few people could take advantage of the information. With computers, attitudes and experience were similar for a long time. Computers tended to be shut away in the domain of the data-processing department. A certain degree of mysticism developed with regard to the technology as between those who claimed to understand it and those, usually the users as opposed to the operators, who did not. There were similar problems too, compared with the book age, regarding the storage of data on computers. In the early days, comparable to the period prior to the invention of movable type, instructions to the computer had to be entered by adjusting the hard wiring of the machine. Later, keyboard entry techniques were developed as programming languages enabled those adjustments to be made automatically.[46] In the future, today's techniques will be judged very slow and inefficient by comparison with automated data-entry capacity, available through optical character recognition and, in the twenty-first century, by direct entry into the computer's memory through the spoken word.

When printing was introduced in the fifteenth century its potential was not at once perceived and the opportunity it gave for improved access to information was not immediately understood. In England, for a while, people clung to the old laborious methods of the scribe. A similar reaction occurred with computers until the technology advanced to the point when the needs of the user could be met and the technology became more accessible to the average person. Further, as printing took off, there was a surplus of newspaper production in London, chasing a market of readers that was unable to sustain every supplier. A shakedown of the newspaper industry was inevitable, just as it has been recently for print workers over the introduction of information technology in the industry. Shakedowns have also taken place in the computer industry, particularly in the early stages of the personal computer and applications-software market. It is interesting to note that the reduction of capacity on the supply side of the personal computer market took place at roughly the equivalent stage as the bankruptcy of some newspaper producers during the eighteenth century. In both instances the mass market for the product in question was just being exploited.

The next comparison between the two periods relates to the problem of how to formulate standards of grammar and vocabulary in relation to both books and computers. A difficulty facing the printers was the time it took to translate manuscript into a coherent format for the populace to use. Dialects and spurious phraseology had to be excised and a language developed using consistent spelling, vocabulary and style. This remains a common problem today as attempts are made to devise common standards in communication and software. The industry has now reached the stage of agreement on the representation of characters in binary code, but the general problem of incompatible computers and communication protocols and software remains.

Also causing controversy during the age of the book was the issue of freedom of access to information, the regulation of international trade in books (trans-border data flows) and the licensing and watchdog mechanisms subsequently imposed. Henry VIII and later Charles II introduced strict controls on the availability of books unless they had been officially sanctioned. The import of information into this country through books and pamphlets, etc., was also suppressed, unless it too met with official approval. Printers and printing presses were tightly regulated and a press censor with enforcement powers was appointed to monitor compliance with these conditions. Today, we can see the parallel of these measures in the controls imposed upon requests by individuals to have access to certain types of computer-stored information, particularly that held on government computers. A further illustration of this comparison can be seen in the protectionist policies of some countries who seek to sustain their domestic data-processing industry against foreign competition. At present, the modern equivalent of the press watchdog appointed in 1663 are those whose function it is to ensure that the telecommunications and data-processing industries operate in compliance with legislation governing the storage and transmission of personal data and the operation of the telecommunications industry, viz., the Data Protection Registrar and the Director General of Telecommunications.[47]

Finally, there is the contribution of the book to the age in which it became prominent- the Age of Enlightenment. In the eighteenth century the world of books and other printed media, such as newspapers, periodicals and plays, provided a new and challenging environment within which the debates of the 'new critical spirit' could take place.[48] The benefits were progressive, gradually fostering links between people and ideas, which, as a result of the interaction of information obtained through books, enabled previously accepted doctrines to be questioned within the spirit of rationalism that fuelled the Scientific Revolution. The contribution of the book has since been described thus:

> The printed book was something more than a triumph of technical ingenuity, [it] was also one of the most potent agents at the disposal of Western civilisation in bringing together the scattered ideas of representative thinkers. It rendered a vital service to research by immediately transmitting results from one researcher to another; and speedily and conveniently, without laborious effort or unsupportable cost, it assembled permanently the works of the most sublime creative spirits in all fields . . . Fresh concepts crossed the whole globe in the very shortest time, wherever language did not deny them access. The book created new habits of thought not only within the small circle of the learned, but far beyond, in the intellectual life of all who used their minds'.[49]

THE GROWTH OF PERSONAL
AND BUSINESS COMMUNICATIONS

THE DEVELOPMENT OF POSTAL SERVICES   While letters and despatches upon the business of the Monarch and for government purposes have been delivered both at home and abroad for many centuries, the development of postal services for the public at large is of more recent origin.[50] During the One Hundred Years' War between England and France (1337–1453), the Kings of England badly needed communication with their forces in France. Privy Council records show that the messengers used were friars and priests, heralds and pursuivants.[51] Similar arrangements were pursued by Edward IV during the war with Scotland. The first traces of private mail services date back to the Middle Ages, when merchants began to develop correspondence routes using their own messenger services and ships between the major trading cities. The universities also made their own arrangements. Henry VIII is credited with the first official appointment of a Master of the Posts, possibly in 1516.[52] The quality of service was very patchy however, as can be seen in a letter by the first holder of the position, Brian Tuke, to Cromwell in 1533, where Tuke complains of 'great defaulte in the conveyance of letters, and of special men ordayned to be sent in post'.[53]

The sixteenth century witnessed some early competition in the provision of postal services as between the official post and that organised by the merchants. This was controlled by proclamation in 1591 to counteract the growing threat to the monarchy from at home and overseas. There were, in those days, the usual complaints about the slowness of the mail, as, for instance, in 1569, when it was said that the posts between London and York 'never come nor go under three days'.[54] The latter part of the century saw the introduction of regulation regarding who should undertake the work, the supply of horses, the quality of saddles and 'furniture' with which to carry the mail, and the use of horns to blow 'by the way'.[55]

The seventeenth century witnessed further development of routes along the major trunk routes to the North and West and into Ireland. Coaches, instead of horses, began to be used on some routes but not across country, where the roads were relatively poor. There was some reluctance on the part of government to invest in roads because it was thought that this might facilitate the mobilisation of troops to move against London.[56] More private packages were carried, but this was controlled by an order of 1637 limiting the use of post to State business alone. This was due to the rising tide of suspicion and uncertainty that culminated in the first Civil War between Charles I and the Parliamentarians, led by Cromwell, from 1642–9.

The Post Office began to develop once more following the restoration of Charles II in 1660, as did the roads with the passage of the first of a series of

Turnpike Acts in 1663.[57] With the accession of William III in 1688 the overseas packet routes grew both into Europe and to the West Indies and Jamaica. By this time a penny post had been introduced for domestic deliveries up to one pound in weight. By 1702–3 nearly one million letters were carried by this arrangement.[58] A form of piracy began to be a problem in the eighteenth century. The conduits of the postal delivery services – the roads – began to be patrolled by highwaymen. One answer was to provide more secure delivery arrangements, characterised by the replacement of foot and mounted post-boys by coaches which were more difficult to intercept. At one stage the Post Office designed experimental forms of conveyance in a 'bullet proof' cart, but apparently robbers even managed to penetrate this attempt to impose an early form of risk management in the transmission of information and funds by mail.[59] A comment at the time stated: 'It was lately the case upon the North Road, where an iron cart, as strong as an iron chest, was stopt, taken out of the road and broke open . . . When desperate fellows had once determined upon a mail robbery, the consequence would be murder in case of resistence'.[60]

The improvement of the roads continuing through the turnpike legislation presented postal delivery with a problem. The new road system was undoubtedly a better one, but the existence of toll gates or barriers every few miles was both a cause of delay and expense.[61] A scheme was approved whereby fast mail coaches would travel uninterrupted along the turnpikes, paying 3d. per mile to the postmasters who in return would prepare the horses at staging points and load the mail. Thus the coaches would enjoy the same privileges as the mounted post-boys, who had always been exempt of tolls as the carriers of royal despatches. The first mail coach to operate under the new scheme left Bristol bound for London on 2 August 1784, covering the distance in seventeen hours which was remarkable for the time.[62] Average speeds increased to eight or nine miles per hour, the toll bars opening as the coach notified its approach by blasting its horn. This approach quickly spread to other routes.[63] The journey of 400 miles from London to Edinburgh was cut from 85 hours north and 131 south c.1750, to 60 hours each way in 1786 when the scheme was introduced to the Great North Road.

The mail coach era lasted approximately sixty years, from 1784 until 1847, when the final coach-run from Newcastle-on-Tyne to Edinburgh took place. In its heyday in the 1820s the central post office in London despatched some 17 coaches daily at 8pm. By 1837 there were 24 departing from the new Post Office at St Martins Le Grand.[64] The last of the London coaches arrived from Norwich and Newmarket on 6 January 1846.[65] The era had established postal delivery services for both private and commercial customers, preparing the foundations for the Rowland Hill reforms of 1839, which led to the introduction of prepaid postage with the penny black stamp on 10 January 1840 and to better financial arrangements for the Post Office. The London office despatched 112,000 letters that night.[66]

THE IMPACT OF STEAM LOCOMOTION   The first pouch of letters ever to be carried on a railway train were loaded on the Liverpool and Manchester Railway on 11 November 1830.[67] Thereafter an elaborate network of mail trains developed carrying a wide range of letters, parcels and packages, including newspapers from the printers in Fleet Street (where the London *Times* was being produced at the rate of 2000 copies an hour following technological improvements in the process, with the introduction of the cylindrical roller).[68] Newspaper and periodical distribution was also encouraged by a larger and more literate populace. More significant still was the reduction in taxation of newspapers when Stamp Duty was reduced from 4d in 1815 to 1p in 1836.[69]

The introduction of steam locomotion also held the key to another information revolution – direct inter-personal communication through personal mobility. Just as books and other printed material provided the conduit for the age of Enlightenment, so the railways served as the engine room of the industrial revolution. The power within that engine room was the steam engine which, as the printing press did for books, underpinned much of the productive effort and innovation that ultimately came together in the industrial revolution. The pioneers of the steam engine were Watt and Boulton, who brought together nearly two centuries of research into the principles of steam power with the launch of the Boulton and Watt pumping engine in 1776.[70] The vital key to the harnessing of steam power for locomotion was the development of the high-pressure engine which could be smaller in size yet achieve comparable amounts of power. This was done by directing the exhaust steam up a chimney from the boiler fire, which raised steam capacity considerably. (Contrast the similar experience with computers in the development of the silicon chip. Computers could be smaller yet much more powerful.)

Early designs of locomotive were tested on the road at the turn of the eighteenth century by Watt, Trevithick and others. In 1804 Trevithick made a locomotive that was able to pull a load of 10 tons on cast iron rails the 9.5 miles between the Penydarran ironworks and the Glamorganshire canal. The vision to make locomotives and railways was taken up by George Stephenson, who had sought the advice of Trevithick having seen his demonstration of a steam carriage in Newcastle in 1804.[71] Ten years later in 1814, Stephenson demonstrated his first machine. He had translated the action of the cylinder power directly to the wheels and pulled eight wagons containing 30 tons of material along a track faster than a horse could walk.[72] The use of locomotive power in the mines was recognised. In 1822 Durham coal-owners opened a railway with 17 wagons pulled by five of Stephenson's locomotives. Sixty-four tons of coal could be pulled on the wagons.[7] Stephenson had realised that the answer to the haulage of heavy loads lay in the grip of the iron wheel on the iron track using friction.[74]

In 1825 Stephenson was discussing with industrialists in the Liverpool and Manchester area the possibility of linking the two centres by rail. It would require a viaduct, 63 bridges and a 600 foot deep cutting through the Pennines to minimise gradients. A Liverpool and Manchester Bill was introduced to Parliament. Concern was expressed about the dangers of travelling at speeds of up to 12 mph and there was worry about the potential loss of jobs to the coaching industry – the coach builders and drivers, the harness makers, roadside inkeepers, horse breeders and dealers. Stephenson's solution was to suggest they become shareholders in the railway.[75] Stephenson wanted the contract to build the locomotive. He wanted to combat other suggestions that he regarded as inferior, such as the use of a stationary engine moving carriages by wire. There were also those who favoured a return to horse-drawn methods. Stephenson's son Robert suggested to his father's backers that a race be organised to demonstrate the capabilities of moving locomotives . The specifications of the vehicle were that it should not weigh more than six tons, should have a maximum boiler pressure not exceeding 60 lb. per square inch, be no more than 12 feet in length and be able to pull three times its own weight at an average speed of 10 mph.[76] A prize of £500 was offered to the winner.

The Rainhill trial took place on 6 October 1829. It was to be run over 20 circuits of a course just over three miles in length. Two hundred constables guarded the course and 10,000 people came to watch. Five locomotives were entered but two were quickly withdrawn. Of the three lcomotives that did compete one proved too light to support the load and the other too unweildy a machine and too heavy on consumption.[77] Stephenson's 'Rocket' was entered by his son Robert and achieved the required speed without difficulty. Uncoupled it reached 30 mph. For the first time in history, man could travel faster than a galloping horse. The success of 'Rocket' lay in the horizontal siting of the cylinders and the increased draught of the high chimney. The success of the trial ensured the rapid growth of the railway system and the conviction that this technology must be implemented if the expanding needs of industry to move goods and raw materials was to be met. Whereas in 1832 only 419 miles of track was either open or sanctioned, by 1840 it had reached over 2500 miles and by 1850 12,500 miles. Within 20 years the lines available doubled and railway usage more than trebled, particularly by passengers travelling third class.[78] Between 1840 and 1880 there was a fourteen-fold increase in steam power throughout the world.[79] In the 1850s speeds of 40 mph were commonplace and within thirty years this increased to 60–70 mph as design improvements were made.[80]

Far from threatening employment the railways produced it, both directly in the construction of the network and the locomotives and rolling stock, and indirectly in all sectors of the broader industrial economy.In 1846–8 railway investment was absorbing 5–7% of the national income. The average cost per mile of track was £40,000 and nationally a £16 million wage bill had to be met for 250,000 employees. The railways helped fuel the development of the construction industry which had a force of 100,000 in 1840 and three times that number seven years later. It also raised demand and therefore the price of raw materials such as coal, iron and bricks. By 1850 one million tons of coal were used by locomotives per annum.[81] However, the investment in the railways was broadly speaking obtained from private investors aided by cheap loans from the Bank of England during the boom period of the 1840s.[82]

Railway companies were set up to undertake construction and management of the railways, but this was not an organised or well-planned scheme. There were too many such companies and no national plan was drawn up. Worst of all, incompatibility in the gauge size of the track was introduced when, in 1847, Brunel brought in a seven-foot gauge on the Great Western Railway. He believed the 4ft. 8½in. narrow gauge was inferior and would be dropped once the broad gauge was introduced. Brunel was wrong and the latter was dropped when the other railways of this country made no move to adopt it.[83] Many more routes were financed than in the longer term could be profitable, but as a result a nationwide network was established. In the Railway Act of 1844, the first steps towards national uniformity were taken in the creation of an inspectorate to enforce certain laid-down minimum standards. However, it was not until a century later, in 1947, that the railways were nationalised.

The impact of the early decades of the railway has been described thus:

> Millions travelled who had never done so before. Without railways the mass distribution of cheap literature would have been impossible. The eating habits of the cities changed, for the price of meat fell, and fresh vegetables were within reach of most city-dwellers for the first time. The railways quickly became the greatest single employer in the country. They created the British export trade of the nineteenth century by making it possible to transport goods cheaply to the docks. They revolutionised methods of government by making Members of Parliament hours instead of days away from their constituencies. They transformed agriculture'.[84]

CARRYING THE MAILS OVERSEAS   The railway was not the only means of transport to benefit from the steam engines of Watt and his fellow pioneer Boulton. As early as 1802 a steam tug had operated on the Clyde, but 16 years elapsed before steam was used for a sea voyage.[85] The change from wood to iron hulls occurred at about the same time such that in 1822 the first iron steamship to cross the Channel was constructed on the Thames.[86] The Post Office commenced a steam mail-packet service in 1821 between Holyhead and Howth in Ireland. This reduced the journey time from 20 hours by sail to eight and a half hours by steam-driven vessel.[87] Five other postal routes introduced steam packet services and in 1837, following criticism of the Post Office for its postage rates, control was transferred to the Admiralty. Distribution of the overseas mails was transferred to Falmouth, though of the 37 Admiralty packets operating from there, 30 were still sailing vessels and only seven were steam driven.[88]

Sailings to Malta left monthly and took seven weeks to complete the journey each way. Services to Brazil would take five months whereas the British West Indies were served twice monthly, the journey lasting three months for the round trip.[89] No steam vessel, however, had yet been used on the Trans-Atlantic route, although in 1819 a full-rigged three-master, with engines supporting the drive paddles, called 'Savannah' had completed the journey in the opposite direction from Georgia to Liverpool.[90] There was considerable speculation and debate in the 1830s as to the dimensions and construction of a steam-ship to take on the Atlantic crossing. One comment of the day was that 'it was easier to go to the moon than to go direct from a port in England to New York'.[91]

A trial very similar to that held in 1829 involving Stephenson's Rocket came out of the competition to be the first to make an Atlantic steam-ship crossing from east to west. The trial was between a newly-formed British and American Steam Navigation Company, whose vessel, 'Sirius' was chartered from a steam packet company who had used it on the Cork to London route. The second contender was Brunel's 'Great Western' built as an extension to the railway construction on behalf of the Great Western Railway Company. 'Sirius' was a 700 ton vessel with 323 horsepower and carrying 423 tons of coal. Great Western was 1340 tons, 450 horsepower carrying 600 tons of coal. Great Western started the crossing four days behind Sirius but both arrived in New York on the same day. Great Western had completed the crossing in 15 days. The return trip was completed in under 12 days, with 68 passengers and 20,000 letters on board. A New York newspaper recorded that 'steam navigation across the Atlantic is no longer an experiment but a plain matter of fact'.[92]

In 1839 the Cunard line was born and regular crossings began with the Britannia in July 1840. In 1851, the tonnage of steam-powered vessels was 185,000 tons compared to an estimated 3.66 million tons of sailing ships with wooden hulls. However, by the 1880s steam ships overtook sailing ships in terms of shipping tonnage registered in the United Kingdom.[93] By then, construction of ships was dominated by iron and, increasingly, steel-hulled steam ships.[94]

For postal services the opening up of the trade routes by the steam-ship was significant, since Britain still had its empire as well as its emigrants, who left to settle in North America or the colonies. The carriers, however, demanded subsidies from the Post Office to carry the mail and this raised the postage rates; for example 4s. per pound for letters, 4d. per pound for printed matter. The Post Office thought this was too expensive and gradually succeeded in reducing the subsidy. This made postal communications overseas more affordable to the wider population. Further improvements to overseas mail services were made when other countries began to adopt the British system of postage stamps and a pre-paid uniform charge. By the start of the 1860s the system was virtually comprehensive. This was subsequently backed by the formation in 1879 of the Universal Postal Union, whose origins date back to the 1860s when the campaign to reduce postage costs was beginning to produce results. Twenty-two states attended a congress in Berne to discuss the matter and following that meeting the Postal Union came into being in January 1875. This basically produced a single uniform rate and weight scale such that a standard letter weighing 15 grammes would cost $2\frac{1}{2}$d. if sent to a recipient in a member country.[95] Some variation from the standard rate was permitted for transit costs but this was subject to controls. Most countries had followed Britain's lead with the penny post for domestic mail, so the margins were there for international transmissions of mail. Transborder data-flow questions were resolved by each country agreeing liberty of transit for each others' mails over land and sea. In 1859, after the Crimean War, arrangements had to be made for soldiers and civilians to send money home from the front, and the Post Office began to carry money orders. This spread world-wide, eventually under the supervision of the Postal Union.

PARALLELS WITH THE INFORMATION AGE   Once again parallels can be drawn here between the birth of the computer industry and the subsequent characterisation of the Information Society, and the invention of steam power and the onset of the Industrial Revolution. Steam power increased the scale of industrial activity as well as engaging with other technologies to produce a new range of manufactured goods and industrial processes. For example, the inventions of the puddling (reverbatory) furnace and the rolling mill by Henry Cort in 1784 enabled pig-iron from the blast furnace to be refined into malleable bar-iron. Prior to this the forges for refining iron ore tended to be located where supplies of water and charcoal were, often away from the site of the iron ore itself. Cort's inventions allowed coal to replace charcoal and water power, and Watt's steam engine to operate the hammers and rollers, such as Nasmyth's double action steam hammer of 1839, used for the production of larger iron beams and plates.[96] The integration of the technologies led to integration of the iron industry, as well as leading to a dramatic increase in production.[97] A similar picture has emerged with the growth and diversification of computers which is most evident in the proliferation of applications and the convergence with other sectors such as telecommunications.

The steam engine was also modified to serve the needs of a number of different industries such as the mobile engines required for transport or the stationary versions used in a variety of industrial sectors. Through its versatility and the increase in rotational speeds, the steam engine also enabled new precision machine tools to be used in manufacturing. For example, using a 30 h.p. steam engine the Admiralty was able to develop machines for making different sizes of pulley blocks, which undertook the tasks of sawing, boring, mortising and scoring. Three different sizes were produced and 130,000 were made on 43 separate machines. The workforce of 110 skilled men was cut to that of 10 unskilled men.[98] The steam engine enabled the process of precision tool making to be carried forward into the industrial sector, even to the point of producing the tools that would be needed for the later versions of the steam engine itself and the tools they would have to drive.[99] The computer industry has similarly served the economy of the Information Society by its diversification into data processing, manufacturing and communications. Practically all industrial and service sectors have been thus affected. Moreover, as with the technology of the past, today's technology is feeding upon itself to fashion the next generation of computers that will perhaps lead to the breakthrough in artificial intelligence and the creation the 'universal machine'.

Another general observation is appropriate at this point. The gestation and take-up periods of the major breakthroughs in technology have shortened as society and time move on. In terms of the information and communication revolutions the point is most evident. Compared with the developmental phase of communication through writing, which began with the linear alphabet of the Greeks and culminated with the book and the printing press some two thousand years later, the exploitation of steam power that was to transform personal mobility was well underway within two centuries of the moment when the first principles of steam power began to be identified. Whereas for centuries man had not been able to travel any faster than a horse, within 20 years of the Rainhill trial of 1829 society had been changed beyond recognition, both in terms of speed and volume of movement. This incremental shortening of societal metamorphosis brought about by technological advance has continued into the 'Information Age', both at the macro level and in terms of the speed of communication and obtaining of information by the individual.

COMMUNICATION IS NO LONGER PROXIMITY-DEPENDENT   Until now we have been tracing the development of communication that is dependent upon the proximity of the recipient to the information and its storage media. Communication was either through drawing, writing or by word of mouth, but in each case the medium that fixated the work, or the person verbally giving the information, had to be within the grasp of the receiver. The first attempts to break this bond and to separate communication of the message from the transmission medium, came with the relaying of visual signals by smoke or fire.[100] Although the recipient had to be in visual contact with the beacon he was nevertheless physically distanced from the source of the medium which transmitted the signal, albeit the case that it could only deliver a very simple message.

The first records of such methods of communication are those of the Greek historian Polybius, who described communication by means of fire-signals.[101] Some seventeen centuries later, the warning of the approach of the Spanish Armada was signalled by a network of beacons across southern England. Many countries used this method to announce danger. The scene has been described thus:

> Shortly after dawn the watchers on the cliff saw the first Spanish ships: fleeting shapes glimpsed far offshore through banks of mist and squally showers. The tar-soaked brushwood of the beacon burst urgently into flame, and within minutes a replying pin-prick of light to the east confirmed that the alarm was passing along the chain to Plymouth and the waiting English fleet: from there the signal would be relayed to all parts of the kingdom.[102]

What is perhaps the first map of a communications network is the Carde of the Beacons, in Kent, which was drawn in the 1560s or earlier to define the beacon points between Beachy Head, London and Folkestone in southern England.[103] In modern terms, the information conveyed by the 'on'/'off' signal of the beacon – 'lit' or 'not lit' was very limited in kind. The recipient, for example, would know what the message contained once the beacon was set alight. In itself it carried nothing other than confirmation that what everyone was looking out for was in sight. It was equivalent to the 'on' or 'off' of a transistor switch within a computer, which either conducts or blocks the flow of an electric current. There was a demand for a more versatile form of communication to enable ships to communicate with shore stations. The future James II, while Lord High Admiral of the Fleet, designed a set of flag-signals for the navy which were later developed and used during the maritime wars against the French in the late eighteenth century.[104] A visual system of sending information had therefore been developed (semaphore) using an alphabetic code based on the position of the signaller's arms.[105] The subsequent use of telescopes enhanced the scope of the system. In 1793 a Frenchman, Claude Chappe, developed what was to become a 3000-mile network of stations, each equipped with semaphore arms and a telescope. The stations were built 10 miles apart, the first link being between Paris and Lille, and before the end of the decade the system extended to Brest and Strasbourg. Initially constructed to support the armies of the French Revolution, the system declined with the onset of the telegraph, and was abandoned in the mid-nineteenth century.

The Telegraph In 1753, in a letter to the *Scots Magazine*, Charles Morrison predicted the discovery of the electric telegraph. His system used 26 wires, one for each letter of the alphabet, to be laid between the transmitting and receiving stations. The message would be spelt out letter-by-letter, each wire being connected to a machine which could generate a static electric current and thereby move a pith-ball attached to the corresponding wire in the receiving station.[106] Twenty years later it was realised that a single wire could replace the 26 if a code was used to define each letter. The key that was to bring these ideas to fruition was the discovery of electricity and its link with magnetism. The ancient Greeks had been the first to realise that by rubbing a piece of amber, a light object such as a feather was attracted to it. In the sixteenth century, the physician to Queen Elizabeth, William Gilbert, discovered other substances which had a similar effect.[107] The positive and negative charges of electricity were identified in 1729 by Stephen Grey and subsequently tested in the 1730s by the French physicist, Charles Du Fey. Later, in 1754, an instrument to measure quantities of electricity was invented by John Canton. Canton was able to show the existence of a current by the repulsion of liked-charged balls of pith suspended by threads. At about the same time, in 1745, Musschenbrook discovered the principles of induction, whereby electro-motive force could be generated by varying the magnetic flux through a closed circuit. His 'Leyden Jar' enabled quantities of electricity to be accumulated and then rapidly discharged. From this and other research, lightning was identified as an electrical discharge and conductors on buildings were introduced. In 1800 the Italian Alessandro Volta discovered an additional source of electricity created by the contact of plates made of different metals, such as copper and zinc, immersed in an acidulated water such as brine. This led quickly to the production of electric batteries in research laboratories from which further discoveries were made.

Oersted, a Dane, who became Professor of Physics at Copenhagen University in 1806, noticed during the course of a lecture that by moving a magnetic compass needle close to a wire carrying an electric current, the needle moved. He had discovered the magnetic field that surrounds a wire conducting electricity. Ampere very quickly demonstrated that the strength of the magnetic field was linked to the strength of the current that produces it. Faraday then showed in 1831 that the motion of a conductor in a magnetic field generated an electric current. His first demonstration involved a wire circling a fixed magnet and his second, the next day, reversed the effect with the magnet circling the wire conducting the current.[108] He had created the electric motor from which the dynamo was developed to generate electricity. This led to Edison and Swan's development of the incandescent light bulb in 1879/80, and to the use of electric motors in industry and transport as an alternative to mechanical power.

The first telegraph system to exploit the possibilities of communication by means of a wire carrying an electric current was developed in 1837 by Charles Wheatstone, Professor of Natural Philosophy at King's College, London, and William Fothergill Cooke, who had sought Wheatstone's help in installing a telegraph for a railway company. (The term 'telegraph' had first been used by Chappe in 1793, to describe his semaphore station network.) Cooke had seen a demonstration of a model of a telegraph during March 1836, developed by the Russian scientist and diplomat, Baron Schilling.[10]Applying the newly-discovered concepts of electromagnetism just discovered (i.e. the flow of an electric current through a coil causing a movement in a magnet adjacent to it) the two demonstrated their 'Five-needle Telegraph' to the directors of the London to Birmingham Railway in late 1837. Earlier, in June of that year, they had patented their invention which worked by deflecting any two of the needles simultaneously, so that they pointed to any one of 20 letters on the grid behind the needle. The deflection of a single needle identified a numeral. (The system could not, however, cope with 26 letters, causing some difficulty with interpretation of messages.) The first system was installed along 21 kilometres of track between Paddington and West Drayton in 1838–9 and subsequently, in 1842, extended to Slough. This was the first time electricity was used for a commercial purpose. By then, a two-needle telegraph had been developed. The system attracted publicity (particularly so when, in 1845, the telegraph was used to apprehend the Quaker murderer, Tarvell, who was identified on board the London-bound train at Slough and arrested upon arrival at Paddington) and the public were charged one shilling to see it in operation. Messages were also accepted from the public for transmission and the telegram was born.[110] The 1830s also saw the development of the telegraph in other countries, particularly Germany and the United States.[111]

In 1846 Wheatstone and Cooke established the Electric Telegraph Company. Several private telegraph companies came into existence at about this time and by 1852 Electric Telegraph alone had installed 4000 miles of telegraph. Writing about the operation Charles Dickens commented:

> 'One hundred and sixty miles of wire are now fixed along parapets, through trees, over garrets, round chimney-pots, and across roads on the southern side of the river, and the other one hundred and twenty required miles will soon be fixed in the same manner on the northern side. The difficulty decreases as the work goes on, and the sturdiest Englishman is ready to give up the roof of his castle in the interests of science and the public good, when he finds that many hundreds of his neighbours have already led the way'. [112]

The telegraph quickly spread to the ports, and in August 1850 the tug 'Goliath' laid the first cable from Dover across the channel into France at Cape Gris Nez.[113] (However, it was fouled by the anchor of a French fisherman within weeks and a new cable had to be laid the following year.)[114] This was the start of a European network connecting Great Britain to other European capitals. The first successful transatlantic cable was laid in August 1858, when two cable-laying ships converged in mid-Atlantic to splice their cables and steam back in opposite directions to land. The cable failed within three months. It took eight more years before a further cable was laid by the 'Great Eastern' between Valentia in Ireland and Trinity Bay Newfoundland, which was to connect Europe and North America permanently by cable.[115]

The United States had, by that time, enjoyed more than 20 years use of the telegraph. Samuel Morse had developed the system of signalling, which became the Morse Code, in 1837, and it was quickly applied, in collaboration with Alfred Vail, for telegraphic purposes. By 1844, the only state east of the Mississippi to be without the telegraph was Florida.[116] In addition to the obvious improvements brought to the US by the telegraph it also had a further impact in that country doing away with local time zones and preparing the populace for nationwide integration in business, government and social affairs.[117] Worldwide by 1862, 150,000 miles of telegraph cable had been laid around the world, including 15,000 in Great Britain and 48,000 in the USA. By 1870, telegraphic connections were underway by private British companies to India, China and Australia. These were complete in 1872 when the Mayor of Adelaide exchanged greetings with the Lord Mayor of London. By the turn of the century more than 17 cables had been laid across the Atlantic, with many more linking other parts of the world.[118]

There was pressure for regulation of the private operators in the 1860s. There were complaints of delays and inaccuracies in transmission and a belief that the system could be expanded and a better service provided. Business echoed these impressions through their Chambers of Commerce calling for the takeover of the private companies by the Post Office and a single charge for telegrams irrespective of distance.[119] Interestingly, the press also felt threatened and exploited by the activities of the private companies in transmitting news to the provinces. Two Telegraph Acts were passed in 1868 and 1869[120] giving the Post Office power to purchase private systems. The first Statute contemplated that, in the absence of agreement on takeover, the private companies could continue their operations, but it then appeared that the Post Office might not get control of the profitable inter-city connections, being left instead with the responsibility of developing the unprofitable routes through the sparsely populated areas. In the 1869 Act the Post Office obtained the exclusive privilege to transmit telegrams in the UK.[121] Foreign cables were excluded from the arrangements in the 1869 Act. The capital expenditure involved in the takeover of the domestic service was £10.9 million. Of this, £7.2 million went to the telegraph companies and £0.8 million to the railway companies. The residue of £1.9 million was spent during the next three to four years on extension and development of the service.[122] The transfer took place on 28 January 1870, and some 60,000 miles of aerial line and 2800 telegraph offices went under Post Office control. That same year Great Britain was admitted to the International Telegraph Union. This had formed just five years before on 17 May 1865, when 20 countries agreed to work towards international co-operation in the field of telegraph communication. (It is now called The International Telecommunication Union, and is the oldest such international body in the field today.)

Initially, the recipient of a telegraph message wrote it down by hand. In 1845, however, a method of printing the message was devised in the United States and in 1860 Wheatstone patented a printing telegraph here.[123] The message first had to be transposed into the form of perforations in a paper tape, and then transmitted and received at high speed. The system was the forerunner of the more modern equivalent which used punched tape as in the early days of computers.[124] By 1880, the Chief Engineer of the Post Office reported that 5000 Wheatstone models were in use in Great Britain, capable of transmitting at the rate of 180–190 words per minute. Estimates put the annual use of the telegraph at this time as equivalent to the transmission of 15 million copies of *The Times*. The tariff was halved to sixpence for 20 words in 1883, increasing the traffic in transmission of telegrams from 33 million in 1883 to 50 million in 1885. This rose to 90 million telegrams by the end of the century. In 1889 money orders were transmitted for the first time.[125] The versatility of telegraph was demonstrated on 17 October 1906 when a photograph was transmitted a distance of 1000 miles by a German Professor Arthur Korn. The transmission was achieved by breaking down the photograph into small parts and producing from each part an electric current corresponding to its shades of grey. This achievement built upon several years of research by physicists and opened the way for the press and news media to obtain pictures much faster than before, particularly to and from the United States. A rapid and affordable method of communication for the business user, and to a lesser extent the private citizen, had been developed, linking the major countries of the world. In 1980, the Inland telegram service was superceded by the 'Telemessage' service offering overnight delivery.

The Telephone The possibility of being able to transmit speech, as opposed to printed messages by wire, had certainly been visualised by a few people by the time Alexander Graham Bell, a Scottish emigrant to Ontario, patented the invention on March 7, 1876.[126] Three days later the first coherent words: 'Mr Watson, come here, I want you', were spoken down the 'telephone line'. [127] Bell's interest in the production stemmed from the interest in the subject of his father and grandfather. For a while Bell had taught deaf children to speak in Boston. Two of the parents whose children he taught financed his research. Bell knew of the work of the German physicist, Helmholtz, into the reproduction of sound and wanted to see whether it was possible to use electricity to send speech by wire connected to an electromagnetic microphone. He had recognised that speech produced small changes in air pressure, and he wanted to see if he could replicate those changes within corresponding electrical signals which could then be transmitted along the telegraph wire. The process involved bouncing the sound waves onto a thin diaphragm, consisting of a circular sheet of iron, which would then vibrate in tune. These could then be translated into electrical impulses and transmitted. His first transmitter was a 'liquid' one consisting of a container of weak acid. The process would produce a corresponding vibration in the diaphragm in the ear piece of the receiving instrument and reconstitute the sound waves matching those falling on the transmitter.[128] Progress was made and within six months of the initial experiment Bell was able to recognise his father's voice over a distance of eight miles.[129]

There were further problems to deal with, however, since the wave pattern of the human voice was very complex and the sound had to be sufficiently clear for the human ear to pick it up. A particular problem related to this was the fact that any electrical conductor faced some resistance in transmission. Each signal would need to be boosted to restore its signal strength if it was to be transmitted over a long distance. There might be other causes of natural interference with the signal too, which would cause distortion on a cumulative basis. The first Bell 'magneto' telephone had a similar mouthpiece and earpiece and which were used in pairs.

In 1878 Thomas Edison improved the efficiency of the transmitter by packing the microphone with carbon granules contained in two small buttons in contact with one another.[130] The resistance[131] of the latter altered quite sensitively with the pressure exerted by the sound waves. With slight contact a high resistance occurred producing a weak current. With the pressure of the sound waves increasing the level of contact between the carbon buttons, less resistance was found and a larger current produced, thus ensuring a more effective reproduction of speech at the receiving instrument. This improved transmitter was still widely used as late on as the 1950's. Further improvement was introduced when Edison developed the induction coil. This combatted the resistance incurred in the wires since, by passing the current through a magnetic field, a current was induced for onward transmission to the receiver. This improved system was still widely used in telephones as late as the 1950s.[132]

In 1877, after demonstrating the device at an exhibition in Philadelphia, Bell came to England to show his achievement to the British Association and the London Society of Telegraph Engineers. Afterwards he took it to Queen Victoria at Osborne House on the Isle of Wight.[133] The Queen had a conversation with Sir Thomas Biddulph, Electrician to the Post Office, who was connected to the main house from Osborne Cottage, a few hundred yards away in the grounds. The Post Office, however, was slow to grasp the opportunity to exploit the telephone which Bell had offered. Instead, with a capital of £100,000, 'The Telephone Company Ltd', was established to be followed quickly by a number of other commercial operations which also capitalised on the invention. Initially private lines were set up with the receivers on property belonging to the same person, such as a line from a merchant's office to his private house or wharf, or to his partner, or a line connecting a head with a branch office or an employer to his employee. Other private lines connected up receivers on property of different persons such as from a doctor's residence to a chemist's shop; from a firm of printers to a bank; from a company to a firm of solicitors; or from a steamship company to excursion and tourist agents. Emergency services could also be contacted from boxes containing a telephone placed in the street by municipal corporations. Police and local householders would have a key to open the box and call for fire, police or ambulance as needs required.[134]

In the United States the Bell Telephone System was able to establish itself almost anywhere throughout the country where the conditions suggested a profit was to be made. This was based on the Bell patents which did not expire until 1894. Service was established mainly between cities where business demand was likely to be strong. In 1884 a long distance telephone service within the country was established. Competition proliferated, however, after expiry with companies vying to wire up the towns and some rural areas as well. By 1902 of more than 1000 cities with phone services over 450 were served by two or more companies,[135] and in 1910 Congress acted to reduce 'wasteful competition' by national regulation.[136] The telephone was of great significance to American culture, giving individuals much greater opportunity for inter-personal communication over long distances and particularly out of rural communities.[137] This was not achieved immediately, however, since the telephone was initially identified as a business utility just as computers were until the arrival of the personal computer.

The first exchange opened in the USA in January 1878 with 21 subscribers. The impracticality of connecting every subscriber directly with every other subscriber had been realised. Instead each would have a direct line to the exchange where the operator could connect the caller with the intended recipient. The first London exchange opened in August of the following year in Coleman Street in the City of London. During the same month Edison formed the 'Edison Telephone Company Ltd', to compete with Bell's company in London. It had a capital of £200,000 to exploit the Edison patents, and shortly after it opened telephone exchanges in Lombard Street and Queen Victoria Street in London. The two companies merged in 1880 to form the 'United Telephone Company'.[138] This later resulted in court action before the Exchequer Division of the High Court in London when the Government succeeded in obtaining an order that the new telephone service was a violation of the Telegraph Acts of 1863 and 1869[139] in the sense that the telephone was, to all intents and purposes, equivalent to the telegraph.[140] This was despite the fact that, at the time of that legislation, the telephone had not been invented and against expert testimony presented in the case on behalf of the defendants. In the words of one such witness, Professor Tyndall:

> 'Prior to the labours of Bell and Edison it had never to my knowledge entered into the thoughts of scientific men to transmit by means of electricity the tremors of the human voice, so as to reproduce audible and articulate speech at a distance. The proof that this was not only possible but practical appeared to those most familiar with experimental physics to be an application of electrical and acoustical science not only new but marvellous. I have, therefore, no hesitation in expressing the opinion that to confound the telephone with the telegraph would be to place in the same category utterly dissimilar things'.[140a]

Despite this, the court held that the legislation had granted the exclusive privilege of transmitting telegraphs to the Post-Master General of the Post Office.[141] Each conversation by telephone was therefore a breach of that right since there was no 'material distinction between telephonic and telegraphic communication, as the transmission if it takes place is performed by a wire acted on by electricity'. The Attorney General, having surprisingly won the argument and an injunction against the defendants, nevertheless recognised the public interest in seeing that the use and development of telephone services prospered. As a result, by agreement signed in November 1884 and backdated to 1 January 1881, the Post Office licensed The National Telephone Company to carry on its operation. The licence had been backdated to within 11 days of the court judgment and conveniently the power to licence was drawn from the court decision in that the Post Office used its exclusive privilege to arrange for the provision of a telegraphic service under the Telegraph Act 1869, to delegate authority to the Edison company. It seemed that the Government was unhappy at the prospect of further State intervention in communications and yet could not suppress the inevitable competition of the telephone service.

This state of affairs ensured that the troublesome relationship continued between the Post Office and the private companies. One particular weapon which the Government used which made life difficult for the telephone companies was to deny them the privileges of the Telegraph Acts which contained wayleave powers to enable the placement of poles or underground lines along public roads or adjacent to the railways. Because of this, the lines had to be laid across private and public authority land, the negotiation with landowners often resulting in large sums being paid for the privilege of taking the lines across. Just as in more recent times, when employees of newly privatised bus companies fought one another on the streets for customers, so too did the gangs of rival engineers competing to install the poles and lines. Recognising the stupidity of trying to compete in the same areas of the country the private companies began to merge. The United Telephone Company and its subsidiaries were amalgamated to form the 'National Telephone Company' in 1889 and in 1894 it controlled more than 73,000 lines compared with 5–6000 which were by then managed by the Post Office.

The Post Office had tentatively entered the market in 1881 when the Government finally authorised it to offer the public a telephone as well as a telegraph service. The first Post Office controlled exchange opened in Swansea in March of that year. In 1896, four years after the decision to do so, and following public complaint about the lack of co-operation between the Post Office and private services, the latter took over the trunk telephone lines[142] of the United Kingdom at a cost of £460,000 in compensation. Following this takeover, it was only a matter of time before the complete takeover of the service would take place. There agitation became particularly strong when the Post Office introduced its own partly competing service in London, supplementing that which already existed under the National Telephone Company's control. Several municipal services also formed during this period, in Hull, Glasgow, Swansea, Brighton and Portsmouth under licence from the Postmaster General, but only Hull and Portsmouth survived beyond 1907.

In 1905 the Government, after negotiations with the companies concerned, and following a recommendation from a House of Commons Select Committee,[143] acquired an option to take over the National Telephone Company and the entire service as from 1 January 1912 at plant cost on that date. The original licence of 1884, backdated to January 1881 was for a period of 31 years, expiring in 1912. The Post Office had acquired 1565 exchanges of which 231 had in excess of 300 subscribers each. Within three years a further 450 exchanges were opened in parts of the country that previously enjoyed no telephone service.[144] Exception had to be made for the surviving municipal telephonic services of Portsmouth and Hull. Portsmouth's service continued until its abandonment in 1913, but Kingston-upon-Hull managed to remain independent and continues to do so today.[145] A total of 19,000 National Telephone Company employees were absorbed by the takeover, and the country, for the first time, could enjoy the benefits of a unified telephone system.

If the telephone service was really going to succeed, a method of connecting one caller with another automatically would have to be found. If this was not done, in due course there would be a recruitment problem in engaging operators to handle every call made. In 1880 Almon Strowger, an undertaker from Kansas City, devised an automatic switch which was operated by pulses of electric current produced by the caller when he dialled a number. The selection was made by the movement of a shaft with a contact arm driven by the action of an electromagnet operated and released by the current produced by the operation of the dial. Known as the 'step-by-step' switching system because it actuated the switches, one by one, until the desired circuit was completed, it was incorporated in the first public automatic exchange at La Porte, Indiana, in 1892. Strowger developed his switch introducing 10 layers to the device, enabling the contact arm to connect in any part of the switch. This increased the capacity of the switch to connect up to 100 telephones with one another. The first automatic exchange in Britain opened at Epsom on 13 March 1912 under the control of the Post Office who, less than three months earlier, had assumed control of the telephone service.

Expansion of overseas connections began with London and Paris becoming linked in 1891 when the first telephone cable was laid across the channel. In 1915, nearly 40 years after the Bell patent, a transcontinental link was made in the USA between New York and San Francisco, having overcome some initial problems of compatability between east and west. The first submarine telephone cable to cross the Atlantic was not laid until 1956. Before that connection to the USA was by radio telephone, established in 1927. The first transatlantic cable carried 37 circuits. Ten years later the number of circuits per cable had risen to 500.[146]

By the mid-1930s Britain had five telephones per 100 of the population totalling two million units. This doubled by 1947. The corresponding figures for the USA were 13 and 23 per 100 respectively, totalling 13 million and 23 million units. It is estimated that the world had 33 million telephones in operation in 1934 and 380 million in 1947. This dramatic development of telephonic communication demonstrates the monumental miscalculation of a Mayor of a small mid-western town in the USA, who commented during the 1880s that one day every town in America would have its own telephone.

'Wireless' Telegraphy   The origins of radio communication can be traced from 1867, when James Clerk Maxwell, Professor of Mathematics at

Cambridge forecast the laws that would prove correct in later research to develop wireless telegraphy. He later published his theories in a work entitled *Treatise on Electricity and Magnetism*. One of the great debates of the latter part of the century was whether forces could operate at a distance without the intervention of any intermediate matter, or whether action between bodies depended upon changes in an all pervasive medium. Maxwell inclined towards the latter minority view and he supported this with his theories that the flow of current within an electrical circuit could produce a corresponding flow in a similarly 'tuned' circuit not connected with the first.[147] He had shown by pure mathematics that electro-magnetic waves could be produced in this way, resembling light waves and obeying the laws of optics.[148] Thus these waves could be reflected, absorbed and focused just as the beam of a torch. His ideas were controversial for the time and not understood or accepted by the majority. In 1879 Edward Hughes walked up Portland Place with a receiver listening to the sounds of radio waves but was persuaded by the Royal Society that it had no significance; it was no more than the sound of 'electromagnetic induction'.[149]

The work was taken up in Germany by the scientist, Heinrich Hertz, who later became Professor of Physics at Karlsruhe in 1895. Without consideration of the practical implications Hertz attempted to create by experimentation the wave motion of the type predicted before by Maxwell. He achieved this in 1887 showing that waves radiated by a transmitter could be picked up by a receiver, the proof of which was the appearance of a spark within a small gap in the receiving circuit. He also was able to show the general similarity between electro-magnetic and light waves as Maxwell had suggested. The basic difference between the two was the wavelength-the distance between the successive crests of the travelling wave which repeats itself at regular intervals. The waves he produced from the sparks of an induction coil produced wavelengths of approximately 24 cm. and were picked up at a distance of 60 feet. He had demonstrated the basic feature of radio communication which is that the electro-magnetic radiation produced by the passage of a current through a conductor travels at the speed of light (c.186,000 miles per second) inducing in any receiver in its path a current similar to that which originally flowed from the transmitter. The current could then be amplified and made audible by the use of a suitable receiver.[150]

The practical application of these experiments in telegraphy was soon recognised and six years later, Oliver Lodge, Professor of Physics at

Liverpool, transmitted signals a distance of 150 yards at Oxford.[151] He refined the process with a tube called a 'coherer'. In his experiment the waves generated by his transmitter produced similar surges of current in his receiver causing iron filings to adhere to one another in the coherer. When this happened current flowed to a battery which flowed into a bell to make it ring. Those who witnessed this trial could see and hear what was happening but they could not understand why it happened.[152]

Quite by accident the Post Office had begun to take an interest in this research, when in 1884, William Preece, Chief Engineer at the Post Office, began to ask why telegraph wires 80 feet above Grays Inn Road in London began to carry messages being transmitted along underground cables below in the street. It was this interest in wireless induction that ultimately led, in 1896, to collaboration with Guglielmo Marconi, the Italian inventor who at the age of 22 had come to London to continue his work, having failed to secure financial support or much interest in his research in Italy. He also obtained help from Captain (later Admiral) H. B. Jackson, who subsequently introduced wireless telegraphy into the Royal Navy. Within the next five years he made rapid progress although it proved necessary to form a company – The Wireless Telegraph and Signal Company – in 1897 when it became clear that the Treasury was not prepared to support Post Office investment in this work. First he developed a tuning device to improve the resonance of the signal and then, conducting experiments on Salisbury Plain, he discovered that the distance over which signals could be transmitted related in proportion almost exactly to the square of the height of the aerial. With larger aerials and increased power longer distances might be achieved. Marconi obtained a patent for his initial system, operating at 300–3000 metres wavelengths, in June 1896 and in 1900 he changed the name of his company to Marconi's Wireless Telegraph Company, with affiliations worldwide.

Continuing his experiments, on 5 December 1897 Marconi erected what he later described as the World's 'first permanent wireless station' at the Needles on the Isle of Wight in southern England. The experimental station exchanged radio messages first with a tug in the bay below, then with the towns of Bournemouth and Poole, some 14 and 18 miles distant along the coast, and finally with a ship in the channel 40 miles away. On 15 November 1899 information for the first newspaper ever produced at sea – 'The Transatlantic Times' – was sent from the Needles station by wireless telegraphy and printed on the US liner 'St Paul' when it was 36 miles distant. This was followed on 3 June 1898 from the same station when the

Scottish physicist Lord Kelvin[153] transmitted the first radio telegram for which payment was made. The station continued experimental work until 26 May 1900, and a stone commemorates this early pioneering work where the station once stood. The turning point for Marconi and for the future of radio occurred on 12 December 1901 when a signal was transmitted from Poldhu, near the Lizard in Cornwall, to Signal Hill, in Newfoundland, a distance of 2150 miles. The company had erected a high power transmission station that was 100 times more powerful than any previous transmitter. An alternator, driven by a 25 horsepower oil engine produced the current. The aerial consisted of wires spread in a fan-shaped position 164 feet above the shed housing the transmitter. In Newfoundland the aerial was 400 feet in the air, supported by a balloon. The equipment remained in place long enough for the three dots of the morse code representing the letter S to be transmitted at five minute intervals and picked up. Once again, however, as with previous advances in communication, little interest emerged immediately (the telegraph was an established form of communication in the first years of the twentieth century and telephones were just beginning to catch the public eye). The achievement, however, was outstanding, leading in 1909 to Marconi sharing of the Nobel Prize with Ferdinand Braun, another pioneer in radio.[154] The Government, however, now committed to the takeover of the telephone service, although the actual assumption of control was still seven years away, took little time to reach a decision on the future of radio. In 1904, a Wireless Telegraphy Act was passed to take control of radio and to establish a policy for its development.

Perhaps the most famous event prior to the outbreak of war, as far as radio is concerned, was its use in July 1910 to apprehend the murderer Dr. Crippen who had taken flight on board the liner 'Montrose', one of the first ships to acquire a ship-to-shore radio. The Captain, having recognised Crippen, alerted Scotland Yard who sent an officer on a fast vessel, the 'Laurentic', to overtake 'Montrose' and arrest Crippen and his accomplice Ethel le Neve. This did much to publicise the new medium. Another interesting event took place four years before, in 1906, when perhaps the first illegal transmission across the air waves occurred. The culprit was a Mr. R. A. Fessenden of Brant Rock who set up a high frequency alternator and transmitted music and a message in his own voice, asking anyone who picked up the broadcast to write to him. It took a further 20 years before the public heard the same again. For the time being the morse code was the language of radio communication.

By the outbreak of World War I many very powerful stations had been set up around the world. During the War the Post Office created direction-finding stations to locate enemy transmitter and aircraft. It was not until after the war that music and speech began to be heard regularly. Under the 1904 Act, the Post Office had control of wired or wireless communication so that a licence from the Post Office was necessary before the BBC could begin broadcasting services to the public who received broadcasts on wireless sets, by then in mass production. The BBC obtained its licence on 18 January 1923. Broadcasting began shortly thereafter. Building on the foundations laid by the radio pioneers, just three years later John Logie Baird was to signal the imminent arrival of a further communications breakthrough when he transmitted the first television pictures along a 700km telephone cable between London and Glasgow.[155]

SUMMARY   We can see throughout this exploration of the history of communications the emergence of factors that have become even more evident with the advent of computers and the onset of the 'Information Society'. One can begin to understand what H.G. Wells meant when he remarked that 'the cardinal fact in history during the past fifty centuries has been the scope, pace, and precision of Intercommunication. Everything else is subordinated to that'. Through the technologies of print, the steam engine and electro-magnetic transmission, first by cable and then supplemented by air waves, communication of information has become a multi-faceted and mass-market phenomenon. Looking at the period commencing with the primeval world of primitive communication, some 2.5–3 million years ago, until the present day, we see a 'big bang' experience in the development of communication and record that operates in reverse to the suggested occurrence of its material counterpart. The reason is that, as far as communication and record are concerned, progress in the relevant parameters that measure development, have accelerated over time as opposed to slowing down as theories suppose is the case with the expansion of the universe.

From the cave paintings of c.20,000 BC, where the volume of information was limited to that imparted by the drawing, society has moved on. First there was expansion in range of information that could be handed on as cuneiform writing and later the linear alphabet developed. Then access to the information expanded as better storage media developed to replace the cave wall and blocks of stone or wood. This came in the form of parchment and later paper. Then, as the rudimentary forms of printing and later movable type developed, a further expansion in the provision of information occurred through books and newspapers. A parallel development at this stage was the gradual decline in the use of languages, such as Latin, that the wider population had difficulty in understanding. The value of the information produced in this way was also enhanced as its currency improved. As a result of these changes, information reached the people quicker than had been the case before. Moreover, works and writings of all kinds, that had existed for some time, but could not be accessed because of language problems or the lack of available copies, were now becoming available. However, the delivery of information was still dependent upon the recipient having access to the storage medium – the newspaper, book or the word-of-mouth report. The requirement that the recipient be next to or in possession of the storage medium had not yet been broken, neither had the problem of speed of transmission which was still no faster than the speed of a horse.

The first attempt to break these rules and to separate the transmission of information from the constraints of fixation to the medium, proximity to the information and the slow transmission rate, came with the Armada beacons and the communications network that developed. Visual transmission at the speed of light across distances that the human eye could perceive had been introduced. However, the problem remained of the limited volume of information that could be transmitted by these methods. In the case in point, it could be no more than a 'yes' or a 'no' to a previously ordained question – 'Do you see the Armada' – or signal – 'The Armada is coming' – depending on whether the beacon was lit. The invention of steam locomotion increased the speed of transmission of information but this required a human carrier who delivered news either by word of mouth or in writing. Real progress in breaking the mould of promimity, time and distance came with the invention of the telegraph where, for the first time, information could be instantaneously transmitted long distances in the time it took to code and send the message. Information had also, for the first time, assumed its chameleon-like characteristics of representation in different forms for the purpose of communication – in this case a series of unmodulated electrical impulses that when transmitted in the form of patterns of long and short signals (the Morse Code) could be reconstituted at the receiving terminal. The telephone was an enhancement of the system with the added feature that the information conveyed by the human voice could be more elaborate and descriptive than that obtained by telegraph. As a more versatile medium, the telephone increased access to information for more people. These developments had also increased the capacity of individuals to obtain or transmit personal information. They could now enjoy better access to general news, ideas and debate through books and newspapers, but now they also had mechanisms for instantaneous communication of personal messages that outstripped the mail in terms of speed of delivery, when speed was of the essence.

The true severance of the proximity relationship came with radio and later television, when the need for an intermediate transmission mechanism was broken. This broke the tie between the tangible transmission medium of paper – for writing; the human being – for word-of-mouth communication; and the wire – for coded signals or speech. The only connection was that which joins mankind, namely the atmosphere within which the transmission and reception of radio wave communication takes place. The story is one of enhanced scope, pace and precision of intercommunication, just as H.G. Wells described it. It is also the story of how the technology extended itself, building upon the existing foundations of discovery about communication mechanisms and finding new ways of using existing media to enhance any one of the factors necessary for development. These include better methods of transmitting information over time from generation to generation, over distance and by volume, currency and access. While these developments were instrumental in the expansion of the system of communication and record in the world, none of the transmission or storage mechanisms could do more than enhance the processes of moving information or storing it. Information was a fixed commodity whose principal source was the human being. No communication or storage medium could create information or process it in any way. It could only hold or deliver it. It was the development of the computer that changed all that.

NOTES

1. Derry and Williams, op. cit., p. 214.
2. Designated as the cultural period beginning with the earliest chipped stone tools, approximately 3–2.5 million years ago, until the beginning of the Mesolithic period c.12,000 BC. In Universal Dictionary, op. cit., p. 1113/4.
3. These date c.20,000 BC. The pictures themselves can be seen in Bronowski, op. cit., fig. 18 and 19.

4. Derry and Williams, op. cit., p. 215. A sketch of the picture itself appears at fig. 91.
5. Remark attributed to Adjunct Professor Sam Sutton, Arizona State University, College of Law, 1982.
6. A character or symbol representing an idea or thing without indicating pronunciation. Universal Dictionary, op. cit., p. 765.
7. Derry and Williams, op. cit., p. 216. Fig. 92 depicts a pictographic tablet from Erech, Sumeria.
8. Universal Dictionary, op. cit., p. 1516.
9. Hieratic – simplified cursive style of Egyptian hieroglyphics; and demotic – simplified hieratic writing. The priestly class used for former and the common people the latter. Universal Dictionary, op. cit., pp. 726 and 416.
10. Derry and Williams, op. cit., p. 218.
11. Ibid., p. 218 *et seq.*
12. Ordinary parchment is made from the skins of sheep and goats. Better quality (vellum) from calf, kid or lamb.
13. Derry and Williams, op. cit., p. 232.
14. The earliest paper was referred to as cloth parchment. Its raw material comprised fibrous ingredients, including straw and wood as well as linen or cotton. In Derry and Williams, op. cit., p. 233.
15. Ibid., p. 234.
16. Derry and Williams, op. cit., p. 237 suggest that the idea probably came from the need to repair damaged inscriptions under the wood-block of a saint. The damaged letters would be cut out and the new one glued in place.
17. Collins, op. cit., p. 318.
18. Derry and Williams, op. cit., p. 235.
19. Febvre and Martin, *The Coming of the Book – The Impact of Printing 1450–1800* (1984) pp. 248–9.
20. Loublinsky estimates that the figure could have been as low as 12 million. Ibid., n. 343.
21. Evidence of private book distribution exists: for example, the Bible by John Wycliffe, who died in 1384. Revised by John Purvey, this text was proscribed by the Convocation of Canterbury in 1409, yet copies spread by unauthorised means throughout the country. Printed translations and other versions appeared early in the sixteenth century. See Mumby, *Publishing and Bookselling* (1930) p. 32.
22. Febvre and Martin, op. cit., p. 15.
23. Mackie, *The Early Tudors 1485–1558* (1952) p. 579.
24. Febvre and Martin, op. cit., p. 278.
25. Cranfield, *The Press and Society* (1978) p. 1.
26. Smith, *The Emergence of a Nation State – The Commonwealth of England 1529–1660* (1984) p. 33.
27. For example, 'The Act passed in 1484 for regulating the trade of foreigners in England carefully exempted every stationer, scrivener, illuminator or printer of books, no matter "of what nation or country he be", and gave him full licence to sell any books, and to settle within the realm for the exercise of

the said occupation'. Mumby, op. cit., p. 44.

28. Blagden, *The Stationers' Company – A History, 1403–1959* (1960) pp. 25–26.
29. Mumby, op. cit., p. 47.
30. Cranfield, op. cit., p. 1.
31. The 1551 Proclamation required the signature of His Majesty or of six of the Privy Council before any book in the English tongue could be printed or distributed. This extended in 1553 to the printing of 'any books, matter, ballad, rime, interlude, process, or treatise, nor to play any interlude, except they have her Grace's special licence'. Quoted in Greg, *London Publishing between 1550 and 1650* (1956) p. 2.
32. Cranfield, *The Provincial Newspaper, 1700–1760* (1962) p. 1.
33. 1662, Chapter XXXIII, 14 Car. II. In Volume 5, *The Statutes of the Realm*, p. 428.
34. For a full history of the Stationers' Company see Blagden, op. cit.
35. Cranfield, *The Provincial Newspaper 1700–1760* (1962) p. 7.
36. 8 Anne c.21 AD 1709. In *5 Laws of the Realm*, p. 256.
37. Feather, *The Provincial Book Trade in Eighteenth-Century England*, (1985) p. 32.
38. Cranfield, *The Provincial Newspaper 1700–1760* (1962) p. 7.
39. Ibid., pp. 19–20.
40. Act of Charles II in 1662, op. cit.
41. Ibid., p. 20.
42. Ibid., pp. 19–20, 32.
43. Febvre and Martin, op. cit., p. 249. See further Steele, 'What Fifteenth Century Books are about', in *The Library* (New Series), Vol. 5, 1903–7, and Lehnart, *Pre-Reformation Printed Books: A Study in Statistical and Applied Bibliography* (1935).
44. Febvre and Martin, op. cit., pp. 323–4.
45. The OTA Report 1990, op. cit., p. 182.
46. For further discussion, see Sprowl, op. cit.
47. The suppression of British Telecom 'Chatline' services in 1989 after complaints to the Director General of Telecommunications, Sir Bryan Carsberg, is an illustration of the 'watchdog' mechanism in action today, although arguably in the interests of consumers rather than the State.
48. Hankins, op. cit., p. 8.
49. Febvre and Martin, op. cit., pp. 10–11.
50. Messenger services date back to the fifth century at least, since Herodotus writes that Xerxes, after the Battle of Salamis (480 BC) used an established government messenger service to report back to Persia news of his invasion of Greece. Discussed in Robinson, *The British Post Office – A History* (1948) p. 3.
51. Op. cit., p. 5. The Universal Dictionary p. 1250 defines 'pursuivent' as, in the British Colleges of Heralds, an officer ranking below a Herald; and secondly a follower, messenger or attendant [Middle English – Pursevant].
52. Op. cit., p. 7. His name was Brian Tuke, who became Clerk of the Signet at the beginning of the reign, and subsequently Master of the Posts.

53. Op. cit., p. 9.
54. Calender of State Papers, Domestic 1566–69 (1856–) p. 109. Quoted in Robinson, op. cit., p. 14, n. 8.
55. Ibid., p. 15.
56. Mathias, op. cit., p. 113.
57. Mathias, op. cit., ibid., p. 113. The turnpike roads were paid for by tolls levied on the users.
58. Robinson, op. cit., p. 85.
59. Reported in Crutchley, *English Institutions – GPO* (1938) p. 49.
60. Report of the Committee on Palmer's Agreement (1797, reprinted 1807) pp. 117–18, in Robinson, op. cit., p. 135, n. 18.
61. Crutchley, op. cit., p. 51, writes that the tolls paid for a carriage-and-four between Bath and London amounted to 18s., or 2d. a mile.
62. Crutchley, op. cit., p. 51.
63. Robinson, op. cit., p. 138, states that the service was extended to Leeds, Manchester and Liverpool in the Summer, 1785 and, *inter alia*, to birmingham, Oxford, Dover and Exeter by the Autumn.
64. Robinson, op. cit., p. 234.
65. Crutchley, op. cit., pp. 54, 58.
66. Ibid., p. 58.
67. Nock, *British Steam Railways*, (1961) p. 46.
68. Robinson, op. cit., p. 245.
69. Ibid. The number of newspapers in circulation increased from 216 in 1821 to 369 in 1833. In 1782 only 61 newspapers had been published.
70. Robinson, *Carrying British Mails Overseas*, (1964) pp. 118–19.
71. Berghaus, *The History of Railways*, (1960, translated into English 1964) p. 10.
72. Ibid., p. 10.
73. Ibid.
74. Mathias, op. cit., p. 278.
75. Berghaus, op. cit., p. 16. Again this is reminiscent of the worries about employment when the computer industry was born.
76. Ibid.
77. The two contenders were 'Novelty', which weighed only 2 tons, and 'Sans Pareil'. See Berghaus, op. cit., p. 18.
78. Evans, *The Forging of the Modern State – Early Industrial Britain 1783–1870* (1983) p. 398. Passengers increased from 77,000 in 1851–2 to 330,000 in 1870. Third class use went up from 40,000 to 224,000. Source: Parl, Papers, 1852–3, XCVIII, pp. 298–9 and 1871, LX, pp. 528–9.
79. Derry and Williams, op. cit., p. 335.
80. Nock, op. cit., p. 25.
81. Mathias, op. cit., pp. 282–3.
82. Checkland, op. cit., p. 36.
83. Nock, op. cit., p. 107.
84. Elton, *British Railways* (1945). Quoted in Berghaus, op. cit., p. 44.
85. Robinson, op. cit., p. 119. William Symington ran a steam tug on the Clyde

in 1802, but the first steamboat was the Rob Roy, of 90 tons and 30 horsepower. It ran between Greenock and Belfast.

86. Derry and Williams, op. cit., p. 370.
87. Robinson, op. cit., p. 119.
88. Robinson, op. cit., pp. 119, 123.
89. Ibid., p. 124.
90. Ibid., p. 124 cites a *Times* report of June 30 1819 stating that the Savannah was chased for a full day off Ireland by the revenue cruiser The Kite, who mistook her for a ship on fire.
91. Attributed to Dr Dionysuis Lardner, a writer on scientific matters. Quoted ibid., p. 126.
92. Ibid., pp. 126–8.
93. Mathias, op. cit., pp. 312–13.
94. Derry and Williams, op. cit., p. 374.
95. Robinson, op. cit., p. 396 *et seq.*
96. Derry and Williams, op. cit., p. 353. It was said in the Catalogue of the Great Exhibition of 1851 that if necessary 'the great hammer could descend with power only sufficient to break an egg shell'.
97. Mathias, op. cit., pp. 123–4.
98. Derry and Williams, op. cit., pp. 349–52.
99. Ibid., p. 349.
100. A similar example would be signals by drum beat.
101. Ibid., p. 621.
102. Martin and Parker, *The Spanish Armada*, (1988) p. 23.
103. Ibid., p. 271, Plate 1.
104. Derry and Williams, op. cit., p. 621.
105. Known as semaphore. Other visual signalling systems using lights or mechanically moving arms developed, as on the railway.
106. Crutchley, op. cit., p. 130, and Derry and Williams, op. cit., p. 623.
107. Gilbert wrote a treatise on magnetism called *De Magnete*. In Derry and Williams, op. cit., p. 608.
108. Ibid., p. 610–11.
109. Anthony R. Michaelis, 'From the First Telegraph to the ISDN'. *Telecommunication Journal*, Vol. 57, 11/1990, p. 92.
110. A typical charge was one shilling for 20 words, excluding the names and addresses of the sender and recipient. To telegraph Ireland would cost six shillings for a similar sized message. In Crutchley, op. cit., p. 135.
111. Steinheil interconnected 'various points in the city of Munich and its neighbourhood' in 1837. By then Samuel Morse had developed his system in the US which became operational in 1843 when a 40 mile connection from Washington to Baltimore was established with a $300,000 grant from the US Government. It was launched on 24 May that year with the words: 'What hath God Wrought'. See Chris Robbins, 'Digital Discoveries of a Shocking Kind', *Computing*, 26 April 1990, p. 26.
112. Dickens, describing the operations of the London District Telegraph Company Ltd., in *All the Year Round*.

113. That same year the world's first central telegraph office was opened by the Electric Telegraph Company. It was sited in Founder's Court, Lothbury, in the City of London.
114. Robinson, op. cit., pp. 271–2.
115. Ibid., p. 272. The cable was laid by HMS 'Agamemnon' and the USNS 'Niagara'.
116. Derry and Williams, op. cit., p. 626.
117. Michigan had 27 time zones, Indiana 23 and Wisconsin 39. James Carey, 'Technology and Ideology: The Case of the Telegraph', *Prospects*, Vol. 8, 1983, pp. 303–25; in The OTA Report, 1990, op. cit., p. 184.
118. Chris Robbins, 'Digital Discoveries of a Shocking Kind', *Computing*, 26 April 1990, p. 27.
119. Robinson, The British Post Office, p. 407.
120. 31 & 32 Vict., c.110 and 32 & 33 Vict., c.73.
121. Ibid.
122. Crutchley, op. cit., p. 136.
123. Derry and Williams, op. cit., p. 627.
124. British Telecom, *Names and Dates for Students* (1984).
125. Robinson, The British Post Office, op. cit., p. 408.
126. He was nearly beaten to it by Elisha Gray, who was also working on the same idea in the USA. He had filed patent documents a few hours after Bell had done so. In *Telecommunications – A Technology for Change*, HMSO (1983) p. 13.
127. British Telecom, *Pioneers in Telecommunications* (1985) p. 12.
128. Williams, *A Short History of the Twentieth Century*, (1982) p. 302.
129. Peter Wymer, 'Seven Words that Changed the World', The *Independent*, 20 February 1990.
130. The vibration of the diaphragm affected the packing of the carbon granules and therefore the electrical conductivity (resistance) of the carbon as a whole.
131. That is, the opposition to the flow of an electric current characteristic of a medium, substance, or circuit element – in this case carbon.
132. Williams, op. cit., p. 302.
133. Crutchley, op. cit., p. 104.
134. Described in *Postmaster-General v. National Telephone Company Ltd.* [1908] 2 Ch. 172 at pp. 174–5. The decision of the Court Appeal was overruled in [1909] A.C. 269 when the House of Lords ruled that private lines connecting two or more separate or independent persons or businesses were not within the exceptions outlined in s.5 of the Telegraph Act 1869 and had to be licensed by the Postmaster General.
135. US Congress, Office of Technology Assessment, *Critical Connections: Communication for the Future*, OTA-CIT-407 (Washington, DC: US Government Printing Office, January 1990) p. 90.
136. Through the Interstate Commerce Commission which shifted jurisdiction to the Federal Communications Commission in 1934. The OTA Report 1990 ibid.

137. The OTA Report, 1990, op. cit., pp. 184–5.
138. Crutchley, op. cit., pp. 104–5.
139. Telegraph Act 1863 (26 & 27 Vict. c.112) and the Telegraph Act 1869 (32 & 33 Vict. c.73).
140. *The Attorney General v. The Edison Telephone Company of London (limited)* (1880–81) 6 QBD 244 CA (Exq. Div.).
140a. Crutchley, op. cit., p. 251.
141. Under s. 4 Telegraph Act 1869, 32 & 33 Vict. c.73.
142. The trunk lines were the direct lines between two distant telephone switchboards.
143. Report from the Select Committee on Post Office (Telephone Agreement) 1905 HC 271.
144. British Telecom, *Names and Dates for Students* (1984).
145. The licences granted to the Municipal services were due to expire as follows: Hull on 31 Dec. 1911; Glasgow on 31 Dec. 1913; Swansea on 31 Dec. 1920; Brighton on 30 Apr. 1926; and Portsmouth on 30 July 1926. Nevertheless, apart from Hull and Portsmouth, the other services were abandoned by 1907.
146. Barnes, *Submarine telecommunication and power cables* (1977) p. 3.
147. Derry and Williams, op. cit., p. 629.
148. He wrote at the time: 'We can scarcely avoid the inference that light consists in the transverse undulations of the same medium which, is the cause of electric and magnetic phenomena'. Ibid., p. 628.
149. *Radio and British Telecom*, p. 3. He was standing of course upon the future site of the BBC.
150. Collins Encyclopaedia and Dictionary, op. cit., p. 325.
151. Others also working in the field were Branly in France (1890–91) and Popov in Russia (1895). In Williams, op. cit., p. 300.
152. *Radio and British Telecom*, p. 3.
153. Baron Kelvin (1824–1907) was a Scottish physicist who prepared the way for James Maxwell in the development of electro-magnetic theory. He also perfected the Mariner's compass and played a major role in the successful laying of the transatlantic cable in 1858.
154. Reported in Williams, op. cit., p. 301.
155. This took place in 1926. In fact, a picture was produced and transmitted a few feet two years earlier. Regular services by the BBC began on 2 November 1936. In Williams, op. cit., pp. 317–18.

CHAPTER 3

The evolution of the new technologies of the 'information age'

THE COMPUTER

The foundation of the technological revolution that is characterised today as the architect of the 'Information Age' can be found in the relationship between information, the computer and communications. The application of microelectronics to these components has generated a convergence between all three that today and in the future will continue to promote the societal transition that has been characteristic of the very short life of the relationship so far. In this section the landmarks in the emergence of that relationship will be explored.[1] This will show how the post war experience with microelectronics has done more than simply expand the potential and capacity of communications, as the technologies explored in the previous information revolutions have done, producing instead a means by which information can be created, transformed and become functional within a concept of a universal machine and a convergence of the component technologies.

A revealing feature of the history of the computer is the fact that it has its roots in two complementary but contrasting activities. The first can be found in the researches of those interested in the laws of human thought and the second in the attempts to build calculation devices that could undertake arithmetic operations for a practical purpose. Unlike the technologies of communication, the computer has always played a functional part in its handling of information, in the sense that it is much more than a passive medium for the retention and communication of the information it carries.

FROM THE UNIVERSAL LANGUAGE – MATHEMATICS, TO THE UNIVERSAL MACHINE – THE COMPUTER   At this point in the late twentieth century man is only just beginning to probe the mechanisms of the human brain. As more is revealed about the way in which it works, computer technology will capitalise upon that information in perhaps its ultimate quest, to try and replicate the brain itself artificially, in both composition and function. It is natural, then, that the science which has become crucial to man's, as yet elementary, attempts to exploit the potential of the computer, should be that of mathematics. Bronowski, described the latter as 'in many ways the most elaborated and sophisticated of the sciences'. He argued that the language of mathematics was a universal language within which the laws of nature themselves could be described as, for example, the laws of motion had been described by Newton and Leibniz in the late seventeenth century.[2] Newton conceived of 'Fluxions' which was a name he gave to what is now called (after Leibniz) differential calculus. With it, Newton calculated that the motion of the moon round the earth was approximately 27.25 days, which confirmed his ideas on universal gravitation. Bronowski comments:

> When the figures come out right like that, you know as Pythagoras did that a secret of nature is open in the palm of your hand. A universal law governs the majestic clockwork of the heavens, in which the motion of the moon is one harmonious incident. It is a key that you have put into the lock and turned, and nature has yielded in numbers the confirmation of her structure.[3]

Leibniz published an essay in 1666 entitled *De Arte Combinatoria* or 'Laws of Thought' describing his attempts to create 'a general method in which all truths of the reason would be reduced to a kind of calculation'. During the beginnings of the period of the Enlightenment in the seventeenth century, Leibniz developed an ambitious programme linking logical thought with mathematical processes. He envisaged 'a universal language based on an alphabet of thought, or "characteristica universalis", a general calculus of reasoning.'[4] He thought that the universal language might take the form of algebraic notation or signs, similar to that of Chinese ideograms, which in combination would ultimately enable the truths of the sciences to be formulated and computed by arithmetic operations. It was within these propositions that the notion of expressing ideas by means of an artificial language and of reasoning by computational methods was developed. In formulating these theories, Leibniz was particularly attracted by the simplicity of binary arithmetic which employs only two symbols – '0' and '1'. This operates to the base 2 instead of the decimal system (base 10), with each of the numbers 0 through 9 being capable of expression in binary. Leibniz saw this scale as reducing the laws of thought to its simplest form. According to the French mathematician, astronomer and physicist, Pierre-Simon Laplace, writing in the early nineteenth century, 'Leibniz saw in his binary arithmetic the image of creation . . . He imagined that unity represented God and zero the void; that the Supreme Being drew all things from the void, just as unity and zero express all numbers in the system of numeration'.[5]

Binary notation has today become a principle component of computer technology. Its 'two-state' or bistable characteristic enables the switching devices of the modern digital computer to indicate one of two possible states: 'on-off' or 'open-closed', upon which the additions can take place that the digital computer is basically constructed to perform, and upon which the entire process of computing and its formidable achievements to date depend.[6]

Further substantial progress towards a recognition of the underlying concepts of mathematical logic was made in the mid-nineteenth century by the self-taught English mathematician, George Boole, who became Professor of Mathematics at Queen's College, County Cork, in 1849. He published a work in 1854 entitled, *An investigation of the Laws of Thought*. He there put forward a symbolic method of logical inference which contributed significantly to the thinking that led ultimately to the design of digital computers a century later.[7] Boole believed that the decisions that individuals take every day of their lives were based on reason and could be expressed in mathematical logic. He developed an algebra of logic in which he advocated a formal calculus that could handle different interpretations. He had in mind two in particular; one which was relevant to relations among things, for example, '$x = y$' means that the classes 'x' and 'y' have the same members, and the other to the relations among facts as expressed by propositions, for instance, '$x + y$' reads 'Either x or y but not both' and '$=$' becomes 'if and only if'. In this way it was possible to extend propositions by adding to them within the formal logic of the algebra, such as 'For all x, either $x = 1$ or $x = 2$', where '1' is a true and '2' is a false proposition.[8] The contribution of Boole to the development of modern computer systems and language has been described thus:

'George Boole, who gave his name to Boolean Algebra – one of the first forms of mathematical logic – thought he was developing the laws of human thought. What he in fact was doing first of all was helping to bring into existence the modern digital computer which is an enormously high-speed calculating machine. But what he was also doing – and this was far less obvious until relatively recently – was developing precisely the laws of human thought. The modern science of Cybernetics owes as much to George Boole as does modern Computer Science. These sciences are both part of what might be called Information Science and have made huge strides in the last twenty years'.[9]

The translation of these ideas into the design of a machine that could undertake the calculations was advanced, in the case of the digital computer, by Von Neumann. He had understood that the two states required for the performance of binary operations could be fulfilled in electronic terms by the 'on–off' sequence of a switch. This led to the development of the stored computer program. Neumann also recognised the difference between the processes of human thought and the artificial computed alternative. It was his belief that if the technology of computing was to advance very far, it would be necessary to understand the difference between the reality, as recognised by the human brain, and the logical environment of computation. With the former, strategies could be devised; with the latter only tactics could be calculated. The difference between the two was judgment formulated upon a system of values. The computer could aid the formulation of 'best' strategies, but it could not reach the decision itself.[10] It is in an attempt to bridge this gap that work in the field of artificial intelligence and in the analysis of the brain proceeds.

THE FIRST CALCULATORS   The earliest machine devised for the purposes of calculation was the abacus. The word derives from 'abax' or 'abakos', meaning a board, tablet or calculating table.[11] The abacus originated c.3000 BC in the Orient and represents the first manually operated storage device for assisting human calculation.[12] However, it was not until the expansion of the physical sciences in the seventeenth and eighteenth centuries, during the Enlightenment, that the fusion between the discovery of mathematical formulae and the design and construction of calculation devices came into their own. There was a demand at this time for machines that could calculate for the purposes of navigation and commerce.

Knowledge of basic arithmetic was not widely spread at this time, particularly in relation to multiplication and division. With this problem in mind, some practical solutions were devised by John Napier, the Scottish mathematician, early in the seventeenth century. In 1614 he discovered the logarithm which described the power to which a base must be raised to yield a given number.[13] This aided multiplication and underpinned the development of the slide rule. The mechanisation of logarithms was also instrumental in the evolution of analogue methods of calculation based on the comparative measurement of quantities to deduce numbers capable of resolving mathematical problems. Three years later, in the year he died, Napier published details of a movable multiplication table which operated by means of rods designed to match a particular multiplicand, and divided into nine compartments to represent the prime numbers. It became better known as Napier's bones, because the rods on which the numbers were printed comprised sticks of bone or ivory.[14]

This was followed soon after by the French mathematician, physicist and philosopher, Blaise Pascal, who successfully built the first desk top calculator while motivated to ease the mental effort required to perform additions while drawing up his father's business accounts. He wrote of his machine in 1642: 'I submit to the public a small machine of my own invention by means of which you alone may, without any effort, perform all the operations of arithmetic, and may be relieved of the work which has often times fatigued your spirit when you have worked with the counters or with the pen'.[15] It operated by means of a series of wheels and gears, the numbers to be added being dialled in on a dial-wheel that activated the mechanism. A more advanced version was produced by Leibniz who devised a prototype in 1671 and completed the final version in 1694. His machine, based on binary rather than decimal concepts, was capable of storing a multiplicand in a register, avoiding the need to engage in successive addition to produce the result. The machine was called the 'Stepped Reckoner', and could also divide and extract square roots, the latter by a system of continuous additions, methods subsequently adopted by many digital computers.[16]

Until Charles Babbage began his research in the early years of the nineteenth century, no one had attempted to move one stage further on, in the development of a machine that could build on its own computation.[17] Until Babbage, all the effort had been put to the construction of calculators that would assist the human operator in his task. Babbage began to think further, following a conversation with John Herschel, the astronomer and physicist, with whom he was working at Cambridge. While checking some calculations connected with their research, Babbage exclaimed in some frustration: 'I wish to God these calculations had been executed by steam!'; Herschel replied, 'It is quite possible'.[18]

Babbage was a controversial figure who devoted most of his time to the development of calculating 'engines'. His first major idea was the refinement of the theory for what he called a 'difference engine' that would be capable of carrying out repeated arithmetic operations, so as to be capable of producing complete sets of tables of figures once set in motion. He planned that it would hold numbers up to 20 digits in length and operate by means of columns of toothed wheels, each one representing, according to its position, one of the digits in the number. He also devised methods for both serial and parallel addition, as well as a means of setting the 'engine' to print the output.[19] Although a pilot model of the machine was built after two years work, the construction of the full version, although elegant in conception, was impractical since the engineering skills of the day were not capable of making the precision parts necessary for it. Babbage therefore found himself having to move one step back, to the design of the tools themselves – cutting tools, lathes, gauges, jigs, ties and taps. Since then, using modern precision instruments, a full-sized replica of Babbage's machine has been manufactured and shown to work. It now stands in the Science Museum in London.

In 1828 Babbage became Lucasian Professor of Mathematics at Cambridge, the Chair occupied most recently by Stephen Hawking. By then he had published a 'A Table of Logarithms of the Natural Numbers from 1 to 100,000', which corrected many errors in the existing tables of the time. He argued that his ideas for the 'difference engine' would remove the risk of such errors creeping into published works. Nevertheless, the project had basically been a failure, and had consumed £17,000 of research money and fourteen years of Babbage's life, albeit with a gap of five years when the project stood still. Undaunted by this experience Babbage continued to devise new methods on paper of achieving his goal. In the early 1830s he started work on the project that he was to be remembered by, namely his 'analytical engine', which is recognised as the world's first digital computer. Babbage wrote: 'The whole of arithmetic now appeared within the grasp of the mechanism. A vague glimpse even of an Analytical Engine at length opened out, and I pursued with enthusiasm the shadowy vision.'[20]

The distinction between this and the difference engine was that the new machine contained a storage unit with a memory device of 50 counter wheels capable of holding 1000 figures of 50 digits each. Its second feature was what Babbage called a 'mill', a carry-over from his earlier work, which performed the arithmetic operation. The concept of separating the arithmetic from the storage unit was clearly significant as modern digital computers have adopted this strategy. Babbage believed that two 50-placed numbers could be added together in one second; a multiplication of similar sized numbers or a division of a 100- to a 50-place number in one minute.[21] Punched cards would operate in effect as the control unit being the mechanism by which numbers were selected from store and fed to the mill for 'data processing'. The cards were based on the Jacquard loom, invented in 1801, which wove flowers and leaves on cloth to produce elaborate patterns. The plungers on the loom would operate according to the sequence of holes on the card through which they passed. Two sets of cards were indicated, one set carrying the coded data and the other the sequence of operations which would determine the variables to be applied to the numbers.[22]

Babbage had envisaged in his drawings the type of sequential control methods used in the programming of digital computers, such as branching and looping, and had gone a long way towards establishing the theory of digital computers that a century later would be uncovered once more in the work and writing of the pioneers of the electronic version. Babbage never built his engine. Once again it proved too complex an exercise for the time. He did pursue his ideas for the engine, however, until his death in 1871. Although they were of no practical benefit directly, they did improve the quality of machine tools which Babbage had worked on in pursuit of his great project. He also helped promote a scientific attitude within industry through his much publicised and controversial activities.[23]

Although Babbage never managed to complete his machine, the use of punched cards to manipulate numbers was not altogether ignored. The statistician, Herman Hollerith, took up the idea to assist him in his work at the U.S. Census Bureau which he joined in 1879. Without the assistance of mechanized methods, Hollerith found that the analysis of a census took 7.5 years, leaving only eighteen months before the next census and the work having to start all over again. Moreover, the problem was likely to grow, as the population of the U.S. was growing rapidly at this time. In preparation for the 1890 Census, Hollerith developed a system whereby certain charactertistics of the population would be represented by holes, punched by the census takers, at a pre-defined location on the card which measured 3 × 5 inches. The machine would 'read' each card by the activation of spring-loaded pins that would locate the position of the holes according to their pattern on the card. Beneath the cards was a tray containing cups filled with mercury. The pins that came through the perforated holes would touch the mercury and in doing so complete an electrical circuit. The system enabled several facts from each census card to be recorded simultaneously. As a result, the time taken for the analysis of the 1890 census was cut by two thirds, despite the population increasing from 50 to 63 million people and the extra work therefore involved. The major difference between Babbage's and Hollerith's ideas was that the latter used electro-magnetic means to read the cards whereas Babbage envisaged mechanical feelers for the detection of the holes.[24]

Following his success, Hollerith set up in business, leaving the Census Bureau in 1896 to establish the Tabulating Machine Company which began to build machines for the market. In 1901 Hollerith introduced the first numerical keyboard for the card punch operation. The Hollerith equipment was used for the first time with the British Census in 1911. That same year the company merged with two others to create the Computing Tabulating Recording Company and in 1924 this became International Business Machines (IBM). The path was now set for the move from mechanical and electromechnical means of calculation to true electronic methods. The technology and the thinking that was to produce the very first primitive electronic computers – the forerunners of those in use and in development today – was now in place.

THE TRANSITION TO DIGITAL COMPUTERS   In tracing the immediate sequence of events that led to the development of the first electronic digital computer, it is important to recognise the contributions of those whose ideas might be regarded as underpinning those of the early inventors themselves. It is also relevant to understand what was motivating this work, in terms of the problems scientists were dealing with which a digital calculating machine might alleviate.

By the end of World War I a considerable amount of research was underway into many electrical questions, particularly in the new field of electrical engineering. Mathematics proved extremely important as a means of expressing or describing the phenomena under scrutiny, predicting a sequence of events or identifying similarities between otherwise unconnected events. However, in the words of Herman Goldstine, who was closely involved in the very earliest computer development at the

Moore School of Electrical Engineering, at the University of Pennsylvania, during the 1940's:

> [whereas] the engineer could write down in mathematical form a description of the phenomenon he was discussing, . . . he had no comparable mathematical apparatus for analyzing this description. In other words the mere expression of a physical situation in mathematical terms does not *per se* lead to any deepening of his understanding. It only does if he can then use the machinery of mathematics to penetrate into the equations.[25]

Among the specific needs for automated computational capacity was the military, and no more so than in the field of ballistics. The latter posed major mathematical problems, for in targetting the firing of a shell it was necessary to calculate the trajectory, taking into account range, velocity, air density, temperature and various other features connected with the flight of the projectile. It was estimated in all that 750 multiplications would be required for a single firing.[26] At the Ballistic Research Laboratory at Aberdeen, Maryland, more than 200 personnel were engaged in producing firing and bombing tables required by the US army and air-force to pursue their wartime operations. A single firing table might contain between 2000 and 4000 trajectories. It was estimated that the plotting of a single trajectory would take a human being, working unaided, two hours to perform the arithmetic and a further twelve hours to apply it. Not surprisingly it was the need to find ways of combatting this task that motivated the construction of one of the world's very first digital computers – the ENIAC (Electronic Numerical Integrator and Computer).

Translating the need from theory to reality was not an easy task. It required a contribution from those who could conceive of the objective and draw together the theories and ideas that up to that point had not been brought together. Three men in particular were significant in this regard: Claude Shannon, Alan Turing and John von Neumann. Shannon was captivated by what he described as 'the interplay between mathematics and electrical engineering.'[27] He had been working at the Massachusetts Institute of Technology on the 'differential analyzer' built by Vannevar Bush. This was an early example of an analogue computer,[28] originally entirely mechanical in conception and later to become an electromechanical device.[29] The machine could set up physical analogues of certain types of differential equation of interest in physics and engineering.[30]

Shannon had chosen to study for his Master's thesis the symbolic analysis of relay and switching circuits as he had perceived similarities between the operation of the Bush machine and the concepts of Boolean algebra. His idea was to see if it was possible to order the switching of arrays of relays and control their 'on' and 'off' states using binary numbers. A simple switch worked by employing an electromagnet to draw a movable electrical contact into a stationary one, thereby completing an electrical circuit at that point. The interconnection of many such switches would enable numerical operations to be performed automatically. Shannon wrote: 'It is possible to perform complex mathematical operations by means of relay circuits. Numbers may be represented by the positions of relays and stepping switches. Interconnections between sets of relays can be made to represent various mathematical operations.'[31] These conclusions contributed significantly to the theory underlying the use of a machine to handle information. He had shown how a computer might be constructed to perform calculations and apply Boolean logic.

Progress in Research Accelerates If Shannon had shown the way to do it, Alan Turing's contribution to the thinking underlying computing was to outline the scope of what such machines might achieve. Turing had studied mathematics as an undergraduate at Cambridge, and subsequently as a research student. In 1936 he published a paper entitled 'On Computable Numbers, with an Application to the Entscheidungsproblem', in the *Proceedings of the London Mathematical Society*. This paper, with it's obscure title, is one of computer science's most important early documents.[32] The origin of this paper derives from an international congress of 1928 in which the German mathematician David Hilbert advanced some fundamental questions about the nature of mathematics as part of his investigation into the foundations of mathematics. The substance of his challenge was composed by questioning each of three propositions: first, that mathematics is complete in that every mathematical statement is capable of being proved or disproved; second, that mathematics is consistent since the statement '2 + 2 = 5' could never be proven correct by any sequence of valid steps of proof; and third, that mathematics is decidable, meaning that there exists the means to prove or disprove any mathematical assertion. His personal view was that the answer to each question was 'yes'. At the same meeting, however, the Czech mathematician Gödel was able to show that the answer to the first two questions was 'no', since assertions existed that could neither be proved or disproved.[33] Further, mathematics could not be proved consistent within its own axiomatic system.[34] The third question, however, had not been answered and it was to this that Turing applied himself.

A year before his famous paper was published, Turing attended a series of lectures given by M.H.A. Newman as part of the Cambridge Mathematics Tripos Part III course on the Foundations of Mathematics. The lectures concluded with proof of Gödel's theorem. Newman speculated as to the answer to the third question, and wondered whether a 'mechanical process' might be applied to determine whether a mathematical proposition might be provable. It was the investigation of this idea that led Turing to write his paper and to contemplate the characteristics of the machine alluded to by Newman. Turing surmised that any 'real number' computed from a definite rule of mathematics should be calculable by a single machine. However he realised that it was not possible to list every such number as each one would simply produce a further set of numbers that had been left out. The job would never be finished as it would never be possible to determine in advance whether, within a table of numbers, all had been listed or whether an infinite sequence existed.[35] Where no rule could be devised to deal with the problem no machine could resolve it. Therefore Hilbert was wrong; some mathematical problems could not be solved by computational means.

What Turing had shown was that no machine could be devised to solve every type of mathematical problem. However, he had to realised that if a problem could be defined in the form of a proper algorithm or computational procedure, then the 'Turing machine' could perform it and in that sense become a universal machine. In the process of coming to this conclusion he had 'discovered something almost equally miraculous, the idea of a universal machine that could take over the work of any machine . . . which, by reading the descriptions of other machines placed upon its "tape", could perform the equivalent of human mental activity. A single machine, to replace the human computer! An electric brain!'[36] Turing had, in his paper of 1936, conceived of the stored-program computer.

Turing won a Fellowship to Princeton University, USA, for the 1936–7 academic year. Among the distinguished members of the Institute for Advanced Study at Princeton were Albert Einstein and John Von Neumann. The latter was a Hungarian who had been a child prodigy in mathematics. Having joined the staff at Princeton in 1930 he subsequently settled in the United States and became a US citizen. His academic interests during the decades of the 1920s and 1930s were wide-ranging within theoretical physics and pure mathematics. His published work touched such topics as quantum theory, mathematical logic, ergodic (logic) theory, continuous geometry and, later on, theoretical hydro-dynamics which led him into defence work including ballistics and in the 1940's to the Manhattan Project connected with the building of the atomic bomb. It was in this field that Von Neumann found difficulty, using known mathematical methods, in achieving the computation necessary for the developmental work. He became interested in devising new and faster techniques of numerical computation, which he needed in particular to demonstrate the theory underlying one of his key contributions to the Manhattan Project, the implosion method of detonation. (It was by this method that the Nagasaki bomb was detonated in Japan at the end of World War II.)[37]

Von Neumann's first exposure to the fledgling science of computing took place, according to subsequent accounts, on a railway station platform at Aberdeen, Maryland, where the Ballistics Research Laboratory (BRL) was located. Herman Goldstine, the liaison officer between the BRL and the Moore School ENIAC project, was on his way back to the University of Pennsylvania where the secret project was underway. Von Neumann was a frequent traveller between the BRL, where he was a consultant, and his other bases at Princeton and Los Alamos – home of the Manhattan project. Goldstine described later his temerity at approaching the great mathematician. In due course, Goldstine, knowing that he could speak about the project to von Neumann who had high security clearance, began to discuss its progress. Goldstine continued: 'When it became clear . . . that I was concerned with the development of an electronic computer capable of 333 multiplications per second, the whole atmosphere of our conversation changed from one of relaxed good humour to one more like the oral examination for the doctor's degree in mathematics.'[38]

Following this chance meeting Von Neumann came to see the work for himself during September 1944. His eminence would add credibility to the project and neutralise opposition to the expenditure involved. Thereafter, Von Neumann took an active interest in the work, becoming a consultant to the ENIAC team. Von Neumann's particular interest lay in the logical design features, and quickly this led to plans for a new machine to follow on from ENIAC. The emphasis in the forward planning for the new machine would concentrate upon the logical dimension – to Von Neumann's liking – as opposed to the technological emphasis that prevailed when ENIAC was set up. The new machine was called EDVAC – the Electronic Discrete Variable Automatic Computer. Later a bitter dispute was to break out between Von Neumann, Goldstine and other members of the team, most notably Mauchly and Eckert, when Goldstine released a paper written by Von Neumann in which he described in detail the underlying features of the new machine.[39] In the minds of the others, not only had Von Neumann failed to give sufficient credit to their contribution to the plans, since he had signed the document alone, but also Goldstine, by passing copies of the report to other American and British scientists, had threatened to undermine any subsequent plans by Eckert and Mauchly to patent what they regarded as their inventions. In the event this dispute led to the break-up of the project team in 1946, and to legal action that was not finally resolved until 1973.[40]

The principle contribution of Von Neumann to the development of computer science was the logical treatment he gave to the subject. He was the first to set out the fact that the logical function of the machine was paramount when compared with its electrical features. Before Von Neumann's exposition the concentration of effort had been upon the electrical engineering aspects of designing the circuits to execute the arithmetic and control operations. Although such designs would be important the crucial breakthrough depended upon setting some design parameters for what he called 'a very high speed automatic digital computing system.'[41] In addition to the importance he attached to the speed of the machine he also identified the importance of the inputting instructions that the machine could sense and operate upon without further human intervention. In short, he set out a complete analysis of an elementary computer system which was to serve as a model for future design.[42] He had also pointed the way towards programming and to the distinction between the processes of human thought in real life and the precise and logical functioning of a digital machine. At the very end of his life, while dying of bone cancer probably contracted as a result of exposure to radiation during experiments on the atomic bomb, Von Neumann expanded upon these themes in a book entitled *The Computer and the Brain*. The text was due to be presented by Von Neumann at the 1956 Silliman Lectures, one of the most prestigious academic lecture series in the United States, organised by Yale University. He was unable to give the lectures but the text was published. Predicting the future, one reviewer remarked: 'In spite of the preliminary nature of this work, it is destined to become the nucleus of a new field of research which will challenge the minds of men for many years to come – the comparative study of the human brain and man-made automata.'[43]

EARLY MACHINE CHARACTERISTICS   Having considered the role of those who conceived of the digital computer, the focus now turns to the builders. What characteristics did the first machines possess and how did the design path unfold to the approaching fifth generation of computers of the present day?

The introduction of fully electronic machines was preceded by an era of electromechanical calculation devices. A Spanish engineer, Leonardo Torres y Quevedo, at the outbreak of World War I, was the first to show that the Babbage concept of a calculator could be achieved by means of electromechanical technology.[44] Hollerith had capitalised on this approach with his tabulator equipment and with the merger of the Hollerith organisation with other companies, into what became International Business Machines Corporation in 1924,[45] the base was created for the further exploitation of the new technology.

In 1929 IBM supported the establishment of a 'computing laboratory' at Columbia University where Wallace Eckert, later among the pioneers in the building of the ENIAC computer at Pennsylvania, connected together an IBM Type 601 punched card multiplier, an accounting machine and a tabulator. This was improved and in 1933 the Difference Tabulator was built, described as the first working universal calculator able to process data and print the output without human intervention.[46]

Research into the defence applications of the technology was also taking place in England at a number of locations, the scope of which has only emerged over the past 15 years.[47] Bell Laboratories, applying the logic, of Boolean logic completed a binary calculator in 1939 and in Germany, working entirely alone, Konrad Zuse was building computers of his own. Translation of his work in the 1960s, together with published papers of the UK war effort, showed that much of the thinking underlying the construction of the first computers in the United States had already been discovered. Whereas the British applied these discoveries effectively in the War effort, particularly in decryption, Zuse's ideas were ignored and plans to use the technology in ballistics did not materialise.[48]

In the United States, IBM extended their support of research by founding a joint project between IBM and Harvard in 1937. Led by Howard Aiken the project team set themselves the task of constucting a general-purpose computer for scientific calculations. It differed from the differential analyser of Bush and Shannon at M.I.T., since it was intended to resolve problems beyond differential equations – the limit of the Bush model. Named the Automatic Sequence Controlled Calculator (ASCC) the Mark 1 version was completed in 1944. The ASCC had, 73 years after Babbage, completed by electromechanical means his conception of the analytical engine. Ironically it was at this precise moment that the technology was about to be replaced by fully electronic computers.

The ASCC was a very large machine weighing five tons and measuring 51 feet long, 8 feet high and 2 feet wide. It consisted of approximately 750,000 parts, 500 miles of wiring and three million wire connections. Different sections of the machine dealt with setting values for constants, counting-adding units representing the machine's main storage, the multiplying and dividing units and finally, behind a control desk, four input tape readers and two electric typewriters upon which printout appeared. The storage of 72 numbers required 1656 counters and the processing speed per addition was 0.3 seconds; multiplication, 6 seconds; and division, 11.4 seconds.[49] The electromechanical operation could be identified in the processes of addition as well as in the transfer of quantities from one part of the machine to another. This was done by a process involving gear wheels operated by electronic pulses. One complete turn of the wheel could be accomplished by 10 pulses. Instructions were executed one by one as the paper tape passed through the system.[50] The machine had cost $500,000 to build and was immediately put to work by the US Navy on calculating mathematical tables connected with gunnery and ballistics. Calculating the trajectory of a missile fired from a battlefield gun was a complex exercise, involving between two and four thousand calculations. Gunners required firing tables for use in action and these were calculated by the Ballistic Research Laboratory. A problem that reportedly took four specialists three weeks to solve was accomplished by the ASCC in 19 hours.[51] Surprisingly it functioned for a total of 16 years, which is a very long time compared with the lifespan of modern computer systems.

THE 'ENIAC' COMPUTER AND THE PATENT LITIGATION Although the machine was a success it did not confront the fundamental challenge of building a computer that contained electronic as opposed to electromechanical circuits. The history of the electronic digital computer identifies the ENIAC machine – Electronic Numerical Integrator and Calculator – as the first of its kind for its comparative high speed, fledgling programmability and generality of purpose.[52] The ENIAC was built at the University of Pennsylvania at the Moore School of Electrical Engineering and completed for the Ballistics Research Laboratory in February 1946. If figures aid comparison, the ENIAC was a much larger machine weighing 30 tons and measuring 80 feet in length, 8 feet high and 3 feet in width. Altogether it occupied approximately 1800 square feet of space. The reason for this was the fact that it used 17,468 thermionic valves,[53] better known as vacuum tubes, to provide the electrical circuits necessary to perform mathematical operations based upon Claude Shannon's work. It had been known since the early years of the twentieth century that vacuum tubes could control electric currents. Their advantage over relay switches was that electrons rather than mechanical switches would move, causing dramatic improvements in response times. Relays could turn on and off hundreds of times per minute, but with vacuum tubes it was in the thousands.[54]

The ENIAC accordingly could perform an addition in 0.2 milliseconds (5000 per second); and a multiplication in 2.8 milliseconds. (This was equivalent to multiplying 333 ten-digit numbers a second.) This was some 500 times faster that its electromechanical counterpart, the ASCC at Harvard.[55] The ENIAC consumed 174 kilowatts of power and some suggested that the lights in the western part of Philadelphia would go out when the machine was switched on. The legend, no doubt fanciful, suggests that they dimmed but did not go out.[56] Despite potential problems, in terms of performance the ENIAC was a breakthrough vindicating the use of vacuum tubes. There was a danger, however, that the tubes would burn out causing constant shut-downs of the machine. This danger was partially resolved by running lower voltages through the tubes, thereby aiding longer life. At its unveiling, the ENIAC performed in 20 seconds a calculation connected with atomic research that existing calculating machines were taking 40 hours to complete.[57] Whereas the Bush differential analyser required 15–30 minutes to complete a trajectory, ENIAC could run it in 20 seconds.[58] ENIAC was in use at the Ballistics Research Laboratory at Aberdeen from July 1947 until October 1955.[59]

There is no doubt that its creators, Eckert and Mauchly together with the thinking of von Neumann, were at the forefront of the pioneering efforts to move the world into the era of electronic digital computers, albeit at the very first and preliminary stages. Many have speculated that the ENIAC was the very first such example of a fully electronic stored program machine. Its memory was indeed very tiny – no more than 10-decimal numbers – which required the replugging of 6000 switches every time a new operation was performed. This laborious task has been described thus:

> Programming ENIAC was a one way ticket to the madhouse. You did not sit
> down at a computer teminal and type in the instructions; instead, you set

thousands of switches and plugged in hundreds of cables (like the cables on old telephone operator consoles) by hand, one at a time.[60]

This hard-wired form of programming the machine could take days to get ready.[61] Nevertheless it did embody the concept and logic of a programmable digital computer. It was in defence of this claim that Eckert and Mauchly applied for a patent in October 1947, but the relevant patent was not finally issued until February 1964. The reason for the delay was the contentious nature of the application, with interference proceedings and controversies with IBM and litigation by Bell Telephone Laboratories.[62] This was highly unusual in Patent Office proceedings which were usually conducted *ex parte*. By then the interest of the two inventors had been bought out leaving the legal battle in the hands of the computer companies (Honeywell Inc. and Sperry Rand Corporation) who wished to break the validity of the early patents in the field so as to promote their own later patents.[63]

Suit was filed by Honeywell in 1967 against Sperry Rand Corporation but the full hearing was not heard until 1971. Extensive discovery proceedings were engaged in during the next three and one half years and over 30,000 exhibits were identified. While this was taking place, Sperry was countersuing for patent infringement by Honeywell after the company failed to pay royalties to Sperry in respect of the former's own computer building projects. The hearing commenced in June 1971 and concluded in March 1973. Judgement was not forthcoming until October 1973. In addition to the attack on the ENIAC, anti-trust misconduct was also asserted against Sperry.

In order to break the ENIAC patent it was necessary to establish that its designers had derived the invention from elsewhere. Sperry Rand had acquired the patent rights from Eckert and Mauchly for $600,000, and Honeywell was fighting the royalties claim by contending that the design of ENIAC was appropriated from another machine, built by a physicist named John Atanasoff and a graduate student called Clifford Berry. The Atanasoff-Berry Computer (ABC) had been under construction since the spring of 1939 at Iowa State College. There had been a number of contacts between Atanasoff and Mauchly from December 1940 onwards when details of the ABC project were discussed. Atanasoff gave Mauchly a demonstration of the ABC and revealed written details of the project which Mauchly examined. Atanasoff claimed that the key elements of electronic digital computing had come to mind one evening while he was resting in a bar during a journey by car from Iowa to Illinois. He claimed to have identified the advantages of vacuum tubes over electomechanical relays, the application of binary arithmetic to recording instructions to a computer, the benefits of serial or sequential calculation with large numbers and a method of regenerating an electrical charge that would provide storage capacity for computer memory.[64] When the ABC was built it had used 300 vacuum tubes together with capacitors (then called 'condensers') to maintain memory comprising 30 binary digits in each of two drums.[65]

In a decision which was bound to cause controversy among the protagonists, Judge Larson ruled that the ENIAC patent was invalid and unenforceable since the essential features of the ENIAC were derived from Atanasoff and the ABC. There was also a technical factor involved which invalidated the patent. The court found that ENIAC had been in public use since December 1945, more than one year before the patent application was made in June 1947. Under US law the period between invention and application had to be no more than one year. Eckert and Mauchly were disappointed, the latter continuing to claim that he had been working on his ideas for at least five years before he met Atanasoff. It is much more likely that the prime motivation for the law-suit was not to satisfy the claims of the inventors as to who first thought of the concepts and applied them, but to remove those patents that might stand in the way of subsequent applications from the computer industry. It is interesting to note that the initiative to sue did not come from Atanasoff himself, but from a lawyer representing IBM who approached him in June 1954.[66] Up to that point Atanasoff seems not to have been bothered to act. The ABC and Atanasoff himself would similarly have faced a challenge had he been perceived as a threat to the interests of the industry. Commenting after the event Mauchly wrote:

'Because I visited J.V. Atanasoff for just two or three days in 1941, the 1974 decision of Judge Larsen was that I had derived all my notions about building electronic computers from Atanasoff. Yet the same judge, one page later in his decision, said that Eckert and I were the true inventors of the ENIAC . . . It is unfortunate that the ABC machine was not completed, and that Atanasoff never gave to the patent attorneys the information that they requested so that the patent application could be filed. When I joined the Moore School in 1941, I wrote to him suggesting that he might join us and possibly have a better chance of developing his ideas, but he chose not to do this. He did no further work in computer development that I know of.'[67]

It is probably a pointless and unnecessary exercise to attempt to seek out one person to acclaim as the inventor of the electronic digital computer. The processes involved required knowledge of mathematics, logic, physics and electrical engineering. Who can say that the work of Shannon, Turing and von Neumann was any less significant in stimulating the discovery than the skills of Atanasoff, Zuse, Bush, Eckert and Mauchly in building the first machines. The fact that, according to the law, Atanasoff is credited with the breakthrough belies the considerable achievements of the others.

Recent history has added yet another name to the list of founders: that of Thomas Flowers. Until classified documents were released in Britain in the 1970s under the thirty-years' rule of non-disclosure, little was known of the wartime activities of the British in connection with computers. Even today the full story has not been made public, so it remains uncertain how much had been discovered in Britain about computers prior to the outbreak of war in 1939. It has emerged however that, with the help of Turing and Professor M.H.A. Newman, who had lectured to Turing at Cambridge in 1935, a computer was built to decipher encrypted messages transmitted by the Germans in pursuit of their war effort. It was built by Flowers and his colleagues between February and December 1943. Named the Collossus 1, it incorporated 1500 vacuum tubes and operated in parallel arithmetic mode at 5000 pulses per second. It might have been faster but for the fact that the prototype reader could not cope and disintegrated when the paper tape reached an entry speed of 60 mph. The machine could accept small programming changes via switch changes on a front panel. For major re-programming, wiring changes were necessary. Eleven Collossus machines were built for decoding enemy signals but none are thought to have survived. The achievement, nevertheless, has been recorded and marked the beginning of some very successful work in Britain at a number of sites.[68]

LANDMARK DEVELOPMENTS IN COMPUTING SINCE 'ENIAC'

It is possible to give both a simple and a highly complex picture of developments since the first generation of computers in the decade of the 1950s. In principle the basic concepts that underpinned the construction of the first digital computers have not changed in the years since; what is different are the techniques employed to achieve those ends. It is interesting to note that nearly fifty years later, the ideas which Atanasoff claimed to have formulated in 1937,[69] have been applied in the development of computers and computer science. The tremendous progress that has been made with the technology in the comparatively short time since the first computers, has therefore occurred because new methods have been found of performing the basic machine functions. This has resulted in major enhancements in the capacity of computers to accomplish tasks, while simultaneously producing a reduction in costs and an expansion in applications. In addition, there has been progress in improving the ease of use of the technology and in automating design techniques themselves. All this has contributed to the convergence of technology generally, as evidenced by the growing importance of information technology in such fields as telecommunications, design, manufacturing, banking, entertainment and, potentially, many other areas too. Essentially these developments have taken place because computers have become much smaller, faster, cost-effective and, by comparison with the first machines, user-friendly and versatile. In addition, much better methods of programming computers have been developed, together with improved means of storing and re-trieving data and outputting results.

THE FIRST GENERATION COMPUTERS   The first generation of computers, based on vacuum tube technology, dominated the period until the end of the 1950s. In 1950 itself there were approximately 20 automatic calculators and computers in existence in the United States, and several other countries were becoming involved.[70] In Britain, significant work was being done at the National Physical Laboratory in Teddington, at the Cavendish Laboratory, Cambridge, at Manchester University and Birkbeck College, London. The vacuum tubes themselves became miniaturized. They were more reliable and consumed less energy and were operated in the central part of the machine hardware that became known as the central processing unit. (The very first computers, built of full-size (non-miniaturized) vacuum tubes, are considered as belonging to the 'zeroth generation'.)

Other problems that were attacked on the hardware side during this period related to the expansion of computer memory and improvements in input and output methods. The ENIAC computer had virtually no memory at all and von Neumann soon recognised the importance of building a stored, programmable memory into the machine concept. It was this idea that was taken up, with the result that a number of technologies were tried out before one emerged in the mid 1950s. Computer memory refers to the capacity of the machine to store and retrieve data. The data is broken down into characters represented by binary digits in the machine, collectively known as bits. The latter are the elements upon which digital representation is expressed. Bits when grouped together in rows of eight are called bytes.

Von Neumann developed the concept of memory hierachies defined according to their speed of operation.[71] Main memory was the fastest kind in direct communication with the central processing unit, and it was realised that methods would have to be found to hold hundreds if not thousands of numbers. All calculations would have to call upon data held in main memory. Finding ways of expanding its capacity was therefore crucial.

The ENIAC team were the first to introduce the concept of delay memory, whereby pulses could be held indefinitely until required. This was done by connecting the input to the output, supported by circuits which amplified and reconstituted the signal. This would be a marked advance upon the vacuum tube approach, where only one bit could be held per tube. Eckert and Mauchly had in mind the transmission of pulses through mercury which research on radar had shown could possibly provide a method. Ultrasonic sound could pass through mercury at the rate of 1400 metres per second so that a tank or tube of mercury one metre in length could comfortably hold at least 1200 pulses at one time. By this method it was possible to increase memory capacity one hundred-fold compared with what was possible with vacuum tubes. It also opened the way to dynamic as opposed to static forms of memory, in which data was represented not in one or other stable physical state, but in lines of pulses in perpetual movement until read at a single point in the device.[72] This concept was applied by Eckert and Mauchly in a computer called the BINAC – Binary Automatic Computer. They formed a company – Electronic Control Company – to develop the machine. This technology was also employed in the Whirlwind computer completed at Massachusetts Institute of Technology in 1955, and in UNIVAC 1, one of the first computers ever to be built for the commercial market, of which 46 were sold to industry.[73] UNIVAC 1 incorporated 100 mercury delay lines. It weighed five tons, incorporated 5000 vacuum tubes and its central processing unit (CPU) measured 8 feet by 15. It performed a calculation in 0.5 millisecond, and a multiplication in 2.5.

The UNIVAC was used by CBS-TV to predict the outcome of the 1952 Presidential election when Eisenhower fought Stevenson. After seven percent of the votes were in, the computer predicted a landslide victory for

Eisenhower. Fearing that the machine was wrong it was decided to repro-
gram the machine and run the results through again. This time it suggested
that the result was too close to call. In the outcome the first prediction
proved correct to within five electoral votes. Eisenhower had demolished
his opponent. The CBS commentator is quoted as saying: 'the trouble with
machines is people.'[74]

Other methods of main memory storage were subsequently developed.
At Manchester University a small team of innovators, later to include Alan
Turing, built what became known as electrostatic tube memory or cathode
ray tube. The concept was invented by Williams and Kilburn, who had
worked on electronics development during the war. The new storage
medium had several distinct advantages over conventional tubes, being
cheap to produce, small in size and also comparatively fast given that the
tube could store between 1024 or 2048 bits. A patent application in respect
of the storage device was filed in December 1946 and incorporated into a
prototype of the MARK 1 computer which was later to spawn a number of
computer developments, including the ICL 2900 range in the late 1970s.[75]
The idea was similar in concept to the operation of the cathode ray in the
television tube which produces a picture on a screen. The electrostatic
charge thus produced could be regenerated to store data. Access time was
no more than 25 microseconds (one microsecond = 1/1,000,000 second).
This concept was used by IBM in the IBM 701 – its first commercial
machine, first demonstrated in April 1953.[76] An addition was achieved in
62 microseconds and a multiplication in 456. Main memory was accessed in
30 microseconds. A total of nineteen 701s were built, eight for the aircraft
industry, four for the government, three for academic research and three
for commercial applications.[79]

Machine breakdown was still a common and indeed an endemic feature
of computing at this time. Williams's tubes were sensitive to electromagnetic disturbance, and under normal circumstances had a life-span of
no more than 100 hours. The IBM 701 ran on average for only 20 minutes
before main memory problems were encountered. The next advance which
introduced greater reliability within the machine employed a magnetic
drum for main memory storage, which consisted of a cylinder coated with a
magnetic alloy capable of being magnetized and demagnetized repeatedly
at high speed. The idea was first developed at Princeton and taken up at
the Georgia Institute of Technology where, in 1950, the ERA 1101 computer first used it in main memory. Up to that point it had been used for
secondary storage, as in the IBM 701, but in main memory distinct

advantages were to be gained. It meant that computers would be cheaper to produce and more reliable, since the number of mechanical parts in the machine were reduced. The mechanics was beginning to give way to the electronics ensuring a better, faster and more efficient product. The ERA 1101 could multiply in 260 microseconds. In 1953 IBM marketed a medium-scale computer with a drum memory. Not expected to sell more than 50 models, the IBM 650 became the first computer to sell more than 1000.[78]

Another pioneering effort with memory was achieved by Jay Forrester who worked on a number of projects at MIT in the 1940s and 1950s, including leading the project to build the Whirlwind computer. The latter took three years to build, deployed 175 people and a budget annually of $1 million. The objective was to create a machine that could operate in 'real time' providing an instant response to a specific scientific calculation. Whirlwind became the fastest machine of the early 1950s, although it used less than 25% of the vacuum tubes deployed in ENIAC. This was because it was the first 16-bit machine calpable of storing 2048 16-bit words in each tube. The short one-month lifecycle of the tubes continued to be a problem, however, despite painstaking handcrafting of the tubes in the project workshop. Cost too was involved, since each tube cost $1000 to make and $32,000 per month to maintain on Whirlwind.

Recognising that he had improved electrostatic technology to its limits, Forrester began work on a new idea after discovering a German product called Deltamax which enhanced magnetic amplification. From his experiments he developed a series of magnetic ferrite cores on a grid of wires. Each core possessed co-ordinates and could be loaded with data when the appropriate intersecting wires were energised. A prototype machine was built to test the new memory with the help of Kenneth Olsen, at that time a graduate student, who later went on to found Digital Equipment Corporation.The system worked and was used in Whirlwind in 1953, reducing access time to six microseconds, a 50% improvement on the electrostatic version, and quadrupling the input data rate. Another significant statistic was the increased operational time now available. Maintenance of the core memory fell from four hours every day to two hours per week.[79] The first computer to be marketed with core memory was the UNIVAC 1103A in 1954 – 50 times faster than the 1101 model of 1951. IBM introduced the 704 series in 1955, increasing capacity from 4096 words of 36 bits to 32,768 words just two years later. The memory had a cycle time of 12 microseconds.[80]

With the introduction of core memory from the mid 1950s attention turned to other areas where advances might be made. One of these was secondary memory devices capable of storing data for subsequent input into the computer. Von Neumann had identified the concept of memory hierachies which he visualised as a means of expanding access to machine-readable data. During this period there were two sorts of secondary memory envisaged: that which was addressable in the sense that it could be called directly when needed; and non-addressable memory that could not. The latter consisted of punched cards and paper tape and has gradually fallen into disuse as more efficient forms of addressable storage emerged. Two such forms of storage media developed during the first generation of computers. These were magnetic tape and disk memories.

Magnetic tape was not in fact an entirely new concept having been used with calculators prior to the inception of computers.[81] UNIVAC 1 used a form of magnetic tape made of steel which frequently broke while in use. The first IBM efforts at tape storage for the IBM 701 model held data at a rate of 100 characters per inch and readable at 7500 characters per second. The IBM 705 series ll machine began to exploit the concept more fully introducing a mechanism for connecting several magnetic tapes to the machine and instructions for controlling the operation, which eased the pressure upon the central processor with regard to the management of input and output.[82] After this, magnetic tape was also used to store data away from the machine. The concept of a 'database' was born when efforts were made to find ways of storing all the data required for a particular machine such that it could be called up without human intervention. This was achieved with the RCA BIZMAC computer launched in 1958 which allowed up to 200 magnetic tapes to be accessed without human intervention using a network of smaller interconnected computers to access the appropriate tape unit.

The key problem with tape systems was the delay in accessing the data. The tape would need to be wound or rewound to the point where the data was held in order to access it. Magnetic disks tackled that problem since data could be held within the tracks on the disk which the reading head could identify and access directly, far quicker than the sequential approach required from tape storage methods.[83] Disks were soon stacked together on a turntable which enabled the reading heads to move in and out between the rotating disks. The IBM 305 business computer, announced in 1956, contained four disk-storage elements with a combined capacity of 20 million characters. Access with this system was calculated at about 125 times faster than conventional tape retrieval.[84] Subsequently the concept of interchangable disk packs were introduced with reading heads lined up opposite each disk, doing away with the vertical movement of the heads in the previous method. This concept was used with the IBM 1311 model in 1962. There were six disks within a pack producing 15 million characters online to the computer.

Developments were also taking place with peripheral equipment that was vital if the increased operational speeds of the first generation machines were to be matched in output. Visual display units, known as CRTs (Cathode Ray Tubes) in the USA, in laboratory use since 1945 in radar and other fields, were deployed and this enabled computer processes to be monitored and directed from a central console. Printers were also developed and by 1953 the UNIVAC 1 printer operated at a speed of 600 lines per minute. Each line comprised 120 characters. Matrix printing which involved the formation of dots representing characters being hammered out on paper was introduced in the late 1950s. The IBM 730 dot matrix printer functioned at speeds of 1000 lines per minute. Non-impact printing by ink jet and laser had not yet been developed.

THE EVOLUTION OF PROGRAMMING LANGUAGES   Up to this point discussion has concentrated upon the hardware developments. Clearly Forrester's magnetic core memory proved a vital step forward in the effort to make computers more reliable machines.[85] It also dramatically increased computer memory and this opened the way to new ideas such as the automatic programming of computers. In the early period of computer evolution, as many concepts were being tried out there was no consistency in construction and little industrial use of computers. Most were constructed in laboratories and used for military applications, primarily as sophisticated calculators for a number of purposes. The lack of a large enough computer memory constrained the development of stored programs, such that, with the early machines, stored computer programs of any size were out of the question. Also, these machines could only operate upon instructions in machine-readable form in binary code – the first generation of computer language (1GL). Simple instructions would require strings of binary digits that would need to be fed into the machine on punched cards or paper tape. A program on ENIAC was set up on a plug board and alterations would require changes to the plugging by a human operator. Major programming changes would require similar amendment to the hard wiring of the machine and might take several days to accomplish. It was this inconvenience that led to greater efforts being put into developing automatic programming operations.[86] There was no consistency in instruction length or formation as this would depend on the organisation of the internal elements of the machine. Initially instructions would be read in sequence being loaded one by one into the computer. Later it was possible to control the order by means of an instruction counter which introduced more flexibility in programming. This concept was used with UNIVAC 1 in 1951.

One of the key problems with the early stages of programming was the risk that an instruction might be incorrectly coded. Turing and von Neumann had been among the first to recognise the need for logical sequencing of instructions to solve problems, and a computer could only operate an algorithmic procedure if correctly instructed to do so by the code it had to work by. The binary concept provided the means by which individuals could communicate with the machine in a form it could respond to, but a single mistake in the coding would undo the entire program. Writers of the code would need to understand exactly how the machine operated upon instructions and the exact form in which they should be given. Writing in machine language was so remote from the objective that no progress would have been made in the technology had better ways not been found by which to simplify the task.

There was little co-ordination of thinking or sharing of ideas among those working in this new area, but plenty of experimentation and hypothesising as to ways of simplifying programming technique. One method that did become widespread in the 1950s among programmers was the 'floating point' system, whereby large numbers could be reduced to multiples of fractions by any power of two, for example, $1000 = .1 \times 10^4$. Although this simplified arithmetic calculation and the programming involved, it inevitably created a problematic side effect, requiring the production of subroutines of code to enable the computer to read the floating point notation. This consumed both human and computing resources.

At Cambridge University pioneering work was done, exploiting the advantages of subroutines. This programming research was undertaken as part of the EDSAC computer project. It was realised that elementary machine functions could be written and held for general use. The concept of a library of 'subroutines' was born – an idea still widely exploited today.[87] A more substantive breakthrough was required, however, if any major progress could be made in simplifying programming. The level of communication would need to be raised to resemble more closely that of language, and better ways would need to be found to obtain solutions to problems given to the computer. The first step towards this goal came with the use of mnemonic codes on the EDSAC project to define instructions as, for example, the letter 'S' meaning 'store'. To achieve this, it was necessary to devise another program that could translate the mnemonic code. Further work was undertaken on this by Grace Hopper while working for the Eckert-Mauchly Computer Corporation, and subsequently when Remington Rand, later the Sperry Corporation, took it over. Mnemonic codes were used in Sperry's UNIVAC 1 machine in 1951, the codes themselves representing an early form of 'assembly language' – the second generation computer language (2GL). Earlier work in assembly language had also been carried out by Alan Turing one of the chief designers of the Manchester Mark 1 computer which successfully ran the first stored program on 21 June 1948.[88]

Instead of coding in binary the UNIVAC 1 used letters, numbers, symbols and short words. The translator programs used to convert the assembly language into machine code took two forms. Interpreter programs converted and executed instructions in sequence which could prove inefficient where instructions and cycles of calculation might have to be repeated. Compilers, on the other hand, were more sophisticated and took whole sequences of code into store, recalling them when required. The concept could take account of the framework of the instructions and focus upon the entire set rather than upon each single one. The first compiler program was created by Grace Hopper and her staff in 1952 and further work over the next five years produced the first English-language data-processing compiler.[89]

Work on evolving simpler terminology than that offered by assembly language continued. Using the latter to formulate instructions still presented problems since it remained closely tied to the machine structure. There was also the problem that programs written in assembly language and translated into machine code on cards or tape would need to be re-entered into the computer by human intervention once the machine code version was ready. This was of course an advance on amending the computer's wiring, but with the development of memory and of elementary operating systems, opportunities arose for improved methods of programming which could be undertaken automatically. Such developments would also assist the programmer as he would need to know less about how the machine functioned in order to program. This requirement in the case of assembly language programming inhibited the user, who found that strict adherence to these conditions did not help the resolution of the problem or the construction of the algorithm to resolve it. A higher level of language than the mnemonic coding of the assembly languages with which to code instructions was needed that conformed more closely to the needs of the user. There was also an economic need as well, since programming and debugging errors were expensive, accounting for up to 75% of maintenance in some cases. The origin of the word 'bug' in the context of a program error is attributed to Grace Hopper. In 1947 while working on the Mark II computer at Harvard, a dead moth was extracted from a faulty relay switch caused by the presence of the insect. The phrase 'debugging' was used thereafter to describe faults in the system.[90]

What in fact emerged were the third generation of computer languages (3GLs), produced to serve particular defined needs which burgeoning demand cried out for as hardware costs fell and machine capacity grew. One of the first to be developed was FORTRAN – FORmula TRANslator – intended as a general purpose language for the scientific community. Its producer was John Backus whose work on computers began in 1950 when he joined IBM. After working on several projects, including the development of an assembly language for the IBM 701 series, he asked himself a fundamental question: whether it was possible to construct a language for programming that contained a sufficient amount of normal mathematical expression to make it easy to use among the scientific community, while keeping within the inevitable constraints of program size and cost.[91] To achieve this objective it would be necessary of course to devise a translator program to go with it that could take coding written according to the higher level syntax of FORTRAN - 'source code' – and translate it into machine code – 'object code'- for execution by the computer. Backus regarded the achievement of this as the bigger of the two challenges.

The project objective was to design the language to enhance programming methods for the IBM 704 machine. It had to be cost-effective and as fast in execution as the most elegant hand-coded programming of the time. Work began early in 1954, and after some delays in getting the product right the basic task was completed in mid-1957. The compiler produced to translate FORTRAN to machine code comprised 25,000 lines of code held on tape. The language proved a major breakthrough for the art of programming and was of considerable value to IBM in selling its computers to those who did not understand particularly well how computers worked. However, as has occurred many times since, the initial version was imperfect, with many programming errors which hindered its effective use. By continued effort to iron out the problems FORTRAN gradually began to operate as intended.[92] FORTRAN is still used today, and in order that it could be operated on other non-IBM computers other compiler programs were later produced, compatible with those machines.

Subsequently other high level languages were developed including COBOL – Common Business-Oriented Language, APT – Automatic Programming Tools, ALGOL – Algebraic Language, and PASCAL a descendant of it, PL/I – Programming Language, APL – A Programming Language, LISP – LISt Processing, and BASIC – Beginners All-purpose Symbolic Instruction Code. Each served a particular programming niche. COBOL provided a language for the business market just as FORTRAN did for the scientific side. PL/I also proved popular as a move towards a 'universal' language and BASIC is known throughout the world as a language for non-experts that later was to become usable on some of the earliest personal computers. Developed by two mathematics professors at Dartmouth College in the mid-1960s, it was placed in the public domain almost immediately and a copyright was obtained by the College who then offered BASIC free to anyone who wanted to use it. The originators of the language, Kemeny and Kurt, did not therefore earn very much money for their achievement.[93]

The effect of these higher level languages was profound. They were crucial to the full exploitation of computers that subsequent hardware innovations enhanced, and they brought some order into the chaotic environment of programming.[94] They reduced the costs of computing and enabled thousands of new applications to be developed for computers that brought them away from the early days, when the machines were perceived as basically number crunchers for complex calculation tasks. However, their development did store up another problem that still pervades today; that of compatibility. A program written in one language cannot easily be translated into another, and the prospect of the task being undertaken automatically by a translator program is only just beginning to produce results.

In summarising the impact of this early period of the industry, in addition to the technical developments in computing, the 1950s were crucial years for management and salesmanship within the industry. It was IBM who led the way in this regard, which was to give the company an unassailable lead over its competitors as the industry took off, initially with transistor technology and subsequently with increased solid state integration. The key to IBM's success was the autocratic yet successful management of the company by its founder Thomas J. Watson. With the high value placed by IBM on its employees and the winning sales methods devised by Watson, the company was able to beat off competition from its main rival, Remington Rand, whose UNIVAC computer was inferior to IBM's 700 series. In 1954 orders for the latter were accepted while the machine was still in development, so that by 1956 the company was ahead in the market, with 76 as opposed to Rand's 46 machines. Just a year earlier in 1955, when Remington Rand merged with the Sperry Corporation, the former had held the lead over IBM with an installed base of 30 large machines compared with IBM's four. By 1961, as transistors began to replace the vacuum tube in the new generation of computers entering the market, IBM had increased its revenues to $1.8 billion, representing 71% of the market compared with the meagre 10% slice occupied by the Univac product range.[95]

And what of the progress of the computer industry in the UK? Whereas the inventiveness of the British was evident in the development of computers, through the contributions made to a variety of the early projects, this did not carry through to the exploitation of that know-how. Two companies, British Tabulating Machine Company which processed the 1911 Census, and Accounting and Tabulating Machine Company, the UK punched card machine producer, were early competitors whose paths merged in 1959 when International Computers and Tabulators was formed – the forerunner of ICL. The latter became the major UK hardware producer from among a number of companies initially active in computing, including Ferranti, EMI, English Electric, Elliott Automation and Leo Computers.[96] The UK industry, such as it was, had of course to face up to the increasing might of the IBM empire as it established its European operational and manufacturing base, followed subsequently by the arrival of DEC.

THE TRANSISTOR ERA   With the decline of the vacuum tube marking the end of the first generation of computers, 1959 is particularly singled out as being the year when the transistor edged out miniaturised vacuum tubes as the state-of-the-art technology serving the central processor. It was the year when several companies announced to the market the availability of fully transistorized machines.[97] Significant progress had been made during the first generation of computers with memory devices able to hold larger and larger volumes of data in machine-readable form, but the processing technology at the heart of the machine function still relied upon vacuum tubes to conduct the binary operations. The tubes had become miniaturised and this of course saved energy, but it still meant that machines would remain comparatively large in size and, prior to Forrester's initiatives, potentially unreliable given the breakdown rate of thermionic valves (vacuum tubes). The thermionic valve was also very inefficient in terms of the amount of energy consumed to produce the required signal.

Interest was growing in the potential applications of 'solid-state' materials as a means of producing electrical circuits for binary operations. Whereas thermionic valves achieved this objective using a heated metal filament, potential alternatives existed in substances possessing similar electrical properties to that achieved by thermionic valves. The objective of course was to provide an electronic means of performing a binary operation by either passing or not passing an electric current through a circuit. Normally a current would pass through a substance as a result of the movement of electrons induced by an electrical voltage. In order to control the flow of the electrons a substance was needed that would both permit and inhibit the such movement – hence the expression semi-conductor. Several substances appeared to offer the necessary conditions of being less conducting than metal and less insulating than quartz, which was known to be non-conducting. One of these was silicon, a plentiful substance from which pure crystals could be produced cheaply. In this form it could prevent the flow of a current, but once impregnated with an impurity such as boron or aluminium, conductivity would reappear. In theory then a solid state alternative existed to the control of an electric current by the switching 'on' or 'off' of a heated metal filament within a vacuum.[98]

The first major step forward in solid-state electronics came with the development of the transistor.[99] The progenitor of the device was William Shockley who, in 1945, became co-director of the solid-state physics research programme at Bell Telephone Laboratories in Murray Hill, New Jersey.[100] He had already worked on some ideas for semi-conductor amplification which had failed largely because of difficulties with the surface of the semi-conductor, which seemed to inhibit the movement of the electrons. Members of Shockley's team then realised that by introducing a positive charge through two small wire electrodes within the surface of a germanium crystal, a 'hole' was produced in the germanium atom by electron movement, thereby transferring the positive to each charged atom in turn across its surface. This drift of electrons produced the electric current and completed the circuit. Shockley and his team had produced a method of controlling the flow of current through a solid substance which could switch between the 'on'/'off' states required for binary calculation. The first transistor worked at Bell Laboratories on 23 December 1947. It was named 'transistor' because it transferred current from a low resistance input to a high resistance output – hence *trans*fer re*sist*ance. The *New York Times* reported it in 1948 on an inside page following a demonstration the day before:

> A device called a transistor, which has several applications in radio where a vacuum tube ordinarily is employed, was demonstrated for the first time yesterday at Bell Telephone Laboratories where it was invented . . . . In the shape of a small metal cylinder about a half-inch long, the transistor contains no vacuum, grid, plate or glass envelope to keep the air away. Its action is instantaneous, there being no warm-up delay since no heat is developed as in a vacuum tube. The working parts of the device consist solely of two fine wires that run down to a pinhead of solid semi-conductive material soldered to a metal base. The substance on the metal base amplifies the current carried to it by one wire and the other wire carries away the amplified current.[102]

A patent was obtained for the 'point-contact' transistor, as it was named, that same year. A further patent was taken that same year in respect of an improved version – the 'junction transistor'. It was this type that went into general use from 1953 in hearing aids and 1954 in radios, and later in a whole range of other electrical equipment. The transistor was 10 times easier to make than a vacuum tube, a 100 times smaller, and required 1000 times less electricity. It would become 10,000 times more reliable.[103] Despite these obvious advantages, its movement into computers was somewhat slower, perhaps because of the significant investment in the prevailing vacuum tube technology and the cost and difficulty of designing and developing a new generation of transistorised machines.[104] It was eventually taken up in early 1956 at the MIT Digital Computer Laboratory, supported by IBM. The initial objective was to replace the substantial 55,000 vacuum tube machine created for the SAGE (Semi-Automatic Ground Environment) Air Defense System. Before the end of the decade the first transistorised computers were available on the commercial market.[105] One such example was the Control Data 1604 computer which contained 25,000 transistors within its central processor. It also had over 32,000 words of 48-bit memory in its ferrite core memory, but curiously little software to go with it. Universities were offered the machine at a low price if they agreed to write some programs.[106]

116

THE BIRTH OF MICRO-ELECTRONICS   The late 1950s were important for the next phase of computer development in preparing the conditions necessary for the subsequent breakthrough in transistor technology which occurred in 1960. This was a development in the production technique of transistors which was more akin to photographic or printing processes than anything else. Another significant advance was the incorporation of transistors on printed circuit boards for use in the processor. Mounting components in this way also reduced the weight of hardware pointing to the direction that the whole industry was about to go in with integration of all the electronics on a single board. The next stage was the production of standardised micro-circuit modules with densities of up to 100 components per cubic inch.[107] From this technology the mass production of transistors of increasing complexity and diminishing size became possible, although production costs remained unacceptably high. It was out of these experiments in design and solid state electronics that the third and fourth generations of computers were to emerge built on the twin pillars of the integrated circuit and the microprocessor chip.[108]

By this time silicon was beginning to take over from germanium as a semi-conductor substance. It possessed some advantages in that it could operate effectively at higher temperatures and was also more stable and less prone to pollution. Instead of placing wires within the semi-conductor to carry and amplify the current, this could be controlled by the injection of impurities (called 'dopants' in this context) into the silicon which would produce similar results on the surface of the semi-conductor itself.[109] When heated in oxygen the silicon formed a quartz layer and this could support deposits of aluminium placed in grooves cut so as to form the circuit connections with the other components. The concept therefore was to do away with external connections so as to integrate the entire circuit within the same piece of semi-conductor material.[110]

One of the key contributors to the breakthrough into integrated circuit chip technology was Jack Kilby whose interest in exploiting the potential of transistors in computers took him to the electronics corporation Texas Instruments in 1958. The latter had been among the first to produce transistor radios four years earlier and silicon as opposed to germanium transistors. Kilby joined a team that was looking to reduce the size of the electronic circuits to increase computer processing capacity. Through his previous experience in designing electronics products he appreciated the difficulties of reducing circuit size, while still relying upon the human hand to perfect the process. The sheer volume of connections to be made were prohibitive both in time and cost, and the growth in applications, particularly in military uses, required more complex designs. These were beyond existing production techniques to accommodate. Finding a means of automating circuit design and construction would enable more powerful and versatile machines to be constructed. The integration of the circuits closer together on the surface of the silicon would mean faster operational speeds as the electronic pulses would not need to travel so far. More instructions could be executed in a shorter time and potentially more could be held in the computer's primary storage. The use of silicon as a semi-conductor, being a solid-state material had, however, tackled the heat problem that would otherwise have prevented the closer packing of circuits on the semi-conductor surface.

Kilby's achievement was to take the essential elements of electronic circuits – the transistors, resistors, capacitors and diodes[111] and produce them in silicon using suitable dopant substances to produce the impurities necessary to operate the circuit. The first demonstration of the technique of integrating the components of a circuit upon a single semi-conductor took place at Texas Instruments on 12 September, 1958.[112] A patent application was lodged at the U.S. Patent Office in February 1959 and the following month Texas Instruments announced their solid-state semi-conductor circuit device which they described as 'no larger than a match head'. (Although the circuit had indeed been fixed upon the semi-conductor, Kilby had not perfected the process for providing the interconnections between the components. In his first device, which measured 7/16 inch across, he had in fact joined the components together by hand with a thin thread of gold wire.) Kilby's patent application had alluded to the alternative approach of making the electrical connections:

> For example, an insulating and inert material such as silicon oxide may be evaporated onto the semiconductor circuit wafer through a mask either to cover the wafer completely except at the point where electrical contact is to be made thereto, or to cover only selected portions joining the points to be electrically connected. Electrically conducting material such as gold may then be laid down on the insulating material to make the necessary electrical circuit corrections.[113]

Two years later, however, he was disappointed when the Patent Office rejected his description as inadequate, supporting instead another patent by Dr Robert Noyce of Fairchild Semiconductor, which contained a more clearly defined description of the process. The latter had filed his application in July 1959, obtaining a patent in April 1961 for a semi-conductor device which included an electrical connection suitable for use with integrated electronic circuits.[114] Thus it was the United States once again that achieved the breakthrough first. In fact, as early as 1952 the concept of an integrated circuit had been put forward by G.W.A. Dummer of the Royal Radar Research Establishment in England. A modest research contract was awarded to Plessey to develop a prototype, but the latter did not work and the idea was not pursued further.[115]

Noyce had studied transistor technology at MIT and in 1956 began work at William Shockley's Semi-conductor laboratory at Palo Alto California. A year later he left the company and with seven other employees, including Dr. Gordon Moore, with whom he later collaborated to found Intel Corporation, joined the Fairchild Camera and Instrument Company. Within three months a new company, Fairchild Semi-conductor[116] was founded and Noyce was appointed head of research and development.

In terms of commercial potential it was the Fairchild 'planar' technology for the production of integrated circuits that proved most successful. Initially the company had used the planar approach to manufacture silicon transistors on wafers that could be cut into chips incorporating a single transistor on each. Whereas Kilby had demonstated that all the components of an integrated circuit could be impregnated upon the surface, it was Noyce who, without knowledge of Kilby's work, overcame the wiring problem so as to give the circuit commercial application. Without the extension of the planar process to accomplish the interconnection of components during manufacturing, it would still have been necessary to wire them together manually which would have destroyed the commercial potential of the new method. Whereas Kilby had referred in his patent application to the possibility that conducting material such as gold could be 'laid down' on the chip surface to create the electrical connections, Noyce defined this more clearly, by describing how the transistor connections could be made by printing lines of metal upon the oxide surface of the silicon.[117] The first planar integrated circuit capable of mass production was introduced in 1961 by Noyce and his colleagues at Fairchild, incorporating a simple circuit that would previously have been made from possibly six transistors and a few other components.[118] With the production problem solved the door opened to the commercial market beginning, as always, with the needs of the military and the space program.[119] The manufacturing process produced a large number of dud chips, but those that did function properly when tested could be relied upon. The elimination of wiring, a feature of the first Kilby device was crucial in this regard.

119

The marketing cost of first planar integrated circuits on a single chip was $120.

As with the transistor, the use of integrated circuits in computers was not immediately taken up, partly because of the availability problem generated by military and NASA requirements. The first commercial product to incorporate an integrated circuit was the Zenith hearing aid in 1964.[120] Thereafter integrated circuits appeared in computers[121] and later pocket calculators and digital watches. The transistor of course was the key component built into the chip, since it acted as a switch for the electric current controlling its 'on'/'off' state. The more transistors that could be connected together with the other components upon a single chip the more binary calculation could be undertaken. The immediate task was to introduce more components within a single chip.

Originally, companies wishing to exploit the integrated circuit technology had to obtain a licence from both Texas Instruments and Fairchild – the respective employers of Kilby and Noyce. These companies began to settle in the Palo Alto/Mountain View region of California in the valley area some 300 square miles in size between San Francisco and San Jose in Santa Clara County. Mountain View was in fact the town where William Shockley grew up, and by 1957 IBM, General Electric, Hewlett-Packard and Raytheon Associates all had operations there together with other electronics businesses spawned by the graduate population of the nearby Stanford University.[122] In all, Fairchild was responsible either directly or indirectly for the spawning of about 100 spinoffs into silicon valley and the semi-conductor industry as it is today in that region: at a 1969 conference for semi-conductor engineers held at Sunnydale, in Silicon Valley, less than two dozen of the 400 present had never worked for Fairchild.

The intensive effort to integrate more and more components upon the surface of the chip began slowly. In 1961 an integrated circuit incorporated just 4 transistors. By 1965 30 components could be placed on a 5 millimetre square piece of silicon. This amounted approximately to 10 integrated circuits. However, three years later 200 transistors were being placed on a single chip. At the same time prices were coming down. A transistor that had sold for £20 in 1954 cost only 20p in 1965. The success of this was also reflected in Fairchild's revenues which grew from a few thousand dollars in 1957 to $130 million dollars ten years later. The original seven who entered the company in 1956 were joined by another 12,000 people in the decade to follow.[124] By 1970 the integrated circuit sector was worth $1 billion worldwide, reaching $3.5 billion in 1976.[125]

THE ·COMPUTER ON A CHIP·   By the end of the 1960s the prospect of a 1000 circuits on a single chip became reality. However, no one had yet developed an insight into what this might mean for the development of the industry if the pace of integration continued. Gordon Moore and Robert Noyce, both of whom had left Fairchild Semi-conductor to found Intel Corporation in 1968, were certainly on the scent but could not envisage the revolutionary potential of what they were about to discover. In particular the idea that sufficient components could be built into a single chip to produce a computational tool was not appreciated, mainly because it was hard to look ahead and identify how the final product should look like. Gordon Moore comments thus:

> At the time it was hard to define any complex integrated circuit that was not essentially unique – you would use them one time in each computer. The technology was capable of making something in greater volume but it was not easy to see what it should be.[126]

Intel initially approached the problem with ideas to develop a memory chip. Gordon Moore felt that it was something that could be made in sufficient number to sell to a broad market. At the time of Intel's formation the most advanced memory devices could store only 64 bits. Within two years Intel had produced the first 1k Random Access Memory chip which produced $9 million in revenue within one year. The man most instrumental in the shift from memory to micro-processor device was Dr Marcian E. Ted Hoff.[127] Hoff had studied semi-conductor technology on the Palo Alto campus at Stanford University and was recommended for a reseach and development post at Intel by his faculty professors. He was keen to produce something in the field that had economic potential and he began to think of a semi-conductor device that could serve as the central processing unit (CPU) controlling the computer operation. Logic chips had begun to appear commercially but these performed specific functions concerned with computer operations such as calculation or printer control.[128] Hoff envisaged that the incorporation of the CPU on a single chip would open up the possibility of many new applications in computing and do away with the need to design a different type of integrated circuit device for every application. Standardised as opposed to custom-built chips, when in mass production, would be considerably cheaper and the diminutive proportions and power of the device would increase the range of uses.

The development of what was to become the world's first micro-processor device began as a result of a project to make components for a programmable desktop calculator commissioned by a Japanese company called Busicom. Hoff did not like the company's rather complicated design proposals which had produced a set of 13 complex chips to operate the calculator. He preferred instead to aim for a general-purpose computer architecture which could be programmed by instructions fed to it from a memory chip built into the equipment. He had recognised from previous experience in hardware design that it was infinitely preferable to incorporate the complexity of computer operation in computer software as the latter was easier to rewrite. Instead of requiring electronics engineers to spend time designing circuit boards using integrated circuits for each specific application, Hoff envisaged a single design which was programmable without altering the design of the processor chip. This could be done by re-programming the memory chips connected to the processor.

The result of this work was a reduction from twelve down to four in the number of chips required to operate the Japanese calculator. These were the micro-processor, a memory chip of 2k bit capacity for program storage and another for processing which could hold 320 bits at one time. There was also a chip for controlling input–output messages. All four chips were mounted on a circuit board of pocket size dimensions.[129] Initially, Intel were tied contractually to Busicom and could not market the chip independently. Agreement was reached, however, in the summer of 1971, resulting in an announcement on 15 November 1971 in Electronic News under the advertising slogan: 'Announcing a new era of integrated electronics . . . a microprogrammable computer on a chip'. The chip was named the 4004: the '4000' identified it as a custom built chip and the '4' signified it was the fourth such chip to be designed at Intel.[130] It was a four bit chip capable of processing no more than 4 bits at a time. This was the capacity of the 2250 transistors built into the chip which operated at approximately 60,000 operations per second.[131] Hoff's 'computer on a chip' was accurate in the sense that he had placed all the CPU functions together on one chip, mounting it on the same circuit board as the support functions of read-only and random-access memory, along with the input/output instruction set.[132] Interviewed in 1986, Gordon Moore described the achievement thus:

> We are generally credited for having conceived of and realised the first Micro-computer or micro- processor as its called on a single piece of silicon. This is a little chip of silicon that is maybe a quarter of an inch square or less, that initially with the first micro-processors had about 4000 transistors on it with all of their inter-connections to make the complete computer function. I remember selling the first 100 transistors for $150 apiece to IBM. Today we

will sell a complete circuit with 150,000 transistors on it for less than the original transistors sold: that is we have decreased the cost of electronics 100,000 fold and given the interconnections away free in the process. Very few technologies have the ability to decrease costs like that, and this tremendous decrease in the cost of doing things electronically has made this technology so important.[133]

A more accurate description of what was done, however, might be to describe it as 'a computer on a circuit board' as it was necessary of course to link up the CPU with memory chips as well as an 'input/output' chip.[134] However, Hoff had challenged the conventional wisdom which had separate chips for keyboard, display and printer control as well as for the logic elements of the computer. A measure of the achievement is demonstrated by comparing the capacity of the 4004 micro-processor with ENIAC or the IBM machines of the early 1960s. The CPU component of the Intel 4004 semi-conductor chip measured 1/8 by 1/6 inches and contained 2250 transistors, more than equal to the ENIAC machine 25 years earlier which weighed 30 tons. Performing as well as the early IBM computers, the chip was sold for less than $100 compared with the $300,000 charged by IBM back in the early 1960s for similar capacity. In the course of the next few years the 4004 chip was incorporated into a range of equipment including traffic lights, video games and cash registers.[135] For Moore this vision of wider applications was the great insight that Hoff had understood ahead of Intel's rivals. Augarten comments thus:

'Although Intel did not realise it at first, the company was sitting on the device that would become the universal motor of electronics, a miniature analytical engine that could take the place of gears and axles and other forms of mechanical control. It could be placed inexpensively and unobtrusively in all sorts of devices – a washing machine, a gas pump, a butcher's scale, a juke box, a typewriter, a doorbell, a thermostat, even, if there was a reason, a rock. Almost any machine that manipulated information or controlled a process could benefit from a micro-processor'.[136]

The Start of Commercial Sales   Intel delayed the launch of the 4004 chip until November 1971 as its marketing division was not convinced how the public would respond. There were fears that the concept would not be understood by the market, which was attached to the idea of large and expensive hardware devices requiring regular maintenance and support. When Noyce predicted at a conference in the late 1960s that a 'computer on a chip' was a feasible proposition, one delegate commented that he would not like to lose his whole computer through a crack in the floor. Noyce retorted that it did not matter if one were lost as there would be 100 more on the desk ready for use. The idea that a defunct or faulty chip could be pulled off the circuit board and replaced by a fresh one for no more than a few dollars was not understood. Moreover, the concept had not been proved and the major computer suppliers such as IBM were hesitant to launch new product lines incorporating micro-processors, with all the additional design expense involved, until the chip had proved itself. By the year end of 1974 Intel was producing in one month more 4-bit micro-processors than there were computers in existence up to that time. This was soon followed by 4-K bit RAM chips and the beginnings of large scale integration, with 10,000 transistors on one chip.[137]

In April 1972, just four months after the 4004 announcement, Intel was ready with another chip – the 8008 – which was the first 8-bit micro-processor chip. This sold for $120 and was used to build the MARK-8 'personal minicomputer'[138] which was more of a prototype than a real computer, although it was the forerunner of the Altair 8800 which really did herald the start of the personal computer industry. The 8008 did not possess a strong technical design but development work continued and in August 1973 Intel launched a much better and more efficient 8080 version. This had begun as a re-design of the 8008 but developed into a complete rebuilding of the micro-processor. With further advances being made in the manufacturing process as well, the 8080 chip became one of the most successful micro-processors ever in terms of sales. It also marked the beginning of large scale integration of components on a single chip which was one of the factors that made the 8080 version so versatile. It was also 20 times faster than the Intel 4004 chip and in its lifespan produced many new products including, of course, the micro-computer.

The 8080 micro-processor chip was an 8-bit device which meant that it could process 8 bits (1 byte) of data at a time. It operated at a speed of 1MHz. which meant that its clock speed operated at the rate of 1 million cycles per second.[139] The chip was originally priced at $360 but this fell towards the end of the decade to no more than about $2.50.[140] For a while Intel monopolised the market expanding sales income to $1.1 billion by 1983 – almost a thousand-fold increase on the initial venture capital investment of $1.3 million fifteen years before in 1968.[141] Today the company retains control of about 8% of the world market for micro-processor devices.

With the foundations of the micro-electronics industry now firmly laid, a number of companies began to market families of chips for a variety of uses. The design of the micro-processor chips rapidly developed, as teams of electrical engineers worked together to cram more and more capacity into the silicon semi-conductor. This marked the start of a second generation of 8-bit processors. Among the companies that began to compete in the semi-conductor market place apart from Intel, Texas Instruments and Fairchild, were Zilog Corporation, formed by ex-Intel engineers in 1975, and other larger micro-electronics companies such as Motorola and National Semiconductor. Zilog produced a rival to the Intel 8080 chip – the Z80. It could process data at the rate of 8 bits at a time and address its memory at the rate of 16 bits at a time. Since 16 binary digits of 1s and 0s combined together could form 65,536 individual combinations, this chip could access a larger memory.[142] Its clock speed was 2.5 MHz increasing to 8 MHz by 1983.

Intel was the first to produce a commercial '16-bit' microprocessor. The 8086 had a 20-bit address space but flaws in its architecture were very costly to the company. The difficulties continued with the next release – the 80286 chip – since it was still based on the compromised architecture. This was to prove costly too for those companies that gambled on the 286 for their hardware or software product range. Microsoft, for example, who built their OS/2 operating system around the 286 suffered accordingly. The 286 was, nevertheless, a commercial success finding its way into the centre of the personal computer sector despite the presence of superior design architectures with other micro-processors.

By the mid 1980s a pattern began to emerge as follows: as chips grew through the 4-bit, 8-bit and 16-bit range, one product would stand out and be taken up. Simultaneous competition would be beaten back by the success of a particular micro-processor which the computer manufacturers and other consumers would purchase. Those producers whose chips had failed to become the industry standard would either miss out altogether or go back to the design stage and seek to improve their original product. They would then compete again with any upgraded version produced by the successful manufacturer, as well as with any later improved versions of the chip produced by other suppliers who had deliberately planned to enter the market later.

Whereas, in its time, the Intel 8080 was a market leader, the Zilog Z80 came later and was designed to out-perform the Intel chip. By comparison, Motorola, who had been the first to respond to Intel's 8080 chip, bringing out the 6800 micro-processor, essentially failed in the market because it came too late and could not compete with the subsequent improved Z80 chip. The Zilog Z8000 micro-processor, designed to compete with other 16-bit micro-processors was unsuccessful but Motorola's 68000 series proved much more in demand. This was an extremely complicated design and led to the development of a series of chips within the 68000 'family' to suit different products. Co-incidentally the chip contained 68000 transistors. With a 24-bit capacity for reading memory it had access to 16 megabytes (16 million bytes) of semi-conductor memory. It also had a 32-bit internal capacity for processing data, although this was halved when transmitting to output devices.

CURRENT MICRO-PROCESSOR DESIGNS   It can be said that, so far as micro-processor development is concerned, the 1980s represented the period during which micro-processors 'grew up from "toy" processors suitable only for low performance, embedded control applications and hobbyist computers to sophisticated, powerful CPUs that challenge mainframe and supercomputer performance levels'.[143] In 1964, Gordon Moore who had co-founded Fairchild Semiconductor in 1957 and Intel in 1968 (and was later to become its President), commented that the number of transistors stored on a silicon chip had doubled each year since the invention of the integrated cicuit in 1959. This pattern of growth became known as 'Moore's Law' and continued to hold true until the 1980s, when the period extended to about 18 months. Whereas a chip in 1970 could store 1000 transistors, this had reached 1 million by 1980. As far as micro-processors are concerned, they advanced in terms of bit size, reading speed, design and function.

The performance capability of the CPU had always been a crucial issue in system design and technologists were now beginning to branch out in their attempt to develop new standards of performance. Micro-processors, for example, were given memory management logic for controlling the allocation of main memory to programs and data in a multi-programming system, as well as floating point support for reduced bit representation in data structures of a large range of real numbers. Another idea that designers looked at was the placing of additional features on the chip that previously were found in separate devices, for example those functions responsible for input–output, disk management and graphics in addition to the space needed for system memory.[144] Another development that built upon the licensed production of chips by other suppliers was the modification of a basic design to suit a user's particular needs. Such products are known as Application Specific Integrated Circuits (ASICs) and have developed a defined market. ASICs can be developed from a successful basic design, thus saving capital costs and providing the user with an application-specific device.[145] ASICs can range from simple controllers to special purpose micro-processors for products such as washing machines, cellular telephones and controllers for chemical plants.[146]

Another difficult problem that designers had to work round was ensuring continuity in design so that software written for a previous generation of chips could be transferred to the latest release. This led to the development of chip families. Account also had to be taken of operating system software currently in use or in the planning stage. Persuading the computer manufacturer to adopt your micro-processor in its new machine was crucial to the success of whichever micro-processor was chosen, particularly if that company was IBM.[147] Motorola and Intel were particularly successful in this regard. In 1984 Motorola introduced the 68020 version of the 68000 architecture. It was launched with both a 32-bit reading and processing capacity. The Apple Macintosh used an 8-bit version of the chip and another version was used by the IBM 3270 personal computer to enable programs prepared for the IBM 370 mainframe to be run on the PC.

The 68000 series was the first family of micro-processor chips to operate across a range of different equipment. This was in Motorola's interests as well as those of competitors and users. Competitors could, by agreements reached with Motorola, capitalise on the demand for the product, share in the research costs, and potentially enable software written for the chip to be run on different equipment using the same basic chip. As far as software compatibility was concerned much would depend upon whether this was the intention of the partners to the sharing agreement. Motorola would benefit from the contribution to its research costs and the payments received from the sharing of the chip. Users would benefit from the increased product choice and the prospect of upgraded versions of the basic design that would enable software written for the simpler chips to be transferred to the more sophisticated range as they were released.[148] This sharing of chip design to enable manufacturing to be undertaken by other firms is called 'second sourcing'.[149] Apart from the benefits already described, second sourcing helps to ensure that demand peaks are met and that research and development activity is not too heavily duplicated.[150]

Following the initial success of the 68000 series, Motorola introduced new generations of the chip with 68030 and 40 versions. The 30 chip was the product of a major redesign of the original architecture while retaining its software compatibility within the family. The 40 chip is a more powerful micro-processor with an integration of more than 1.2 million transistors. Its performance level is four times that of its predecessor.[151] The chip has been adopted by 35 computer manufacturers and Motorola claim that the hardware base of the family is worth $160 billion.[152] The chip entered volume production for the market in 1990 at a single price of $759.

Intel also came back strongly, with the 32-bit 80386 chip in 1985, followed in 1989 by a more powerful i486 version with a i586 in the pipeline. The i486, however, was not the runaway success that Intel had hoped for, because a minor bug in the design inhibited manufacturers from designing personal computers to the new chip specification.[153] Despite this setback, which cost the company millions of dollars, plans were announced in June 1990 to build a $187 million manufacturing facility in Dublin under the second phase of its 10-year programme designed to supply Intel's chips in Europe. The European operation is expected to be worth $1 billion within 2 years.[154] The chip has been warmly welcomed by the industry which is set to adopt it on a wide scale.

RISC versus CISC Chips   The prospects for the 1990s suggest continued improvement in chip performance levels and applications, as designers continue to exploit current technology until it reaches the silicon 'wall' sometime around the turn of the century. After that time, the increases in chip performance that we have all grown used to since the late 1970s will abate, unless a new technology is unlocked in the meantime to replace the existing silicon technology. Currently this means that the effort in micro-processor design is concerned, not only with developing techniques for packing the chip with more and more components, but with introducing new architectural features that make the chip respond more effectively for particular purposes.

For example, designers are trying to see how chip design can contribute to tackling some of the bottlenecks that have become apparent beyond CPU speed, which in the new language of the area is defined as 'cache size, memory size and latency, bus bandwidth, I/O speed and latency, software algorithms, file system structure and compiled code efficiency.'[155] 'Cache memory' speeds up execution of instructions; 'latency' is the delay between the instant a request is made for an item of data and the instant the transfer starts; 'bus bandwidth' is a measure of the amount of information that can

128

be transmitted between digitally based devices in one cycle; 'I/O speed' is a measurement of input–output cycles.[156]

What has been described as 'the most significant micro-processor event in the latter half of the eighties'[157] is set to develop further in the nineties. It was pioneered at the University of California, Los Angeles, partly in an attempt to minimise the risks and expense involved in micro-processor development which Intel in particular experienced with its 86, 286 and 386 chips. This is the Reduced Instruction Set Chip which has become known as the RISC processor. The underlying concept is to increase performance by reducing the design complexity of the micro-processor to a condensed set of basic instructions operating through a large register set.[158] This makes the chip smaller and cheaper to produce than the traditional Complex Instruction Set Chips (CISCs), exemplified by the two market leaders in CISCs – the Intel i486 and Motorola 040 products. Moreover, because the RISC chip responds only to simple commands it can do so faster than its more complex rivals.[159] For example, the 32-bit micro-processor developed in California is designed to operate 10-times faster that the Motorola 68000 chip which, through its speed, more than compensates for its simplicity. This has considerable appeal as users look for enhanced performance at lower cost. It also attracts designers if the prospect exists of reduced development costs and faster implementation of designs. The RISC chip developed at another University in the United States – Berkeley – was designed, for example, in six months, requiring only 20% of the manpower of comparable CISC architectures.[160]

A commercial battle is now in full swing for control of the argument as to which approach is the best, as well as control of the market, particularly that of the mainstream desktop-computing, executive 'workstation' and computer-aided design sectors.[161] RISC advocates point to its suitability in processing high-level language code which generates a large number of machine instructions once translated into object code. The straightforward design creates simpler control measures, rendering microcode unnecessary while being well-placed to respond to technological innovation ('Microcode' is a level of computer instruction below that of machine code, responsible for the management of the chip functions).[162] CISC supporters point to the substantial hardware and software base around their products, the considerable experience of the major producers in high performance design, and the uncertain future of the comparatively new RISC architecture. The issue is crucial for once a producer settles on a particular chip family for its product range it becomes very difficult to change.[163]

Both Intel and Motorola are safeguarding their position by developing their own RISC micro-processors. At Intel there is the i860 64-bit chip with one million transistors. The combination of bit capacity (64 bits manipulated at a time) and simplified instruction sets means the new chip can be run at very high speeds with one instruction being completed per processor clock cycle. This means that the i860, at its operating speed of 40MHz, can process at the rate of 40 million instructions per second (Mips) whereas, by comparison, the 25 MHz. 80386 chip runs at only 5 Mips. The extra space made available on the chip by the new design will enable other features to be added, for example, special functions for 3D graphics work or memory management and floating point processing for mathematical processing. There is a theoretical possibility of the chip reaching a speed of three 64-bit instructions per clock cycle – 120 Mips. Since this new micro-processor is not compatible with the CISC 80000 family the prospect of a new generation of computer workstations is possible. Intel currently claims a 66% share of the 'micro-processor for PCs' market and it hopes this will increase to 83% by 1992.[164]

By contrast, Motorola has developed the 88000 RISC micro-processor chip and a consortium of more than 50 hardware and software vendors has formed the 88/Open group which seeks to build a common standard for 88000 RISC-based machines and software. Successful RISC architecture has been produced by Sun Microsystems for its Sun-4 family of workstations. Known as SPARC – Scalable Processor Architecture – it has a set of register 'windows' that can be switched into according to the task and context of the function. This capacity is particularly relevant to real-time responses.[165] However, the real significance of the RISC design became apparent in January 1990 when Norsk Data announced that it was adopting Motorola's 88000 chip in the development of a logic circuit of 8 chips capable of delivering up to 1000 Mips with parallel processing at a speed of 25MHz. The company claims that this will produce mainframe performance for £500,000 – much cheaper than current mainframe prices (Mips means 'millions of instructions per second. It is a crude measure of system performance since the term "instruction" does not always mean the same between producers. Mips is a better measurement of performance between chips of the same family'.)[166] The next series of fast processors are well on the way too. Intel's i960 chip uses a new superscalar architecture which supplies four full 32-bit instruction words to the decoder/scheduler at a time. This enables multiple instructions to be executed per clock cycle which operates at rate of 66 million instructions per second.[167] With the arrival of these and other micro-processor chips, particularly Intel's 80486 CISC chip and i860 RISC/i960 SUPERSCALAR micro-processor, the prospect of moving from the 'computer on a chip' to the 'supercomputer on a chip' is now in sight, with revolutionary implications for existing demarcations between product ranges, operating systems and the industry's structure. The advance will have been achieved in little more than 20 years.[168]

DIGITAL STORAGE   It is important not to lose sight of the implications of this advance in micro-processor performance. It will bring with it new generations of computer systems and will challenge the dividing lines between existing systems as processor power accelerates. Running parallel of course with micro-processor development is the need to make advances in the capacity of both primary and secondary digital storage media. This is vital if the micro-processor is to be served efficiently and fast. In the case of primary storage, the development of dynamic Random Access Memory (D-RAM) chips has occurred at the same rapid pace as that of micro-processors. Intel's first manufactured component, the 1103 memory chip first distributed commercially in the early 1970s stored just 256 bits. By 1972 a 1024-bit dynamic memory chip was introduced, formed from 32 × 32 squares of cells. Known as the 1K D-RAM chip, sizes have increased by a factor of four with each new generation of memory chip. (RAM refers to random access memory: either the directly accessible memory of a comput or those parts of memory which can be examined and changed as opposed to merely read. A ROM – read only memory – Chip describes a chip which cannot be altered ('written to').)

In 1977 the 16Kbit chip was launched, followed in progression by production samples of the 64Kbit in 1980, the 256Kbit in 1983, the 1Mbit in 1986, the 4Mbit in 1989 and the proposed 16Mbit chip scheduled for 1992. The capacity growth from the initial 16Kbit chip to the current 4Mbit device is substantial, and equivalent to an increase in storage capacity from a newspaper column to an average-sized book, all in the space of approximately 12 years. Semi-conductor analysts are now predicting the 64Mbit chip in 1996 emanating from up to six independent sources of supply.[169] Development costs remain high though, growing at an average rate of 50% for each new generation of device. The cost of the 4Mbit chip, which is currently in production will be $2 billion, rising to $5 billion or more for the 64Mbit chip.[170] This adds to the pressure on companies to engage in joint project work similar to the agreement between IBM of the US and Siemens of West Germany who are currently collaborating in the development of a 64Mbit chip, with a view to having 'a world standard 64Mbit D-RAM ready for commercial production in the mid 1990s.'[171] Collaborative ventures like this also have a political motive as they ensure that competition against Japanese producers continues despite their effective takeover of the D-RAM industry in the late 1980s. Toshiba, for example, had 50% of the world's 1Mbit market all to itself for the first 18 months of the chip lifecycle. A subsequent trade dispute between the US and Japan caused major shortages which forced some suppliers to hold back on production plans and product launches.[172]

Developments in Secondary Storage Reference has already been made to the accleration in capacity and performance of micro-processor devices and memory chips (D-RAM) – the latter providing fast direct CPU access for both storage and accessing of data. Rapid improvement has also taken place in the capacity of secondary storage media to hold data which is held for transmission to D-RAM when required. Magnetic tape and subsequently disk storage has for the past 20 years or so provided the media by which data could be stored in digital form. In the early years of digital storage of data, users experienced a low level of data storage using cumbersome hard disks. Tapes provided the back-up storage off-line, stacked on shelves for call-up if needed. As time went on, continued advances in the technology provided more versatility, increased storage capacity and reduced costs. Methods were also found through hardware techniques of enabling disk storage to simulate semi-conductor memory, allowing, for example, 1 megabyte (1 Mbyte) of the latter memory to use programs occupying 16 times as much space. Known as virtual memory, this enabled programs written for larger machines to operate on smaller computers.

In the 1970s with the advent of micro-computers, floppy diskettes were introduced providing storage for about 100k bytes of data. Originally on 8-inch diskettes, subsequent versions have been 5.25, 3 and 3.5 inches in size routinely holding 1.2 Mybtes when serving conventional personal computers. High density floppy disks have since been developed for back-up purposes. The original was the 10Mbyte Bernoulli developed by Iomega on a 5.25-inch floppy. This has now increased to 40Mbytes, with data recoverable at speeds equivalent to hard disk retrieval.[173] For small data handling

132

needs this offers a flexible alternative to the non-removable hard disk which took over from floppies with the development of the Winchester magnetic disk drive.

Whereas floppies were used to deliver mass-market software to customers and to enable personal computer users to back-up small quantities of data off-line, the Winchester disk was a rigid magnetic disk system sealed in a dust-free chamber with the magnetic head floating very close to the surface of the disk. Larger storage requirements could be met by stacking several disks on the same shaft with a detection head for each.[174] Currently the top of the range is the IBM 3390 disk family with a maximum capacity of 22 GBytes (22 billion Bytes). This represents a three-fold increase in storage density compared with the previous 3380K series and massive storage capability in multi-disk formats. Single units are also available with capacity in excess of 300 Mbytes,[176] although some large-capacity hard disks can store up to 900 Mbytes individually.[177] Currently, it is common to find in excess of 65 Mbyte hard-disk capacity on personal computers selling for £1000–£2000.[178] Another possibility today is the removable hard disk cartridge which can store 40Mbytes, or double that if a two slot chassis is involved. Up to this point tapes have continued to offer cheap and efficient off-line back-up with 60–100 Mbyte units available, but this must now decline as removable hard drives and other mass media storage units including optical media take over.

In the 1980s optical storage systems began to challenge as an alternative to magnetic tape and disk. Optical disks initially became popular with the consumer as compact disc music players, but the technology can also operate to store very large amounts of digital information on small, robust and inexpensive disks. Two types of system have emerged – the 'Write Once Read Many' (WORM) drive and the 'Erasable Optical' (EO) drive. The WORM is essentially a Compact Disk Read Only Memory device that can be written to. Apart from phenomenal storage capacity – its advantage over a conventional hard disk – the optical disk can be removed from the drive and another added, thereby increasing the capacity of the drive to read new data. (The hard disk of course cannot be removed from its casing.) Current storage capacity of WORM discs nudges 1 Gigabyte (1 billion bytes), or more in multiple attachment. Digital Equipment Corporation, for example, has introduced a high capacity WORM disk attachment for its VAX computer which can be accessed through a network. It can hold 64 cartridges of 2 Gigabytes each, totalling 128 Gbytes altogether and initially costing £142,000. But there is much more to come.

ICI and disk manufacturer Iomega have developed a WORM prototype which ICI, who invented the medium, have called 'digital-paper'. This is because the medium of reflective plastic film is so cheap and its storage capacity so great that a user could back-up his files every day for one year on a single cartridge. Preliminary estimates suggest a cost of £30 for a 1.5 Gigabyte capacity. Increases in storage media capacity of this magnitude will herald major changes in the way we access and distribute pre-recorded information.

In 1989, for the first time, erasable optical (EO) otherwise known as magneto-optic disks came on the market. One of the first was designed for a new range of workstations using the Unix operating system. The cost of the 5.25-inch removeable disk was $250, giving a storage capacity of 600 Mbytes. Sony in collaboration with the American company 3M have developed a 650Mbyte cartridge. The disk retails at £225 or just under £4000 complete with the drive unit.[179] This produces a figure of 40 pence per megabyte of storage space on the disk. Since it is now possible both to read and write to the EO disk, costs will be reduced, because the resource is more flexible and data, perhaps previously held off-line, will now be available to users through on-line access.[180] The capacity is equal to that of 1000 average-sized floppy diskettes, and many of the large processor suppliers are now supporting the new storage media. The optical disk has great commercial potential with its capacity to store large amounts of information such as encyclopaedias, business information and biblio-graphic databases. Moreover, in addition to text, the optical disk will be capable of holding any digital data, including sound, graphics and video. Already Sony are among the first to produce a portable compact disk player – the 'Data Discman' – which displays data from the disk on a liquid crystal screen. The company is looking at ways of combining music or sound with text as well as graphics and video. Such products will develop into portable databases, updated regularly by the distribution of a new disk. It also has tremendous commercial potential for the distribution of business and technical information to field personnel.[181]

It is with optical technology that digital alternatives to conventional paper-based storage on a routine basis is likely to become a reality.[182] Supported by scanner machines that can digitise up to 25,000 pages of A4 text per day, Electronic Document Management Systems otherwise called 'document image processing' (Dip), could obtain widespread commercial acceptance in the next decade. These can store, not just the representation of the document in the structured data format of the computer, but the

document itself, including the multiple type faces and sizes, logos, letter-
heads, diagrams, annotations and signatures. The process requires the
scanning of a document in order to capture its electronic photograph which
is then stored as a digitised image. Software can then be introduced to
enable the operator to access and update the record from a desk-top
computer. Given the pressure of the daily storage requirement, combined
with the increased storage consumption of Dip systems, much higher
storage capacity will be required than is conventionally necessary to store
the digital representation. For example, image processing requires 0.5
Mbytes per page at 200 dot per inch resolution, or 500 Gbytes for 1 million
pages, although this can be reduced to only 50 Gbyte using complex image
compression technology.[183] However, whereas conventional optical character recognition techniques can operate at speeds of approximately two
pages per minute, image scanners are much faster and can scan an A4 page
at 200 dot per square inch resolution in two seconds.[184] A top-of-the-range
machine could in theory scan 25,000 pages a day at this rate although the
problem of high storage consumption remains.[185] It is likely that these
drawbacks will be tackled and that Dip technology will integrate with other
office systems as the nineties progress.[186]

SUMMARY   Thus far we have traced the development of the computer
from its origins with ENIAC and the other early machines. What was
unthinkable then in terms of system performance is a reality today.
Computational speed has increased beyond all recognition compared with
what was achieved by ENIAC. The dream of the computer scientist just
after World War II to build a machine that could execute one million
instructions per second has been well and truly shattered. The development of processing power since then can be illustrated by comparing the
time it would have taken ENIAC to calculate the three dimensional
supersonic flow past an aeroplane wing. It is estimated that this complex
calculation would have taken ENIAC 27 years to compute, compared with
two days in 1969 with the CDC-7600 computer and one hour in 1985 with
the Cray-2 supercomputer. This artificial comparison will probably reduce
further to nearer 20 minutes in the 1990s with the Cray-4 model.[187]

At some stage this constant advance in processing speed, storage capacity and CPU power will reach its limits so far as semi-conductor technology is concerned. The 'silicon wall', as this phenomena is called, will be
confronted soon after the end of the century. At that point, if Moore's Law
had been carried through, a storage capacity of 100,000 million transistors

on a single micro-processor would have been produced – equal to the number of neurons active within the human brain.[188] This is of course fanciful with existing technology although Intel has speculated that a 'super-fast' micro-processor with up to 100 million transistors will be possible by the year 2000. The projections are moving upwards, however, for this appears to be a lower target than that aimed for by some in the industry. Research laboratories are now looking at both improved production techniques and whole new technologies.

As far as memory chips (D-RAM) are concerned, IBM and its competitors are now spending hundreds of millions of dollars on identifying new ways of delivering the first of the 256Mbit-chip generation. New techniques for etching the circuitry are being investigated that are likely to go beyond the achievements of optical lithography, which has produced line widths of 0.8 microns (millionths of a metre) in the 4Mbit chip, 0.5 in the 16Mbit and, if the 64Mbit device is to come about, 0.35 microns at that stage. If that is the limit of optical techniques, some form of X-ray lithography will be required to capitalise on its shorter wavelength. When compared with optical ultra-violet methods this will theoretically enable finer lines to be etched on the chip than is possible by optical means.[189] In the meantime it has not escaped the industry's attention that 150 of the 64Mbit D-RAMS, connected together upon a single board, would reach the significant milestone of 1 billion bits (1 Gigabyte) of main memory on a single board – equivalent to a storage capacity of 50,000 single-spaced typewritten pages. This will be highly important for high-volume storage/processing applications such as high definition television, voice recognition, image processing and other 'intelligent' purposes.[190] The technology is certainly approaching this capacity from other directions given the announcement by IBM, in December 1989, that it had produced an experimental magnetic disk capable of storing 1Gbyte per square inch of disk surface. This may be achieved with D-RAMs too, within a few years, if the Director of the semiconductor design and development centre at Hitachi Corporation is correct. Dr Tsugio Makimoto believes that memory chips will reach this level early in the next century.

Research with micro-processor technology is also very promising. IBM, for example, claims to have a prototype transistor capable of 75 billion cycles per second made from a silicon alloy to which a small quantity of germanium is added.[191] (The ultimate possibility so far as semi-conductor technology is concerned is to reduce component size to atomic proportions so that single electrons could carry the data.) Alternatives to binary logic as a means of exploiting such increased chip densities is also being examined.[192] Meanwhile AT&T's Bell Laboratories is looking at glass lenses, mirrors and 'photonic' devices as a replacement for silicon chips. The objective is to produce a digital optical processor in which computational calculations are performed using laser beams and lenses, compared with the slower speeds of electrical signals and electronic chips. Theoretically, scientists believe that it may be possible to create an optical supercomputer that could be 1000–10,000 times as powerful as existing state-of-the-art electronic computers.[193]

To concentrate discussion upon increased computational speed and capacity is of course an artificial measure of the degree to which information technology has come on during the past 40 years. This capacity to process instructions at very high speed must be harnessed to produce an output before any true assessment of the extent of its influence can be measured. Software must be developed that can exploit the power that the hardware can deliver. The following chapter begins to consider this question, looking at the growth of further areas of the computer industry and the reliance of the world economy on the products and services that the digital revolution has produced.

NOTES

1. For an illustrated history of the chain of discovery leading up to the invention of computers, see Stan Augarten, *Bit by Bit – An Illustrated History of Computers*, (1984, George Allen and Unwin).
2. Bronowski, op. cit., pp. 184–5 and 222–3. Leibniz, (1646–1716) studied law at Leipzig (1661–66). He soon became interested in mathematics and metaphysics and as such must be one of the very first lawyers ever to engage in the analysis of 'information theory' and its application in 'computer science'.
3. Ibid., p. 223.
4. *Encyclopaedia Britannica*, 15th Edition, (1979) p. 64.
5. Williams, *The History of Technology – The Twentieth Century c.1900–c.1950*, Part II, p. 1192.
6. George, *Machine Takeover* (1977) p. 8. George comments that 'adding is a surprisingly general operation, since virtually all mathematics can be reduced to the operation of addition. Subtraction involves the addition of negative numbers, while multiplication is repeated addition and division is the inverse of multiplication. Other more complicated mathematics can similarly be reduced to the operation of addition. So we see that an "adding machine" has surprising generality. This is where counting – which is where arithmetic started – takes on enormous significance'.

7. *Encyclopaedia Britannica* – Ready Reference and Index, Vol. II, 15th Edition, (1979) p. 156. Boole was born in 1815 and died in 1864. His other work of note was 'Mathematical Analysis of Logic' published in 1847.

8. For further description see 11 Encyclopaedia Britannica op. cit., p. 67.

9. George, *Machine Takeover* (1976) p. 5.

10. See discussion in Bronowski, op. cit., pp. 432–6.

11. Encyclopaedia Britannica, op. cit., p. 1046.

12. It consists of rows of wires through which are threaded beads representing, on one side of a bar perpendicular to the wires or rods, units and, on the other, fives or tens.

13. For example, the logarithm of 100 to the base 10 is 2, written as log 100 = 2.

14. See Williams, *A History of Technology*, op. cit., pp. 1151–2.

15. Ibid., p. 1159.

16. Ibid., pp. 1162–4.

17. Augarten, op. cit., p. 42, does suggest, however, that designs of a calculator had been invented in Germany around 1786 by a captain of engineers in the Hessian army. The sum of money needed to build the machine was never raised. The invention was described in a book published in 1786 written by E. Klipstein, entitled *Description of a Newly Invented Calculating Machine*.

18. John North, ed., *Mid-Nineteenth Century Scientists*, (1969) p. 5.

19. North, op. cit., pp. 5–10.

20. Ibid., p. 21.

21. Williams, op. cit., p. 1176.

22. Known as 'number cards' and 'directive cards'. See 4 Encyclopaedia Britannica op. cit., pp. 1046–47.

23. An actual model of the mill of Babbage's analytical engine was built by his son H.P. Babbage in 1910. See Fig. 48.12 in Williams, op. cit., p. 1177.

24. See further, Williams, *A Short History of Twentieth Century Technology*, pp. 348–9.

25. Goldstine, *The Computer from Pascal to Von Neumann* (1972) p. 86.

26. Ibid., p. 138.

27. Slater, *Portraits in Silicon* (1987), p. 34.

28. Encyclopaedia Britannica, p. 1048. Household thermostats are analogue devices that measure temperature and convert these measurements into electric currents that vary in strength according to the rise and fall of the temperature. A speedometer in a car is an analogue device in which speed is measured by the strength of the voltage output of the generator connected to the drive shaft. Analogue machines operate similarly solving problems by measurement of continuous variables. This contrast with digital computers which count rather than measure the presence or absence of discrete signals. The digital computer has become the dominant machine by comparison.

29. Wilkes, *Memoirs of a Computer Pioneer* (1985) p. 124.

30. Hodges, *Alan Turing – The Enigma of Intelligence* (1983) p. 155.

31. Quoted in Slater, op. cit., p. 35.

32. Ibid., p. 15.

33. Hodges, op. cit., pp. 91, 93.

34. Ibid., p. 93.
35. Fifty years earlier a mathematician named Cantor had shown how attempts to list numbers within a table would always produce numbers that, although capable of being defined and written down, could never be predicted in advance and included in the list. There was always the possibility of unlisted numbers existing. Only trial and error could deduce this. Readers wanting to investigate this in more detail should read Hodges, op. cit., pp. 96–110.
36. Hodges, op. cit., p. 109.
37. Metropolis, Howlett and Rota, eds, (1980) pp. 95–6.
38. Goldstine, op. cit., p. 182.
39. J. von Neumann, 'First Draft of a Report on the EDVAC' (Philadelphia, 1945). In Wilkes, op. cit., (1985) p. 108.
40. *Honeywell Inc. v. Sperry Rand Corp. and Illinois Scientific Developments Inc.* (1973) 180 USPQ (BNA) 673 (US DC DM 4th Cir.). *Iowa State University Research Foundation Inc. v. Sperry Rand Corporation and Control Data Corporation* (1971) 444 F.2d. 406 (US CA 4th Cir.).
41. Quoted in Slater, op. cit., p. 28.
42. Goldstine, op. cit., pp. 191–8.
43. *Applied Mechanics.* Bronowski op. cit., p. 433, described von Neumann as 'the cleverest man I ever knew'.
44. Moreau, *The Computer Comes of Age* (1986) p. 26.
45. For a detailed account of the rise of IBM, see Augarten, op. cit., Ch. 6.
46. Moreau, op. cit., pp. 26–7.
47. See Metropolis, Howlett and Rota, eds, op. cit., pp. 52–64.
48. Slater, op. cit., pp. 41–50.
49. Moreau, op. cit., p. 31.
50. Ibid., pp. 1184–7. Aiken subsequently built Mark II, III and IV versions and contributed to such new fields as mathematical linguistics, automatic translation of languages, switching theory and the use of magnetic drums and cores as components.
51. Slater, op. cit., p. 87.
52. Augarten, op. cit., p. 122.
53. There were also 70,000 resistors, 10,000 capacitors and 6000 manual switches necessary for the logical, arithmetical and transfer circuits of the computer.
54. Slater, op. cit., p. 56.
55. Moreau, op. cit., pp. 34–5.
56. This is no doubt fanciful since the energy, 174 kilowatts, is no more than that produced by a 174 horsepower motor (the average four cylinder engine was 75hp.) Quoted by Augarten, op. cit., p. 125.
57. Slater, op. cit., p. 74.
58. Reported by Augarten, op. cit., p. 128.
59. Moreau, op. cit., p. 34.
60. Augarten, op. cit., p. 128.
61. Slater, op. cit., p. 28.
62. *Sperry Rand Corporation v. Bell Telephone Laboratories Inc.* (CA 2nd Cir.) (1959) 272 F.2nd 29 and (1963) 317 F.2d. 491. See also *Sperry Rand*

Corporation v. Bell Telephone Laboratories Inc. (DC SD NY) (1959) 171 F. Supp. 343; 173 F. Supp. 714; (1962) 208 F. Supp. 598.

63. The action was between Honeywell Inc. and Sperry Rand Corporation.
64. Slater, op. cit., pp. 56–57.
65. A capacitor is an electric circuit element used to store a charge temporarily, consisting typically of two metallic plates separated by a non-conducting element. In Atanasoff's time the term used was 'condenser'. Universal Dictionary op. cit., p. 243.
66. Quoted in Slater, op. cit., p. 61. The lawyer's name was A.J. Etienne.
67. J. Mauchly, 'The Eniac'. In Metropolis, Howlett and Rota, eds, op. cit., p. 549.
68. Metropolis, Howlett and Rota, eds, op. cit., pp. 47–93. See also Stevens, *Understanding Computers – A User Friendly Guide* (1986) pp. 29–30.
69. Quoted in Slater, op. cit., p. 57.
70. Goldstine, op. cit., p. 321 mentions various countries in Europe as well as Israel and Japan.
71. Wilkes, op. cit., p. 120.
72. Moreau, op. cit., p. 51.
73. Ibid., pp. 51–5. BINAC was built for the Northrop Aircraft Company. Whirlwind was originally built for the control of flight simulators but subsequently developed as a general purpose machine. UNIVAC was launched in 1951 as the world's first business machine. Manchester University in collaboration with Ferranti had produced the very first commercial machine in the Ferranti MARK I, but it was more limited than UNIVAC. Altogether 45 UNIVAC machines were sold to industry.
74. Augarten, op. cit., p. 164 reports that the UNIVAC awarded 43 States and 438 electoral votes to Eisenhower and 5 States and 93 electoral votes to Stevenson. In the final tally the result was 442 against 89 in favour of Eisenhower.
75. S.H. Lavington, 'Computer Development at Manchester University'. In Metropolis, Howlett and Rota, eds, op. cit., pp. 433–43.
76. Moreau, op. cit., p. 58. Its main memory on Williams tubes consisted of 2048 words of 36 bits each.
77. Augarten, op. cit., p. 192.
78. Moreau, op. cit., p. 62.
79. Statistics in Augarten, op. cit., p. 202.
80. Moreau, op. cit., p. 65.
81. Moreau, op. cit., p. 75.
82. Ibid., p. 76.
83. See Stevens, op. cit., pp. 116–9.
84. Moreau, op. cit., p. 81.
85. Goldstine, op. cit., p. 310.
86. Moreau, op. cit., p. 35.
87. Wilkes, op. cit., pp. 142–3.
88. Augarten, op. cit., p. 148, reports the eye witness reaction thus: 'When [the machine was] first built, a program was laboriously inserted and the start

switch pressed. Immediately the spots on the display tube entered a mad dance. In early trials it was a dance of death leading to no useful result, and what was even worse, without yielding any clue as to what was wrong. But one day it stopped and there, shining brightly in the expected place, was the expected answer'.

89. Slater, op. cit., p. 225. Known as 'Flow-matic' it was later incorporated into COBOL – one of the first higher level languages.
90. Ibid., pp. 223, 234.
91. Ibid., p. 233.
92. Augarten, op. cit., p. 216.
93. The full story is told in Slater, op. cit., pp. 241–9.
94. Steve Roche, 'Moving closer to the Fifth Generation', *Computing*, 8 February 1990. Roche states that one book published in 1969 identified 120 3GLs, but few survived very long commercially.
95. Figures quoted by Augarten, op. cit., pp. 217–20.
96. Nicholas Enticknap, 'Tales of Future Past', *Computer Weekly* 22 March 1990 – a review of Martin Campbell Kelly, *ICL: A Business and Technical History* (1990, Clarendon Press, Oxford).
97. Moreau, op. cit., p. 92. The first such machines were General Electric's GE 210, International Business Machine's IBM 7090, IBM 1401, and IBM 1620 models, National Cash Register's NCR 304, and Radio Corporation of America's RCA 501.
98. Stevens, op. cit., pp. 83–6.
99. The background to the invention of the transistor is described in: 'Nostalgic Thoughts on the Heart of the Matter', *Computing*, 15 February 1990, pp. 16–17.
100. Slater, op. cit., p. 143–6.
101. Ibid., p. 146.
102. Reported in: British Telecom, *The Microchip Revolution* (1985) p. 4.
103. *Equinox*, Channel 4 TV, 'The History of the Computer', 3 November 1986.
104. Mackintosh, *Sunrise Europe* (1986) p. 12.
105. Augarten, op. cit., p. 230 states that the first transistorised computer to appear was introduced by UNIVAC in 1957, a second following from Philco Corporation in 1958.
106. Moreau, op. cit., pp. 91–2.
107. Chris Robbins, 'Keeping track of all the Transistor Technology', *Computing* 22 February 1990, p. 18. In 1962 a computer used by the US Army contained 10,000 of these modules reducing the weight of the hardware to 90lbs, compared with the half a ton that is equivalent would have weighted using miniature valves.
108. First generation hardware operated with vacuum tubes; second generation with transistors; third generation incorporated thousands of transistors on a single chip; fourth generation involved very large scale integration (VLSI) of transistors on miniaturised wafers of silicon.
109. Phosphorus, for example produced a negative charge whereas boron promoted a positive one. Since unlike charges attract each other, this controlled

the movement of electrons through the silicon. As little as 10 parts per million of a dopant substance was sufficient to produce the intended result. See British Telecom, *The Microchip Revolution* (1985) pp. 6–7.

110. Stevens, op. cit., p. 86.
111. Transistors amplify the signals within the circuit; resistors regulate the flow of signal energy; capacitors store it and diodes provide the path in a single direction for the electric current to pass, thereby detecting the presence or absence of a binary digit, in 'The Microchip Revolution', op cit., p. 11.
112. Slater, op. cit., p. 170.
113. *Noyce v. Kilby* 416 F.2d 1391 (1969) CCPA at p. 1394.
114. Ibid., at pp. 1391–92.
115. W.H. Mayall, *The Challenge of the Chip* (1980) p. 5. See also: Jack Schofield, 'On the Ninth Day: The Chip', The *Guardian*, 6 June 1990.
116. Larsen and Rogers, *Silicon Valley Fever* (1984) p. 101.
117. For details of how the process works, see 'The Microchip Revolution' op. cit., pp. 8–9.
118. A photograph of the first integrated circuit can be found in Stevens, op. cit., p. 87.
119. Integrated circuit chips were first used in the Minuteman Intercontinental Ballistic Missile which needed 2500 circuits for its guidance system, and in the Apollo Space Program. Nearly all the chips produced went on these two projects at that time. See Slater, op. cit., p. 171.
120. Ibid., p. 159.
121. For example the ICT 1900 series computer built in the mid-1960s used integrated circuits, op. cit., p. 5.
122. Augarten, op. cit., p. 241.
123. Larsen and Rogers, op. cit., pp. 43–4.
124. Augarten, op. cit., p. 245.
125. Chris Robbins, op. cit. World consumption of integrated circuits reached $3.5 billion by 1976.
126. Interview with Terry Dodsworth, *Financial Times*, 8 November 1989.
127. It was called the 4004 since the 4000 meant that it was a custom built chip for a particular client and the 4 signified the fact that it was the fourth custom chip to be designed by Intel. In Larsen and Rogers, op. cit., p. 106.
128. For example the Texas Instrument 7400 range of chips could perform these functions. Larger operations could be performed by linking logic chips together. In Stevens, op. cit., p. 86.
129. Augarten, op. cit., p. 264.
130. Larsen and Rogers, op. cit., p. 106.
131. The unit of frequency is called a Hertz.
132. The original advertisement of the 4004 described the computer on a chip as a family of four: 'Using no circuitry other than ICs [integrated circuits] from this family of four you can create a system with 4096 8-bit bytes of ROM storage and 5120 bits of RAM storage . . . The heart of the system is a Type 4004 CPU which includes a powerful set of 45 instructions . . . The system interfaces easily with switches, keyboards, displays, teletypewriters, printers

. . . and other popular peripherals.'

133. *Equinox*, Channel 4 TV, op. cit.
134. Hoff was assisted by two other former Fairchild employees – Stan Mazor and Frederico Faggin. See Larsen and Rogers, op. cit., pp. 105–6.
135. Stevens, op. cit., p. 70. A photograph of the 4004 micro-processor can be seen on this page.
136. Augarten, op. cit., p. 265.
137. Chris Robbins, op. cit., p. 19.
138. Augarten, op. cit., p. 269. The inventor was Jonathan Titus and the article announcing the product appeared in the July 1974 issue of *Radio Electronics*.
139. Another way of putting it would be to say that it could read one 8-bit instruction in 1 MHz. Since its clock speed was 10 times quicker than the 4004 micro-processor and it read 8 instead of 4 bits at a time, it could be said to be 20 times faster than the 4004. It was capable of 290,000 operations per second, bearing in mind that more than one instruction would be involved such as 'add two 8-bit numbers together.
140. Larsen and Rogers, op. cit., pp. 108–9.
141. Terry Dodsworth, op. cit.
142. Stevens, op. cit., pp. 71–6.
143. Michael Slater, 'Micro View – The View from 10,000 Feet', *IEEE Micro*, February 1990, p. 96.
144. Martin Banks, op. cit., p. 8.
145. Within Europe, Philips and Seimens and a three-firm partnership calling itself Silicon Structures have co-operated in the production of ASIC chips. See Morgan and Sayer, *Microcircuits of Capital* (1988) p. 65.
146. William P. Birmingham et al., 'The Micon System for Computer Design, *IEEE Micro* October 1989.
147. Terry Dodsworth, op. cit. The adoption by IBM of the Intel micro-processor for the IBM PC back in 1981 all began following a routine salesman's call to IBM's development team in Florida. At the time Intel had no appreciation of the opportunities about to open in personal computers.
148. Stevens, op. cit., pp. 77–9.
149. The second source makers of the Intel 8088 chip were NEC (1980), AMD (1982), Fujitsu (1981), Siemens (1982), Matra (1982), Mitsubishi Electric Corp., (1983), etc.
150. Morgan and Sayer, *Microcircuits of Capital* (1988) p. 64.
151. Robin W. Edinfield et al., 'The 68040 Processor – Part 1. Design and Implementation', *IEEE Micro*, February 1990, p. 66–78 at p. 66.
152. 'Motorola ships new 20 mip 68040 cpu', *Computing*, 1 February 1990.
153. Darrell Ince, 'Millions of Mistakes to Make', The *Independent* 23 April 1990, p. 16.
154. 'Intel to make Chips in Dublin', *Computing* 14 June 1990. The plant is to cost $187 million and will ultimately employ 2600 people.
155. Longley and Shain, *Macmillan Dictionary of Information Technology*, Third Edition (1989, Macmillan).
156. Stephen C. Johnson, 'Hot Chips and Soggy Software', *IEEE Micro* February

1990, pp. 23–6 at p. 23.

157. Michael Slater, op. cit., at p. 95.
158. Longley and Shain, op. cit., p. 430, defines 'register' as: 'a memory device, usually high speed, and of limited specified length (eg. one byte, one word); used for special purposes (eg. arithmetic operations)'.
159. John L. Rynearson, 'Risc Versus CISC', *Computer Systems Europe*, April 1990, pp. 16–17.
160. Beatrice Lazzerini, 'Effective VLSI Processor Architectures for HLL Computers: The RISC Approach', *IEEE Micro* February 1989, pp. 57–65 at p. 57.
161. Executive 'workstations' are personal computers providing a range of desk-top business applications, including word-processing, spreadsheets, graphics and database facilities togehter with communications.
162. Lazzerini, op. cit.
163. Michael Slater, op. cit., p. 94.
164. 'Intel Superchip', 9 *Computer Systems Europe* No. 4, April 1989, pp. 7–8.
165. Rynearson, op. cit. The chip contains 7 register windows containing 24 32-bit registers in three groups of 8 to perform specific functions.
166. 'RISC Wars: 88000 to hit 1000 Mips', *Computing*, 4 January 1990, p. 2.
167. Glenis Moore, 'Superscalars Clock it up', *Computer Systems Europe*, December 1989, p. 31.
168. Louise Keheo and Alan Friedman, 'Intel Takes on RISCS with the Wizard', *Financial Times*, 1 March 1989, p. 34.
169. Clive Cookson, 'A Fast Expanding Game', *Financial Times*, 8 February 1990, p. 22. Competitors Hitachi, in a joint venture with Texas Instruments, The European Community through the JESSI (Joint European Submicron Silicon Programme) and at least one Korean company are also involved.
170. Clive Cookson, op. cit. Estimate of Dataquest, the international electronics consultancy. The Japanese electrical group Toshiba are investing $553 million on production of the 4Mbit D-RAM. Capacity is expected to reach 3 million per month by April 1991.
171. Ibid.
172. David Manners, 'First Round to Japan in the Chip Wars', *Computer Weekly*, 22 February 1990, p. 30.
173. Charles Seiter, 'Hard Disk Alternatives', *MacWorld*, August 1989, pp. 12–22 at p. 15.
174. Stevens, op. cit., p. 122.
175. 'Front End', *Computer Systems – Europe*, December 1989, p. 5.
176. For example, the Priam Corporation offers a hard disk of up to 337 Mbyte in one unit. See 'Storage – The Story so Far', *Computer Systems – Europe*, October 1988, p. 20.
177. Charles Seiter, op. cit., p. 12.
178. Hard disk drives on PCs usually store between 10 and 100 Mbytes.
179. Charles Seiter, op. cit., p. 21. The drives that write to and read the cartridge are manufactured by Sony, Ricoh and Maxtor. Magstore sell the product as the Cosmos 600 at £3950. This includes a 568Mbyte EO which has reduced

disk space, compared to the 650Mbyte potential of the cartridge, because of the software format deployed.

180. George Stokes, Megabytes on the Cheap', *Computer Systems – Europe*, March 1989, p. 25.

181. Clive Cookson, 'Moying to the Beat of a Different Mix', *Financial Times*, 29 November 1989, p. 20.

182. Dennis Moralee, 'Image of Document', *Computer Systems – Europe*, March 1989, p. 11.

183. Ibid., p. 11.

184. Ibid., p. 13.

185. Commercial scanners operate at 150 dot/in., requiring 0.25 megabyte per page; 300 dot/in., at 1 megabyte per page; and 600 dot/in., at 4 megabytes per page.

186. Peter Knight, 'Fast Route to Efficient Filing', *Financial Times* Survey: 'Using Computers in Business and Industry', 24 November 1989.

187. Dr Edwin Galea, 'The Speed Kings jostle for a place in the Fast Lane', *Computing* 16, February 1989, pp. 30–3.

188. Stevens, op. cit., p. 6.

189. Clive Cookson, op. cit.

190. Cookson, op. cit.

191. Known as the Heterojunction Bipolar Transistor (HBT). *Computer Systems – Europe*, April 1990, p. 8.

192. Chris Partridge, 'On a New Wavelength', *Computing*, 28 June 1990, pp. 18–19.

193. Louise Keheo, 'Through the Looking Glass to Silica Valley', *Financial Times*, 1 February 1990, p. 22. See also John Kaye, 'Light Years from Today', *Computer Weekly*, 8 February 1990, pp. 23–3.

CHAPTER 4

The information technology industry and its significance today

DEFINITION AND ORGANISATION OF THE INDUSTRY

Today the major economies of the world are heavily dependent upon the success of their IT industries. Some nations are pouring huge resources into further research and development, and into collaborative projects on a transnational basis. Meanwhile, multi-nationals like IBM have developed into substantial economic forces in their own right. IBM, for example, has a turnover in excess of the national incomes of many countries, and profits, running until recently at the rate of £100 million per week worldwide. This chapter asks how the IT industry is defined and organised today and what are the influences that have shaped its structure. Where is research and development heading and what movements are there towards convergence and standardisation of industries, products and protocols? How is all this translated into the tangible products and services that, together, have generated the 'Information Society'? And finally, what does the future hold?

THE GROWTH OF THE MODERN COMPUTER INDUSTRY

Mainframes People's perception of the computer has changed remarkably over time. In the early days few individuals, outside those directly involved, knew what computers were. In November 1958 the *Harvard Law Review* published the first article ever to refer to 'information technology'. One aspect of the concept was epitomised by the

147

'high speed' computer which the authors considered would lead to a 'recentralisation' of management within the large organisation:

> By permitting more information to be organised more simply and processed more rapidly it will, in effect, extend the thinking range of individuals. It will allow the top level of management intelligently to categorize, digest, and act on a wider range of problems. Moreover, by quantifying more information it will extend top management's control over the decision processes of subordinates. If centralisation becomes easier to implement, managers will probably revert to it. Decentralisation has, after all, been largely negatively motivated. Top managers have backed into it because they have been unable to keep up with size and technology. They could not design and maintain the huge and complex communication systems that their large, centralised organisations needed. Information technology should make recentralisation possible. It may also obviate other major reasons for decentralisation. For example, speed and flexibility will be possible despite large size, and top executives will be less dependent on subordinates because there will be fewer 'experience' and 'judgment' areas in which the junior men have more working knowledge'.[1]

All machines in existence in the immediate postwar years were, by definition, large pieces of equipment, given the thermionic valve technology of the day. The word 'mainframe' was coined for large configurations supporting the major user, and this took on the character of a distinctive market sector as size reduced and processing power increased with the advent of the semi-conductor and micro-electronics breakthroughs of the 1960s and 70s. IBM has from its earliest machines dominated the world mainframe market. In the 1960s mainframes offered the customer on-line facilities, replacing gradually the system whereby the user handed his program to computer operators written out on punched cards to be processed and the results collected some time later as computer printout.[2] By 1985 mainframes supported on average up to 120 users at one time, accessing the computer on terminals linked to it. The average value of such machines was $1 million, although much more expensive configurations could be obtained depending upon what was provided by way of storage, processing capacity, software and speed.

The roots of IBM's success can be found in a very important decision taken by the company in the 1960s to develop computers that would be compatible with one another. Compatibility had to be achieved between different-sized machines within the same family and between the old and the new generation of machines. The policy began with the 360 series and has been described as 'an enormous gamble' on the part of the company, but one which clearly paid off. Before IBM's decision mainframe producers manufactured computers that were incompatible with previous models, and IBM was no different. However, the customer was put to enormous inconvenience since his software and data would have to be converted for use on the new machine.

The new policy was therefore popular, particularly with the smaller user, who could add processing capacity to his original equipment base as his computing needs grew. If the latest machine had a similar architecture to its predecessors then the user would have little difficulty in transferring his operation to the new machine, or in upgrading accordingly.[3] That policy, to an extent, continues to the present day, despite the problems of having to live with the difficulty of upgrading what is likely to become an old and out of date design. IBM has built the company around this approach since the policy encourages customers to 'lock in' to IBM machines. If a user wished to change to something new he would be faced with the expense of a redesign of his system and possibly of his data files and software too.[4]

A mark of IBM's dominance and evidence of its rapid growth can also be seen from its contribution of more than 600 products in the first 20 years of the electronic data processing industry and more than 10,000 patents up to 1973 alone.[5] This level of performance quickly set the company apart from its competitors who became known as 'The BUNCH'. These were Burroughs, Univac, NCR, Control Data Corporation and Honeywell. Subsequently, as a result of takeovers and mergers, the BUNCH changed, although the number of manufacturers in the mainframe market remained small. Later on these companies were to spawn others just as had occurred in the semi-conductor industry. For example, Gene Amdahl, who designed the system 360 series for IBM in the early 1960s left to form Amdahl Corporation in October 1970, competing in the marketplace for powerful mainframe computers. In 1981, having left Amdahl he formed a new company ACSYS which became linked to CII Honeywell Bull, recently re-named 'Bull'. Another illustration is Seymour Cray who left Control Data Corporation in 1972 to found Cray Research, concentrating on high speed supercomputers for the scientific community. Currently companies competing in the mainframe marketplace include: Amdahl, Bull, Control Data, DEC, IBM, ICL, NCR, National Advanced Systems,

Prime Computer, Tandem and Unisys (formerly Burroughs and Sperry Rand who merged in mid-1986).[6] Hitachi Data Systems has also entered the mainframe sector with a mid-range machine designed to compete with IBM's 4391 model.[7]

Whereas in 1975 IBM controlled 75% of the mainframe marketplace, it still controlled 62% in 1985.[8] The company was successfully able to retain its dominance of the market with its 370 architecture which became an industry standard in the 1980s and this has been followed by the 3090 range.[9] However, during that period the proportion of the market as a whole devoted to mainframes reduced from 83% to 36%, although its value has increased. In the United States, IBM's share of the large commercial systems market was 72.8% in June 1989 (57% in Western Europe[10]) accounting for 38% of the company's sales and up to half its net profits, according to estimates.[11] The relative decline of the mainframe sector by comparison with the rest of the market for computers is accounted for by the rise of other types of computer, particularly the personal computer and workstation sector, which have grown by 74% and 1100% respectively in the period from 1985 to 1990.[12] The increase in micro-processor capacity has also blurred the distinctions between sectors, as well as inviting new configurations involving distributed processing and networks. The widespread assumption, though, that mainframes would give way substantially to distributed systems, such as workstations connected to a network or a series of mid-range machines servicing particular specialist applications, has not materialised. In fact a sluggish growth rate of only 3.7% in 1985 has increased to 6.9% in 1989 with predictions of over 8% by 1993.[13] The expected future upturn in the market is supported by the figures for western Europe which point to a reversal of the decline in the installed base of mainframes from 8018 in 1988 to 7885 in 1990 rising to 8550 by 1994.[14]

Gene Amdahl believes that mainframes will continue to offer advantages over other arrangements with high storage capacity, as well as the potential for increased performance and flexibility. As organisations begin to integrate computer use and exploit what the technology has to offer, there will be a demand for a high level of data storage and processing capacity which the mainframe may be able to meet in competition with the alternatives.[15] The demand for central processing power may increase if the new concept of 'client-server computing' takes off. This involves the provision of local processing needs by small front-end machines linked by a user interface to larger back-end machines with more powerful processor and memory capacity. No hierachical relationship is involved though, with the front and back-end processors operating within the network as equals. The server processor is likely to develop into a specialist machine offering large database, transaction processing or graphics modelling capability.[16]

What happens in this portion of the market is extremely important for IBM as it is in the mainframe sector where the company made its name. In the 1980s analysts suggested that IBM might become a $100 billion organisation by 1990. The high-water mark in expectation was in the first quarter of 1988 when the company turned in profits up 10.4% above the comparable 1987 figure. Since then turnover growth has been declining with figures of 4.3% and 2.3% respectively for the last two quarters of 1989. The company maintains above 50% of its assets in the US and conducts 40% of its business there. Its poor 1.6% improvement in turnover in the US sector was therefore significant for the final results. Increased competition, consolidations and restructuring within the company and increased competition, particularly in the personal computer sector, forced IBM (nicknamed 'Big Blue') to write off a staggering $2.42 billion of the profits from the last quarter of 1989. Although this meant a reported loss of $0.3 billion on the year from US operations, the company was still able to record a profit on the quarter of $529 million and a total profit for 1989 of $3.75 billion compared with nearly $5.5 billion in 1988. The company reported a turnover of $62.7 billion for 1989 which, although a long way short of predictions, still leaves the company earning more than its next 10 US rivals put together and four times that of its major competitor Digital Equipment Corporation. Its workforce is estimated to be in the region of 400,000 people.[17]

Mini-computers Another product of the increased performance of micro-processors is the mid-range market. It was inevitable that the industry would try to develop new products as the technology created a wider range of choices. The mini-computer was first launched commercially in 1963 when Digital Equipment Corporation came out with the PDP-8 computer. It was built out of the aging hardware of transistors and magnetic cores, could run only one program at a time and possessed only 4k words of memory.[18] The machine which measured about the size of a refrigerator was used to control chemical flows in refineries, machine tools in factories, inventories in warehouses, and other operations not requiring the full power of the mainframe as it was in the mid-sixties.[19] The machine sold for $18,000 and helped DEC to develop into a company worth more than $225 million by the time it became a public corporation in 1966. By 1975 DEC sales reached $1 billion. Gradually the software packages written for the mainframe market were modified for the mini range and new operating system software enabled minis to become multi-user machines. 75 companies existed in 1971 competing for a share of the mini-computer marketplace, but not all succeeded.

As the micro-computer made its debut, a new range of 'super-minis' was introduced at 32-bit standard.[20] In 1978, DEC launched its highly successful VAX architecture – a 32-bit computer. This was a 'virtual' machine (standing for 'Virtual address extension') designed to allow larger programs to be run than the semi-conductor memory could otherwise handle. Within a short time DEC had 40% of the market with VAX becoming an industry standard, particularly so in science and engineering.[21] IBM competed in the 1980s with a number of products including the series 1; the 4300 and 8100; systems 34, 36 and 38 (the 'System 3X' range); 6150 and 9370. Different operating systems were developed for these machines which contributed to the success of the DEC strategy to market a unified range of machines supported by a single operating system known as 'VMS'. IBM replied with the AS400 in June 1988, aimed at small- and medium-sized business. At the outset the AS/400 family comprised six members, from B10 to B60 machines. The B30/40 models upgraded to B/35/45 in 1989 and a top end B70 was added too.[22] The new family is an evolution of the System 38 which had sold 30,000 machines worldwide. It was significant as it provided increased power for System 38 users and a new route for 370 mainframe users to migrate to. The System 3X market was a major revenue earner for IBM generating an estimated $75 billion in sales. The arrival of the AS400 increased the user base of System 3X and the AS/400 combined from 285,000 to 410,000 by the end of the 1980s.[23] While it remains incompatible with the current 3090 mainframe, the forthcoming 'Summit' replacement to the 3090 range may be able to run AS400 programs in 'emulation' mode.[24] ('Emulation' takes place where one system is able to act as if it were another, and minimises the disruption otherwise involved when a new system replaces an old one.)

The market for computers has changed considerably in the past 10 years as more powerful machines have been developed, supported by a wide range of applications software. The old distinction between mainframes, minis and micros is no longer valid. Desk-top machines as powerful as mainframes were in the 1970s are on the way.[25] It is now a matter for every user to build his system according to the configuration most likely to meet his requirements. The increase in the power of the personal computer chip, such as Intel's i486 32-bit micro-processor, brings mini/mainframe performance to the desk top with machines that can provide shared computer resources within a local area network.[26]

The centre of the competitive battle for mid-range processors has traditionally joined IBM and DEC. Hardware technology improvements have enabled both companies to provide powerful mid-range systems supporting up to 800 users. DEC has concentrated upon developing a single architecture based upon the VAX range of computers and the VMS operating system, which is compatible – from the powerful workstation at the bottom of the range to clusters of VAXs in the 'supercomputer' class, capable of supporting thousands of users.[27] This reduces conversion costs if customers want to re-organise their computer use, and encourages software development which has a stable and firm base upon which to evolve. IBM has settled on four main hardware standards across the entire range of its products, with the 370 mainframe (and 'departmental' 9370 computers); AS/400 minis (System 3X replacement); RS 6000 workstations and PS/2 personal computers. This effort to standardise design by IBM follows criticism from its customers who called for a unified vertical structure, not simply one that supported migration between mainframes upon which IBM's initial strategy was based. To meet that criticism IBM is developing unified standards for programming and user interfaces which it calls Systems Application Architecture (SAA) announced by the company in September 1987. This set of rules and protocols which will gradually evolve is intended to give all IBM systems and programs running on them a similar 'look and feel.'[28]

IBM suggests that by 1994 multiple AS/400s could support between 2000–3000 users and will be well placed to compete with more than 5000 software applications available through the AS/400s OS/400 operating system. However, more companies are now in the mid-range sector which is in a volatile state. After cutbacks and product redefinition, competition is intensifying from the established mini-computer manufacturers as well as from the powerful workstation producers with mid-range 'network-server' ambitions. There is also the underlying pressure away from proprietary hardware and software to UNIX-based 'open systems' using standard micro-processors, memory chips and software.[29]

153

IBM recognised this after several key competitors expanded into UNIX in the mid-range sector. The company's research indicated that the UNIX grip on the operating system market would increase from 6% in 1988 to 22% by 1991.[30] Accordingly IBM is now developing new UNIX-compatible machines with RISC technology for the mid-range sector using AT&T's AIX UNIX-compatible operating system under licence. The company launched its initial attack on the UNIX market in 1987 with an interim model – the AIX 6150 RT multi-user machine which it upgraded from the PC RT. New machines will be launched in due course but it is not clear whether they will allow cross-over from the AS/400. If IBM do not provide one, others will.

Industry analysts believe that the mid-range sector will grow more slowly than any other, including mainframes, at 7.5% per annum, as users re-think their strategy in this sector. Some specialisation is expected with companies targeting their products for particular applications. IBM for example, has promoted the AS/400 range on the computer-aided design market whereas Wang has gone for image processing. Other companies have gone for increased processing power offering a mainframe challenge to IBM. DEC have done this with the VAX 9000 which will compete with the IBM's 3090. Hewlett Packard, the number three in this sector, have rebuilt their product line incorporating RISC chip technology for increased speed. Compaq have gone for competitive products at economy prices claiming that their Compaq Systempro outpaces DEC's VAX 6300 by a factor of six, Hewlett Packard's HP9300 by three and IBM's AS/400 by nine. The benchmark in this comparison was the performance of a typical file operation within a network server domain.[31] Some companies have reported losses to which this sector contributed. These include Data General, Wang and Prime. Others claiming a share of the market are Unisys, Olivetti, NCR, and the major Japanese computer corporations. In 1987 IBM had revenues totalling $18.3 billion for mid-range machines followed by DEC at $3.6 billion.

Super-computers From the early 1970s when Seymour Cray founded Cray Research, designers have attempted to build fast processors for a specialist market. The demand for very fast machines has never diminished given the enormous computing requirements of, for example, the military and scientific sectors. The accolade 'supercomputer' is awarded to machines that possess a very substantial primary memory, large bit-word size for addressing memory and very fast processors. The yardstick against which to measure performance in this range is the Cray-1 machine launched in 1976. This operated at a clock cycle of 12.5 nanoseconds (thousand millionths of a second) and contained 200,000 semi-conductor chips, 3400 integrated circuit boards and 60 miles of wiring in a box only six feet high and eight feet across.[32] It retailed at $8.8 million. 13 were sold in 1981, 15 in 1982, a similar number in 1983 and 23 in 1984. The total number of supercomputer installations world-wide on 1 January 1989 were Cray Research (220); Fujitsu (83); Control Data (57 – including 34 ETA machines); Hitachi (26); and NEC (23).[33] In April 1989, Control Data dropped out of the sector being unable to support the high level of research and development necessary to stay in the race. The company linked up with Cray giving its customers access to Cray supercomputers and Cray reciprocal access to Control Data's mainframes and workstations.[34] A total of 3100 employees lost their jobs representing 10% of the company's entire workforce. Included were 800 employees of the ETA Systems division of the company.[35] The company had earlier suffered spectacular losses of $567.5 million in 1984 on revenues of $3.68 billion reducing its assets from $7 billion to under $1 billion. Such losses demonstrate the volatility of the industry which can make a company as fast as the market can break it.

Currently, the biggest users of large systems are research institutions with 24% of the installed base of just over 400. This is followed by the Universities – 18%; Defence – 16%; Aerospace – 12%; Petroleum – 10%; Environment and Nuclear Energy with 7% each and service bureaus with 3%.[36] Since the first generation of Cray machines perform-ance has increased regularly and this is likely to continue as multiple processors are harnessed to work together in parallel. Cray-II contain-ing two billion bytes of internal memory was 6–12 times faster than Cray-I, according to the model in question, and the later Cray-II version 5–10 times faster than its predecessor with 8 billion bytes of memory. In terms of arithmetic operations per second (as opposed to instructions per second) Cray-1 operated at 190 megaflops (190 million floating point operations per second)[37] whereas the early Cray-2 model reached over 700 Megaflops. The Cray-II of 1985 had a peak performance of 1.7 gigaflops (1700 million) and the 1988 Y-MP version – 3 gigaflops (at a cost of $20–30 million).[38] In late 1989 Cray created a new company – Cray Computer Corporation – under the direction of Seymour Cray himself, to develop a Cray III machine using gallium arsenide as the solid state conductor instead of silicon. The former is several times faster than silicon and more tolerant of changes in temperature.[39]

Today there are projects aiming at achieving the 'Teraflop' – million million operations per second, which would be of interest to the code breakers at GCHQ or the National Security Agency in the USA.[40] Architectural and programming methods are also undergoing change since circuit speeds have reached their limit with conventional technology. Work is now going on to link micro-processors, known as transputers, together in a parallel processing array. Transputer boards when programmed in Occam – the only computer language to date designed for programming parallel algorithms – can achieve very high processing speeds. For example, an experiment in linking transputers at Southampton University in 1989 produced 250 Mips of processing capacity.[41] A single transputer board loaded into an IBM PC can give it the power of a DEC VAX 11/780 mid-range computer. In 1985 a machine that could process in excess of 40 Mips was credited with supercomputer status,[42] whereas mainframes operating at speeds up to 70 Mips are commonplace now.[43]

Given the cost today of these machines at $20–30 million, the market for supercomputers at the top end of the range will remain small at around 1000 in the world in the 1990s.[44] Nevertheless, the market for supercomputers was worth $3.87 billion in 1986 and is expected to reach $11.8 billion by 1991. This contrasts with the mainframe projections which, despite the downturn in overall percentage of the computer market it enjoys, is set to rise from the 1986 figure of $140 billion to $205 billion in 1991.[45] Two new trends, however, are beginning to reshape the supercomputer market in the 1990s. First, the Japanese are now challenging Cray quite strongly for supremacy, with NEC of Japan announcing the SX-3 model at $24.2 million which the company claims will run at 22 Gigaflops per second, five times quicker than the fastest Cray in commercial production – the YMP-8. Cray's response is a successor to the YMP-8 planned for 1992 – the C-90, which will have a speed of 16 Gigaflops.[46] Although at present the US still has the predominant market share in supercomputers, analysts believe that Japan will take over by the turn of the century.

The second trend in this sector arises directly from the growth of micro-processor power, particularly Intel's new iPSC/860 chip. This was launched at the 1990 'Supercomputer Europe Show' at Olympia in London, and marked a new phase in chip technology.[47] This will broaden the scope for faster machines providing parallel processing alternatives to the multi-processor approach to supercomputing. Multi-processors link large numbers of powerful processors together to share computational load whereas parallel processing uses a variety of processors for particular tasks so that several functions can be performed simultaneously. A dozen or more companies are currently involved in developing large scale parallel processing capacity for carrying out tasks involving massive computational input such as weather forecasting, 3D simulations, aerodynamics, computer speech and vision, and artificial intelligence.[48]

One of these companies is Intel Corporation's Scientific Computer subsidiary division which is seeking to build what the industry now calls a 'massively parallel computer' with up to 2000 processors each as powerful as the Cray 1. Intel aims to improve performance 100 fold compared with present day technology.[49] The iPSC 860 chip will be used by the machine which is expected to notch up speeds of 7.6 Gigaflops for no more than $3 million. Intel believes that with design development a 150 Gigaflop machine is in reach by 1992.[50] Such machines will be required in the scientific sector particularly climate and environmental modelling of such phenomena as the 'greenhouse effect'.[51] The company already has a stake in the multiple CPU market with over 100 installations based on its 80386 chip, consisting of between 16 and 128 processors. Called the 'Hypercube', this has now been upgraded with the 860 RISC chipset. The machines are used primarily in computational mechanics and simulation.

The latest chip generation has led to new possibilities and a broader market in supercomputing with the high performance 'mini-super-computer' for scientific and commercial use. This can deliver substantial processing power at a much reduced price compared with supercomputer costs.[52] The challenge from companies like Convex in the new 'minisuper' market has prompted Cray research to diversify its product range so as to appeal lower down in the market. The new Cray Y-MP2E offers a one- or two-processor alternative to its eight-processor Y-MP supercomputer, with operational speeds of between 80–100 megaflops. Such machines are for sale much more cheaply, at between $2 and $5 million.[53] This trend to diversify at the top end of the range has been brought about by the ability to pack additional power of considerable magnitude within existing configurations. As a result the industry is beginning to broaden its focus away from exclusive attention on the supercomputer to that of 'superperformance' at all levels of machine performance. The concept has been defined as: 'the highest performance computer system or subsystem available at a given price point'.[54]

Accordingly, 'super-status' can now attach to top range processors represented by Cray and others; augmented mainframes (eg the FPS 5800 connected to a Digital 'host' mainframe); mini-supercomputers (eg. Convex C-210 machines); super-workstations (eg as supplied by Ardent; Stellar, Silicon Graphics and Sun Micro Systems); high performance parallel architecture machines (eg Thinking Machine's NCUBE-2 with the iPSC/860 chip); software based supersystems (eg the Multiflow VLIW architecture) and super PC's (eg as likely to result from collaboration between Intel, AT&T, Olivetti and Prime).[55] This will mean that applications previously only available via top of the range machines will become affordable on less expensive and comparatively smaller computers. The potential applications of these products are illustrated as follows: for example, the UK Royal Armament R&D Establishment operates a Cray X-MP (EA/416) supercomputer for batch-processing of fluid dynamics calculations; British Aerospace has an augmented mainframe for cockpit simulation research; Jaguar Cars is using a mini-supercomputer for software engineering in design; the European Southern Observatory in West Germany has a super-workstation to digitise information obtained from photographs of different areas of the sky; the Edinburgh University Concurrent Supercomputer Project is using Meiko of Bristol's parallel architecture in supplying a national facility; software based systems are locating a market in mechanical and chemical engineering and super PCs are just coming into production. In May 1990 ICL, who were at one time the UK's biggest builder of mainframes, launched a 64Mbyte 'super-micro' using Intel's powerful 486 standard 32-bit micro-processor.[56] The latter will offer much by way of enhanced graphics, office applications and communications.[57]

The Micro-Computer   Once the secrets of solid-state semi-conductors were unlocked to produce a reliable micro-processor chip it was only a matter of time before someone would come up with the idea of a micro 'personal' computer. However, in the late 1960s some lateral thinking was required on the part of those in the industry at that time to conceive of such a machine. It must be remembered of course that at that time all computers were large and expensive. Surprising as it may seem today most members of the public did not really know what computers did other than that large organisations had them and that in some cases they paid their monthly salary cheque into the bank. On top of this no concept of either a market or an application for micro-computers as yet existed. Those that were interested in the subject approached it more from curiosity to see how far the technology might be stretched than from any clearly defined game plan to produce a pre-determined product. Nevertheless, the opportunity was there. Between 1960 and 1970 computer costs had fallen significantly. Whereas at the start of the decade it took $75 to perform one million operations in an elapse time of one second, by 1970 the cost had fallen to six cents with the elapse time halved.[58]

Micro-computers or PCs entered the market in the mid 1970s, at first in kit form and later in mass production. The kit was that of the Altair micro-computer which was advertised in the January 1975 issue of *Popular Electronics*. The model was based on the Intel 8080 micro-processor linked to a tiny amount of memory – approximately 4Kbytes. It was manufactured by a firm called MITS in New Mexico and sold for less than $400.[59] It was designed by a former air-force instructor in Albequerque who also operated a small electronic kit company making calculators, which were micro-processor devices with fixed programs. When the cost of calculators dropped down to no more than a few dollars the company found itself in debt to the sum of $350,000. However, in 1972 Ed Roberts, who had designed one of the first programmable calculators, was looking for ways to exploit this potential and salvage something of the company. Within a period of no more than 30 days after the 1975 article appeared the company had turned from an overdraft of $200,000 on its books to a positive cash-flow of $250,000. Les Solomon, Editor of *Popular Electronics*, who wrote the cover story on the Altair described the reaction to the announcement:

> The response to the article was totally unbelievable. What bothered me personally I guess was why would anybody in their right mind send $400 to an unknown company in Alberqueque, New Mexico, for a product that nobody really knew very much about. And there were thousands of guys out there: frustrated engineers, software developers, computer users, digital enthusiasts who suddenly saw their first opportunity to have a computer for essentially the cost of the micro-processor.[60]

The Altair was a powerful catalyst for those enthusiasts interested in computers. Once they had built their machines, they would have to maintain them and to do that they would have to make contact with other people who knew about these things. In the words of Steve Wozniak, co-founder of Apple Computer Corporation, 'these were people who dreamed of possessing a computer before a computer could do anything other than be a computer. Just knowing you had one mattered. The fact it could not run a single program did not matter'. In 1975 a computer club that, because of the anarchistic state of the industry at the time, never 'officially' existed grew up in Santa Clara called the 'Home Brew' club, whose members continued discussions in the Oasis Bar afterwards. It was the first such group in the United States and two of its most famous members were Steve Wozniak and the other Apple pioneer, Steve Jobs. The Altair had shown to all those who wanted to make their own computer and do things with them that this was possible, but to achieve this they had to talk to each other to discuss ideas and find out the missing pieces of detail that they needed to complete their project. The 'Home Brew' Club was the place 'where for two years it was possible to get the entire industry in one room'.[61]

It was one thing, however to come up with wild ideas for products; it was another to translate these into reality and into hard cash. To do that it was necessary to seek the help of marketing people who could create a market for the product. All the companies that successfully came through the early days were the ones that recognised this need. The innovators among the 'Home Brew' club were not professional products designers as the industry was too new. They were the technical fringe who essentially scraped a product together using whatever know-how they could lay their hands on. This was exactly how Apple Computer Corporation was started in the mid-seventies by Jobs and Wozniak. They began in a garage and developed the enormously successful Apple PC Computer, which later became Apple Macintosh. It was not the first personal computer, but it was the one that caught the public imagination, launching the PC industry in the process. Its success was its simplicity and several years after its launch the Apple 2 version was still a best selling PC. In the words of Regis McKenna, the most successful publicist in Silicon Valley who made his name by taking on the marketing of the Apple computer, 'Steve Wozniak created the perennial volkswagon or the polaroid that's continuing to sell'.[62] Apple grew from a tiny entrepreneurial activity in a garage, absorbing Wozniak and Jobs for 16–20 hours a day, day after day, into a world industry in less than 10 years. The market was educated and expanded to accept the product which was improved through the feedback of a small core of customers who reported back their comments on what improvements they wanted to see. In Regis McKenna's words, it was 'market driven not marketing driven'.

Commenting on the birth of the personal computer industry, Steve Wozniak said this:

> We were into one of those rare periods when a company can grow to be a billion dollar company in five years. It occurs only when a market expands out of nowhere. So we are kind of a big success story. We represent the American dream. People started gathering together and exploring the idea there was going to be a revolution in technology that was going to change society so drastically. None of the real professional world recognised how important this was going to be. People were finally going to have home computers . . . It went up and up and up until one day we looked at ourselves and said 'gees look what's happened: this is a real success'. We thought it was a real success when we got our first $50,000 order. Then one day we could look at ourselves and we had more money than our parents had ever earned, and it was still just the start.[63]

Until the launch of the Altair no one had succeeded in putting the Intel chip in a computer configuration, using it instead in traffic lights or computer peripherals such as printers or visual display units to assist their functioning.[64] Initially there was no software for these machines, requiring the enthusiast to write small programs for himself in either machine or assembly code direct from the keyboard. The development of the CP/M operating system developed by Gary Kildall, who had acquired military experience with computers and subsequently as consultant to Intel, introduced a standard that was easily transportable from one micro-computer system to another. This enabled software producers to fix on a standard and to begin to produce applications for these computers. A major advantage of the first version was its size, since it only required 3Kbytes of memory to run. Kildall marketed CP/M through Digital Research which he formed with his wife in 1975. The company offered the operating system to manufacturers by license and more than 900 such licences were purchased by the end of the decade. In the mid-1980s 300 computer models used CP/M and 3000 applications programs had been written for CP/M-based systems. In its time more than 200 million copies were estimated to be in existence and it remained dominant until the early 1980s when MS-DOS took over as the most popular operating system for micros.[65]

MS-DOS (Microsoft Disk Operating System) was developed by Bill Gates, the co-founder of Microsoft which produced programs for suppliers such as Apple and Commodore. When IBM decided to move into the PC market place, having seen somewhat late in the day the expansion of the market outside mainframes, it commissioned Microsoft to produce its operating system. Gates and his partner Paul Allen had earlier written a BASIC interpreter for the Altair, the first version of which ran required only 4Kbyte memory. MS-DOS was written for a 16-bit PC architecture which IBM had planned. Despite an argument between Kildall and IBM over allegations that IBM had copied his CP/M interface, with its proprietary form of MS-DOS called PC-DOS, the new system quickly dominated as companies fought to produce IBM-compatible alternatives. The IBM personal computer was launched in late 1981 for the business user followed by the PC junior (PCjr) for home computer use in 1983. This marked the formal recognition by the industry leader of the importance of micro-computers. Perhaps partly due to IBM's diffidence in this sector, neither machine was admired. Within two years of its launch IBM was forced to withdraw the PCjr following a disappointing sales performance.[66]

In 1987 IBM launched its PS/2 range of personal computers, moving away from the standard set by the IBM PC. The new standard is based upon a high speed method of organising the transfer of data and flow of instructions through the PC known as Micro-Channel Architecture (MCA). This is patented by IBM who intend to licence compatible PC manufacturers wishing to use MCA, charging up to 5% on PS/2-compatible sales.[67] To support this advance IBM launched the OS/2 operating system, again written by Microsoft Corporation. OS/2 allows several PCs to link up within a network, offering a pathway for the user to upgrade out of MS-DOS. Since May 1990, OS/2 has been in competition with Microsoft's own 'Windows 3' software which is arguably more advanced than OS/2, particularly in running standard software. Windows 3 emulates some of the screen-based features of the Apple Macintosh.[68]

Desk-Top Machines in the Nineties From its uncertain beginnings the PC sector has now established itself as the fastest growing section of the computer industry, with current annual growth of desk-top machines running at 14.7%. This is almost twice the growth of both the mainframe and mid-range divisions.[69] This contrasts with the standard PC market in which growth in sales is now declining from 7.4% in 1988 to about 2% in 1990. Following the pattern of the other markets, what began as a straightforward product offering modest office applications, has diversified into a powerful tool, which once again challenges established industry demarcations between machine performance and applications. The development of PCs has today blurred the distinctions between small and large systems as processing power gravitates inexorably down through the market to the bottom range. As far as revenues are concerned, the PC sector has grown in value particularly in the business/professional field. In the United States, for example, PC sales generally have more than doubled in the period 1986–1990, with 8.5 million machines in operation. Sales of PCs by US manufacturers were expected to exceed $23 billion in 1988, a rise of 17% on the previous year. At the top end of the range, growth was an estimated 33% in 1988 reflecting the increase in micro-processor capacity. Worldwide sales are expected to exceed 12 million units per annum by 1993 with revenues around $25 billion.[70]

For the business/industrial user the market has diversified in two ways. First of all, desk-top machines now offer many more facilities than before. Users are now looking, for example, at networked PCs or 'workstations' as a way of distributing data processing operations without necessarily opting for a more expensive alternative such as the mini-computer. Software development, computer-aided design, graphics and desk-top publishing have all now entered within workstation capability, supported by high-quality low-cost laser printers. Producers include Sun Microsystems, DEC, IBM, Pyramid and Apple – the latter with a high-end Macintosh brand machine.[71] IBM has been in the workstation market since 1985 with the RT family of machines. With only 3% market share the company launched the 'System/6000' family in February 1990, codenamed 'Rios'. The new machines are UNIX-based in recognition of the dominance of UNIX in the small/mid-range marketplace and are IBM's response to a poor performance up to now in a sector currently worth $6.5 billion.[72] Its top range PS/2 personal computer is also beginning to look increasingly like a workstation, with networking capacity, multi-tasking operating system capability and high grade graphics. What used to be the mark of the workstation in the eighties – one Mbyte of memory; one MIPS of performance and one million pixels for high definition screen display (the 3 Ms) – looks decidedly marginal today and will inevitably need to be revised upwards as PCs begin to rise above their station.[73]

The workstation concept has also spawned the 'executive information system' (EIS) in a market currently growing at 30% per annum. Targeted at the senior executive, the idea is to provide him with a window into his company's performance by extracting from the web of corporate data in circulation and from external data sources, information that will enable him to assess what is going on. The key to EIS performance is the software, which can be introduced into a wide range of hardware. Attributes of EISs include the ability to convert information into pie charts, diagrams or graphs, and the monitoring or tracking, with screen-based indicators, of particular types of information according to pre-set parameters. These systems are likely to develop further as software improves. IBM has indicated it will enter the EIS sector, expected to be worth $230 million by 1992.[74]

The second form of diversification in the commercial sector is in the growth of portable 'laptop' computers with optional telecommunications access through to central processors or networks. This has been dubbed 'the second personal computer revolution'.[75] The sight of a passenger on a train or aircraft working away at his keyboard rather than fritter away the time is no longer a novelty. Todays products 'range from laptop to desktop portable, luggable and, more recently, mobile, hand- held and palm-top models'.[76] The success of the portable is due largely to the ability of manufacturers to give it something close to PC capability without the drawbacks of earlier machines. For example, a range of machines just launched by Compaq weighing no more than 7lbs., pack the power of an IBM PC/XT and AT.[77] Other companies producing laptops are Apple Computer with the Macintosh portable; Toshiba with the T1000SE high specification 'notebook style' PC; Psion – the UK portable computer manufacturer with the Psion mobile computer; Epson with the HX20; Atari, Hitachi and Zenith.[78] There is an obvious demand for the right product. A company sales force needs the communications with head office; many employees whose job takes them away from central facilities need access to information on a day to day basis as well as a means to transmit it. Typical features on current models include liquid crystal display screen and long battery life as well as increased processing power in a smaller, lighter box. The number of units sold per annum is expected to rise from 817,000 in 1988 to 3.5 million by 1993 in a market worth $2.3 billion in 1988.[79]

Analysts believe that the market will diversify as the product range begins to stretch. At the top of the range will be the portable PC offering an improved range of spreadsheet, word processing and other PC applications, followed by smaller cheaper 'personal organisers' with modest spreadsheet and word processing facilities. These will retail either for personal use or for business as a 'data capture' device. Inevitably, before too long, the technology will link up with portable compact disk players such as Sony's 'Data Discman' to extend the laptop into a portable PC with a substantial digital Read Only Memory. As laptops become more user friendly their popularity will grow. IBM is thought to be reconsidering its entry into the market after two earlier failed attempts. Certainly the market is growing fast. One UK research organisation has revealed that the UK market grew by 229% in 1988 compared with the year before, with sales up by another 69% in the first half of 1989.[80] Estimates suggest that 70% of all PC sales will be laptops by 1999.

OTHER INDUSTRY SECTORS – THE 'PLUG' COMPATIBLES It is of course entirely misleading to describe the framework of an industry simply by the breakdown of its products. Just as the products shade into one another without total clarity in categorisation, so too does the industry itself in the way it organises and produces. Although IBM has clearly dominated in terms of its revenues and market share, it now faces competition in an industry that is becoming ever more specialised and extended in the products it makes. One of the key areas within which competition occurs is the 'plug-compatible' sector. A plug-compatible manufacturer is one who produces equipment that can be operated in conjunction with that of another manufacturer when connected by plug or cable.[81] It applies not only to complete computer systems but to peripherals such as storage media, printers and various 'add-on' facilities designed to enhance machine performance.

Manufacturers of complete systems will frequently design their products around components produced by a number of different makers. Producers who obtain components, and add value to them by building a plug compatible computer for resale are examples of Original Equipment Manufacturers, otherwise known as OEM's. (OEM also refers to manufacturers who purchase equipment and add to its value by enhancing its capabilities or adapting it for a specific application.)[82]

165

Indeed OEMs might have agreements with particular hardware manu-facturers to purchase their hardware, add features or enhancements to it, such as expansion cards for increased performance or capability, or additional applications software, and then sell it as their own brand. More recently, OEM producers have tended to operate in reverse, supplying peripherals or even central processing units to major com-puter manufacturers who then distribute complete systems in their own company name. In fact, the IBM AT, which launched the company in the PC market, was built mostly by sub-contractors using 'Off-the-shelf' components.

The company most affected by the activities of the plug-compatible industry has, of course, been IBM. By setting the *de facto* standards for the industry for such a long time, there have always been good economic reasons for designing systems that can interact with IBM equipment in terms of operating systems, applications software, equipment for the storage and transfer of data, communications standards and a range of other features. At the top end, Amdahl Corporation provides IBM plug-compatible mainframes such as the 5890E mainframe which sup-ports IBM's new Enterprise Systems Architecture (ESA/370 TM) and the MVS/ESA TM operating system. More recently the Japanese have sought agreements with IBM to strengthen the plug-compatible industry in Japan. The electronics giant, Fujitsu, which has a 49% stake in Amdahl, has recently agreed terms with IBM that will give it access to IBM operating system microcode.[83] This followed a settlement in September 1987 under the auspices of the American Arbitration Association after accusations that Fujitsu had violated IBM's operating system software. The agreement allows Fujitsu and its customers to continue using its operating system which is compatible with IBM's MVS mainframe system and for appropriate payments to be made to the latter.[84] Hitachi has also moved closer to IBM, and following negotia-tions commenced in 1982, which took four years to complete, has rewritten its VOS operating system which has similarities to IBM's. It has now joined the US software corporation Electronic Data Systems in a takeover of the plug-compatible hardware manufacturer National Advanced Systems to form Hitachi Data Systems. Since Hitachi no longer uses 'informal' means of copying IBM operating systems, IBM now provides Hitachi with information to enable it to produce systems compatible with IBM applications software.

The real centre of the plug-compatible industry, however, is found in the PC or workstation sector. The pattern has been for manufacturers to produce competitive compatible products to match each strategic move by IBM in product development. Companies include Apricot, Samsung, Compaq, Amstrad, Olivetti, Phillips, Tandy and others. The objective of these manufacturers is to produce a consistent but better product than IBM at a reduced price. Improvements might be found in levels of performance, in add-on facilities or enhanced software. As early as 1964 IBM was faced with plug-compatible competition in respect of input–output peripheral products (tapes, disks, memories, printers) that were matched with IBM central processing units. In 1969 it designated peripherals as a 'key corporate strategic issue' (KCSI) and began to examine ways of reducing its exposure to this market.

The IBM/Telex Antitrust Litigation As a result of IBM's response to the inroads of the plug-compatible manufacturers, a test case was brought in 1972 by Telex Corporation and Telex Computer Products Inc., alleging IBM's 'monopolization and attempts to monopolize the worldwide manufacture, distribution, sale and leasing of electronic data processing equipment since 1954' in contravention of the Sherman and Clayton Anti-trust legislation. In the action which followed Telex was awarded \$259.5 million in anti-trust damages in respect of the various anti-trust violations which had allegedly damaged their market share and its rental and sales profits. (The true figure was only one third of the amount, but this had to be trebled under US Anti-trust law. The Telex case provides a fascinating historical account of the nature of the computer industry up to the early 1970s.)[85] This decision was reversed in part on appeal and eventually settlement reached between the parties. The appeal court regarded the product market as wider than that for peripheral products plug-compatible with IBM's CPUs. The relevant market should have been defined at first instance to include those peripherals compatible with other systems. In the context of the entire market there could be no ruling of monopolization or of 'predatory' behaviour since IBM was doing no more than engaging in the type of competition prevalent throughout the industry.[86]

The case was significant since it established the right of competitors to test monopoly practices within competition law. Whilst IBM's practices were not found to be illegal, this and subsequent cases did introduce base-line standards for adjudicating between acceptable and unacceptable competitive behaviour, that contributed towards the development of competition within the industry.[87] It also underlined the distinction between the regulation of competition and the assertion of proprietary rights in intellectual property. The court at first instance in the Telex case found that there had been trade secret violations by the latter in respect of confidential IBM information and copyright infringement in respect of IBM copyrighted manuals. Damages of $13 million were awarded in respect of the advantages secured by Telex in the development of its products through trade secrets misappropriation. It also awarded $13,700 for copyright violations as well as a destruction order in respect of all Telex manuals found to have infringed. A total of nearly $22 million inclusive of attorney's fees was awarded against Telex, though reduced to $18.5 million on appeal.

At the same time, however, on competition grounds, the court ordered IBM to provide technical information describing the design of the electronic interface of its central processing unit, and other information that would be necessary for independent plug-compatible producers to manufacture products interchangable with IBM equipment. The sharing of technical data by IBM relative to its systems and software has occurred regularly since. This enables IBM to dictate the terms of any technology transfer while deepening IBM's own profile in the market as its products become the *de facto* standard to which other computers and systems must comply. The extent to which manufacturers of leading products within the market can expand the scope of proprietary rights in the technology as a means of maintaining or expanding market share, while avoiding any challenge under competition rules is, however, a matter that remains under discussion, particularly over computer software. From the competitor's perspective it remains equally difficult, within the volatile climate of intellectual property law, to know where the line is drawn between legitimate reverse engineering, and infringement resulting from any similarities between the new product and the market leader.

Meeting the IBM Standard The difficulties and dilemmas created by these tensions are evident today in the efforts of the plug-compatible industry to manufacture computers compatible with IBM's PS/2 microcomputer range, representing the second generation of IBM PCs. To succeed in producing a compatible PS/2 clone, manufacturers must emulate not only the PS/2 design but also IBM's proprietary Micro Channel Architecture which defines the standard for data flow to and from the processor and throughout the whole system, and which is the standard to which future non-UNIX based generations of business PCs from IBM will comply. Designing a 'clean' compatible that does not infringe proprietary rights requires, first of all, the creation of a similar Basic Input Output System (BIOS). This is the group of routines that are implemented when the user first gets the machine up and running. It is located in a BIOS chip within the memory map of the micro-computer and is called up by the operating system when it needs any input/output routines. Developers must therefore produce compatible circuit designs for the BIOS and other logic chips within the PS/2 as the first step towards a machine that is functionally equivalent to the IBM range. This did not prove difficult in the case of IBM's first generation of PCs, since they were essentially put together from components bought in by IBM from other producers and did not enjoy the protection of the proprietary technology that surrounds the PS/2 and MCA package. It has been estimated, for example, that IBM included over 100 patentable features in the mechanical design of the Micro Channel Architecture used in the PS/2 Models 50, 60 and 80.[88] IBM also has copyright in the logic of MCA and has indicated that it is prepared to use its proprietary rights to preserve its market share.

One chip manufacturer, Chips and Technologies (C&T), produced a compatible chip-set for the first generation PC AT which was built into more than one million AT compatibles and used by 60% of all manufacturers of AT clones. This cost IBM part of its market share for the AT which it would not want to repeat with the PS/2. Instead IBM has offered selected manufacturers licensed access to its patented technology in return for a royalty of 5% on subsequent sales. In effect the objective is to grant access to the ideas while not necessarily permitting the copying of the logical design directly. Olivetti is one company that has reached an agreement with IBM designed to share technologies across the entire range of products – from typewriters to mini-computers.[89] Other chip manufacturers and systems producers must decide whether to negotiate licences or go ahead with a compatible product and risk legal action on the basis that IBM's intellectual property rights have been infringed. One chip-set producer, Western Digital, has invested 'tens of millions of dollars and probably 100 man years' in developing the core logic for Micro Channel Achitecture compatibility, and claims to have added functionality and flexibility over and above the IBM original.[90] In developing a compatible BIOS and core logic to the

169

IBM PS/2 MCA range, the company has adopted two different design approaches in an effort not to infringe IBM's intellectual property, as described thus:

> To make a compatible BIOS, Western Digital technicians reverse-engineer IBM's code, creating design specifications that are then passed on to a separate group of 'forward engineers' through company lawyers. The second group creates a 'clean' BIOS from the specifications. Because it has not seen IBM's own BIOS code – only Western Digital's specifications for it – they can claim that they did not copy IBM's designs directly. Hardware design, on the other hand, starts with forward engineers, who pore over the specifications IBM provides for third party developers. They create a paper design and then go back to the PS/2 and perform various electronic and software tests to validate their assumptions about the way it operates. From that process come the specifications used to create Western Digital's own original PS/2-compatible designs.[91]

In contrast, a true 'clone maker' will purchase an IBM PS/2 and deprocess its components by chemical, mechanical and electrical means, the object being to copy the circuit design without amendment: 'core logic dyes are stripped away layer by layer; the circuits are extracted, and electron microscope photographs are taken of input and output circuitry traces.'[92] The product is a schematic database that can be taken by a semi-conductor manufacturer to produce a compatible chip. It is this method which contains no originality in the process of producing a compatible design that is most likely to infringe proprietary rights. The battle between legitimate competition and unfair competitive practices and the promotion of and challenge to intellectual property rights within that process remains a central feature of many of the legal disputes within the industry today. In fact basic reverse engineering of products is an endemic practice within the computer industry. It is practiced all the time by companies wanting to assess the quality and competitiveness of their own products. It is when the results of such practices are taken and used without amendment in a cloned product or complete system that legal action becomes almost inevitable, although far from easy to utilise successfully. The copyright treatment of reverse engineering is currently under consideration by the European Commission who are preparing a Directive on the Legal Protection of Computer Programs.[93]

Other Industry Sectors In completing the description of how the computer industry functions it would be inappropriate to ignore the many other sectors that have established niches within the overall framework. Apart from the software and telecommunications industries which will be discussed later, there is a substantial peripherals industry providing equipment that interfaces between the user and the computer. These range from printers, terminals, storage media, display units and a wide range of additional office equipment. Other service sectors have developed concentrating on equipment maintenance or facilities management – whereby an independent service organisation manages and operates the computing installation. This is estimated to be worth between £200–400 million in the UK alone,[94] and growing domestically at the rate of 25% per annum.[95] Another is the leasing industry by which users lease computer systems from a company over a period of say seven years subject to a range of credit terms, some more risky than others. The sector was rocked in 1990 with the collapse of the billion-dollar Atlantic Leasing with 2,500 customers.

The semi-conductor components industry is, of course, another division dominated by the growth of the large chip producers, initially in the United States. This industry too has divided as companies have begun to develop different chip products either for their own use or for sale to machine manufacturers. IBM, for example, is the biggest chip producer in the world whose output is built into its own machines. Another is Sun Micro-systems whose chips appear in the company's workstations. In 1984 the Japanese took the lead in the strategically important memory chip (D-RAM) sector. This occurred when NEC brought out the 256K D-RAM a year ahead of the American companies. A 'chip famine' resulted in 1988 when the two countries became embroiled in a dispute about price fixing and jobs.[96] The result was a Trade Agreement between the US and Japan designed to limit the dumping of Japanese D-RAMs in the US market. However, this attempt to sustain a market price for Japanese chips in the US backfired, for by that time several US D-RAM producers including Motorola and the chip's original inventor – Intel – had withdrawn from the market leaving only Texas Instruments and Micron Technology in the field. US companies are now renewing their efforts to obtain market share by joint ventures and licensing deals including ones with Japanese companies. Meanwhile, much political manoeuvring is continuing as companies and their domestic national governments fight for control.[97]

These rapid fluctuations in company fortunes in the chip sector are not unusual within the industry as a whole. Fortunes can be quickly won and lost depending upon a range of factors, not least of which is luck in getting the right product with the right technology and marketing together at the most suitable time. Apart from IBM, Apple Computer Corporation was a prime example of success in the market with the launch of the PC, as were Compaq[98], Sun Microsystems and Lotus in other fields. On the downside, failure in design or the choice of the wrong standard in hardware or software can lead to substantial and rapid losses, as can external influences arising from cutbacks in defence budgets, and political and economic decisions arising from international events. The market is not always ready to accept a new product even though the technology can deliver it. Unexpected factors may be relevant that the designers have not considered.

IBM has experienced its own share of failures over the years as have many other companies, as the following illustrations show. The world's second largest computer company DEC suffered a 90% decline in profits in the third quarter of 1989 to $25 million. A slowdown in the market combined with strong sectoral competition in the workstation sector is blamed and this has resulted in a 'business simplification programme' to streamline the company's operations.[99] Unisys the defence, mainframe and maintenance company – the merger between Burroughs and Sperry Rand – is trying to shake-off debts of $4 billion[100] and Wang, the US office automation manufacturer, has restructured following falling sales and a $425 million loss over 1989.[101] In the same sector, a similar fate ensued at Olivetti after a 40% decline in profits up to June 1989.[102] The German micro-computer company Nixdorf, which now specialises in systems integration based on common industry software standards, suffered a 90% slump in profits in 1988 when world market conditions worsened following the rise in D-RAM-chip costs during the trade dispute between the US and Japan. The company had, allegedly, failed to move across towards 'open systems' compatibility with its machines as soon as it should. As a result it too has streamlined its operation. The UK division of Nixdorf is now planning collaboration with Siemens' Data and Information Systems to strengthen the company's existing product lines.[103] Apple succumbed to a small fall in profits from $140 to $125 million in 1989, due to its slow product development cycle, which led to a tardy response to the laptop market and low-end PC sector.[104] The UK-based Apricot Computers resisted industry standards and settled on the wrong workstation technology in the mid-1980s. The company's recovery to profitability in 1989 (£6 million) was achieved only when it diversified beyond workstations into software and services. This move was underlined when Apricot bought Information Technology (ITL) in October 1989, whose base was in health-care software and computer maintenance.[105] In March 1990 Apricot itself was bought by Mitsubishi, who want Apricot to be the company's worldwide centre for design and manufacture of desktop computers.

These examples show how successful companies, often started by engineers, programmers, venture capitalists or groups of like-minded enthusiasts can outgrow the creators and flounder because subsequent decisions about strategy or product development are misguided. This might be because the initial enthusiasm in designing a winning product has dissipated once day-to-day management, together with an entirely new set of skills, is called for. They also suggest that the computer industry, like any other business is not sacrosanct to market conditions brought about by a down-turn in the world economy. In fact it could be said that it is likely to be among the first to feel the draught.

COMPUTER APPLICATIONS TODAY

In contrast with the highly specialised marketplace for supercomputers and the decline in the relative size of the overall market for mainframes, the personal computer has enjoyed an unprecedented rise to become an established part of the hierachy of data-processing equipment.[106] A number of factors are responsible for this. First and foremost has been the advance in the technology that permits substantial computer power to be placed on a desk-top machine. Second, as ways were found for non-technical users to be introduced to the benefits of computers, and as prices fell with mass production and reduced hardware costs, the PC became an attractive proposition for businesses and home users. Operating System standards centred on a few proprietary systems – CP/M, MS-DOS and OS/2 not to mention the wider appeal of the UNIX 'open systems' alternative. The ability of the smaller manufacturers to build machines that could run the standard operating system of the day, with add-on features available for a competitive price, ensured that the market developed, offering products at lowest price.

Until the late 1980s it might have been appropriate to define the centre of gravity in computer use as being at the level of the PC.

Certainly personal computers have brought technology to the masses through the ingenuity of individuals like Sir Clive Sinclair with his popular range of home computers, later to be eclipsed by Amstrad. The contribution that the PC has made in developing attitudes among users towards the technology must also be recognised, most notably an acceptance of its role and contribution in daily life. Whilst the hobbyist interest was about all that could be catered for by early home computers, the business user was encouraged to adopt some simple applications in the workplace as software was created to provide it. The Apple Macintosh was particularly important in that regard and continues to be so today. However, as if like a bouncing ball, just as soon as the technology hit the ground with the birth of the PC, it appeared to extend away again as performance levels of mainframe proportions found their way onto desk-tops. This, combined with developments in networks and advances in telecommunications, means that the picture of grass roots computer use today is much harder to read than it was.

Users in particular have a wider choice regarding the way they equip themselves than they once did. The increase in computer power exploited by the ingenuity of software producers has opened up applications to the public previously beyond reach because of cost, incompatibility or lack of a genuine product. The networked workstation, the executive information system, the desk-top mini, etc., have all contributed to the range of options and configurations available to today's user. New technology uses in the office and in the commercial environment have broadened considerably as systems have become affordable. Activity has extended beyond wordprocessing and accounts, database development and design, into electronic mail and networking, business analysis, stock, and quality control, machine control and job scheduling.[107] In support of these needs the software sector has designed a set of applications programs for retail distribution and in so doing created a separate market for each. In the 1990's it would be very surprising indeed to find any area of business that did not find the technology of value in its day to day operations. The major applications will now be described.

WORD-PROCESSING PACKAGES   The most popular application of computer technology has always been word processing and this remains the position today. For many it remains synonymous with computing itself, having acted as a stepping stone to more sophisticated computer uses.

Wordstar, the word processing package written in 1978 and sold by MicroPro for the CP/M *de facto* standard operating system, was highly successful despite widespread copying of the program. The company estimates that more than 3 million copies have been sold since then. Wordstar is now in version 5.5, retailing at £399 in the UK and remains competitive.[108] Currently, Microsoft Word and particularly Word-Perfect are popular packages. WordPerfect overtook Wordstar 1512 in sales through dealers in the UK in July 1987, with a unit share of the market in that month of nearly 18%.[109] Currently WordPerfect is at version 5.0. Distributed by WordPerfect Corporation of Orem, Utah, the company maintains 19 separate authorised distributors on a world-wide scale. The corporation is now considering development of a Windows 3.0 compatible version of its word processing software. Microsoft's Windows, 3.0 released in May 1990, enhances the DOS industry standard operating system with an interface to the user. However, WordPerfect is not altogether compatible with Windows in its present form, hence the need for a version able to compete with Microsoft's own word processor.[110] In addition to business use, word processing is now widely available on PCs designed for the home user, in addition to other regular home computer applications which include entertainment with computer games, education software for home or school, household finance and programming tools such as BASIC.

SPREADSHEET APPLICATIONS Spreadsheet applications refer to PC business programs designed to assist the business user with financial forecasting, analysis and business planning. The first major success in this area was VisiCalc developed by Daniel Bricklin and Robert Frankston within their own company, Software Arts, and marketed by Personal Software. The product was launched in October 1979 costing $100.[111] It had sold 800,000 copies by 1985, when – at a time when the company was in difficulties – VisiCalc and other assets were acquired by Lotus. Thereafter Lotus 1–2-3 took over as the market leader, although it has since had to face strong competition from alternative spreadsheet packages such as Microsoft's Excel and Borland's Quattro-Pro.[112] Other competitors include SuperCalc and Symphony.[113] Lotus 1–2-3 is now in Releases 2.2 and 3, running under the DOS and/or OS/2 operating systems.[114] To remain competitive such products must move with new industry standards such as OS/2 – the IBM operating system designed for its Microchannel Architecture – MCA. In April 1990 Lotus launched an OS/2 version of its Presentation Manager Spreadsheet – the 1–2-3/G, and others are available for the IBM System 370 mainframe, DEC Vax VMS mini-computers, UNIX based Sun workstations and Apple Macintosh.[115] Release 3 of Lotus 1–2-3 includes 3 dimensional worksheets, file linking which allows the user to retrieve figures from other files for use in calculations, and a database for importing data from external sources without leaving 1–2-3. Enhanced analytical graphics are also featured.

The Lotus strategy today is to establish communications protocols to enable users to access all information held on external databases through its 1–2-3 spreadsheet. To achieve this it is releasing details of its data exchange architecture to enable other software suppliers to design products that will be compatible. One company with which Lotus is doing this is WordPerfect Corporation. The plan is to develop common user-interfaces for the two companies' spreadsheet and word-processing packages. This collaboration will strengthen the two companies in their competitive battle with Microsoft who are at the centre of the industry so far as setting standards are concerned.[116]

It is likely that the next generation of products in this area will extend beyond 'spreadsheets' into 'Decision Support Systems' (DSS). These, it is argued, offer more than 'stand alone' analyses of cash flow, profits and forecasts. Instead, DSS will have capacity to import data from throughout an organisation and thereby offer a much more sophisticated output than is available today with the conventional spreadsheet.[117] DSS are available today and becoming increasingly popular with executives through computer workstations on the desk-top. The term 'DSS' is beginning to take over as the name given to a range of software products designed to help the business user gain access to and make sense of management information.

DSS vary in sophistication from simple spreadsheets to the coming systems which will employ artificial intelligence techniques to improve the quality of the information provided.[118] These concepts are of course a feature of the Executive Information System (EIS) workstation already discussed. The overall view of the market in 1990 is that Lotus is well ahead in spreadsheet applications with an estimated 55% of the market. However, this dominant position is being eroded at the margins by the products from Microsoft and Borland International. For a while it was thought that a merger between Lotus and fellow software producer Novell in 1990 would displace Microsoft as the largest software company in the world, with product sales of $950 million. The link-up fell apart at the last minute so that Microsoft retains its top position. Merger and partnership rumours will nevertheless intensify the competition between the two industry giants.

DATABASE MANAGEMENT SYSTEMS Other established applications designed for the business user are database management systems (DBMS) that manage the storage and retrieval of information. These systems enable the user to organise his data and to store it in a variety of forms and locations. The minimum requirement is to create a database file and index it, then add retrieve and update facilities.In the early days DBMS were designed for larger computers given the demand for storage and high speed retrieval. A standard for storing data was developed by Dr. E.F. Codd at IBM in the early 1970s. The concept known as the 'relational database' proposed that data should be stored in simple two dimensional tables. The theory behind it is that the data should be kept distinct from the applications that use it.[119] Programs that manipulated data stored in this form were comparatively easy to write since the data was not stored in complicated structures. Users found this advantageous.

The original database product for PCs was Ashton Tate's dBase which came to pre-eminence just as Wordstar and Lotus 1–2-3 did in the spreadsheet market. This was written by Wayne Ratcliff and was developed at the Jet Propulsion Labs in the late 1960's and run on a mainframe. There was never a commercial version of dBase I, so that the first version for micros was dBase II. It provided in effect a 'toolbox' of pre-written data handling routines representing the 'back end' of the system, with a menu-driven 'front-end' 'help' system and other features designed to simplify the user's task.[110] It gave the user options to link files together or select data from different files and form new ones. Such products are useful when the user needs for example to know how many employees drive a certain model of company car, when they received it and when tax must be paid on the benefit. However, early versions of Dbase were a real struggle to operate. Users recall its sheer user-unfriendliness compared with the later releases.

The dominant database product in recent times has been dBase III, but this is now facing competition with the growth in popularity of IBM's DB 2 public domain language – Structured Query Language

(SQL) which has emerged as the industry standard for relational databases. SQL emerged from IBM in the late 1970s and started as a mainframe and departmental computing product before expanding into the PC environment. DBMS products written in SQL also allow databases to be distributed across machines linked up within a network. For instance access to a network of databases might be controlled from one computer, while other nodes in the network might contain different 'back end' features to minimise network traffic.[111]

Today the 'back end' of any DBMS must be accessible through SQL to compete within the industry standard. The hardware leaders supporting SQL distributed database applications are DEC with its VAX clusters supported by the VMS operating system, IBM, Tandem and International Computers Limited (ICL) – the UK company.[112] Competitors of IBM and Ashton Tate include Cincom, Cullinet, Applied Data Research and Software AG[113] – all of whom will support the IBM standard through licensing agreements. DBMS suppliers who have moved their SQL-based products to the PC include Oracle with SQL*Star and Relational Technology with Ingres.[114] It is important for established dBase users to be able to extend through dBase into SQL and thereby retain their compatibility within the database market. This is because SQL will serve as a kernel around which other facilities will be developed.[115] Ashton Tate has done this by embedding SQL and a compiler into its current dBase IV version while licensing the necessary interface technology from other relational database suppliers to achieve the link up. In 1988 the value of the worldwide database management systems market exceeded $2 billion. 1987 projections suggested approximately 56% of DBMS usage ran on IBM and plug-compatible mainframes, 21% on minis, 12 % on micros and 11% on other mainframes.[116] The proportion of the micro-based usage is expected to grow rapidly in the next five years.

Database management is required right across the range of hardware from the comparatively small relational database requirements of the PC market to the systems required to look after large numbers of files linked together and accessible to many PCs within a network. Products are now coming to the market that incorporate IBM's structured query language with the other features necessary for the top end of the database category. Another trend is to add some database management capacity to other business applications such as spreadsheet. Lotus 1–2–3 offers an add-on database extension called @Base which can read data directly from a dBase-compatible file or from a 1–2-3 spreadsheet.[117] Also Ashton Tate has a product called 'Framework II' which allows dBase files to be examined while importing and exporting 1–2-3 files.[118] Others include Symphony 2; Enable; SmartWare 11; and Open Access II. Each integrates word processing, spreadsheet, graphics, telecommunications and a database manager.[119] The market also attracts 'clone' products which are not confined to operating systems or hardware. Fox Software has produced a clone of dBaselV. Whilst the language of dBaseIV is repeated the product retains a distinct 'look and feel' in an attempt to avoid copyright litigation that has resulted in a series of running battles between producers in recent months.[120]

Another form of information management that is catching on is the 'personal information manager'. These are software products that are designed to produce reminders for tasks, appointments and meetings within a workgroup. Products include The Co-ordinator Version 11 by Azlan; Higgins by Enable; Right Hand Man by Custom Micro; and WordPerfect Office by WordPerfect Corporation.[121] Such applications frequently offer a shared calendar for flexible monthly, weekly or daily reference, electronic mail or gateways to other electronic mail systems. When the system receives a message it automatically updates the record, scanning for priority subjects and reminders. Where information needs to be distributed to a group, the product does so, updating files as it goes along. An alarm system can be built in to alert the user about incoming mail or messages.

One assessment of the future is of PCs or workstations becoming the focal point of all database systems, supported by IBM's OS/2 operating system and linked to optical disk storage media. Users will be able to select from a range of facilities including customised user interfaces for ease of use, assisted by a new generation of software able to optimise performance automatically.[122] The Lotus objective is to continue to seek innovative ways in which to expand the use and utility of desk-top computers for a large sector of the community. The Lotus President believes that the key to this strategy is building software bridges 'that are upwardly and downwardly compatible' with current products, so that the user can operate successfully within the mixed computing environment of the 1990s.[123] However, the future for Ashton Tate looks uncertain. The company is currently looking for a buyer after first-quarter results in 1990 showed a drop in revenue of $33.8 million to $57 million and a loss of $1 million which the company blamed on overselling and over-stocking by dealers in 1989. Analysts believe that the company's 45% share of the PC database market will fall further as products from Borland International, Microrim and Gupta Technologies gain market share.[124]

GRAPHICS AND GRAPHICAL 'USER INTERFACES'   One of the most interesting developments in computing over the past ten years has been the way in which graphics are now used both in improving screen displays and, to a lesser extent, output. So far as output is concerned, graphics originally entered the scene with the simple pie chart and line and bar graphs common today. These features were part of the original Lotus 1–2–3 spreadsheet package launched in 1982. Today the presentation of graphics is much more sophisticated, with a range of specialist graphics packages on the market, and high-quality laser printers offering many different fonts and typestyles. Graphics functions are now an endemic feature of many other applications, most obviously spreadsheet products providing scope for importing images into text-based applications and enabling such images to be transferred out of specialist graphics applications.[125] Database management systems have also responded to the growth in graphics output with products capable of handling graphics files. One example, Precision Software's Superbase 4, is an interactive database that allows the user to define and manipulate database tables.[126]

Such is the rate of growth in the use and popularity of graphics that micro-computing has started to turn away from character-based methods to graphics-oriented formats.[127] The deployment of icons, menu bars, and overlapping windows on the computer screen has been highly significant in making computers much more user-friendly machines than they once were. The concept has become known as the 'graphical user interface' (GUI). It comprises the screen layout controlled by hidden software that also defines how programmers should write their programs for that particular GUI.[128] The approach was particularly successful for Apple Computers with their Macintosh PCs which led the market in the 1980s. Largely because of this technology, Apple's revenues from sales grew from $1 billion in 1983 to $5.3 billion in 1989. Despite Apple's entrepreneurship, the initial pioneering work on the visual interface is claimed by Xerox, following work done at the company's Palo Alto research centre in Silicon Valley in the 1970s. It was Apple Computers, however, with the Apple Macintosh that brought graphics interfaces, and with it PCs, into their second generation. Since then there has been a strong and sustained challenge from Microsoft with their series of software products aptly named 'Windows'.

Windows, which was originally designed for the MS-DOS operating system, has been described in these terms:

> 'Windows is an operating environment that provides for the control and management of all computing resources, specifically the screen, memory, disk storage and interaction with peripheral devices. In simple terms, the application program interacts with Windows rather than with the underlying operating system or directly with the hardware. Because it controls memory management, Windows enables multi-tasking – running more than one application at a given time . . . Windows is named well. The Window is where all the action – and user interaction – is. Each window provides the facility to display text and graphics, to select command options from a menu, to change the window's size, to 'put the program away' – displaying only a representative icon – and to display messages or prompts for specific user input.'[129]

Given the company's central position in setting standards for operating systems, it is not surprising that Windows, which sold 2.5 million copies in 1989, has acted as the bridge between the old (character-based) interfaces and the new generation. It has the advantage that users can gradually convert to the new generation while continuing to operate under the old regime using existing equipment. Microsoft intend Windows to become the standard graphics environment for the PC range, supported by 'Presentation Manager' – the version designed with IBM for its proprietary OS/2 operating system. Presentation Manager, offers all the graphic devices now standard in such products – moveable overlapping windows, pull-down menus, icons, scrollable list boxes, pop-up dialogues, variable text fonts and sizes and a complete range of colour graphics. It also follows the complex graphics standards requirements built into the user access portion of the IBM Systems Application Architecture, enabling graphical constructs to be transferred to all other IBM equipment and software. It is likely that a growing number of software products over the next few years will be written to Windows specifications, which are expected to have an important influence upon system design over this period.[130]

What is unclear, however, is the extent to which Windows 3.0 will affect competition between the rival MS-DOS and OS/2 operating systems, both of which were developed by Microsoft and continue to be served by Microsoft graphical user interfaces.[131] The launch of Windows 3.0 in 1990 also signals more intensive competition with Apple for dominance in the graphics user interface sector. Many software developers want Macintosh applications to run under Windows, which could distract Apple in its development of Macintosh. The battle has now spread to the courts with Apple alleging copyright infringement by Microsoft of its Macintosh screen display.[132]

A further trend in the development of the GUI is the drive towards a standard. This will of course be of considerable interest to the developing UNIX environment. What started as an academic project at Massachusetts Institute of Technology to find ways of passing files across campus regardless of hardware or networking environment, has translated into a potential GUI standard.[133] The idea is that each user should share a common screen layout independent of machine type, size and screen resolution. To achieve this MIT developed a directory of 260 instructions for drawing lines and shapes capable of accommodating the interface requirements of the diverse range of machines and systems. A user should now be in a position to access different applications through the same GUI. Within a network a user should have access to multiple applications available through one or more host computers, which could be UNIX based. The software has been called 'X Windows' and release 3, issued in November 1988, has been proposed for adoption by the X/Open Standards Organisation as part of the Common Application Environment. If recognition is also given to X-Windows by the International Standards Organisation and the American National Standards Institute it will enhance the drift towards workstations, PCs and terminals already underway as potential 'X-servers'.[135] Release 4 of X-Windows took place in January 1990, and this is regarded by analysts as the 'definitive' X implementation.[136]

Another area with promising potential for the user interface is character recognition of handwriting. An integral part of the user interface up to now has been the 'mouse' – the hand-held device for operating and controlling the cursor. Now US manufacturers are investing considerable sums of money in developing a pen interface system able to understand normal cursive handwriting. IBM has already developed a prototype called 'paperlike', able to track handwriting and reproduce it on screen.[137] Apple, Compaq and other venture start-up firms are also engaged in this field. Another US company called Grid Systems has become the first to offer a pen interface machine called 'Gridpad'. This can recognise hand-printed upper case letters. Designers are working towards interface software that can fit into a laptop and automatically correct text after the reader has corrected the proof copy on the screen. The California-based Infocorp market research organisation predicts that annual sales of pen interface notebooks will reach 3.4 million units by 1995. Grid Systems predict the market will reach $200 million by 1991.[138] Voice processing technology can also be expected to develop as the 1990s progress. It will be particularly useful in the provision of customer services.[139]

DESKTOP PUBLISHING   It is but a short step from graphics output in the form of good quality printout, to what has become known as desk-top publishing (DTP).[140] The results of this technology are visible, not just in the disintegration of Fleet Street as the UK national press moved to Wapping, but in the thousands of newsletters, in-house reports and briefing papers now appearing from every imaginable source. Each year on budget day, the firms in the financial, accounting and legal community vie with one another to be the first to deliver their analysis of the budget, usually next day. This appears in high quality glossy format, complete with graphs, tables, charts and commentary. This is the result of DTP technology which gravitated from mainframe and minicomputers to the PC as the latter increased in processing capacity, memory and sophistication. Telecommunications links were also of help, enabling text to be transmitted electronically from all corners of the globe provided the connections worked. Newsletter production is one of the most popular applications of DTP systems, which involve the user keying in his text to a PC and, with the help of a proprietary publishing package such as PageMaker, then producing typeset copy for output through a laser printer or higher quality typesetter.

Today, DTP is a generic term for a whole range of desk top publishing products, some much more sophisticated and worthy of the term than others. In the UK the major growth area has been in newspapers, magazines and graphic design. In the United States, the production of newsletters followed by business and technical documents, internal company reports and sales literature have been the most popular.[141] Of all the products developed for this application, the most influential has been PageMaker. Produced by Aldus UK and adopted by the Apple Macintosh PC, PageMaker was responsible for defining the market for DTP whose inventor, Paul Brainard, thought up the expression to launch his product in 1985.[142] It enabled text to be integrated on screen with graphic images and translated into a page layout for output in a variety of typefaces and print sizes. Later PageMaker was adapted for IBM compatible computers.[143] However, PageMaker does not allow the user to put pages together at the same time the text is written and it offers only a limited amount of editing thereafter. Alternatives now exist in the enhanced wordprocessor packages that combine word processing facilities with quite sophisticated DTP capacity, but there will be some deterioration in the quality of printed output with these products.[144] At the other end of the scale are typesetting languages such as 'Just Text' by Knowledge Engineering and 'Textures' by Addison Wesley for mainframes and minis. These languages are not easy to learn but offer very high quality results and options once mastered.[145] High quality printing is also available now on the Apple Macintosh from companies like Crosfield Electronics, Scitex of Israel and Hell of West Germany.[146] Such products offer high quality graphics, printing and high definition colour scanners for colour photo insertions.

The mainstream battle for DTP continues to revolve around PageMaker, with the Xerox Ventura Publisher package the most successful in the IBM environment.[147] Another centre of gravity is the link-up between Apple and Microsoft in the design of a text format for display and printing. Its previous partner was Adobe Systems of California which produced display software known as Postscript and adopted by DEC, NEC, Wang and Fujitsu. Adobe claims 600,000 sales and incorporation of Postscript in 60 separate products. The company is now trying to retain its status by releasing its typefacing codes to the public domain.[148] In the future it is likely that there will be increased integration of desktop publishing with graphics interfaces, word processing and spreadsheets giving the user increased capacity and flexibility no further away than the PC on his desk. The cost of colour printing will also come down with advances in both laser and ink-jet technology. Image-processing technology is also on its way, providing consistent typesetting based on the digital dot images produced by the technique. This produces a resolution quality of 2000 dots per inch, compared with an average of 300 with laser printers.[149] Expectations are that the PC DTP market will grow at an average 28% per annum until 1995 in the US.[150] The market for ink-jet printers in the US will top $1 billion by 1991.[151]

COMPUTER INTEGRATED MANUFACTURING

Design Systems   Another feature of the increased versatility and performance of computer technology can be found in the domain of design and manufacture. The potential of artificial intelligence offers much in terms of automated techniques of manufacture upon the factory floor and, in the hands of designers, many products and processes. Computer Aided Design, or CAD, provides a screen-based 'electronic' drawing board for designers to work with. Essentially the user can produce a drawing on screen by instructing the computer to produce the lines and curves, either through keyboard entry or with the aid of a 'light pen' or 'mouse'.[152]

The history of CAD emanates from research undertaken in the late 1950s and early 1960s on interactive computer graphics. A key product in CAD development was a program called SKETCHPAD, which was financed by the US Department of Defense, and demonstrated for the first time at the Massachusetts Institute of Technology in 1963.[153] This employed the 'light pen' approach and enabled the user to draw and manipulate pictures on a screen. At that time such products were expensive as they required considerable hardware resources in terms of the performance levels of the day. CAD technology was therefore limited to major industrial sectors such as aerospace, automobile and electronics industries. Initially CAD programs could only produce two-dimensional drawings but this has since been extended into 3-D capacity which is necessary for complex imaging. As computer performance has increased, CAD has extended, in the same way as other applications, through mainframe and mini-computers to stand-alone or networked micro-computers. Currently, CAD systems will typically oflafer a 'library' of stored shapes and commands with facilities that allow the user to move and replicate shapes within a design, enlarge one sector of the drawing and change its size or proportions in relation to the rest of the model, and rotate the end product so that the user can view it from a number of different perspectives.[154]

One of the most successful CAD products developed in the UK is Gino. It was launched in 1972 by the Computer Aided Design Centre at Cambridge as a programmer's tool for building graphics capability into a whole range of applications. It was the first of its kind to implement 3 dimensions, and since then has been used on a range of computers for the purposes of 3-dimensional modelling, process plant design, architectural drawing, electrical schematics and business graphics.[155] However, at the time when the International Standards Organisation was discussing a possible standard for CAD, the Cambridge Centre was being run by the Department of Trade and Industry, whose civil servants did not grasp the implications of the products. Lack of understanding of the commercial implications of Gino allowed a German product – GKS (Graphical Kernel System) to become a world standard.[156]

Since the mid-1970s CAD systems have expanded into a whole range of specialist applications for different industrial and service sectors including engineering, building, electronics and manufacturing. The graphic arts industry has also exploited the technology. This has proved useful in clothes design, ceramics, advertising and packaging.[157] A third generation of CAD systems have also emerged during the 1980s, known as 'Solid Modellers'.These products can rotate an object in 3-D, but also retain its image as a solid object. CAD has contributed greatly to design efficiency and to the speed of development of many different products. For example, Pedrick Yacht Designs of Newport, Rhode Island, designers of one of the next America's Cup boats, have used 3-D modelling software from Parametric Technology of Massachusetts. This reduced by 75% the amount of scale-model and tank testing required in testing design performance and isolating trouble spots.[158]

3-D modelling until recently required powerful computers with almost half the capacity of mainframes. This was because the software could require up to ten times the computer power of its 2-D equivalent. Now 3-D modelling can be accomplished on workstations at a total cost of no more than £16,000. Systems are available from Sun Microsystems, Apollo, Hewlett Packard and DEC.[159] CAD systems for the PC include, Autocad version 10 by Autodesk, Cadkey version 3.12 by Engineering solutions and Microstation PC version 3.0D by Intergraph.[160] Crude comparisons of the design time involved using CAD techniques compared with manual techniques show the former to be between 0.5 and 100 times faster than the latter.[161] The cost saving on prototypes can be enormous using CAD techniques. One technique employed in the production of the European Fighter Aircraft is Rapid Prototyping. This has helped immensely in the management of this complex project where inevitably the design parameters have had to be developed from initial concepts that, at times, inevitably lacked direction or cohesion. New ideas could be fed in and tested at a saving of up to 1000 times the cost of producing a conventional prototype. The system also helped the design team to access detailed aspects of the project which which would not have been possible otherwise.[162]

Keeping track of all the documentation involved in engineering design is itself a problem which technology can counter. Engineering Data Management (EDM) is a product developed by the US software producer, Sherpa Corporation, to manage the design files and the mass of other data generated about the product. EDM software is used by large companies such as General Electric, Hughes Aircraft and Philips. Others are developing their own systems to meet individual requirements. Ford, for example, has spent $77 million developing an 'engineering release' system to cope with the administration of release statements that certify the design as ready for manufacture. With up to 10000 components in a single vehicle, this form of information management has proved essential to Ford. The Ford system, dubbed the 'Worldwide Engineering Release System' (WERS), will serve 20,000 users through a network of 10,000 terminals. The UK software house, SD-Scicon, have taken this a stage further for Ford, with a system called Computer Aided Process Planning (CAPP). This brings together EDM data with manufacturing design instructions showing how the product should be made. The system contains both text and graphics and can switch to different languages when required.[163]

One of the major benefits of computer modelling today is the opportunity it provides for reducing the R&D time cycle. In the aircraft industry, for example, the development of a new aero-engine can take upwards of ten years from design concept to full certification, at a base cost of £500 million. Rolls Royce, makers of the successful RB-211 engine have invested significantly in computer-aided engineering and manufacturing techniques. In the 1960s the company expected to build and break up to 20 developmental engines in the course of bringing a new engine forward. The company has now reduced this to seven or eight engines and expects to reduce it further to about five. It has achieved this by conducting more and more of its testing on computer, thereby confining any design problems to the simulation of the engine rather than the real thing. A computer can test a component by simulating the conditions under which it might operate in real conditions. For example, in the past, the standard way of testing the performance of an engine blade in the presence of a foreign body would be to pass a flock of 1.5 lb. gelatine 'birds' into the fan at 160 knots to simulate the impact

187

of birds getting sucked into the engine while at full thrust during take-off.[164] A simulation of this process can produce very clear evidence of what might happen in reality. It also enables testing to be taken much further, by providing a cost-effective means of testing a variety of components made of different substances and designs without the normal consequences of delay and expense that would otherwise be incurred if this was done by the old methods. These techniques of component modelling and simulation are making the traditional boundary between design and manufacture increasingly artificial.

Although solid modelling of CAD systems has contributed significantly to the capacity to develop complex design specifications, the possibility now exists of adding 'intelligence' to such products. 'Smart' CAD systems could contribute to the process of design by, for example, comparing a design to an existing one, storing and using data on standard dimensions and sub-parts of a design and assisting the designer to produce the best possible design according to all the parameters that should be taken into account in the process. Such systems might enter into inter-active dialogue with the user during the design activity, commenting upon the impact of choices in terms of cost, efficiency, integration and ease of construction.

Manufacturing Systems Artificial intelligence techniques are also likely to play an important future role in connecting CAD systems to other parts of the production process, most notably computerised systems of manufacturing. The trend is moving inexorably towards the integration of computers at all stages of the production process, from design to delivery. The success in this field comes not only as a result of the increased performance levels of computer hardware, but improved software developed with the aid of a new generation of computer languages. This is also the cause of heightened expectations for developments in expert systems. For some time the industry has tended to link together automated design with manufacturing, using the abbreviated expression 'CAD/CAM' for Computer aided design/Computer aided manufacturing. CAM is a generic term used to describe the migration of information technology onto the factory floor for operation in an aspect or aspects of the production process. The most visible example of such applications can be seen in the car industry, where robots are used on the production line. Japan has proved to be a world leader in the design and use of industrial robots, which have been defined as: 'reprogramm-able multifunctional manipulator[s] designed to move material, parts, tools, or specialised devices, through variable programmed motions for the performance of a variety of tasks'.[165] This definition covers a large number of machine tools, the design of which is far removed from any resemblance with human beings that the expression 'robot' is inclined to conjure up. Indeed the less emotive term to describe these machine tools might be 'programmable manipulator'.[166]

A typical robot consists of a controller which is usually a micro-computer or micro-processor which guides the movement of the robot and allows an operator to input instructions. The manipulator compris-ing the 'hardware' part of the machine is the apparatus itself, which will undertake the task it is programmed to perform. The third element is known as the 'end effector' and consists of either a tool manipulator or material handler attached to the robot arm, according to the process it must perform. Such parts may well be supplied independently of the main apparatus and may consist of a gripper of some sort, or a weld gun or spraying device. Current robot applications include material hand-ling, machine loading or unloading, spray painting or welding, machin-ing and assembly and rudimentary measurement and inspection tasks.[167] The largest 'robot populations' are located in Japan and the United States, with only a comparatively token use elsewhere in the world at this stage. In 1985, for example, it was reported that Japan had 93,000 robots in use, compared with 20,000 in the USA, 8,800 in West Germany and only 3,208 in the UK.[168]

Europe is now beginning to deploy the technology to an growing extent, and overall worldwide projections point to a five-fold increase in robot sales between 1988 and 1992.[169] Other estimates suggest that up to 150,000 robots could be operating in the USA by 1990 in an industry worth between $1 and $2 billion.[170] Installations in Europe are growing at 35% per annum.[171] The Fiat car plant at Cassino in Italy deploys 439 robots able to build different models at random.[172] British investment in robots is monitored by the British Robot Association. It reports that in 1987 Britain had 4,300 robots in use – just on third of the number deployed in West Germany and two thirds that of France and Italy. The figure reached 5000 in 1988 although this still represents a very slow rate of growth compared with other European producers.[173]

The future of these techniques, when linked to the prospects offered by artificial intelligence, point towards a revolution in the methods used

189

by companies in the design, development and manufacture of their products. The costs involved in the R&D cycle can be substantial and there may be financial consequences if any design deficiences or other mistakes need correction along the development path. For this reason there is a strong incentive to look towards the technology for ways of controlling this risk and reducing the design time and development path through to full testing and production. The solution to this requirement appears to lie in using the technology to integrate the process through-out the cycle as described. For this reason the term 'Computer Integrated Manufacturing' (CIM) is today a more accurate description of the objective than the divided concept of CAD/CAM.

With CIM, the boundaries between the use of these systems in design and manufacture are blurred, since the objective is to communicate the design information direct to the machine tool on the factory floor that manufactures the part. Movement in this direction has been impeded, however, by the fact that the separate components of these systems were not designed originally with integration in mind. These barriers are now beginning to break down as the need for communication becomes evident. Two standards that appear to be tackling the problem of machines that cannot communicate with each other in the factory environment are MAP and FMS. MAP – Manufacturing Automation Protocol – was developed by General Motors to enable computer controlled devices on the shop floor to link up, reducing the need to rewrite communications protocols before such integration could occur. FMS – Flexible Manufacturing System – is described as the building block of the factory of the future. This envisages the partitioning of robots and machine tools on the factory floor, with the scheduling of work initiated and controlled by computers supported by automated collection and delivery of parts by vehicles guided by computers.[174] These standards could also offer automated links with component suppliers on other sites providing an automated environment for linking the supply of components to the requirements of the factory floor. Thus a picture emerges of extensive use and diffusion of microelectronics technology in a range of process and production applications, linked through communication systems to generate the manufacturing data necessary to orchestrate the entire operation.[175]

In the future the links between research, design, product definition, manufacture, test and production are likely to become much more closely integrated as these techniques become more widely accepted.

Substantial research into CIM is currently underway in the United States and Japan. In the former, the National Bureau of Standards is working as a test bed in CIM techniques, particularly in the development of standards for communication between systems and interface strategies that will determine the framework for the development of CIM techniques in industry as a whole.[176]

In July 1989 the Ministry for Trade and Industry in Japan announced a 10 year programme worth Y150 billion to promote the growth of world standards in networked systems integration. There is a feeling that, despite advances in using technology in manufacturing, companies have only gone half way towards full integration. Materials requirements, data collection on the factory floor, supervisory control of robotics and production, computer aided design and process planning need to be joined within a common manufacturing control environment. IBM, has spent between $500–600 million on developing a CIM architecture (ICA) and launched 56 products under the ICA standard in October 1989.

In the UK there is a computer-aided production management project at Polytechnic South-West in London supported by the Science and Engineering Research Council to develop software tools. Other liaisons have formed between DEC and Allen Bradley, the US factory control supplier, and other similar suppliers. UK software house Hoskyns, and Oracle, US supplier of relational databases, are also involved. Manufacturers are also looking at the engineering workstation market, worth $1.83 billion in 1988 rising to $4.5 billion by 1992.[177] Electronic Data Interchange (EDI), the new standard in electronic business communication, can also be expected to enter the frame as a means of ordering and paying for supplies, contacting customers and linking retailers into a distribution network.[178]

SUMMARY In the 1980s, computers were able to perform ten million operations per second at a cost of one cent. In the 1990s, as speeds accelerate further, computer costs are expected to decrease by a factor of 100, with manufacturing costs becoming 20%-30% cheaper.[179] These powerful statistics go a long way towards explaining why the computer industry has experienced success in the 1980s with new products and new markets. Indeed, with technological advances of this magnitude it would have been hard not to develop products that the market wanted. This has certainly been the story to date so far as office automation is concerned. Whilst the 'paperless office', widely predicted as coming in the 1980s, never arrived, there are better prospects in the 1990s, as image processing generates digital paper. This will bring with it a whole cluster of new problems which the technology and society will need to address. Desk-top machines in a variety of clusters and groupings have appeared, some networked and others not, to provide an entirely new environment within which to discharge business, design and manufacturing functions. As the industry has searched for standards it can live with, so too has the user demanded that some of the increase in computer power be used to devise more user-friendly machines. The position has certainly improved as the industry begins to identify interface standards, and contribute better software, more explanatory manuals, and more specialised hardware for the job in hand.

The challenge for the user will be in finding out what is going on and applying technology efficiently within his organisation. The user will also need to educate himself to think freely about the technology and its potential and not in terms of rigid perceptions of a market gone by, dominated by mainframes and central processors in which the only role for the PC was wordprocessing or computer games. That would be foolish, for by 1992 the worldwide office automation market is expected to be reach $150 billion. Meanwhile, the faithful typewriter, mainstay and symbol of the traditional workplace for a century, is expected to drop out altogether, as numbers dwindle worldwide.[180]

NOTES

1. Harold J. Leavitt and Thomas L. Whisler, 'Management in the 1980's', *Harvard Business Review*, November–December 1958, pp. 41–8 at p. 43.
2. Stevens, op. cit., p. 185.
3. Architecture in computer terms refers to the arrangements and interconnection of the micro-processor elements with the system as a whole.
4. Arnold and Guy, op. cit., p. 19.
5. *Telex Corp., v. International Business Machines Corp.* 367 F.Supp. 258 (1973) at p. 306.
6. See chart of competition in *Computer News*, 15 October 1987, p. 13.
7. 'Hitachi Prepares Attack on IBM Mainframe Line' *Computing*, 15 March 1990, p. 2.
8. Arnold and Guy, op. cit., p. 19.
9. The 3090 replacement is a 500 Mips machine code named 'Summit'. It is uncertain whether it will appear in 1990. A final upgrade to the 3090 may

give IBM more time. This will be the 3090J with 1Gbyte memory and 4Mbyte D-Rams. Source: Nicholas Enticknap, 'The Year Ahead for IBM', *Computer Weekly*, 25 January 1990, p. 22.

10. International Data Corporation (IDC); in Clive Cookson, 'Mainframe Systems – Definitions are Changing', *Financial Times*, 24 November 1989, p. 111.

11. Nicholas Enticknap, 'Crisis Point in a Crucial Market', *Computer Weekly*, 25 January 1990, pp. 32–3.

12. Ibid., p. 32.

13. Clive Cookson, op. cit.

14. Figures by International Data Corporation.

15. Richard Sharpe, 'Power Points', *Computing* Special Report, 15 June 1989, pp. 4–5.

16. Clive Cookson, op. cit.

17. Source: Jonathan Green-Armytage, 'Just a Business Like any Other', *Computer Weekly*, 15 January 1990, pp. 24–5.

18. Augarten, *Bit by Bit – An Illustrated History of Computers*, (1984, George Allen & Unwin) p. 257–8.

19. Ibid., p. 258.

20. The 32-bit micro-processor is, of course, now to be found in the micro-computer range.

21. Slater, op. cit., p. 213.

22. Dennis Keeling, 'Straight Down the Middle' *Computer Systems Europe*, October 1989, pp. 14–16.

23. 'Demarcation Lines are Fading', *Computing* 29 March 1990, p. 14.

24. Nicholas Enticknap, 'Riding in the Middle of the Range', *Computer Weekly*, 25 January 1990, pp. 30–31.

25. Greg Wilson, 'Connecting to a Workstation in Every Home', The *Independent*, 24 April 1990, p. 33.

26. Louise Keheo, 'PC Chip that packs a Mainframe Punch', *Financial Times*, 12 April 1989, p. 17.

27. Richard Sharpe, 'IBM and DEC – Fierce Battle for the Mid-Range Ground', *Financial Times*, 26 May 988, pp. III–IV.

28. Alan Cane, 'Medium-Sized Systems' Market – A Flurry of Newcomers', *Financial Times*, 26 May 1988, p. III.

29. Nick Gill, 'Generating High-Quality Results in the Mid-Range', *Computing*, 15 February 1990, pp. 20–21; Louise Keheo, 'Minicomputer Makers face a Dilemma', *Financial Times*, 24 November 1989, pp. 2–3.

30. Dennis Keeling, op. cit., p. 14.

31. Louise Keheo, op. cit., p. 3.

32. Slater, op. cit., p. 199.

33. Roderick Oram, op. cit. The approximate market share for supercomputers in 1988 was Cray (63.4%); Fujitsu (18.1%); NEC (9.1%); Control Data (6%); and Hitachi (3.4%). Revenues have grown from $323 million in 1984 to $495m (1985); $784m (1986); $861m (1987); $967m (1988). Source: Dataquest – In Donald Mackenzie, 'The Race is on for the

Teraflop', The *Guardian*, 25 May 1989, p. 27.

34. Alan Cane, op. cit.

35. Roderick Oram, 'Big Brain Power Blows a Fuse', *Financial Times*, 21 April 1989, p. 33.

36. Alan Cane, 'The Supercomputer Sector – Entering a Traumatic Period', *Financial Times*, 24 November 1989, p. 11.

37. Floating point arithmetic was invented by George Stibitz, a mathematician at Bell Labs, in 1942. It enables machines to handle numbers that would otherwise be too large. Each floating point operation consists of large numbers of smaller calculations lending itself well to binary concepts. In Moreau, op. cit., p. 29.

38. Edwin Galea and Susan Clinnington-King, 'Supercomputer Show Sets the Scene for the Coming Decade', *Computing*, 8 February 1990, p. 9.

39. Edwin Galea, 'The Speed Kings jostle for a place in the Fast Lane', *Computing*, 16 February 1989, pp.30–33 at p. 33.

40. Donald MacKenzie, 'The Race is on for the Teraflop', The *Guardian*, 25 May 1989, p. 27.

41. For background see Phil Manchester, 'Parallel Lines', *Computing*, 21 January 1988, pp. 18–19.

42. Stevens, op. cit., p. 189.

43. James Connolly, 'The Big Band Sound', *Computer News*, 15 October 1987, pp. 13–15 at p. 13.

44. Ibid., p. 30.

45. Source: *Electronic Trend Publications*. Reported in *Computer News*, 17 March 1988, p. 1. Readers will note the different projections for the supercomputer market compared with that given earlier. This illustrates the need to define the term before drawing conclusions. Obviously, this statistic is based on a wider definition of 'supercomputer' than that referred to in the former case.

46. Edwin Galea and Susan Cunnington-King, op. cit.

47. Louise Kehoe, 'PC Chip that Packs a Mainframe Punch', *Financial Times*, 12 April 1989, p. 17.

48. Source: Dennis Longley and Michael Shain, *Macmillan Dictionary of Information Technology*, 3rd Edition, 1989, pp. 379–380.

49. Louise Kehoe, 'Unrelenting Struggle to stay in the Lead', *Financial Times*, 9 August 1989, p. 9. Among the leaders in this sector are Thinking Machines of Cambridge, Mass.; Active Memories of San Diego; and Ncube of Beaverton, Oregon.

50. Edwin Galea and Susan Clinnington-King, 'Supercomputer Show Sets the Scene for the Coming Decade', *Computing*, 8 February 1990, p. 9.

51. Philip Hunter, 'A Silver Lining in the Storms', *Computer Weekly*, 15 March 1990, p. 24.

52. Alan Cane, op. cit.

53. Edwin Galea and Susan Cunnington-King, 'New Challenge in Supercomputer War', The *Guardian*, 24 May 1990.

54. Glenis Moore, 'Superalternatives', *Computer Systems – Europe*,

September 1989, pp. 25–27 at p. 25. Comment by Michael Burwen, President of the Palo Alto Management Group.
55. Ibid.
56. Guy Kewney, 'Giant's Miniature Vision', The *Independent*, 28 May 1990, p. 15.
57. Source: Glenis Moore, 'Super Alternatives', *Computer Systems Europe*, September 1989, pp. 25–27.
58. Quoted in U.S. Congress, Office of Technology Assessment, *Critical Connections: Communications for the Future*, op. cit., p. 46. Source: *Communications Week*.
59. Slater, op. cit., pp. 265–6.
60. *Equinox*, Channel 4 TV, op. cit.
61. Comment by Lee Felsenstein, a computer designer in ibid.
62. Ibid.
63. Ibid.
64. Stevens, op. cit., p. 178.
65. MS-DOS stands for Microsoft Disk Operating System.
66. Matthew May, 'A Cheap and Easy Second Shot', *The Times*, 28 June 1990, p. 33.
67. Margaret Coffey, 'Computer Giant establishing a New Standard', *Financial Times*, May 26 1988, p. 11.
68. Guy Kewney, 'Double Blow to IBM Hope', The *Independent*, 30 April 1990.
69. Louise Kehoe, 'Minicomputer Makers Face a Dilemma', *Financial Times*, 24 November 1989, p. 11.
70. Della Bradshaw, 'A Crisis of Identity', *Financial Times*, 24 November 1989, pp. 3 and 6. Source: IDC and MIRC.
71. Guy Kewney, 'Apple's Way out of a Jam', The *Independent*, 30 April 1990, p. 18.
72. Louise Kehoe and Alan Cane, 'Big Blue Puts the Byte on Workstation Market', *Financial Times*, 8 February 1990, p. 37.
73. Della Bradshaw, op. cit.
74. Della Bradshaw, 'The Director's New Best Friend', *Financial Times*' 25 October 1989, p. 17. EIS producers include: Metapraxis; Execucom of Austin, Texas; Pilot of Boston (sold in the UK by Thorn/EMI Computer Software); Comshare of Ann Arbor, Michigan; and Planning Sciences of London.
75. Paul Abrahams, 'A Rush for Portable PCs', *Financial Times*, 24 November 1989, p. IV. Comment by Atsutoshi Nishida, Senior Manager of International Operations for Information and Telecommunications Systems at Toshiba.
76. Ibid.
77. Adrian Morant, 'Lightweight Laptops are a Boon Away From the Office', *Financial Times*, 24 November 1989, p. IV.
78. Ibid.
79. Paul Abrahams, op. cit.

80. Paul Abrahams, op. cit. Figures by UK researchers Romtec.
81. Longley and Shain, Data & Computer Security – Dictionary of Standards, Concepts and Terms 1989, p. 264.
82. Ibid., p. 241.
83. Patricia Tehan, 'Japanese Stars Rise in West' *Computing*, 6 July 1989, p. 12.
84. See 'Arbitration – IBM v. Fujitsu Ltd.', [1987–88] 5 *Computer Law and Security Report*, p. 27, and Cliff Dilloway, [1987–88] 6 *Computer Law and Security Report*, pp. 32–4.
85. *Telex Corp. v. International Business Machines Corp.*, 367 F. Supp. 258 (N.D. Okla. 1973), aff'd. in part, rev'd. in part, 510 F.2d. 894 (10th Cir.), cert dismissed, 423 U.S. 802 (1975) at pp. 363–64.
86. *Telex Corp. v. International Business Machines Corp.*, 510 F. 2d. 894 (1975) at pp. 919 and 928.
87. Cases brought by peripherals manufacturers include: *California Computer Products, Inc. v. International Business Machines Corp.*, 613 F.2d. 727 (CA-9 1979); *Memorex Corp., et al. v. International Business Machines Corp.*, 458 F.Supp. (ND Cal 1978). Litigation by leasing companies include: *Greyhound Computer Corp. Inc. v. International Business Machines Corp.*, 559 F.2d. 488 (CA-9 1977), cert. den. 434 U.S. 1040 (1978); *Transamerica Computer Co. v. International Business Machines Corp.*, 481 F.Supp. 965 (ND Cal 1979). Issues concerning software include: *Symbolic Control Inc. v. International Business Machines Corp.*, (CA-9 1980)
88. Michael Hogan, 'State of Play in the Blue's Clone Series', *Computer News*, 3 May 1988 pp. 17–20.
89. Ibid., p. 19.
90. Comment by Collier Buffington, Vice President, Western Digital. Ibid., p. 19.
91. Ibid., p. 20.
92. Ibid.
93. OJL Com (88) Final- SYN 183 Brussels, 17 March 1989.
94. Della Bradshaw, 'Ways to Ease Company Computing Burdens', *Financial Times*, 24 November 1989, p. X.
95. John Kavanagh, 'An Alternative to the Old Ways', *Computer Weekly*, 23 November 1989.
96. David Manners, 'First Round to Japan in the Chip Wars', *Computer Weekly*, 22 February 1990.
97. See Tom Foremski, 'Fighting to be Heard in Congress', *Computing*, 31 May 1990, p. 15. A group of 11 US computer companies including IBM, Hewlett Packard and Sun Microsystems have established a trade group called Computer Systems Policy Project to press their views in Congress.
98. Compaq's sales for 1989 were up 39% at $2.9 billion compared with $2.1 billion in 1988. Sales in Europe topped $1 billion for the first time. Reported by Louise Kehoe, *Financial Times*, 2 February 1990, p. 21.
99. David Martin, 'When the Going Gets Tough', *Computing*, 21 June 1990,

p. 12.

100. 'Mitsui Helps the Ailing UNISYS', *Computing*, 5 July 1990, p. 10. Mitsui has agreed to buy $150 million of UNISYS stock.

101. Louise Kehoe, 'Wang Reveals Heavy Losses and Plans to Restructure', *Financial Times*, 1 August 1989, p. 20.

102. Terry Dodsworth, 'Olivetti to Target Markets Rather Than Technology', *Financial Times*, 14 September 1989, p. 42; Also Alan Cane, 'Three Keys to Olivetti's Fight Back', *Financial Times*, 25 October 1989, p. 27.

103. Andrew Fisher, 'Surrounded by Speculation', *Financial Times*, 19 December 1989, p. IV.

104. Louise Kehoe, 'New Man to Put the Shine on Apple', *Financial Times*, 2 February 1990, p. 21. This was despite 36% international growth in 1989.

105. Alan Cane, 'Apricot to Buy ITL for £12.7 million', *Financial Times*, 19 October 1989, p. 27; 'Restructuring Costs leave Apricot Halves', *Financial Times*, 31 October 1989, p. 26.

106. Alan Cane, 'Competition Intensifies – Personal Computers', *Financial Times*, 16 September 1988.

107. Chris Batchelor, 'The Right Program is Found on the Cards', *Financial Times*, 26 June 1989, p. 15.

108. John Lombardi, 'Brave New Word – Wordstar 5.5', *PC Business World*, 29 August 1989, p. 25.

109. *PC Business World*, 20 October 1987, p. 1. Other wordprocessing packages include Multimate Adv; Wordcraft; Wordstar 2000+; Displaywrite 4; Word; New Word 2. Wordstar 1512 has been revamped and called Wordstar Express.

110. Tom Foremski, 'A Merger to Worry Microsoft', *Computing*, 19 April 1990, p. 19.

111. Slater, op. cit., p. 291.

112. John Walkenbach, 'Spreadsheet Lightning', *PC Business World*, 28 November 1989, pp. 27–30.

113. A survey of spreadsheet use among *PC Business World* readers in December 1988 showed that whereas, at the beginning of 1988, 54% of readers were using Lotus 1-2-3, this could be down to 42% by the end of 1989. Comparable figures for Excel were 1% in January 1988 and over 20% of the market by the 1989 year end. *PC Business World*, 13 December 1988, p. 1.

114. Features include: multi-dimensional and linked worksheets; data import capabilities; mouse support; extended customisation facility; character interface. Its OS/2 version also offers advanced financial modelling; data sharing; analytical tools and a graphical interface. Source: *PC Business World*, 5 May 1987, p. 1.

115. 'April Release for 1-2-3/G makes Lotus Strategy nearly Complete', *PC Business World*, 6 February 1990.

116. Tom Foremski, op. cit.

117. Rod Wyte, 'Information on Tap', *Computer Systems*, April 1988, pp. 31–3.

118. Alan Cane, 'Technology Reduces the Paper Mountains', *Financial Times*, 26 May 1988, p. IV. The term 'Executive Support System' is becoming popular, describing a workstation DSS for the top executive. The term DSS was invented in the late 1970s by Peter Keen, an information systems specialist.

119. 'A truly relational DBMS must regard its data as a set of two-dimensional tables at the logical level, no matter how it implements this scheme at the physical level. The database's structure must be defined in another table, known as the database dictionary, and it should be possible to satisfy any request by referring to the table name, an index key, and the column heading.' Nick Lees, op. cit., p. 19.

120. Nick Lees, 'Seen not Heard', *PC Business World*, 12 January 1988, pp. 18–19.

121. Ibid.

122. Jim Hackett, 'Distributed: True or False?' *Computer Systems – Europe*, April 1989, pp. 67–70 at p. 67.

123. The database product for Cincom is Supra; Cullinet – IDMS/R; ADR – Datacom/DB; and Software AG – Adabas.

124. Charles Babcock, 'Arch Enemies battle for Database Market Share', *Computer News*, 9 April 1987, pp. 24–5.

125. Comment by Shaku Atre, President of New York-based Atre Consultants. In Russell Lipton, 'Micros move in to dominate the Databases', *PC Business World*, 29 September 1987.

126. Jenny Mill, 'Embracing a Relational Future', *Computing*, 25 September 1986.

127. James Toole, 'Acrobatic Lotus add-in', *PC Business World*, 26 April 1988, pp. 32–3.

128. Karl Dallas, 'Supercalc prospers but Lotus Reigns Supreme', *Computer News*, July 9 1987, pp. 18–19.

129. Don Crabb, 'Trial by File to find the Master among Jacks of all Trades', *PC Business World*, 28 June 1988, pp. 65–72.

130. Apple Computer Corp. is suing Microsoft Inc. and Hewlett Packard alleging infringement of the Macintosh 'user interface' (*Apple v. Microsoft, et al.*, ND CA San Francisco Div., No. C-88-20149-WWS); meanwhile Xerox Corp. is suing Apple on the grounds that the Macintosh 'user interface' is improperly based on Xerox's copyrighted 'Star' and 'SmallTalk' software developed in the late 1970s (*Xerox Corp., v. Apple Computer Inc.*, ND CA, San Francisco Div., No. C-89-4428-WWS) Source: *Computer Industry Litigation Reporter*, 12 February 1990, p. 10787.

131. Sebastian Rupley, 'Mind You're On Time – Workgroup Software', *PC Business World*, 30 January 1990, pp. 23–6.

132. The new software is categorised as belonging to the 4th generation of computer languages.

133. Karl Dallas, op. cit., p. 19.

134. 'Ashton Tate Faces Bleak Future', *Computing*, 10 May 1990, p. 8.

135. Kevin Townsend, 'Graphics – A Major Influence', *Financial Times*, 16 September 1988, p. VIII.
136. Mike Farrow, 'Working More with Windows – Superbase 4', *PC Business World*, 16 January 1990, pp. 20–22.
137. Kevin Townsend, op. cit.
138. Jim Costello, 'A Friendlier Face to go on your Front End, *Computer Weekly*, 16 November 1989, pp. 26–7.
139. Harry Miller, 'Windows with no Hot-Air', *PC Business World*, 1 November 1988, p. 13.
140. Michael Guttman, 'An exciting Problem that Can't be Ignored', *PC Business World*, 4 October 1988, p. 13.
141. Louise Kehoe, 'Window of Opportunity', *Financial Times*, 24 May 1990, p. 25.
142. *Apple Computer Inc., v. Microsoft Corp., et al* (1988) ND CA San Francisco Division No. C-88-20149-WWS.
143. Jim Costello, op. cit.
144. The X Consortium that is promoting X-Windows comprises DEC, AT&T, Hewlett Packard and, with cautious approval, IBM. Users including the US Government, the European Community, Ford and Shell also belong. Source: Jim Costello, op. cit., p. 26.
145. Keith Jones, 'A Window with X Appeal', *Computer Weekly*, 22 February 1990, pp. 44–5.
146. 'The Missing Piece of a Long-Standing Puzzle', *Computing*, 25 January 1990, pp. 12–13.
147. 'Character Recognition in hand from IBM', *Computing*, 28 June 1990, p. 3.
148. Tom Foremski, 'Taking up the Pen in the Crusade for Friendly Systems', *Computing*, 5 July 1990, pp. 22–3.
149. Adrian Morant, 'How to Provide Services Around the Clock', *Financial Times*, 24 November 1989, p. VIII.
150. Desktop publishing is a method whereby documents can be prepared using a computer, page composition software and a printer for output. The objective is to offer 'wysiwyg' capacity, ie. what-you-see-is-what-you-get, so that the layout as seen on screen is actually what prints out on page.
151. Delia Bradshaw, 'Growth Forecast Scaled Down', *Financial Times*, 23 October 1989, p. 18.
152. Andrew Bluhm, 'Technology Has its Uses', *Financial Times*, 23 October 1989, p. 18.
153. Karl Dallas, 'Has Desktop Publishing lost its Way?, *Computer News*, 30 July 1987, pp. 20–23.
154. Enhanced wordprocessor packages include: Spellbinder DTP by Lexisoft, Microsoft's Word and Samna IV.
155. Steven Sonsino, 'Desktop Publishers Learn a Language', *Computer News*, 23 July 1987, pp. 14–15.
156. Delia Bradshaw, op. cit.

157. Karl Dallas, op. cit., p. 22. The Apple Mac PageMaker has faced serious competition from products such as Letraset's Ready, Set, Go3 and Heyden's Quark Express.

158. Della Bradshaw, op. cit.

159. Andrew Bluhm, op. cit.

160. Source: US market research organisation Dataquest.

161. Source: The UK technical consultancy, the Technology Partnership.

162. A 'light pen' is a pen-shaped object wired to a computer capable of locating points on a screen. A 'mouse' is a small hand-held device that when traced on an adjacent surface has the ability to move a pointer around on the screen.

163. *Computerized Manufacturing Automation: Employment, Education and the Workplace* (1984, Washington, D.C.: U.S. Congress Office of Technology Assessment, OTA-CIT-235) p. 43.

164. Ibid., p. 44.

165. Richard Sarson, 'New Life for an Old Pioneer', *Computing*, 17 July 1986, p. 21.

166. Ibid.

167. Terry Ernest-Jones, 'Art Transplants', *Computer Weekly*, 30 Novembeer 1989, p. 30.

168. Della Bradshaw, 'A Step Nearer the Design Miracle', *Financial Times*, 19 September 1989, p. 17.

169. Ibid.

170. Jeffrey Gile, 'Quick on the Draw – The Best CAD', *PC Business World*, 29 August 1989, pp. 18–21.

171. *Computerized Manufacturing Automation*, op. cit., p. 47.

172. Lynton McLain, 'Getting it Right the First Time', *Financial Times*, 24 November 1989, p. 22.

173. Alan Cane, 'Keeping Tabs on Worldwide Production', *Financial Times*, 16 August 1989, p. 25.

174. David Fishlock, 'Confining the Failures to the Computer', *Financial Times*, 13 June 1989, p. 17.

175. Definition coined by the RIA (a Trade Association of robot manufacturers, consultants, and users, formerly the Robot Institute of America). In *Computerized Manufacturing Automation*, op. cit., p. 48.

176. Ibid., p. 50.

177. Ibid., p. 54. Source: Tech Tran Corp., *Industrial Robots: A Summary and Forecast*, 1983.

178. *Robots out of Wonderland – How to Use Robots in the Age of CIM* (1987) p. 16.

179. Computerized Manufacturing Automation, op. cit., p. 53. Source: Tech Tran Corp., *Industrial Robots: A Summary and Forecast*, 1983.

180. Ibid., p. 296.

181. Nick Garnett and John Dwyer, 'The Factory of the Future is at Hand', *Financial Times*, 15 August 1989, p. 14.

182. John Griffiths, 'Vision of Cars Produced Almost Entirely by Robots',

Financial Times, 13 September 1989, p. XIX.

183. Richard Sarson, 'Learn to Love the Robot', *The Times*, 1 June 1989, p. 32.

184. Andrew Lawrence, 'A Shopfloor Revolution – But not Yet', *Computing*, 24 September 1987, pp. 24–5.

185. *Government Policies and the Diffusion of Microelectronics*, OECD, 1989, p. 12.

186. *Computerized Manufacturing Automation*, op. cit., p. 82.

187. John Dwyer, 'Production Controls Improved', *Financial Times*, 24 November 1989, pp. IX–X.

188. Clive Cookson, 'A Good Fit for the Factory Floor', *Financial Times*, 6 June 1990. p. 15.

189. OTA Report 1990, op. cit., p. 46. Source: CMP Publications Inc.

190. Source: Clementson/Nu Markets and Wharton Information Systems.

CHAPTER 5

Computer software – the emerging industry

THE RISE OF THE SOFTWARE SECTOR

Up to now discussion has focussed upon the high rate of development in computer hardware, the products and applications that came out of this effort and the markets which have emerged. But what of the software sector itself? Just as productivity gains have been made in computer performance by hardware evolution so too are substantial gains to be had with software. It is easy to forget that the hype about hardware achievements, encapsulated in the advancement of the micro-processor, would count for nothing without the software to drive it. Whereas programming the computer used to be an arcane task attracting little of the limelight, the position today has been reversed. The centre of gravity has moved a stage further on from the pre-occupation with extending raw computer power towards improving ways of advancing its exploitation. This has been achieved through the development of programming languages, combined with advances in programming techniques. The industry has glimpsed, somewhat distantly at present, that the tools it has created could become self-sustaining with the advent of artificial intelligence. So what are the trends in relation to the software sector, and what progress has been made in developing standards within the industry? What are the dynamics of the industry in terms of how competition develops and what does artificial intelligence research promise in the decade ahead?

THE VALUE OF THE INDUSTRY   Figures are of course hard to quantify, but the best estimate of the software component of the total data processing industry market is that, in 1988, it represented expenditure of $102 billion within an overall world market of $330 billion (of which $172 billion represents hardware and $56 billion the rest). If these figures are correct the world software market has increased in value very quickly for in 1985 the market at supplier level was valued at about $30 billion with US based suppliers and their foreign subsidiaries accounting for over 71% of worldwide revenues.[1] Western Europe has also developed a significant interest in software with domestic revenues of nearly $10 billion in 1985 compared with $2.8 billion in Japan.[2] European software markets were high in the first half of 1989 with record sales for US companies. Growth in European sales increased by more than 36% during the period compared with only 11% in the United States.[3] In Europe the combined turnover of the top ten computing services companies was £3.1 billion, with the largest- CAP Gemini Sogeti (CGS) – earning revenues approaching US$1 billion. This means that it is strong enough to challenge the large US computing service/software companies such as Computer Associates and Electronic Data Systems (EDS – a subsidiary of General Motors).[4] Japan has not, traditionally, been strong in software development, but both Fujitsu and Hitachi are now competing with development of IBM compatible operating systems that in years to come could establish a market share in the West as part of their drive to enter the compatible hardware sector. 1987 sales of the top ten software companies in Japan totalled $3.31 billion, employing just under 25,000 staff.[5] Worldwide, there is every prospect of growth in the software market continuing at 20% per annum, well up compared with the predicted average 12% annual growth rate in hardware and 6% in telecommunications for the ten years 1985–95.

Growth estimates for marketed production of software and services in 1990 is $175 billion, rising to $400 billion by 1995. Comparative figures for hardware, including computers, office automation and private telecommunications equipment are $380 and $730 billion respectively. (Hardware includes: 'electronics, all kinds of computers, office automation (including text- and data-processing machines) and private telecommunication equipment (including telex, telefax, modems, etc.); these figures also include user expenditure associated with the introduction of IT'. Software and services include: 'value-added networks and services and maintenance'. Telecommunications 'refers to switching and transmission equipment owned and operated by telecommunication administrations and Recognised Private Operating Agencies'.)[6] One survey predicts, somewhat optimistically perhaps, that by 1993, packaged software and professional services will outstrip all other expenditure on systems hardware.[7]

According to one software developer this is a natural consequence of the growing maturity of the hardware market, which will pressurise the industry to look for the maximum return on its hardware investment.[8] Currently, hardware and salary costs dominate data-processing budget expenditure, with software just behind.

In the UK, the computing services industry achieved sales of just under £3 billion in 1989 at £2.95 billion. The major share came from sales of software at £1.24 billion. Bureau services and other professional services accounted for £1.34 billion and hardware £365 million. This amounted to a rise of 23% for software and 63% in the case of hardware over the 1988 figures. This has continued into 1990 with software up by 17% at £358 million and hardware up 42% at £127 million in the first quarter of the year.[9] Britain's only mainframe producer, ICL, owned by STC, had profits of £145 million in 1989.[10] The company is currently the subject of takeover talks with the Japanese producer Fujitsu who also own Amdahl Corporation in the United States.

THE MIGRATION FROM HARDWARE TO SOFTWARE   The shift in the balance of power from hardware to software is evident from the UK figures just set out, and reflects the importance of software in the development of any new computer application. In the past, as computer performance levels developed, the key objective of the industry was to accumulate users. In the early days this was confined to a relatively small market of large corporate users as machines were expensive and difficult to maintain, requiring a lot of space and offering limited processing capability. The market changed significantly when the PC was developed, since this enlarged market potential introducing computers to the small business user and to the individual. As perceptions changed and computers became much more widely used and accepted,[11] the demand to do more with the technology grew. Reference has already been made to the achievements of the software pioneers who, in the early years of the history of the modern digital computer, looked for ways of improving communication with the machine itself. The first generation of software, used in the computing environment of ENIAC, comprised programs written entirely in machine code and entered by physical re-ordering of the switches in the hardware.[12] Stored-program computers of the kind envisaged by Turing and von Neumann replaced these early methods. The second generation referred to programs made up of mnemonic codes and symbolic addressing (for defining locations in memory), collectively known as assembly language where the code proved a little more intelligible than the 1s and 0s of machine language. This covered the period from the late 1950s to the mid 1960s.

The third generation (3GLs) comprised the high-level programming languages which were introduced to overcome the very 'hit and miss' performance levels of the earlier crude forms of programming in the first two generations. These emerged in the 1960s in particular, at a time when people doubted the possibility that languages could be produced that were free of the constraints of assembly language and capable of automatic machine translation for execution of the program. Up to that point programmers were used to having to produce code closely formatted to the structure of the machine they were using. The first of the third generation were described as the evolved languages, since they were gradually built up over time in a haphazard manner extending their scope as particular requirements were met. FORTRAN, for scientific applications, was built up in this way.[13] Once the possibility became reality other languages evolved, but this time in a more structured form. COBOL – for management applications, and ALGOL and PL/I – multi-purpose languages, were examples of this more conceptual approach. The same could be said for RPG and BASIC for simple applications, and for LISP – where the language contained a notation very close to that of mathematics. LISP together with APL – designed for complex scientific and engineering tasks, were languages where a formal specification of the objective was set out in development.[14]

Later 3GLs emerged that were structured languages designed as such to reduce complexity, ease modification and simplify debugging. Among these was PASCAL, named after the physicist, mathematian and philosopher Blaise Pascal, which originated from the Federal Institute of Technology in Zurich in 1970.[15] The language has been popular in teaching as it demands the use of good programming practices. Another was ADA produced by the US Department of Defense in the late 1970s used in computer control and communication systems. It was particularly suited for long-term use where modification and maintenance was a concern.[16] A third language was C, developed at Bell Laboratories in 1972. The programming language of C has closer affinity with assembly language and operates faster than compiled languages like PASCAL. It is widely used today in its later versions.[17]

Essentially these high level languages represented the first step in the automation of programming. They enabled the user to produce code in terms close to normal English which could be translated into machine code

206

by 'translator' programs devised for particular languages and hardware. 3GLs marked the starting point for the programming industry, which up to that time was fragmented, machine tied and task specific. High level languages created opportunities for a wide range of applications software, which steadily increased as participation developed. For many individuals it was an attractive industry to enter, requiring little capital investment in order to get started. 3GLs are still widely used. It has been estimated, for example, that some 70–77 billion lines of COBOL have been written up to now, much of which will remain in use well into the 1990s, more than 30 years after the development of the language.[18] Indeed it may well extend into the 21st century as the language is adapted to new approaches such as object-oriented programming.[19] Another estimate puts the value of COBOL programs at $100 billion by 1982.[20] In 1988 it was suggested that almost 70% of UK data-processing installations operated COBOL as the dominant language. Though that figure is more likely to be closer to 50% today, the suggestion is not surprising, since 80% of business applications in use in 1982 were written in the language.[21] At that time, according to a US survey, more than 65,000 people were employed by the US Government specifically to program in COBOL.[22]

By the early 1980s it was clear that a huge accumulation of software had built up, valued at $500 billion. This software had been written in the early high-level languages and was based on the computer architecture of the 1960s and 1970s. The main reason for this was that, until the 1980s, the configuration of computer systems did not alter substantially, being based on the concept of a central system through which all computing activity took place. The core consisted of a central computer, either a mainframe or a mini, supported by systems software developed from this earlier period. Maintenance and sometimes modification of the software might prove necessary, but once it was established for the task in hand and any program errors were eradicated, there was little incentive to change if the system worked tolerably well. Another factor detracting from change in this respect, were the policies of the computer manufacturers. These tended to stabilise architectures, operating systems and the stock of compiler programs in favour of consolidating the customer's software usage, while encouraging him to migrate within successive generations of hardware from the same supplier.[23] This created a reasonably stable environment for the software industry as the portability of software between a single manufacturer's hardware enhanced the longevity of the product. IBM pursued this policy with the launch of the third generation of IBM machines, embodied in the System 360 product line announced in 1964 and first sold in 1965.[24] During this period there were limited opportunities for small-scale independent software producers helping customers to produce their own applications software. These services enlarged in the 1960s as user needs became more specialised.[25]

Another factor that influenced the early stages of the software sector of the data-processing industry was the system whereby customers purchased hardware and software 'bundled together' as a single package[26] and invoiced without separate entry. Applications software would be handled by supplying it as part of a turnkey contract in which the complete system would be delivered. This was encouraged by the main hardware suppliers, led by IBM, who could see the advantages of tying a customer into their set of in-house products. Following an anti-trust complaint launched in 1969 against IBM by the United States Department of Justice,[27] this practice came to an end with the result that the independent software industry found a firm base upon which to develop. Rapid growth has taken place since the early 1970s. The OECD reports that independent suppliers have grown strongly since that time in most of the member countries of the organisation. The services offered have shifted gradually away from time-sharing[28] into consultancy and engineering, turnkey systems, custom software design and implementation and software packages. Since the convergence of telecommunications with computing such companies have moved into network services as well.[29] Having been responsible, by these measures, for the gestation of an independent market for software, computer manufacturers have inevitably retained an interest in the market, particularly on the systems software side. In 1988 IBM derived $7.9 billion from sales of software, which increased to $8.4 billion in 1989. Whereas in 1985 software accounted for only 7% of the company's turnover, this had increased to over 13% by the end of the decade.[30]

THE SOFTWARE INDUSTRY TODAY

THE PRODUCTS AND THE MARKET   A reasonable view of the software industry today is that it is slowly maturing from the turmoil of its early years. The industry is now just 30 years of age. Within that time it has matured against a background of extremely rapid advances in hardware performance and the growth of an eager market for the technology and its many potential applications. The period has also experienced the convergence of computing with telecommunications, providing the user with a range of choices as to the configuration of his data processing and communications needs. Thousands of small software and software-related start-up companies have come and gone since then, and a few have grown very rapidly into substantial forces within the market. Building up such a company to a reasonable size has always involved intense competition with success dependent upon making the right choices about which market niche to aim for, the type of service to provide and the particular range and type of hardware to link with the product. Categorising software for the market usually draws a distinction between its function and method of supply. In terms of function the basic distinction is between systems and applications programs. The picture is changing, however, since new categories of software are developing to support the changing environment of automation, integration and network communications. As far as supply of applications software is concerned, distinctions turn on whether the software comes in packaged or standardised form, is customised to meet a single customer's requirement or is offered as part of a turnkey system of hardware and software comprising a complete system for the customer.[31]

The second category, that of systems software, is important to the fixing of standards by the computer industry for all ranges of machine. Many crucial decisions are taken by developers and users of computer products based on which system or systems predominate. Software houses writing applications software must decide which operating systems to write for and what level of computer to target. The collective choice of the software houses, the purchasing decisions of the market or the strength of the big players such as IBM, will determine whether an operating system is to become the standard for that particular sector. At a functional level, systems software is a vital component of the computer, comprising the combination of programs necessary to exploit the machine and its peripherals to the fullest extent.

The operating system takes precedence over other software since it provides the user with the basic facilities he needs to operate the computer. These include control of the interaction between the central processor, peripheral memories and user interfaces, together with the provision of a stable environment for applications software to exploit the machine's resources. In addition, compilers and interpreters must be added to enable programs written in one of the high-level languages such as COBOL or BASIC to be read and performed by the computer. A variety of other aids and supports are also likely to feature. These vary according to requirements but include diagnostics aids for detecting faults, as well as utility programs and debugging aids which are used for general housekeeping tasks such as copying files from one medium to another and for program development testing.[32] Colour graphics for word-processing or file management are also available, among many further features.

Up to and including the third generation languages (3GLs) no one had thought of a way of producing a language for everyone to use, professional and non-professional programmer alike. What was needed was a language that concentrated not on the method by which a programmming objective might be achieved but on what the objective was in terms of the desired end result. The outcome were products defined as fourth generation computer languages (4GLs). The first to appear was RAMIS in 1969 followed, in the 1970s, by FOCUS and NOMAD and RAMIS II shortly thereafter. Described at the time as non-procedural software, it was only in the 1980s that the term 4GL appeared to mark the break with the previous generation. During this period many so-called '4GLs' entered the market in a variety of specifications and for a wide range of purposes. Although the concept is reasonably well understood, many products with dubious credentials have been presented under the 4GL banner. Although responsible, to an extent, for introducing 'end-user programming', the benefits of 4GLs have not escaped the professional either. Estimates suggest that at the end of 1989, 45% of all applications software under development in the UK were using a 4GL language.[33] Claims have commonly been made that 4GL's have achieved productivity gains of up to ten fold compared with COBOL and other 3GL counterparts.[34] While the traditional role of the programmer has not changed fundamentally, 4 GLs will continue to be used extensively in software engineering, expert systems, and artificial intelligence research. They will also play a role in integrating between systems by developing settled codes consistent with the emerging standards.

COMPETITION FOR OPERATING SYSTEM SUPREMACY Until distributed computing broke the established arrangements of centralised facilities, common in the 1960s and 1970s, most of the mainframe and minicomputer manufacturers maintained their own proprietary operating systems. These included Prime, Data General, Burroughs and Sperry (now Unisys), HewlettPackard, Wang, Honeywell (now Bull), and IBM.[35] Operating systems owned and operated by a single computer manufacturer are still to be found , but the picture is changing in favour of systems that are more portable enabling different makes of computer to communicate and interact with each other without major difficulty. Given the volatile state of the stock market, in which corporate takeovers and mergers are common, there is increasing pressure from users for the introduction of standards that will enable systems to work together, take each others' data and software, and integrate activities with a minimum of reorganisation.

However, although computer manufacturers like to market the idea that the 'proprietary migration path' from one machine to a larger one is the least troublesome method of ugrading one's computer operations, it can involve unnecessary expense and effort. Taking IBM as an example, the path might be from an IBM PC operating PC DOS, to a network of IBM PCs, then to an IBM mini AS/400 running the OS400 operating system. From there the user would migrate to an IBM 4321 mainframe running on IBM's VM operating system and finally to the IBM 3090 mainframe operating on MVS. One IBM software supplier has commented that such a migration path would involve the rewriting of software and the conversion of files. Moreover new screens, peripherals and perhaps cabling would be required and staff might need re-training.[36] In contrast, with common standards representing an 'open systems solution', a user might 'begin with a Compaq 386 micro, upgrade to a Motorola 8800, then a Sequent Symmetry, and finally to an Amdahl 5890 mainframe'.[37] In this example the only requirement would be to upgrade the software for the larger machine, as all run the 'UNIX' operating system and Uniplex office automation software.

The Creation of UNIX The ability of computers to communicate with those of other manufacturers is the key to much of what users have been demanding for the past decade, since the advent of the PC and subsequently of the networked workstation, mini or mainframe. There are two pre-requisites if this objective is to be met: first, the need for a portable operating system able to function across different models and levels of performance; and second, the existence of a common communications standard that all manufacturers can use to transmit files, data, messages and software between computers. In the past the operating systems developed by IBM or licensed to the company, have tended to create a *de facto* standard which the plug-compatible industry has adopted. Today, however, a greater degree of democracy has crept into the industry as it begins to make collective decisions about its future policy regarding standards for 'open systems'.

The overwhelming evidence is that UNIX is destined to become the standard to which all manufacturers must comply in the future if they are to sell their machines. UNIX is an operating system for both small- and medium-sized computers that emanated from AT&T's Bell Laboratories in the mid-1970s. Today it is possible to run UNIX on anything from a Cray supercomputer to a micro. It was devised by two researchers, Dennis Ritchie and Kenneth Thompson, and grew out of an earlier project to look at ways of enabling a number of users to share time on a mainframe computer simultaneously. They were trying to find solutions to the drawbacks of traditional arrangements whereby a user would punch his instructions onto cards, deliver it to the computer centre and come back later on to get the results. In the words of Dennis Ritchie:

> What we wanted to preserve was not just a good environment in which to do programming, but a system around which a fellowship could form. We knew from experience that the essence of communal computing, as supplied by remote-access, time-shared machines, is not just to type programs into a terminal instead of a keypunch, but to encourage close communication. . . . We had become used to interactive environments where you could actually type things on the machine and get instant responses. It is just more satisfying to work that way. This is as opposed to taking our deck of cards and handing it over a counter, and coming back in an hour, and getting a big pile of listings.[38]

The result was UNIX, which proved successful because of its success in realising user needs for a portable, multi-user system. The authors had also chosen to develop the operating system on the DEC 'PDP' computer range which was a popular machine in the 1970s because it was reliable, compact and inexpensive. When users could not satisfy their needs with DEC software they would turn to UNIX as an alternative.[39] The popularity of UNIX grew steadily,but AT&T did not set out to market the product aggressively, so allowing time for improvements to be made to the original design of the system. One such improvement was the development of a high level language called 'C', which Richie and Thompson wrote specifically in order to re-write UNIX, replacing the assembly language version of the original UNIX.[40] Having identified those parts of the system that were specific to the PDP 11 machine, the authors were able to re-write them in a form that was independent of particular models of computer. The coding of UNIX in assembly language made it difficult to transport the system to other machines. 'C', however, overcame that problem, providing a powerful and versatile tool for programmers. It was much easier to use than assembly language, with its combination of high- and low-level terminology, efficient use of instructions and modern design.

The central kernel of UNIX was written in only 8000 lines of code of which only 10% were retained in assembly language. It also contained more than 200 programmed commands and proved less rigid than other systems in permitting combinations of commands to be strung together.[41] The power of UNIX has also transferred to the applications it supports. One estimate put forward suggests that a program written in 10–1000 lines of 3GL code might, with UNIX , be operable with less than 10 instructions. The success of UNIX has promoted the development of C itself, which became popular as a 'systems programming' language for professionals seeking portability and compact results. Subsequent versions of C, in particular C++ are being heralded as the most significant recent event in the programming environment, allowing the maximum re-use of code in program development as well as ease of code maintenance.[42] (C++ has been described as one of the first 'Object-Oriented' languages that are discussed later.)

UNIX Competition   The C version of UNIX was completed in 1977 and subsequently all the main computer manufacturers produced versions of their own. By 1989 AT&T estimated that between 1.2 and 1.3 million user licences had been issued, with an expected growth in new licences of 60% per annum.[43] It is expected that the global expenditure on UNIX-based computer systems will grow from 6% in 1986 to 21% by 1991 and 30% by 1993.[44] Initially UNIX was strong in the academic market with approximately 80% of universities with computer science departments holders, operating UNIX as early as 1984. Since then it has spread to the workstation and small business systems market, and since 1988–89 it has begun to make a strong showing among larger equipment purchasers including McDonalds, Burger King and Federal Express, the latter with operations in more than 100 countries. UNIX is now a viable alternative to IBM's OS/400 and DEC's VAX operating systems in the mid-range of computers and is expected to achieve an almost equal market share of the operating system market by 1991. At that point UNIX will have 22%; IBM's 370 system 24%; MS DOS and OS/2 23%: VAX VMS 6% and others the rest.

Compared with the 1988 figures, this represents a fall of 2% for IBM 370; an increase of 5% for MS-DOS with OS/2 and a 16% increase for UNIX. Most significant of all, though, is the gravitation to UNIX from other systems. In the three year period to 1991 the UNIX migration is expected to rise from 23% to 41%.[45]

UNIX will also compete against the proprietary systems of the mainframe producers – an inevitable fact following IBM's decision to support UNIX with its own version called 'AIX'.[46] IBM plan that AIX will ultimately be available across the majority of its range of computers. AIX has now been implemented on its 6150 workstation, PS/2 PC range and subsequently on IBM's System 370, from the 9370 up to its largest mainframe, the IBM 3090.[47] The decision to introduce AIX and to commit itself to UNIX was taken by IBM in the knowledge that proprietary systems were losing market share at a significant rate. Projections show that by 1993 the IBM share of the mainframe operating system market will have fallen from 24% to 19%, and down to 4% in the case of its systems for minis. Users can today begin with a PC based on the Intel 80286 micro-processor and move up to a mainframe as big as an Amdahl supercomputer remaining in UNIX throughout. Software migration aids are now available too which help with the transfer from single- to multi-user systems. For example, Microsoft, who originally developed MS-DOS, the successor to CP/M, as the *de facto* industry standard for PCs, have developed Xenix- a popular UNIX-based operating system, developed for the IBM AT in 1985.[48] Xenix attracts MS-DOS users wanting to move to a multi-user system. SCO, one of the main suppliers of Xenix in the United States, produced SCO-Xenix in 1986, which enables users to operate Xenix beside MS-DOS in the same computer, enabling users to transfer to the UNIX standard at their own pace.[49] Other suppliers too have developed tools designed to connect PCs with UNIX-based machines in a network where files can be exchanged.[50] The big question, however, is whether IBM will provide a cross-compiler to bridge across from the AIX-UNIX family to its proprietary Systems Application Architecture via its mid-range operating system OS 400. It seems only a matter of time before this facility is provided.

The world's third most popular operating system behind MS-DOS and UNIX is 'PICK'. Between 1983 and 1988 it grew annually at a compound rate of 58.6%, marginally better than UNIX at 57.9%. Designed by Richard Pick it is a virtual-memory multi-user operating system that is particularly relevant for business applications and information processing.[51] The operating system is sold through about 3500 systems houses worldwide and claims a \$2 billion share of the market.[52] Pick was developed for transaction processing in which the user operates from a remote terminal, frequently over a communication link. As such it is better suited for this environment than its two competitors. An advanced version of PICK appeared in 1990,[53] together with a 'seamless interface' to UNIX for the AT&T 5x, IBM AIX and SCO Xenix versions. This will allow both operating systems to run simultaneously, supporting open systems concepts and UNIX strengths in scientific and process control applications, with the high performance levels of transaction processing offered by PICK.[54] Another proprietary operating system is the Unisys owned CTOS, acquired by Burroughs prior to the merger with Sperry-Rand from Convergent Technology. CTOS workstations are the third most popular behind IBM PCs and Apple Macintosh machines. However, whether a fourth operating system can survive in the longterm in this competitive sector of the market remains to be seen.[55] Apple Computers are also working on a new version of its operating system – System 7.0 to be released in late 1990.[56]

PROPRIETARY SYSTEMS OR UNIX: WHICH WAY FOR 'BIG BLUE'? The question of proprietary or open systems is one of the core issues on IBM's mind as it develops its future product strategy. Up to now it has pursued a largely sales-driven approach, aimed at fitting the customer to the product. Regis Mckenna, the man behind the marketing of the first Apple PC, which established Apple Computer Corporation in the late 1970s, believes the position is changing in favour of a market-driven approach in which the product is selected to fit the customer's strategy. Whereas, historically, IBM dominated the mainframe market and customers moved between products, upgrading as necessary, the emphasis today on the development of standards points strongly towards the linking of systems from a range of manufacturers. With UNIX at the centre of all the major advances in supercomputers, parallel processing, networking and graphical user interfaces, as well as the RISC chip, new companies have been encouraged to enter the market selling systems and software that are strongly competitive with the products of IBM. Customers can have more confidence in a smaller manufacturer than they did before, since adherence to the developing industry standards gives the customer the confidence to 'shop around', knowing that if a particular supplier fails, he can reorganise his acquisition policy without the potentially catastrophic results that could face the user in the days before the commitment to compatibility was very strong.

IBM and SAA – Systems Application Architecture A good illustration of the dilemma facing IBM in relation to its future policy on product development concerns its response to UNIX. Whilst embracing the reality of the industry move towards UNIX, IBM has not abandoned its comparable OS/2 proprietary operating system, developed jointly with Microsoft, or its Systems Application Architecture (SAA), announced in the spring of 1987. OS/2 (Operating System 2) is a multi-tasking operating system that provides IBM with the alternative to its AIX 'bridge' to UNIX. It is aimed at capitalising on the higher memory capacities and performance levels of the PS/2 range of personal computers, offering an upgrade path for the 20 million DOS-operating system users, who might be looking to improve on the 640K limitation on main memory. In contrast to DOS, OS/2 offers 16Mb of main memory, which will be necessary for the multi-tasking characteristics of the system. This will allow several applications to be run simultaneously, compared with the single job capability of DOS. A more powerful operating system is also required to cope with some of the new applications coming along in the automated office and factory environment of the future, where integration of tasks and of access to systems and data within networks will be required.

IBM's SAA is closely linked to OS/2, providing in IBM's words: 'a common framework for developing and using the same applications programs across the broad range of IBM systems, from personal systems (PS/2) to mainframes'. However, its critics argue that the concept has yet to become a technical reality, as a hardware-independent applications environment would have to overcome the immense difficulties of interfacing with the four IBM SAA-targeted operating systems VM, MVS, 3X and OS/2 – in order to represent a single enterprise-wide software architecture.[57] If the architecture did succeed, however, it would be tempting to the software companies as they could market almost the same version of an application throughout the IBM customer base. This would be very attractive to the software producers, which is of course precisely what the 'open systems' movement is trying to achieve right across the vendor community, not only vertically within a single manufacturer's range of machines.[58]

Despite the statements of intent from IBM, that the company would shortly be introducing SAA, bringing to its customers a common unified architecture with portability across the hardware range, the realisation of this objective is still to be achieved. Evidence of the problems that IBM are facing has come with the delayed release of the first SAA application of new office software, designed to capture the 'electronic office' systems

216

market in competition with DEC and Apple. The software, called 'Office-Vision Version 2.0', an upgrade of version 1.0, was first announced in February 1990. However, it will not be ready until 1991. The application has taken more than two years to develop and has cost millions of dollars to build. In a three-year program IBM intend to offer it on their full range of machines from PS/2 workstations, to mid-range AS/400 computers and finally on to its mainframes running on MVS and VM operating systems.[59] Version 1 provides an incoming mail service, address book, correspondence processor and file service, and Version 2.0 is intended to incorporate a number of enhancements and optional products including facilities to transfer mail to a colleague during the user's absence, a calendar, with security features enabling a colleague's diary to be inspected by an authorised person, and optional contextual search facilities enabling documents to be retrieved by keyword identification within the text. Further releases, say IBM, will provide business project planning facilities and improved statistical and forecasting features.[60]

The problem for IBM, however, is the sheer magnitude of the task it has set itself. Full implementation of SAA requires IBM to provide co-operative processing, common user and programming interfaces, and integrated software development tools for faster growth, across its whole range of hardware. More than three years into the project, Officevision is the only application nearing completion. Anxieties about the strategy have led users to demand a much clearer definition of SAA and of the timing for releases. Users complain that they still do not know exactly how SAA will affect them on a day-to-day basis. The strategy has led to competition too, for other companies have started to announce their own 'unifying' computer architectures, albeit of a lower order of complexity compared with IBM's SAA. Competing software houses have also jumped in with products designed to fill some of the applications gaps produced by IBM's slow delivery. Software AG, for example, has developed 'Predict', a computer-assisted software engineering tool, as an alternative to IBM's 'AD/Cycle' product definition for SAA compatible software engineering.[61] The latter is central to IBM's strategy for SAA, for it defines a series of software development tools designed to help the user operate effectively within SAA and to meet his corporate objectives applying the technology.

In an attempt to influence software development, IBM has invested about $500 million in approximately 40 software companies over the past two years. The figure could go higher, to something approaching $1 billion. One such company is Knowledge Ware, in which 10% of the share capital was purchased by IBM in August 1989 for $10.5 million.[62] IBM hope that by taking minority stakes in strategic companies they will be in a position to influence and support the development of the right products. Knowledge Ware is central to IBM's plans to develop a 'repositary' – an industry standard common interface for Case tools and the key aspect of AD/Cycle, being the data dictionary designed to feed the code generator and thereby produce code automatically.[63] The repositary is due for release in the latter part of 1990.[64]

Other 'Standards' Battles Another battle is being fought between IBM and the rest of the industry over the 'bus' standard for the next generation of personal computers. The 'bus' in data communications is the common group of hardware lines used to transmit information between digitally-based devices and components, such as disk drives and internal memory.[65] The new generation will operate at twice the capacity of PCs currently in use, enabling 32 bits of data to flow to and from the central processor per cycle, instead of the standard 16 bits common today. IBM has introduced a proprietary bus architecture – Micro Channel (MCA) for its PS/2 range of PCs which it would like to develop as the standard. It seems, however, that IBM's competitors are settling for an alternative, 'Extended Industry Standard Architecture' (EISA), using state-of-the-art microprocessors such as Intel's 386 and 486 chips.

The EISA initiative began in September 1988 when nine suppliers got together to standardise on a 32-bit bus architecture. EISA provides a faster response to high performance applications, including direct memory access for multi-user systems or servers operating via UNIX.[66] British Aerospace, for example, has adopted an EISA-based Compaq Systempro running Novell Netware 386 and supporting more than 40 PCs. Although both the EISA and MCA standards are equally good, technically the difference is that EISA is in the hands of several suppliers whereas MCA is proprietary to IBM.[67] Intel, is the world's leading microprocessor producer for PCs, and will now manufacture chip sets for both EISA and MCA. The company has reported that more than 20 PC producers are now designing machines that incorporate the EISA standard, including Compaq, Zenith Data Systems, Olivetti, Tandy, Hewlett-Packard, AST Research, NEC and Epson America,[68] whereas only IBM is a volume producer of MCA-compatible PCs.[69] At present, IBM has 90% of the market, with Apricot taking almost all of the remainder.[70] Nevertheless, approximately

218

one dozen suppliers have announced MCA-compatible machines, including Olivetti. It may take between three and five years before it is clear whether one or both standards have survived.

The strength of IBM's influence within the industry may become more apparent when it is clear how well SAA is doing. Its initial impact has clearly not inspired customers, who are waiting to see what materialises. Much depends on the software products coming forward within its umbrella and how competitive OS/2 is in the market, compared with the alternative UNIX-based upgrade, for DOS users in the Xenix VP/ix product and in the other UNIX-based derivatives for larger systems users. Some comparisons of the two systems have shown that UNIX can be faster than OS/2 in performance,[71] although OS/2 is recognised as being a major improvement over DOS. The real test will come in the months ahead as the open systems movement begins the attempt to turn objectives into reality, reflected the movement's development and IBM's reaction to it.

In one sense SAA, with its emphasis on building a consistent environment within which users can migrate, accords with the open systems approach, especially as it could theoretically support AIX with a pathway to UNIX. The drawback, however, lies in how far IBM might be prepared to allow SAA to develop as an open, rather than proprietary standard, and whether they will continue to sell AIX as only of interest to technical computer users, rather than as a general purpose operating system, as X-Open intends for UNIX.[72] Certainly, if IBM is serious about the latter it needs to develop AIX more quickly in order to catch up with AT&T's UNIX System V release 4, which has arguably been a couple of versions ahead.[73] However, IBM wants to become the most comprehensive supplier in the worldwide telecommmunications field and for that reason it seems unlikely that it will accept a non-IBM standard without a fight. Instead it is much more likely that IBM wants SAA standards to spread, whilst providing interconnection links through AIX to the UNIX-based community.[74]

Despite IBM's public commitment to standards, and the publicised difficulties IBM is having with SAA, the combination of OS/2 and SAA perpetuate. At least, this is the position for the time being, with the company telling its customers that they can achieve all their requirements within the IBM environment.[75] In sharp contrast, companies like Data General are putting all their effort into open systems having lost ground in the mini-computer market in recent years. The company plans to link all its machines, from the 17 Mips single-CPU workstation to the 40 Mips multiprocessor computer, to UNIX and to the 88/Open BCS. The company believes that sales of computers compatible with these standards will sell up to four times faster than the proprietary systems of IBM and DEC. Only time will determine whether the substantial installed base of the latter will diminish significantly as a result of the movement for compatability in hardware and software that the open systems movement is seeking.[76]

THE PRESSURE FOR INDUSTRY STANDARDS

The Rival Camps   The question to be decided now is whether the computer industry either wants or can be persuaded to agree on a common version of UNIX that all manufacturers can support. Until late 1989 there appeared to be two main contenders: AT&T's System V and IBM's AIX. The competition between the two versions intensified in 1988 when AT&T announced that it was collaborating with Sun Microsystems, the fast growing US manufacturer of workstations, to develop a definitive standard. This move intensified the rift between AT&T and the rest of the industry over UNIX that had begun when the former charged formidable licence fees to potential customers wishing to use the operating system. This encouraged the other manufacturers to develop alternative, largely incompatible, 'UNIX-based' systems that deepened the whole problem of developing an open, non-proprietary, common UNIX standard. The response of the rest of the industry to the AT&T announcement was to form the Open Software Foundation (OSF),[77] committed to the development of a competitive standard based on the IBM version of UNIX-AIX.[78] The founder members were seven manufacturers – Apollo Computer, DEC, Hewlett Packard and IBM from the United States, Siemens and Nixdorf from West Germany and Groupe Bull from France. Retaining their independence on this issue were Unisys and Olivetti. In its first response to this impasse, AT&T formed UNIX International/Unix Software Operation (UI/USO) in early 1989, comprising manufacturers and users, with responsibility for directing the future product requirements of UNIX.

At this point three outcomes seemed possible: first, that OSF would continue with AIX, leaving AT&T outside and the industry divided; second, that OSF would agree to embrace System V, leaving the position of IBM uncertain; third, that a compromise would be found enabling the best components of the two systems to be brought together in a composite version that all sides could embrace.[79] It now seems that the third and most unifying outcome is indeed possible, after the rival organisations narrowed down to two the versions they wished to promote. The IBM AIX version of UNIX was abandoned by OSF after frustration grew within the organisation about the lack of progress with its implementation. This, combined with fears about the potential domination of the UNIX market if AIX were adopted, led to the organisation turning to the Mach operating system developed at Carnegie-Mellon University in Pittsburgh, Pennsylvania as the kernel for UNIX.[80] Code-named OSF/1, the OSF plan to release it in late 1990. UI/USO have agreed on AT&T's Release 4 as its definitive product.[81].

Convergence on X/Open   In May 1989 both the Open System Foundation and UI/USO announced that they had been accepted as members of the X/Open Consortium, following undertakings that they would conform to the X/Open common applications-environment specification.[82] X/Open was founded in 1984 as an independent, non-profit-making consortium of international computer systems vendors, whose objective is to work towards a common applications environment, that is vendor-independent and based on *de facto* and international standards. All members of the organisation are committed to supporting the environment as defined, and more than 300 software companies worldwide are developing compliant products. Before the organisation could operate, however, it had to satisfy Article 85(1) of the Treaty of Rome, which prohibits, as incompatible with the common market, 'all agreements between undertakings which may affect trade between Member States and which have as their object or effect the prevention, restriction or distortion of competition within the common market'.

In December 1986 the European Commission agreed to X/Open's application for exemption under Article 85(3) of the EEC Treaty on the basis that the advantages involved in the creation of an open industry standard – 'in particular the intended creation of a wider availability of software and greater flexibility offered to users to change between hardware and software from different sources' – easily outweighed the distortions of competition which arose from membership of X/Open.[84] Any distortion of competition that might be caused by the competitive advantages available through membership and by the power, within the rules of X/Open, to restrict access to the group, were reduced by the Group's intention to make available as soon as possible the results of the cooperation. The

Commission considered this commitment as an essential element in its decision to grant an exemption.[85]

Following these developments, a platform now exists for a common UNIX standard to develop in the 1990s. The real issue, however, is exactly what the industry and the user community are looking for from open systems. Is UNIX the only component to standardise before the era of open systems arrives, or is it simply a part of what is needed to bring about interoperability between systems and portable applications that can be run on more than one system? The latter is certainly the bigger challenge, and is just what the X/Open common-applications architecture is concerned with in defining a set of interfaces, protocols and conventions for this purpose.[86] However, there is a considerable amount of work to be done before any prospect of a truly open UNIX system emerges. AT&T has relaxed its proprietary interest in UNIX, which began in 1985 when the company published a 'System V Interface Definition', aimed at providing a standard application interface to the UNIX operating system. This could be seen as a move towards a standard form of UNIX, or an attempt to establish the AT&T model as a front runner within the market. Clearly a new level of co-operation between competitors, not seen hitherto within the industry, will need to develop soon, and will probably result largely from upward pressure from the user community.

Agreement that something must be done is also a matter of inexorable logic, since an estimated 30–35 commercial versions of UNIX are available today on machines of different capacities. This means that applications software written for one version must be modified before it can run on another. However, for AT&T's Release 4 or OSF/1 to work themselves into a single unit within X/Open will not be easy. Release 4 has evolved through generations of development whereas OSF/1 is designed specifically for the multi-processor and network-oriented environment of the nineties. Clearly these and other differences between the rival standards organisations need to be resolved quickly. In July 1990 the AT&T UI/USO grouping offered to open talks with the OSF camp, partly as a result of growing user frustration. This came to a head at the end of May 1990, when in excess of 40 of the world's leading petrochemical companies announced that they were forming their own Petrochemical Open Software Corporation, in part due to the lack of progress within the rival computer industry sectors.[88] Analysts now believe that UI/USO holds the dominant position on UNIX, with OSF contributing on the periphery with additions and extensions.[89]

Closing in on a Standard   Among the wider matters to be settled if full portability and inter-operability are to be achieved, is the selection of a standard display interface and the parameters for networking services in relation to remote file access and job execution. Microsoft's X-Windows is rapidly becoming a *de facto* standard for the former,[90] as is TCP/IP for transmission control in communications (i.e. programs concerning methods of communication between networks). A major discussion is also underway to standardise the 'real-time' functions of the system. The problem is that proprietary systems have tended to contain the innovation which the standards organisations have sought to exploit. Potentially there are in any case too many standards bodies and UNIX 'open systems' groups, although for political and economic reasons, securing reduction in the numbers of these organisations seems remote. Currently, in addition to X/Open, a proliferation of Unix standards bodies exist, representing almost an industry in themselves. Perhaps the strongest of these is that of the American Institute of Electrical and Electronics Engineers (IEEE), which is advancing a UNIX standard called Posix (Portable Operating System Interface). The IEEE's efforts in this respect have gathered strength since the US National Bureau of Standards adopted its own Posix Federal Information Processing System (Fips) Portability Architecture in 1988. The IEEE has had seven working groups concerned with Posix, each addressing different areas (such as complete open systems, interfaces, conformance testing and military requirements),[91] but with the common general aim of helping systems developers and vendors to move towards open processes.[92]

It is now a possibility that the next X/Open portability guide will fall into line with a single worldwide Posix standard. This means that a fully-fledged international UNIX standard that is Posix compliant could emerge soon, although it still requires approval from the other standards bodies- the International Standards Organisation (ISO) and the American National Standards Institute (ANSI).[93] Responsibility for standardising 'terminology, problem description, programming languages, and communications characteristics' was assigned to ANSI by the ISO in 1960. ANSI therefore provides the framework within which sectoral groups can work cooperatively in developing standards within an industry sector.[94] The ISO pursues similar objectives within the international community, free of governmental influence. Its work includes standards for software, hardware and languages.

The obvious reason for this effort in relation to UNIX is to provide an environment within which applications can be obtained 'off-the-shelf' in object code format, usable immediately on a wide range of systems with different levels of performance, and manufactured by any one of a number of vendors. The PC clone market has achieved success in this respect, but if it is to happen throughout the entire market, it will also be necessary to approve a standard for the micro-processor architecture within the central processing unit. The rapid success of the Reduced Instruction Set Chip (RISC), especially Motorola's 88000 RISC micro-processors, has encouraged movement in this direction too, so that discussions are taking place with more than 50 systems vendors and software houses to try and establish a binary compatibility standard (BCS) for the 88000 chip.[95] The 88/Open Consortium aims to provide independent software vendors with access to the 88000 design technology to enable applications to become immediately available on 88000-based systems. Hardware developers supporting the 88/Open Consortium are Data General, Motorola, NCR and Sanyo/Icon. Work on implementing the BCS, which covers data types, file formats, signal handling and installation procedures, was started in 1988, prior to the availability of systems to meet the standard.[96] Its advance publication will enable software producers to adopt it before committing their applications to code. It also lines up with existing standards for Unix, so far as they exist, being compliant with Posix, X/Open and AT&T's System V Interface Definition. More than 26 independent software vendors planned to deliver new applications for the 88000 architecture during 1989, and Motorola expected to sell more than 50,000 of the 88000 micro-processor family during the same period.[97] Other micro-processor producers can be expected to pursue the same goal with '88000-compliant' open systems processors.

The long-term objective must be to provide portable applications that are independent of operating system and of micro-processor architecture. The first such products could be on the market in the 1990s if the current moves towards common standards are successful.[98] The X/Open consortium has taken the first step with the launch in September 1988 of its 'verification and branding' programme, which aims to provide an open systems standard for applications software. Vendors seeking recognition of compliance to this standard must submit their products for testing before being permitted to display the relevant X/Open logo on the product. Among the first to pass conformance tests for software have been Bull, Hewlett-Packard, ICL, NCR, Olivetti and Siemens. The immediate objective is to provide the market with a greater degree of choice in software and hardware, reduced reliance on a single vendor, plus decreased expenditure on training, maintenance and support, together with simpler and quicker integration of multi-vendor equipment.[99] Whether suppliers can bring themselves to participate truly within such an open competitive market, without the security of having customers locked in to their proprietary systems, applications and architectures, remains to be seen. There may be political pressure to do so. Already the European Commission has adopted an open systems policy and is encouraging the individual Member States to do so too.

However, as if to stress IBM's competitive ambitions for proprietary architectures, it added a new one to its list in March 1990 when it announced its Systems Management Architecture for the utilities software market worth $1.2 billion and currently growing at 30% per annum. Utility programs provide support for the routine operations of the computer system, and have been strongly exploited by Computer Associates with at least one application in 80% of IBM mainframe sites. IBM claims that the new architecture will integrate 'hundreds of presently incompatible utility programs'.[100] To strengthen its chances, IBM plans to release its SMA programming interfaces to encourage third party tie-ins.[101]

FULFILLING THE POTENTIAL OF SOFTWARE

ISSUES CONFRONTING THE INDUSTRY After a period of adolescence, the software industry is beginning to settle down into an identifiable business. It has a large number of participants and is in a sense more democratic than the hardware sector, since there is room for the smaller competitor with the good idea to gain a foothold. The threat of competition law suits or other forms of regulation has opened up the market considerably in the past 20 years, particularly once computer power and third generation languages developed to the point where a viable industry could be formed. A degree of economic self-interest was also involved, in the desire of the computer suppliers to win over the successful and strategic software releases to their own proprietary standards. As the range of machines has grown and as more specialised hardware has appeared, so too has the battle intensified among the software producers and the computer supply industry for market share in each software sector. The industry has experienced substantial growth as micro-processor developments extended the technology to a very significant extent.

As with the hardware sector, when a new market develops, some companies grow quickly into industry leaders.[102] The American corporation Computer Associates claims to be the world's leading independent software company. Its turnover revenue exceeded $1.3 billion in 1989–90, up by 21% on 1988–89, when figures had been up by 45% on the previous year. In September 1989 the company took over Cullinet Software Inc. for a fee of $333 million. This has strengthened the company's interests from business software and utilities to applications and databases.[103] Microsoft and Lotus Development Corporation are other examples of substantial software producers. For the large-scale competitor the pressure is growing for collaborative ventures in product development or even mergers, because the R&D development costs are becoming high.

With the continuing debate on standards for software, there is a strong level of investment in 'off-the-shelf' software which is growing more rapidly than expansion in custom-built products. New developments occur rapidly in the industry so software developers must monitor the market carefully to keep up with the trends and with the competition. In this respect the software sector remains volatile. As suggested before, competition laws both in the United States and Europe have ensured that the hardware producers cannot monopolise the market by illegal practices. This has given the software sector its independence and companies now must rely on taking the right decisions about their products in an intensively competitive environment. When designing new applications software for example, many choices are available. These include which operating system and which version to support, what features to incorporate in the application, which hardware to support, whether to be IBM-compatible or seek X/Open compliance branding, and if so at what level. There are also complex marketing considerations involving timing, updates, cost, maintenance and sales strategy.

It is now clear that the lack of good software is a bottleneck to the full exploitation of the performance capabilities of modern hardware. Execution rates of instructions have demonstrably improved to such an extent that software is now the key concern for the client. The time may even come when the user obtains all his software on a micro-chip with the rest of the hardware almost given away at the time of purchase. (Some photgraphic developers are now giving away free cameras every time the customer develops a film – 50 years ago this would have been unthinkable). IBM, which grew to its present dominance through its strength in hardware and particularly mainframe systems, now recognises the importance of the

226

software sector to its own future development. Back in 1987 the company established a US-based Application System Division to become a world-wide centre for IBM's software applications on all models. At that time software accounted for under 12% of IBM's revenues and the company did not want to be too heavily reliant upon outside software developers for the supply of applications software for its machines, unless it had a stake in those companies.[104] Currently, within both proprietary and open-system configurations, IBM is targeting office systems, manufacturing automation and systems for the financial markets (including banking and securities) as the key areas over the next few years. In 1990 the company estimates that these three sectors will account for 50% of the revenues from software sales. One of the problems of serving these areas, however, has been in producing reliable software, able to do the kind of things that users want, and produced at a sufficient speed to satisfy the needs of the market. The twin pressures of portability and interoperability between systems have further contributed to the overall difficulties.

With the growth of global communications networks, financial trading systems, for example, need to be capable of reacting swiftly to international trading conditions. In London, the Stock Exchange requires the reporting of transactions within five minutes. However, in the United States some dealers believe that five seconds would be too slow for a transaction to be processed.[105] The Stock Exchange would like to see a single communications channel and a single terminal with common coding standards for securities and counterparties, as well as transaction and bargain references, to replace the diversity of standards that exists today. The advantages would be the introduction of automated 24-hour global trading. To achieve this, however, will impose a significant challenge to the software producers to develop the products within the time schedule desired by users.[106]

NEW TECHNIQUES – SOFTWARE ENGINEERING   For some years now, as a response to such user needs, software developers have been looking at ways of using software tools as an aid in the process of maintaining, testing and indeed creating software. Since the mid-eighties there has been a rapid growth in the availability of software tools which, to a degree, have significantly advanced the process of software development. Their use today, together with fourth-generation languages and powerful desk-top computers, makes software development possible at a much reduced cost than before. The pressure for greater sophistication in computer software, to capitalise on developments in hardware, is a reflection of the growing reliance of the business user on computer systems and a realisation that software has not delivered all that it could in the past.

It is more than 20 years since the first conference on software engineering. As early as 1968 there was criticism that software maintenance and development was patchy and inadequate. As 3GL software brought with it larger and more complex programs, so too did the cost of detecting and correcting errors increase. Once a product went beyond the design phase into production, it became much more expensive to correct than errors uncovered before. Every effort was made to sort out problems during development. Unless performance requirements were critical, a 'fix it later' approach tended to be adopted, with the emphasis on correctness rather than high efficiency in performance.[107] The legal position now needs to be considered too. Liability can accrue if a producer is found to have fallen manifestly below the standard of care as exemplified in the industry, by failure to use recognised testing and correction techniques.

The attempt at harnessing automated techniques to combat the problem began with tools for testing the reliability of codes to ensure that they worked as the programmer intended. One tool of this type is known as a 'program instrumentor' or 'dynamic analyser'. This analyses a program to find its structure and then tests to see that branches and statements within the program are executed correctly. It can also identify 'hot spots' within the code, which are areas within the program that are brought into use more often. If these can be identified, the project manager can check to see if the run-time of the program can be reduced by relatively minor alterations of the code in these hot areas.[108] Another method is that of mutation testing, whereby the original program is tested against a number of mutants which have had errors inserted into the code. These are then operated with the original test data and the output compared with the results of the original program. If any mutant program produces identical results, this is a sign that the original code is faulty and work can continue until all mutant results can be distinguished from the correct version. A third method is the assertion processor which is a piece of code inserted into the program that contains a statement which must be true in relation to the program variables operative at that particular point in the coding. A number of such inserts can check whether the program is operating as it should, pinpointing errors more accurately.[108] In addition to testing for accuracy, testing for performance is also important and could save a lot of money. A software tuner was able to help a New York bank to reduce its batch processing window by more than three hours, while online systems were maintained to the West Coast without the need for additional hardware.[110] In another instance, software modelling of a proposed electronic funds transfer system showed that it could process no more than $50 billion per night, and not the $100 billion that the bank wanted. Had the system been implemented without the test, the bank would have faced interest charges on $50 billion each night.[111]

ROLE OF FOURTH GENERATION LANGUAGES   Running parallel with these aids were *ad hoc* methods, introduced by the programmers themselves to aid the often tedious and painstaking work that programming involved. It was useful to maintain a library of common routines for implementing regular programming requirements such as screen handling and field editing. Gradually these productivity aids became more formalised, the objective being to remove as many programming tasks as possible, while assisting the programmer to accomplish those tasks which remained. It was from these roots that fourth generation languages (4GLs) were born. In effect, 4GL products provide a 'tool kit' of components, all designed to improve the productivity of the user.[112] The concept of a fourth-generation language embraces an ancestry which began with machine code programming in the 1940s and 1950s. This was followed by assembler languages, input/output controllers and file management techniques of the late-1950s and early/mid-1960s, supplanted by the high level languages of COBOL, BASIC and FORTRAN of the period thereafter.[113]

The objective of 4GLs is to ease the burden of having to remember the detailed programming syntax of the high level languages. Instead, the user should be able to develop a prototype of the program without having to specify in detail how the processing should actually be performed.[114] A typical 4GL software tool should include a data dictionary enabling the user to specify fields, files and database formats without lengthy data description statements. It should offer a screen 'painter' to specify the format of any online displays, and a report generator controlling printout, formats of reports, graphics and tables, etc. The user language itself should also be consistent in style and convention throughout, and incorporate natural words and syntax. Where the user enters variants or simple errors, the 4GL should be able to handle this by drawing assumptions, applying defaults and deploying helpful error messages to guide the user in the direction he wants to go.[115]

229

In a report published in 1987 by the consultancy group Xephon, 25 4GL tools were listed as fitting the 4GL criteria.[116] Altogether hundreds of so-called 4GL products were marketed as such in the 1980s, but only a small proportion of these can hope to survive once standards governing the characteristics and capacities of these products are imposed. The nearest that the industry has come to with a 4GL standard is IBM's data manipulation language- SQL- Structured Query Language. It is thought, however, that SQL is too complex for the end-user programmer, and in any case difficult to use for large applications.[117] It is, perhaps, best regarded as a standard interface to relational databases, producing a combination which is rapidly becoming the primary programming medium.[118] Put crudely, the relational database protects applications from distortion by changes in file structure, while ensuring that data is stored in a logically sensible manner and that standard access paths are maintained. Among the tools incorporating an SQL interface are Unify Corporation's 'Accell/SQL'; Information Builder's '4GLFocus' and Cognos's '4GLPowerhouse'. Most major 4GL manufacturers now offer their own relational databases with their 4GL product. In one instance, a 4GL and relational database have been used to design a data management system for a hospital which distributes test results on blood, body fluids and specimens. Results will be available on-line, avoiding delays that delivery by post or courier inevitably involves.[119]

When the fit is good between the user requirement and the 4GL product, productivity in software development has been known to increase ten-fold. 4GLs main role will probably be in improving the portability and inter-operability of each product produced. To demonstrate the plus side of such 4GL programming, grand prix have been held where developers demonstrate the power of their products. In 1986 11 contestants, each using their own 4GL, had to take an unseen specification for an airline booking system and produce a working system within 24 hours that was capable of handling account customers, booking them in to a fixed number of destinations. The competition took place in a London hotel over a weekend and, on completion, contestants had then to see how many other machines they could run their system on. The judges estimated that what had been achieved in 24 hours with 4GL programming would have taken four to five months with COBOL.[120] In practice, however, 4GLs have not so far provided the comprehensive answer people want and for many they have simply been ignored. Some applications produced by 4GLs have been found to run comparatively slowly, perhaps because of a lack of performance testing. In addition, up to now, 4GLs have not proved to be particularly portable, or to be popular among programmers, whose skills are cherished.[121] There is also the cost of re-training to handle 4GL programming techniques.

Perhaps the most serious drawback of 4GL programming is its limited functionality. The key role of 4GLs has been to provide an aid in program design and coding within the programming phase of development – tools such as analysers, generators and translators. These can be useful although the task is incomplete since the writing cycle must be preceded by the all important development of the operational requirement and specification stages where 4GLs have made little contribution.[122] The resolution of this problem by artificial intelligence techniques and expert systems will herald the arrival of the 5GL. In the meantime, the horizons of programming aids, encapsulated by the 4GL generation, are gradually expanding as Computer Assisted Software Engineering (CASE) concepts are introduced to help speed up software development.[123] However, as frequently happens with the introduction of new products, the exact dividing line between a comprehensive 4GL and database and a basic CASE tool is hard to draw. This is not altogether surprising given the imprecision of industry definitions and the speed at which developers like to jump on a bandwagon when someone thinks up new terminology.[124] A user might be better off changing his 4GL than switching to a CASE tool. Both are complex products and evidence that developing an application is not just a matter of generating the code but of satisfying user requirements. 4GLs can be immensely valuable in database design, screen and report formats, and menu structures etc., whereas CASE techniques will help in all the developmental stages from design to writing the actual program. The real benefits may be in a marriage of the language and the tool that crosses the standards divide.[125] Information Builders are going in this direction with their re-packaged 4GLFocus product called Focus Application Construction Tool (FACT).[126]

COMPUTER ASSISTED SOFTWARE ENGINEERING (CASE) CASE tools purportedly take the automation process a stage further than the coding phase, where 4GLs have tended to operate, by focussing on the wider range of design and development concerns that operate throughout the implementation cycle. The two phases are known as 'upper' and 'lower' CASE respectively. The first group of CASE products is concerned with the schematic design of software. These are run on PCs or workstations and are languages which assist the programmer to describe a problem and devise a model solution. Schematic design systems incorporate graphics, tools to aid prototyping, and a design dictionary and analysis capability for error checking. One claimed advantage of such tools is that they can present the logic and data elements of the program in diagrammatic form which both programmers and users can discuss together. This enables decisions about the program to be reached faster, and for changes to be made more easily.[127] The second type of CASE tools – the 'Upper CASE' products – are those which take the logic design of the software and automatically convert it into program code.[128] Known as code generators, these tools also offer facilities for the automatic generation of documentation, the means for error checking and a data dictionary or repositary. The latter defines the data structures required for the program including database records, file structures, screen and report formats and their inter-relationships.[129]

The main advantage of code generators is of course their ability to write the code, easing the cost of programming resources. If the CASE tool can do it this is clearly an important step forward, for one estimate suggests that the cost of employing computer professionals has increased 60 fold by comparison with the cost of computer power over the past 20 years.[130] It is of course fanciful to suggest that code generators will ever supplant the skills of programmers 100% of the time. Claims have been made, however, that between 40% and 60% of code for certain applications have been automatically produced.[131] It is likely that the role of the programmer will tie in much more closely with that of the systems analyst in future, so that gradually the two roles will merge into a single job description. One product that generates COBOL code has been estimated at five- to ten-times quicker than a human programmer working at the height of his abilities.[132] Automated techniques also have the effect of removing a source of potential confusion between analyst and programmer, as the former tries to explain his requirements to the latter whose job is to translate it into code.[133]

Another area where code generation is proving useful is in restructuring and translator programs designed to upgrade older code to modern standards or convert it into another language altogether. Restructuring of code is particularly needed to upgrade the aging stock of COBOL code which is still at the heart of many business applications today. Such tools can re-organise a COBOL program by eliminating inefficient or poorly-structured code such as 'backward jumps in the logic path, recursive or wandering logic or GOTO loops within a paragraph'.[134] One clear advantage of such tools is the reduced cost of software maintenance after restructuring has occurred.[135] The function of translator applications is to enable the user to transfer software to a new computer system, overcoming any incompatibility that might otherwise cause those programs to be discarded. Frequently this stock of software will represent a major investment for the user, and translation may be infinitely preferable to re-programming. A good example would be the migration from a DEC PDP-11 computer with a library of BASIC programs, running under the RSTS operating system, to a DEC VAX machine that operates under UNIX.[136] The translator would convert the BASIC code into the C language, which is much more widely used today and can commonly be read by many UNIX-based computers.[137]

Sometimes this process will involve loading the translator into the original operating environment then running the conversion and loading the new language version into the replacement system. An alternative would be to locate the translator package within the UNIX unit so that it can simulate the old environment and translate the code with the aid of a compiler program.[138] Such methods are, of course, a stage beyond the routine conversion that takes place when, for example, a word-processing package is upgraded. There, the new version will automatically convert all files produced by the discarded application into the new format, so that the data can be retrieved within the upgraded environment.[139]

Getting the Most out of CASE In reality, as with 4GLs, many CASE tools have not lived up to expectations, as distributors race to produce a product or upgrade an existing one that they can quickly package as CASE technology, while ultimately falling short on performance. It may be for these reasons that only 5% of staff engaged in software development in the UK are estimated to be using CASE tools in the process.[140] A survey in 1989 by Price Waterhouse suggested that more than 40% of IT Managers in the UK had no plans to use CASE methods. Of 32% who had used CASE tools 20% gave them up.[141] That is despite the availability of more than 600 products in the UK in an industry that, according to forecasts of industry analysts Frost & Sullivan, was worth approximately $1 billion in 1989.[142] The UK market was expected to reach $245 million in the same year. Another assessment by London-based consultancy Ovum Ltd., puts the figure much lower – at only $140 million in the USA in 1987, although doubling in size annually. The company predicted, however, that it would be a full 10 years before CASE products were used routinely in software development. This was despite another finding that suggested that the average large software project ended a year late and cost twice as much at its budget.[143] CASE tools have also been found to be error prone themselves and not particularly easy to use.

Dennis Fife, Director of the Institute for Defence Analyses, which carried out a study of five design tools on behalf of the Strategic Defence Initiative Organisation, found lack of flexibility to be a continuing problem:

> The problem with all these tools is that someone up in the clouds has assumed the position of saying what's best for everyone. The tools should be more adaptable so that a user could make up new language forms and new graphics to express aspects of the system's design or behaviour that no one else has thought of.[144]

One way out of this may be to adapt CASE tools to meet particular user requirements. Some companies are looking to apply the same techniques to the analysis and design of applications as has occurred for some time now in regular programming where the software writer draws on a library of sub-routines to incorporate in the program. CASE is perceived as supporting an organisation's own development methods, adopted standards and hardware mix, through a customised approach.[145]

One of the severest problems in software development is the control of the management process itself. This applies both within the vendor organisation and subsequently in the user domain where maintenance and upgrading of software takes place. It is not just a question of integrating new applications, or system software, upgrading through a development path. It can mean an entire reconfiguration of the organisation's computing activity, perhaps associated with a move towards networking or clustering according to user requirements. This might result from technological advance where, what used to require a mainframe, can now be accommodated through networked workstations. Known as 'down-sizing', this can involve considerable effort by the user to get the system working to specification. The future, then, lies in developing aids that can offer support in tackling the broader problem, especially as the scope of systems and of development projects grow ever more complex. Even tiny savings on efficiency in a large project can translate into substantial savings later on. Many such projects, as indicated already, do not work out as expected and delays occur. Management complexities in the development of Version 3 of the Lotus 1-2-3 spreadsheet, for example, caused a delay of one year in its completion. The original version had involved no more than a dozen designers, but problems grew as the development team got bigger ending up at more than 100.

Developing a CASE Standard   The future now seems to lie in the creation of fully integrated case tools. The market is moving tentatively towards this approach, which it identifies as the 'Integrated Project Systems Environment.'[146] Although simple in concept, the realisation of the ambition is more difficult, especially as the issue of common versus proprietary standards is bound to interfere. The aim of the approach is to support a project team throughout the process – from design to specification and from coding to documentation. Projects to build IPSE products have themselves fallen into precisely the difficulties that they are designed to tackle. One example is the long running project at IBM to build an application development toolkit called 'Repositary', which was delayed even after eight years in development.[147] One reason was to ensure it complied with IBM's software architecture – SAA. It was finally announced in September 1989, for release in late 1990.

The Repositary in concept is an 'application development environment' (ADE), within which developers can 'engineer' software. To begin with it will store a wide range of information such as project control data, details of earlier versions and those planned, in a form which will allow for careful comparisons to be made of all products developed within the Repositary and for code to be re-used later on.[148] Using CASE tools integrated within the Repositary, design staff will develop documentation and code which can then be tested against the design specification as previously set out and defined within the Repositary. The system will track the development of the product, providing a more rigorous, flexible and efficient environment within which to produce the product. IBM's Repositary will also incorporate 'life cycle' support tools,[149] including aids for prototyping, quality assurance and testing, configuration management, planning and monitoring.[150] IBM believe that this structured method will provide the organisational framework within which software can be developed. The first of these development environments is the AD/Cycle,[151] consisting of tools and a data repositary for IBM's range of hardware compatible with its proprietary Systems Application Architecture.

The strategy is that as artificial intelligence and fifth-generation languages are deployed, these systems will become more interventionist in advising and directing the development process. One result, as already described, may be the return of customised or bespoke software, or the marketing of more specialised applications, either through the modification of packaged software or, perhaps, through access to substantial amounts of code held in modular form in repositaries served by such tools. Currently the vast majority of standard applications are upgraded and redeveloped by the software vendors themselves. In the 1990s it is anticipated that users will be able to licence 'application system generators', through which a specification is produced tailored to the customer's needs to be followed by the finished application.[152] This trend will certainly strengthen if CASE can develop a standard of its own,[153] not to mention compatibility with the key industry standards that are gradually emerging elsewhere in operating systems, chip design and communications. There is a move already to offer an alternative to IBM's initiative, in the British Government-backed 'OpenCase/SSADM'. Based on Structured Systems Analysis and Design Methodology (SSADM), this has been developed in the UK and offers a potential European approach to software engineering. OpenCase/SSADM is described as 'an analyst/designer workbench' for software development across the product life cycle.[154] The US software producer Informix will support the standard which is intended to be open and non-proprietary.[155]

Object-Oriented Programming   The introduction software engineering tools as a means of resolving what has been called the 'software crisis'[156] is not the only significant recent development in the software field. New approaches are being tried in programming methods themselves, which could have a major impact on future software development.[157] The most promising of the methods being explored is that of 'object-oriented programming' (Oop), pioneered at Xerox's Palo Alto Research Center (Parc) in California.[158] The programming technique has been around since the 1970's when Dr Alan Kay developed 'Smalltalk' at Parc. Another early influence was 'Simula', which emerged in the 1960s and was the first to have the term 'object' in its classification.[159]

Oop is structurally different from conventional programming in that it purports to be more flexible, by not differentiating between the data and the procedures which operate on and modify that data. This compartmental approach, prevalent in conventional programming, makes it difficult to use the latter to modify an application in line with the needs of the often-changing user environment. This is because in restructuring a program using conventional techniques, one must go back to basics when even minor alterations are proposed. Oop attempts to overcome these problems by focussing, instead, on a series of objects or modules which are defined according to their internal states and their relationships with other objects.[160] A set of in-built procedures define the attributes and behaviour of these objects providing a level of artificial intelligence not present in conventional program modules.[161] Programs developed in this way can be extended more easily since new objects can be added which attract the same characteristics – data and procedures – that other objects within the same class already have.

One of the key benefits of the Oop's approach is that it parallels more closely the thinking of the software designer, by allowing him to define his ideas in code in the same order as they come to mind. An illustration of how Oop works is seen in the Ohio-based paper producers, Combustion Engineering, who operate a measurement system to run the paper-making machinery. By classifying the sensors in a single object class, the message 'start measuring' is transmitted to all sensors at once. Each responds in its own time according to the general and specific parameters applicable to the 'sensor' object.[162] Other aspects of the process carried out by the machines are represented by separate objects. By adopting objects in this manner, programmers have a base upon which to build an application. Errors and wasted code are more likely to be detected, particularly in the development of complex systems where modelling the requirement using conventional methods is hard to achieve. A study has cautiously suggested that Oop techniques, which are intended to be re-usable, maintainable and designed for change, can increase productivity by as much as 15 fold.[163] Oop is also capable, it seems, of reducing the level of code needed to complete an application. One user claims a five-to-one improvement as a result of being able to re-use Oop's modules.[164] Whether or not these levels of economy become widespread, it is true that the industry badly needs a breakthrough in programming techniques, perhaps more that the software engineering technology that has already been described, for the latter cannot build effective applications if the underlying programming concepts are dated.

The prediction is that Oop could become a mainstream technique from the mid-1990s, with support from the major hardware vendors and CASE suppliers, who would want to exploit the new programming method if it works. Currently a growing number of developers, working in software development and artificial intelligence, are acquiring the techniques.[165] They include Apple, Bull, ICL and IBM. The latter has based its AS/400 SAA-compatible mid-range computer system on Oops principles. There is also to be an object-oriented component to IBM's proprietary Systems Application Architecture which links part of its hardware range together under a common operating environment.[166] Microsoft and Borland International head the software industry's response, backed by other small artificial intelligence-based development companies. In 1989 Microsoft announced collaboration with the Dublin-based software development company Glockenspiel, to produce a version of the Oops programming language C++.[167] This will bring Oops programming techniques to all software developers.[168] Inevitably, another 'standards' battle will commence if Oop fulfills its potential.

A large number of Oop languages already exist, exploring different features of the object-orientation concept.[169] Apart from the limited success so far with fourth-generation languages, the software sector has not moved very far from the conventional techniques of programming, built around the third-generation high-level languages such as COBOL which are now growing older despite modernisation.[170] However, the hardware sector is moving into new designs, too, built around parallel processing and innovative RISC and CISC chip technology. Oop could do the same for software and provide the all-important linkage that is needed to bind the technology into a more productive force. The industry is hoping that new programming concepts such as Oop will achieve the breakthrough necessary to advance software performance and resolve any log jams that exist, while opening the way to some significant advances in products and services. Currently it is applied in a wide range of packages including expert systems, publishing systems, micro-processor and window managers.[171]

FUTURE PROSPECTS – INTELLIGENCE AND INTEGRATION

MORE TO COME FROM SOFTWARE The driving force in computing, responsible for delivering the technological achievements that we experience today, has always emanated from a perception that there is more to come. In the immediate post-war period the limit of the ambition among those working in the fledgling computer industry was the dream of machines capable of executing one million instructions per second (Mip). That objective has been overtaken for some time now, so that today, the ability to deliver 20 Mips to the desk-top is regarded as inadequate for the kind of applications currently in demand – from drug synthesis to economy modelling, and decision support and just-in-time scheduling to CAD/CAM applications.[172] Now the industry is not sure how far the technology can go, although it knows there is a lot more performance to be captured. Today, the ambition is not so bound up with crude and simple pre-occupations about improving performance levels, but with the more subtle issue of linking targets to user needs. What the industry has recognised is the importance of data in relation to software. This manifests itself in the drive to develop new languages and forms of data-holding to secure the anticipated benefits of the increase in computer performance.

What continues to be impressive to the lay observer is the apparent scope of the technology to overcome the natural human barriers of time, distance, volume and calculation to produce tangible results. This is illustrated by the achievement of humanity to gather information from space. For example, when the Magellan space mission gets to Venus in December 1995, some 67 million miles away from the sun, it is expected to map 85% of the planet's surface in only 243 days, transmitting this back to Earth. It follows the Voyager 2 space craft which reached Neptune in August 1989, having completed a 4.4 billion-mile/12-year journey into space, and successfully beamed back pictures to the earth using new 'image motion' camera techniques. This method of picture compensation, designed to prevent blurring, was programmed into the Voyager 2 computer during its mission and was not even invented when the craft was launched in September 1977.

Second, there is the improvement in techniques of information processing. Large information systems of terabyte proportions, supported by relational database techniques are now delivering precise high-value information on an increasing scale. The mapping of the human genome over the next 10–15 years, for example, will involve the storage of a massive 3 billion characters.[173] Rapid accessing and analysis of precise data will be imperative if the benefits of the investment in extracting the information are to be realised. The objective today, then, is to close the gap between the intelligent, forgetful but intuitive human being and the fast, efficient but dumb 'artificial intelligence' of the universal machine. Mankind requires better tools than he has at present to process and use the high value information that the technology is striving to deliver. Although organisational issues such as that of industry standards will continue to be debated, it is also likely that discussion of how to bridge the gap between the technology and human intelligence will grow too. The key to closing that gap is software and its capacity to handle information. Whereas hardware can deliver the opportunity, only software and advanced, interactive information-storage techniques can bring about that fulfillment.

ARTIFICIAL INTELLIGENCE   The computers of the 1990s are extracting themselves from the lineal connection that they once had with the calculation machines that began with the abacus and progressed through those envisaged by Pascal, Leibnitz and Babbage. Traditionally, the strength of computers has been their ability to assimilate rules and execute instructions according to the mathematical model of the task. The 'mindless' execution of interminable logical sequences of instructions, enhanced further by parallel processing techniques, is now giving way in research attempts to use processing power to imitate the architecture of the human brain. The concept is to devise a means whereby the computer can develop a picture of the world through statistical observation and other forms of data analysis, such as imagery, and thereby 'learn by experience'. In this way the benefits of parallel processing – the means whereby more than one process is active in a given instant – could now be applied in a neural network of individual cells interconnected like the brain.[174]

'Artificial intelligence' was given its name in the 1950s when a movement developed arguing that intelligence could be modelled so that a machine could simulate it. The concept has been described as follows:

> Artificial intelligence is the study of how to make computers do the sorts of things that human minds do. Some of those things that we normally think of as requiring a lot of intelligence – like doing maths or playing good chess . . . or working out a scientific problem – we are used to thinking a computer might be able to do [early in 1990 a chess computer called 'Mephisto-Portorose' became the first machine ever to beat the former world champion, Anatoly Karpov]. And those are things being done by computers in artificial intelligence now. But there are other things, which people do not normally think of as requiring intelligence, because we can all do them without really thinking about it, that have turned out to be very very difficult to make computers do. These are things like talking, seeing, . . . moving around the room without walking into things – which a robot would have to do, if it was the sort of robot that could wander around a factory floor as opposed to being one that is clamped onto a work bench. So today's computers can do all sorts of things the human mind can do, but only up to a point . . . and only to a very limited extent.[175]

At present the success in artificial intelligence has been in taking computers and increasing their capacity to intervene in some of the tasks that human beings routinely do. In a very limited way computers are beginning to make decisions and react to those decisions in a way that one would normally accept required a measure of intelligence. Scientists are experimenting with computers that can simulate speech, sight and hearing to a primitive degree. It is anticipated that in due course products will emerge that are sophisticated enough to do away with keyboard methods of entering data, replacing it with data entry through speech. IBM, for example, has developed a 'speaker-dependent' system capable of recognising up to 20,000 isolated words.[176] Capacities of 60,000 words are thought to have been achieved in research.[177] Simultaneous translation from one language to another is also distinctly possible once computers can develop a reasonable vocabulary. The translation of visual experience into digital format will enable machines to be built that can undertake complex assembly tasks bringing a new generation of factory automation to the shop floor. There will also be a host of other applications that have not yet perhaps even been contemplated.

Alan Turing was the first to propose a test for an 'intelligent machine', suggesting that if a person could converse with it through a teletype machine and believe he was talking to another individual, then the machine would be 'intelligent'.[178] Programming attempts at joining this conversation between humanity and a computer have had some success. For example, with a program called 'Shrdlu', researchers have created a form of 'dialogue' in conversational English. Other research continues with visual images, natural languages, and robotics. The puzzle that still awaits an outcome is how far artificial intelligence can go in this direction. Is the replication, for example, of the formal structure of the brain ever going to make up for the absence of bio-chemical features; and to what extent can simulating the model of the brain ever capture its reality and copy the true mental processes that operate within it? The debate is of fundamental importance between those who believe there is a scientific answer to the modelling of human actions by computers and those who consider that there is no coherent theory of human behaviour equivalent to those within the physical sciences. The latter argument runs that simply because man has gone a long way towards understanding the properties of matter and the interaction of particles within the physical world, this does not mean that anything that possesses physical characteristics can be understood and replicated by scientific means. The challenge lies in whether it is possible to capture mental states through symbolic manipulation, which is the centrepiece of what digital computers can do. If so, would this amount to the thing itself, or does the process merely simulate thinking in the absence of an equivalent and required biochemistry?[179] Furthermore, why should people believe that it is possible to get to the root of what intelligence is by looking at a set of rules, for how can one simulate common sense and all the other expressions of feeling and intuition within a non-human domain?

The proposition that the human mind is conditioned by an underlying set of rules was first examined by Socrates and, later, by Plato. If man has freedom of choice, he is not controlled by any underlying mechanism that determines his thoughts, feelings, actions and behaviour. Moreover, as a social being, his performance is conditioned by external as well as internal stimuli. Supporters of artificial intelligence methods believe, however, that since man is a physical entity within a physical environment, his mental processes must be capable of artificial recreation. The answer, they claim, may not lie in the identification of any particular rules or principles, but in the creation of an artificial environment within which the biochemical conditions underlying brain function can be simulated. No one knows how far the isolated representations of artificial intelligence so far produced suggest that this is ever capable of being accomplished.

The debate goes on at the philosophical level as to what the future may hold in terms of the potential of artificial intelligence. In the meantime it is clear that work in this field has a very long way to go before any firm answers are available to the questions posed. For the moment it may be preferable not to get side-tracked by directing artificial intelligence research too strongly towards creating a simulated human intellect. Pragmatically, the concern should be to try and make better products, rather than to pursue such abstract arguments. There is nevertheless much that artificial intelligence techniques can offer, through modelling and simulation techniques, that in the long term may generate entirely new concepts. Currently, this is an area that falls within the domain of 'expert systems'.[180]

EXPERT SYSTEMS   If the long-term goal of developing and harnessing the potential of artificial intelligence seems way off at present, lacking the rewards of any 'Newtonian' breakthrough, equivalent to that of the physical sciences, what can be expected to come out of this area of research in the immediate future? The answer seems to lie in the development of 'expert systems', perhaps the first genuine product of artificial intelligence to reach the commercial marketplace.[181] As with all generic terminology there is always a rush to claim it for every related product on the market, whether or not it fits. In essence an 'expert' system, otherwise known as as 'knowledge-based' or 'intelligent-knowledge-based', is a computer system that exploits human expertise through inference techniques applied to very large volumes of data. The latter form the inference 'engine' of the computer program using problem-solving algorithms developed from analysis of the techniques or rules applied by the expert (the user). The knowledge base consists of the data stored in the computer and selected by the expert as relevant to the decision making process. The 'expert' information must then be ordered and stored in the form appropriate to the methodology of the inference techniques.

The first expert system is usually claimed to be DENDRAL, developed at Stanford University in the mid-1960s. The program was designed to assist chemists in the selection of compounds based upon spectrometric analysis.[182] A number of programming languages have also developed that are particularly suited to work in artificial intelligence applications. These include, LISP (LISt Processing), PROLOG and LOGO.[183] Since then expert system 'shells' have developed, too, allowing the user to create his own system by adding to it the knowledge base relevant to the proposed field of use.[184] The market has now diversified into small-, medium- and high-range shell systems. Products include: small – 'Crystal' by Intelligent Environments; mid-range – 'ESE' by IBM and 'Xi Plus' from Expertech; and high-range – 'Art' by Inference Corporation, Los Angeles.[185]

The introduction of these products has provided a potential 'do-it-yourself' alternative to the complete, off-the-shelf system, the development of which normally requires extensive interviews with the participating expert and a lot of additional work besides. During this exercise the interviewer will be interested, not only in what the expert says he does, but also in what he may unconsciously do when reaching a decision. It is vital for the 'knowledge engineer' to uncover the true picture of how decisions are made so that the system can be more effective in accomplishing its task. In practice, shell packages have not provided the user with the complete answer to expert system building as, frequently, the inference techniques built into it have not matched the characteristics of the knowledge base. As a result more complex products known as 'systems builders' have been produced, offering a more sophisticated toolkit for the specialist user.[186] Another area of promising research for expert systems is in 'fuzzy logic'. This is the attempt to reduce ambiguous information into numerical values. In Japan, researchers have been working on this in a number of fields. The approach could be extremely useful, for example in the financial sector, where it could help to avoid the kind of difficulties experienced during the stock market falls of the late 1980s, when computerised selling, triggered by the share price reaching a pre-determined level, contributed to the problem. Several Japanese companies are building systems that could extend consideration to a wider range of factors such as exchange rates, underlying trends etc. For the moment, however, these are being targeted as decision-making tools for investment and the assessment of credit risk.[187]

The result is that, today, highly complex systems are in use that have cost large sums of money to develop. These include MYCIN (Antimicrobial therapy); CASNET (Glaucoma assessment and therapy); INTERNIST-1 (Internal medical diagnosis); PROSPECTOR (Geological exploration); HASP and SIAP (Ocean surveillance – signal processing).[188] The real growth in such products has had to wait until advances in computer design and, in particular, the techniques of parallel processing, have produced the speed necessary to exploit knowledge bases at an adequate level of performance. Parallel computing is the ability to execute many steps of a program simultaneously rather than in sequence. The parallel processing of instructions thus speeds up the completion of the task which the computer has been directed to perform. ICL in the UK have been developing a computer called ALICE which is intended to support the exploitation of expert systems. The company is also involved in a consortium, working at six different sites, to design computer software which will support Department of Social Security personnel in the application of benefit rules to more than seven million people annually. Meanwhile, GEC have backed a project at Westminster Hospital that assists in the detection and early selection of patients admitted with chest pains who require urgent treatment for control and prevention of heart attacks. It is anticipated that tools like this will enhance the process of decision-making in many different environments.

Expert Systems for All　With the advances in the power of personal computers, expert systems are already being modelled for the PC marketplace. The merger of expert systems, for example, with decision support applications offer exciting prospects. One such illustration of an 'expert support system' is a product called 'Financial Advisor', developed at Cambridge, Massachusetts by Palladian Software. The system has had built into it a knowledge base of management and accountancy 'science'.

The user feeds relevant corporate data into the system, which then responds to rudimentary questions about business projects. These deal with such matters as the impact upon competition of a particular project strategy and its preferable duration.[189] Another example which experiments with these concepts is a system called MARION, designed to assist the user in the analysis and control of computer risks.[190] The capture and storage of data in machine-readable form from hard copy is also fertile territory for 'intelligent' applications. The Kurzweil Intelligent Character Recognition System, for example, is able to analyse the way characters are formed, learn to recognise that character for future reference, and make intelligent guesses about a character that is not immediately recognisable.[191] Systems are also being developed to convert written text into audible speech.

Similar kinds of improvements can be expected too in the field of relational databases The development of systems equipped with both data and a set of rules with which to interpret that data, represents a significant opportunity in certain fields where rules have meaning. In the commercial context this includes automating sales, service and marketing, including analysis of mailing lists, integration of statistical and tabulation packages, and access to geographic information data for sampling to produce names and addresses of those most likely to respond to a marketing campaign.[192] Another application might be in the legal field, providing advice to a company upon the rules governing statutory sick pay, or dismissal.[193]

The overall impact of these developments will be to provide the user with more accurate and sophisticated tools with which to obtain and access information, co-ordinate business decisions and operate equipment. Organisations, whether large or small, inevitably have complex information needs. Developments in information technology have changed the face of management and administration techniques, so that today, these functions, together with the information applied in the process of their performance, are likely to be distributed throughout the organisation. Expert systems linked to a clearly defined and considered information strategy, will ensure that organisations develop an appropriate system linked much more closely to corporate objectives. It should mean, for example, that data will only need to be captured once by the organisation to be available automatically thereafter within the information system, for whatever use the organisation or the system dictates. An organisation might have a number of 'what if' questions to put to the system. The expert system features would then come into play. This would enable the information system to develop its own strategy for answering the questions posed, based upon the parameters given to it both by the software and the user. Areas of business activity and planning hitherto inadequately supported with high-level information, either because of cost or lack of means, will now become routinely much better supported with the detailed information necessary to make appropriate choices. This is particularly true for companies or institutions with concerns about environmental factors- toxic waste, water, weather forecasting etc. – where computer modelling, the development of large databases, remote sensing and computerized mapping will all contribute to improved management and responsiveness to environmental pressures.[194]

The last and perhaps most important aspect of this research is developing transparent and responsive technology for the benefit of the user. There is much that can be done to make computers more accessible and less forbidding tools than they have been up to now. In Japan and elsewhere, research is underway to advance this cause. The intent is to move away from simply making computers faster and more efficient at storing and processing data, to machines that are more accessible and adaptive to the way human beings think and respond (described as the 'sixth generation' project).[195] It may be that the combination of expert systems, databases and fourth-generation languages will lead to a more enlightened and trouble-free relationship. If that is accomplished, it will mark the arrival of fifth-generation computer languages. If the 5GL tag is to be deserved, the software must provide for the non-expert communicating in natural language through a variety of interfaces including multilingual speech recognition and conversion of text into speech.

SUMMARY   Computer software is only just beginning to flourish and it has infinite potential. The history of communication has been one of inexorable improvement in the speed, volume and method of collecting, storing and transmitting information by distance and time. The development of information technology during this century has provided a new dimension, with the discovery that data can be represented in a form which is readable by a machine. Since that discovery, the story has been one of finding better methods of harnessing its benefits through improvements in machine performance and in the techniques of orchestrating that power to accomplish a wide range of functions. With the development of automated data-processing techniques, computers have introduced a precision in the obtaining and distribution of information that has not been possible, hitherto, by manual processes. Equally important has been the reduction in the cost of doing this which has contributed substantially to the growth of the products and services of the information society. That process will continue as the technology continues to build on these foundations. Artificial intelligence, new programming languages, software engineering tools, and micro-processor and other hardware improvements, will all contribute to a future that will put a rising value on the delivery of information.

Obtaining the correct data, from the most appropriate sources, followed by instant processing and transmission for the maximum impact, is what the information technology revolution is about. It is also about developing the use of information in a functional way to implement and control processes which hitherto have either not been possible to achieve or, if they have, not with the accuracy and efficiency of automated as opposed to other manual or mechanical methods.[196] Herein lies the concept of the universal machine envisaged by Turing and Von Neumann half a century ago.[197] The key to this future lies particularly in what can be achieved through software. A glimpse of one aspect of this potential environment is given by the software developers themselves:

> When you walk into an office in 1998, the PC will sense your presence, switch itself on, and promptly deliver your overnight electronic mail, sorted in order of importance . . . Suppose that the most urgent message concerns a lost shipment from Osaka. You load an English-to-Japanese word processor, speak into a microphone, and 'write' a letter simultaneously in both languages. End the session and the program automatically telecommunicates the message to the client in Japan, copies your boss, and files a copy away in the company's cross-indexed optical disk archives.[198]

The fulfilment of these objectives is inseparably connected with the future of telecommunications. Without the latter, the former would be a technology locked in a box, unable to get out. Just as the individual found ways of improving dialogue with humanity, so too has the computer found ways of exploiting its own digital expression to communicate with other computers and through the digital medium to man himself. The work of pioneers such as Morse, Edison, Bell, Marconi and others has already been discussed. The next chapter moves forward to outline the important developments in telecommunications that have taken place in the twentieth century, during the same period as the initial stages of the computer revolution.

NOTES

1. *The Internationalisation of Software and Computer Services*, OECD Information Computer Communications Policy Series No. 17, pp. 9 and 39–41.
2. Ibid., p. 41, Table 15.
3. Tom Foremski, 'Doing Very Nicely Over Here', *Computing*, 11 January 1990, p. 16.
4. The companies are CAP Gemini Sogeti (France) £680m. (estimated turn-over in 1987); followed by SD Scicon (UK) £427m.; Sema Group (UK) £408m.; Finsiel (Italy) £407m.; Sligos (France) £228m.; GSI (France) £225m.; Datev (West Germany) £200m.; CISI (France) £188m.; Thorn EMI (UK) £186m.; Logica (UK) £185m. In Alan Cane, 'Hard Heads Conquer the Software Jungle', *Financial Times*, June 1989.
5. The companies are: Nippon Business (affiliation Hitachi) US$575m.; Nomura (aff. Nomura) $420 m.; Computer Services (aff. Independent) 405 m.; JIEC (aff. IBM/CSK) $360 m.; Hitachi (aff. Hitachi) $305 m.; Toyo Joho (aff. Sanwa Bank) $280 m.; Intec (aff. Independent) $275 m.; Fujitsu (aff. Fujitsu) 235 m.; NEC (aff. NEC) $230 m.; Japan Business Automation (aff. Toshiba) 225 m. In Patricia Tehan, 'Japanese Stars Rise in West', *Computing*, 2 July 1989, p. 12.
6. *Information Technology and New Growth Opportunities*, 1989, OECD Information, Computer, Communications Policy Series No. 19, p. 20. Source: OECD Secretariat estimates based on IT industry sources.
7. Worldwide Information Technology Industry Growth by Major Market Segment 1984–1993. Source: IDC 1987 *Annual Review*, p. 25.
8. David Moschella, Vice President, Processors, Peripherals, Software IDC. In IDC 1987 *Annual Review*, p. 25.
9. Computing Services Industry, Quarterly Survey in *Business Bulletin*, 23/90 (23 March 1990), and 43/90 (25 June 1990).
10. *Computing*, 1 March 1990, p. 1.
11. It is estimated that in 1986 27 million people had access to some form of PC technology. This is likely to double in the period up to 1993. There will also be a 45% increase in the supply of multi-user systems according to estimates. Source: IDC 1987 *Annual Review*, pp. 25 and 26.
12. Steve Roche, 'Moving Closer to the Fifth Generation', *Computing*, 8 February 1990, pp. 14–15.
13. Moreau, op. cit., p. 150.
14. *Software – An Emerging Industry*, op. cit., p. 30.
15. Dennis Longley and Michael Shain, *Macmillan Dictionary of Information Technology*, 3rd Edition, 1989, p. 381. The language was named after the physicist Blaise Pascal.
16. Ibid., p. 7. ADA was named after Babbage's assistant Augusta Ada Countess of Lovelace. Typical uses include 'production lines, data recording in laboratories, navigational systems, networking and interfacing of multiple processors'.

17. Ibid., p. 71.

18. Christopher Robbins, 'Coup de Grace', *Datalink*, 6 April 1987, p. 18.

19. Gary Flood, 'Cobol Gets Set for an Object-Oriented Future', *Computer Weekly*, 15 February 1990, p. 19. The Codasyl Cobol Committee that sets standards for COBOL met in Scottsdate, Arizona in November 1989 and established the Object Orientated Cobol Task Group to oversee the project.

20. For this reason a market has developed of products that can modernise or translate COBOL applications to bring them up to date, reduce maintenance costs and enable applications to be transferred to computers running some of the newer operating systems such as Unix.

21. Barbara Primrose, 'Staying with COBOL', *Computer Systems*, January 1988, p. 32.

22. Jerome Garfunkel, 'Cobol in the Nineties', *Computer Systems – Europe*, June 1990, pp. 17–20. COBOL 85 is the latest American National Standard's Institute/International Standards Organisation approved standard for the language.

23. *Software – An Emerging Industry*, op. cit., p. 44.

24. The operating system for the IBM 360 had several million instructions and took 5000 man years to develop. This contrasts with the IBM 650 in 1955 which ran on no more than 5000 instructions. Machines in the 1980s require in excess of 20 million instructions to run. Source: Moreau, op. cit., pp. 134–5.

25. U.S. Congress, Office of Technology Assessment, 'International Competition in Services – Banking, Building, Software, Knowhow', OTA-ITE-328 (Washington DC: U.S. Government Printing Office, July 1987), p. 160.

26. This was of course the approach IBM took until the judicial ruling. For a historical account of IBM's development and policies see: David Mercer, *IBM: How the World's Most Successful Corporation is Managed*, (Kogan Page, London 1988).

27. *U.S. v. IBM* Civil Action 69-200 (S.D.N.Y. 1969). With the backing of President Reagan the case was dismissed on 8 January 1982 after a protracted fight between the two sides and a number of court hearings. For discussion see Robert P. Bigelow, 'US Versus IBM: An Exercise in Futility?' 1 *Yearbook of Law, Computers and Technology*, 1984, pp. 57–77.

28. Time-sharing, which became popular since the 1960s when computer CPU performance increased, is the technique whereby a computer can handle simultaneous users and peripherals in which each operation is performed in sequence, giving the impression of a multi-user service.

29. OECD, op. cit., p. 15.

30. Jonathan Green-Armytage, 'Just a Business Like Any Other', *Computer Weekly*, 25 January 1990, pp. 24–5.

31. *The Internationalisation of Software and Computer Services*, (OECD, 1989). Information Computer Communications Policy Series No. 17, p. 16.

32. *Software – An Emerging Industry*, op. cit., pp. 22–3.

33. Philip Manchester, 'A Boon for Programmers', *Financial Times*, 24

November 1989, p. V.
34. Steve Roche, op. cit., p. 15.
35. Julian Patterson, 'Trumpet Voluntary', *Informatics*, May 1989, pp. 36–40.
36. This is the reported view of Uniplex whose office automation software is backed by IBM. In Schofield, 'A Unix Twist to IBM's Future', The *Guardian*, 15 June 1989, p. 27.
37. Ibid.
38. Slater, op. cit., p. 276.
39. Ibid., p. 279.
40. For a description of UNIX and of C, see Stevens, op. cit., pp. 137–8 and 160 respectively.
41. Slater, op.cit., p. 281.
42. Hugh Griffiths and Colin Walls, 'C++; A Language for the 90's', *Computer Systems – Europe*, June 1989, pp. 57–8.
43. Julian Patterson, op. cit., p. 38.
44. Estimates of the International Data Group and the Gartner Group, reported in ibid.
45. Dennis Keeling, 'Straight Down the Middle', *Computer Systems – Europe*, pp. 14–16.
46. Tom Foremski, 'IBM Knocks its Critics over Open Standards', *Computing*, 9 March 1989, p. 11.
47. Philip Manchester, 'Open Question', *Computing* 20 April 1989, pp. 8–9.
48. Dennis Keeling, op. cit., p. 16.
49. Philip Manchester, op. cit., p. 8.
50. For example, Altos – a Unix based supplier, whose product 'Adlantes' provides this opportunity.
51. Neil Ratcliffe, 'Is PC Pick Top of the Ops', *Computer Systems – Europe*, March 1990, pp. 28–30. See also, Dennis Longley and Michael Shain, op. cit., p. 390.
52. 'Pick Learns the Art of Living with UNIX', *Computer Weekly*, 1 February 1990.
53. Advanced PICK will run with AT&T's System V 386 PC Version and its 3B2 mid-range hardware.
54. Neil Ratcliffe, op. cit., pp. 29–30.
55. 'Unisys Misreads Signs of Open Systems Road', *Computing*, 28 June 1990, p. 13.
56. 'Apple's Troubles Grow with System 7 Delays', *Computing*' 17 May 1990, p. 10.
57. Perhaps this explains why some people are referring to SAA as 'Save Aker's Ass' in relation to IBM Chairman John Aker's attempts to retain customers with SAA undertakings. Source: Tom Foremski, 'More Fear, Uncertainty and Doubt', *Computing*, 5 July 1990, p. 14.
58. Discussed by Francis Gens, 'Will IBM take SAA from Vapourware to Reality', *Computer News*, 11 February 1988.
59. Mark Hamilton, 'Big Blue Unveils Package for Office of the Future', *PC Business World*, 23 May 1989, p. 3.

60. Ibid.
61. Michael Powell, 'A Case For Further Development?', *Computer Weekly*, 30 November 1989, p. 29.
62. Nick Gill, 'Getting on Top of the Case with a New Cycle at IBM', *Computing*, 1 March 1990, pp. 22–3.
63. Michael Powell, op. cit.
64. Nicholas Enticknap, 'Cleaver and the Art of Glasnost', *Computer Weekly*, 25 January 1990, pp. 22–3.
65. Longley and Shain, op. cit. note ante, p. 47.
66. David Barlow, '486 Good Reasons to Move Up', *Computer Weekly*, 25 January 1990, p. 42.
67. Keith Jones, 'EISA Lays its Foundations', *Computer Weekly*, 5 April 1990, pp. 44–5.
68. Novell has announced the first '32-bit bus master Ethernet network adaptor card' for the EISA bus, available commercially for the first time in 1990. Source: *Computer Weekly*, 16 November 1989, p. 51.
69. Louise Kehoe, 'Intel Challenge to IBM "Bus" ', *Financial Times*, 12 July 1989.
70. Keith Jones, op. cit., p. 45.
71. Jack Schofield, 'A Unix Twist to IBM's Future', *Guardian*, 15 June 1989, p. 27.
72. Martin Banks, 'Europe X/Open for Business', *Computer Systems – Europe*, September 1988, pp. 66–72.
73. Phil Manchester, 'IBM Versus (Almost) All the World', *Computer Weekly*, 25 January 1990, p. 34.
74. David Guest, 'Is IBM Hoping for Too Much?', *Computer Systems – Europe*, October 1988, pp. 66–8.
75. Natalie Taylor, 'SAA Points the Way to IBM's Strategy', *PC Business World*, 31 March 1987, p. 9.
76. The comment was made by Ed de Castro, Founder and Chief Executive of Data General Corporation: 'Once DG has achieved parity with the largest system vendors as regards the applications software base, it will be able to compete effectively on the basis of performance, reliability, etc . . . We will drive deep into the hearts of the proprietary system vendors, as our level of integration begins to rival theirs.' In 'DG's Open Opportunity', *Computer Systems – Europe*, April 1989, p. 7.
77. The origins of the OSF was the Hamilton Group which included Apollo, Hewlett-Packard and DEC, Data General, Silicon Graphics and Mips. It was set up in response to the ties between Sun and AT&T, which the other companies believed would give Sun an 18-month lead over rival workstation producers, In, Claire Neesham, 'Unix World Wakes up to a Divided Future', *Computing*, 26 May 1988, p. 17.
78. Alan Cane, 'Computer Makers Seek Accord', *Financial Times*, October 1988.
79. Ibid.
80. Douglas Millison, 'A Gigantic Attack on Double Standards', *Computing*, 12

April 1990, pp. 26–7.

81. Andrew Rutter, 'Mission Impossible', *Computing*, 7 June 1990, pp. 22–3.
82. For a good background article on the political battles being fought out within the industry over UNIX standards, see Dominic Dunlop, 'Sorting the File on Unix', *Computer Systems – Europe*, January 1989, pp. 59–64.
83. Members include: AT&T, Apollo Computer, Bull, Digital Equipment Corporation, Fujitsu, Hewlett-Packard, Hitachi, IBM, ICL, NEC, NCR, Nixdorf, Nokia Data, Olivetti, Philips, Prime Computer, Siemens, Sun Microsystems and Unisys.
84. See Commission Decision of 15 December 1986 relating to a proceeding under Article 85 of the EEC Treaty (IV/31.458 – X/Open Group) *Official Journal* L35/36, 6 February 1987 and Notice [1986] 3 C.M.L.R. 373.
85. *Official Journal*, 1987 L35/36, 6 February 1987, para. 42.
86. Andrew Rutter, op. cit., p. 22.
87. See *Official Journal*, 1987 L35/33, 6 February 1987, paras. 3–5.
88. Companies include: Shell, BP, Texaco, Ex..on and Mobil. Source: *Computing*, 7 June 1990.
89. 'OSF Comes to Europe for a UNIX Extension', *Computing*, 19 July 1990, p. 6.
90. A transmission control program is one within a computer network that defines the formalised methods of communication between networks. Source: P.B. Brown, *Dictionary of Electrical, Electronics, and Computer Abbreviations*, Butterworths, 1985, p. 212.
91. For example, one group is looking at defining complete open systems at a general level – including operating systems, development tools, languages and networking facilities etc. Another is concentrating on interfaces – how to build applications that are hardware-independent, and another is considering the development of a Posix 'shell' and the tools systems developers will use. There is also work underway on conformance testing methods, 'real-time' Unix extensions, military requirements and security standards.
92. For a full discussion of the Posix standard proposals, see 'Rallying to the Standard', *Computer Systems – Europe*, July 1988, pp. 64–5.
93. Ginny Fraser, 'Year of the Curate's Egg', *Computer Systems – Europe*, December 1988, pp. 53–9, at p. 57. The issue now it seems is whether there will be options and subsets within Posix that should have the effect of producing products which are 'Posix compliant' but which are very different in character. This would work against the objective if carried too far.
94. Gerald W. Brock, *The U.S. Computer Industry – A Study of Market Power* (1975) p. 143.
95. A summary of the BCS is given by Richard Foden in Steven Heath, op. cit., p. 28.
96. Steven Heath, 'Source, Object or Binary?', *Computer Systems – Europe*, July 1989, pp. 27–8. (Includes a summary of BCS by Richard Foden.)
97. 'Open Systems Processor', *Computer Systems – Europe*, April 1989, p. 7.
98. This issue is discussed in more detail by Peter Mitchell, 'Unix leads OS shake-up', *Computer Systems – Europe*, May 1989, pp. 17–22.

99. 'X/Open Branding Programme', *Computer Communications*, (6), December 1988, P. 333. In addition to the application software standard, X/Open has also produced three equipment standards at different conformance levels to enable the user to purchase a system that directly meets his requirements.

100. Editorial, *Computer Weekly*, 22 March 1990, p. 19.

101. Charlotte Klopp, 'IBM Draws Up Utilities Architecture', *Computer Weekly*, 22 March 1990, p. 1.

102. *Software: An Emerging Industry*, op. cit., p. 13.

103. Cullinet is strong on applications software and database products, R&D, marketing and client support. Prior to the takeover it operated in 22 countries, in 10 languages and from 100 offices.

104. David Bicknell, 'IBM Targets Software for Development and Growth', *Computer News*, 10 September 1987, p. 10.

105. Philip Manchester, 'Big Challenge for Software Creators', *Financial Times*, 10 November 1988, p. VIII.

106. There is likely to be yet another scramble between IBM and the rest of the industry to get in first with a standard. IBM has already been working with Logica since 1987 on a General Trading Architecture for the financial market, but the time factor has caused the project to be scaled down in order to produce results in the short-term. Full implementation is seen as a longer term initiative. See Patricia Tehan, 'IBM Limbers up to Build City System', *Computing*, 18 May 1989, p. 17.

107. Connie Smith, 'Software Fire Prevention', *Computer Systems – Europe*, June 1990, pp. 27–31.

108. This technique was developed by an American academic named Donald Knuth, who found that by improving the code in the hot spots, run times could be reduced from hours to minutes. See Darrel Ince, 'Testing Times for Software', *Computer Systems – Europe*, May 1989, pp. 31–4.

109. David Ince, 'Testing Times for Software', *Computer Systems – Europe*, May 1989, pp. 31–4.

110. Connie Smith, op. cit., p. 27.

111. Connie Smith, op. cit., p. 27.

112. Russell Jones, 'Marking the 4GL Card', *Datalink*, 9 November 1987, p. 11.

113. George Schussel, op. cit., p. 16.

114. This is defined as a non-procedural component since the user need only explain what he wants the program to do, without having to specify how it should accomplish it. See Russell Jones, 'DEC's End-Users Thirst for Power', *Computer News*, 28 January 1988, pp. 13 and 16.

115. For a good description of 4GLs see Longley and Shain, op. cit., p. 150.

116. Quoted by Sean Hallahan, 'A Generation that few Understand', *Computer News*, 21 January 1988 pp. 13–16 at p. 13.

117. Steve Roche, 'Moving Closer to the Fifth Generation', *Computing*, 8 February 1990, pp. 14–15.

118. Glenis Moore, 'The Next Step', *Computer Systems – Europe*, January 1990, pp. 9–12.

119. Ibid., p. 9.

120. '4GLs Return to Defend their Title', *Computer News*, 17 March 1988, p. 22.
121. Cognos's 'Powerhouse' is, however, being extended for Hewlett-Packard, DEC, and Data General mid-range systems, plus IBM PC/AT systems, 386 machines and HP-UX. UNIX platforms are also being developed. Source: Glenis Moore, op. cit., p. 9.
123. Sean Hallahan, op. cit., at p. 15.
124. Russell Jones, 'Pruning with a 4GL Power Tool', *Computing*, 17 November 1988, pp. 28–9.
125. Tony Rundle, 'CASE Tools and 4GLs', *Computer Systems – Europe*, April 1990, pp. 34–8.
126. Philip Manchester, 'A Boon for Programmers', *Financial Times*, 24 November 1989, p. V.
127. Rebecca Hurst, 'CASE Systems Near Fruition', *Computerworld*, Focus No. 27A, 8 July 1987, pp. 27–9. Examples of Schematic design tools are: Information Engineering Workbench (Knowledgeware Inc. – Atlanta Ga.); Case 2000 Designaid (Nastec Corp., Southfield Ma.); and Excelerator (Index Technology Corp., Cambridge Mass.).
128. The best known Upper CASE product is Knowledgeware's 'Information Engineering Workbench' (IEW) widely used at mainframe sites. Source: Michael Powell, 'A Case For Further Development', *Computer Weekly*, 30 November 1989, p. 29.
129. Russell Jones, 'Linchpin With a Future', *Datalink*, 2 March 1987, p. 14. Some code generators include: Gamma (Knowledgeware); Transform (Transform Logic Corp., Scottsdale Az.); and Vax Cobol Generator (Digital Equipment Corp., Maynard Mass.).
130 Julia Vowler, 'A Case That Has To Be Taken Seriously', The *Independent*, 3 July 1989, p. 14.
131. Leslie Tilley, 'Coders Must Change', *The Times*, 25 May 1989, p. 35. Claim by the West German software house, Software AG, in relation to the capacity of their own code generators.
132. In the US Navy the standard for human COBOL coding is 23 lines per day. A top level analyst/programmer could produce 100 lines, whereas James Martin Associates claim that IEF can generate 500–1000 lines per day without difficulty, Rolls Royce are using IEF to generate code for new systems for use in manufacturing engines. See Leslie Tilley, op. cit.
133. The produce is Information Engineering Facility (IEF) produced by James Martin Associates. The company claims that a Danish Bank used it to produce an online banking application without engaging a single programmer. See Leslie Tilley, op. cit.
134. Charles Babcock, 'Authors Meet Head-On to Settle their COBOL Differences', *Computer News*, 5 March 1987, p. 20.
135. COBOL restructuring tools include COBOL Structure Facility (IBM); Recorder (Language Technology, Salem Mass.); Retrofit (Peat Marwick, Chicago Ill.); and Superstructure (Group Operations, Washington DC).
136. Anthony Westbrook, 'Taking a High-Jump over the Language Barrier', *Computing*, 31 March 1988, pp. 16–17.

137. See ante, p. 212. 'C' was developed at Bell Labs in the early 1970s to assist in the writing of Unix. It has subsequently been extended as is used widely today not least in writing CASE tools themselves.
138. Migration Technology (formerly MS Associates) market a translator called 'C-Gen' and Tetra Business Systems offer C-Base. Another product is Sector 7's B-Tran The intense interest in these products led these companies to court in 1986–87 over allegations of copyright and trade secrets infringement. The disputes were settled at the interlocutory stage without ever going to full trial.
139. For example, the conversion from Word Perfect Corporation's 4.2 wordprocessing package to the 5.0 version.
140. Katherine Spurr, 'Case: A Culture Shock', *Computer Bulletin*, June 1989, pp. 9–10.
141. 'CASE is Unpopular', *Computer Systems – Europe*, July 1989, p. 7.
142. Philip Manchester, 'Better Systems Faster', *Computing*, 26 February 1987, pp. 16–17.
143. Clive Cookson, 'Program to Solve the "Software Crisis" ', *Financial Times*, 20 September 1988, p. 21.
144. Quoted ibid.
145. Tony Hill 'Customising Case', *Computer Systems – Europe*, (5) 1990, pp. 29–32.
146. Martin Whybrow, 'Ipse Facto', *Informatics*, April 1989, pp. 28–32.
147. Kenneth MacIver, 'IBM Postpones Coding Future', *Datalink*, 17 April 1989, p. 1.
148. It is estimated that up to 40% of code can be identified and re-used where structured design methods of software engineering are employed. See George Walker, 'How to get the msot out of IBM's Repositary', *Computing*, 4 May 1989, pp. 24–6
149. A typical product lifecycle begins with the user requirement and moves to individual program specifications. When approved this is then coded, checked and tested before passing to the user. Maintenance is then provided for the duration of the product.
150. George Walker, op. cit., p. 25.
151. See Sarah Aryanpur, 'Get To Work On Your AD/Cycle', *Computer Weekly*, 25 January 1990, p. 36.
152. George Schussel, 'Software's Future', *Computer Systems*, January 1988, pp. 16–19 at p. 19.
153. Europe and the United States are both promoting standards within CASE. These are the Portable Common Tool Environment (PCTE) proposed by the European Computer Manufacturers Association and the US Department of Defense single common programming language 'ADA', which provides tools within the 'ADA Program Support Environment' (APSE), the current version of which is 'CATS-A'. On ADA, see Stevens, op. cit., pp. 160–61. On the broader issue, see Special Report: 'PCTE as a proposed ISO' *Computer Systems – Europe*, January 1989, pp. 17–20.
154. 'Informix Gets on the Case with SSADM', *Computing*, 28 June 1990, p. 1.

155. The software methodology is based on 'Virtual Software Factory', developed by the UK software producer Systematic.
156. Alan Cane, 'Software that Builds on the Real World', *Financial Times*, 5 July 1989, p. 37.
157. Other approaches being considered are 'logical programming' – based on the logical description (of the nature and relations) of the system to be computerised; and 'functional programming' – based on high-level functional instructions, suitable for developing expert systems which manipulate largely non-numeric lists, information and symbols. Quoted from *Software: An Emerging Industry*, OECD, 1985, (Information Computer Communication Policy Series No. 9) p. 34.
158. Alan Cane, 'A Promise of Big Gains in Productivity', *Financial Times*, 24 November 1989, p. V.
159. John Samson, 'Starting with the Human End Instead', *Computing*, 1 February 1990, pp. 20–23.
160. *Software: An Emerging Industry*, op. cit., p. 34.
161. Alan Cane, op. cit.
162. Ibid.
163. Ovum Ltd., 'Object-Oriented Systems: The Commercial Benefits 1989'. Quoted by Alan Cane, Ibid.
164. Ibid.
165. The first Oop language is 'Simula' developed by a Norwegian Company of the same name. Xerox also have a product called 'Smalltalk'. The fastest growing Oop language is 'C++' developed by AT&T, who also created 'C' used in the design of the operating system Unix. For discussion about C++, see Hugh Griffiths and Colin Walls, 'C++; A Language for the 90's', *Computer Systems – Europe*, June 1989, pp. 57–8.
166. The Oop's link to SAA is an architecture for data connectivity called Distributed Data Management. Alan Cane, op. cit.
167. See ante, p. 213.
168. Judith Jeffcoate, 'Software For the Real World', *Computer Systems – Europe*, August 1989, pp. 29–30.
169. Steve Cook, 'Mastering Computers', *Computer Bulletin*, May 1989, pp. 21–2.
170. In November 1989 the COBOL standards committee – CodaSyl established an Object Oriented Cobol Task Group (OOCTG) to oversee the adding of object orientation to the COBOL language. Source: Jerome Garfunkel, 'Cobol in the Nineties', *Computer Systems – Europe*, June 1990, pp. 17–20.
171. Judith Jeffcoate, op. cit., p. 29.
172. Adrian Lincoln, '20 MIPS is Not Enough', *Computing Systems – Europe*, May 1990, pp. 38–41.
173. Source: Steve Rogerson, 'Terabytes Hold No Terrors', *Computer Systems – Europe*, November 1989, pp. 46–8.
174. Christian Tyler, 'Make Way for the Thinking Machine', Weekend FT *Financial Times*, 30 June/1 July 1990, pp. I and VIII.
175. Professor Margaret Bowden, Sussex University, BBC TV *Horizon* pro-

gramme, 1987. For a full investigation of Artificial Intelligence, see Philip Leith, *Formalism in AI and Computer Science*, (Ellis Horwood, Chichester, 1990).

176. Gideon Summerfield, 'Voicing Objections', *Computer Systems – Europe*, October 1989, pp. 23–4.

177. Alan Cane, 'Computer with a Good Line in Chat', *Financial Times*, 14 December 1989, p. 12.

178. The Turing Machine is also discussed in Aleksander and Burnett, op. cit., pp. 34–9.

179. John Searle comments that what matters is the specific bio-chemistry. He believes that the simulator approach 'neglects what is so fantastic and amazing about the human brain, namely that the specific bio-chemistry of the brain causes us to have specific thoughts and feelings and so on'. BBC TV *Horizon* Programme, 1987.

180. Expert systems have been described as a 'sort of theoretical lowering of sights within the artificial intelligence research community'. In, Noak Kennedy, *The Industrialisation of Intelligence*, (Unwin Hyman, London, 1989), p. 116.

181. Aleksander and Burnett, op. cit., p. 107.

182. Ibid., p. 108.

183. LISP does not distinguish between program and data formats – the kind of rules and concepts that AI researchers believe parallel human thought. PROLOG is a predictive language that states properties of rather than procedures necessary to attain an answer. Logo is used as a teaching language, particularly with graphics or a robot turtle.' Source: Dennis Longley and Michael Shain, *Macmillan Dictionary of Information Technology*, 3rd Edition 1989, p. 28–29.

184. IBM have developed products called 'Knowledgetool' and 'Expert Systems Environment'.

185. Source: Bruce Andrews, 'The Expert Needed a Few Lessons', *Financial Times*, 12 October 1989, p. 23.

186. Examples include: ART (Automated Reasoning Tool) by Inference; KEE (Knowledge Engineering Environment) by Intellicorp; Knowledge-Craft by Carnegie Group; and Goldworks by Gold Hill Computers. These are all small California-based companies. Source: Rory Johnston, 'Intelligence with Less Brain Strain', *Computer News*, 24 September 1987.

187. Michiyo Nakamoto, 'The Clear Sense of Fuzzy Logic', *Financial Times*, 5 June 1990, p. 16; Bruce Andrews, 'The Growing Role of Computerised Expertise', *Financial Times*, 14 September 1989, p. 26.

188. Duda and Shortliffe, 'Expert Systems Research', *Science*, April 15 1983.

189. Russell Jones, 'Expert Support Systems – A Marriage of Convenience made in Heaven', *Computer Weekly*, 26 March 1987, pp. 20–21.

190. It is distributed by Coopers and Lybrand for use on an IBM OC or close compatible and costs £600 for the software and supporting documentation.

191. Kevin Townsend, 'Artificial Intelligence – Ever-Expanding Experts', *Computing*, 12 March 1987, pp. 22–3.

192. David Madden, 'Poised to Close in on the Customer', *Financial Times*, 7 June 1990.
193. Paul Beynon-Davies, 'The Logical Next Development for Databases', *Computer News*, 14 April, 1988.
194. Peter Knight, 'A Deal on the Green Market', *Financial Times*, 31 May 1990.
195. Aleksander and Burnett, op. cit., p. 284.
196. For discussion of this important issue see: U.S. Congress, Office of Technology Assessment, *Intellectual Property Rights in an Age of Electronics and Information*, (1986, OTA-CIT-302, Washington, DC: U.S. Government Printing Office) p. 78.
197. See also Aleksander and Burnett, *Thinking Machines*, pp. 22–4.
198. Eric Knorr, Robert Luhn, Ros Davidson, Daniel Ben-Horin, Charles Seiter, 'When Hal Becomes Real', *Computer News*, 30 June 1987, p. 15.

CHAPTER 6

Telecommunications – the global transition

NEW LINES OF COMMUNICATION

SWITCHING ON THE GLOBAL VILLAGE   It is difficult to grasp the effect on society from developments in telecommunications this century, for the impact has been so great. Communication, as the basic means of all human interaction, defines and extends our culture and the opportunities that the individual and the state have for economic and social autonomy.[1] The point has been described thus:

> The explosion of telecommunications in the second half of the twentieth century may be compared to the transition that humans made thousands of years ago from hunting to agriculture, or, more recently, from an agricultural society to an industrial society. The transition of industrial societies, via the limbo of the 'post-industrial' society into fully-fledged information societies – as we witness now – makes telecommunications the hallmark and defining characteristic of our society. It is a measure of a society's wealth or poverty, and a major factor in a society's capacity for change.[2]

The onset of digital communication, combined with the development of computers, is about to introduce a new much more personalised information culture, in which the individual will have a greater degree of personal choice and opportunity for accessing and distributing information than he has known before. New transmission media will provide choices that neither the printing press, the telephone nor even television has delivered up to now.[3] The root of this transformation lies in developments in transmission media and in the convergence of picture, sound and text in digital format. The days when the individual was the passive recipient of information into the home according to the preset formats of the broadcast

259

media are, according to many sources, numbered. [4] The plan is to introduce a single integrated services digital network (ISDN) as the cornerstone for worldwide digital transmission. This will provide unparalleled opportunities for communication and sharing of information and for the exploitation of the processing and future artificial-intelligence capabilities of computers and the databanks that the technology will serve.

EXPANSION IN NETWORK CAPACITY   Apart from verbal communication by telephone, prior to the 1970s telegraphy was still the principal electrical form of communication for the instantaneous transfer of messages for reproduction in a material form. In the main, until the 1930s, when simple teleprinters were introduced, messages had to be relayed within the network from switchboard to switchboard and laboriously translated by the recipient operator into the dot and dash code developed by Samuel Morse for conveying information. [5] In coded form, the message could be converted into electrical signals for transmission to the point of receipt where it could be deciphered and written down. [6] It was thus the first example of an electronic digital network for the transmission of information.

With the advent of automatic switching of messages after World War II, whereby the call could be dialled through direct to its destination, public exchanges were set up, interconnected throughout the world in a separate network from that of the telephone. There was AT&T's TWX service in the USA and Telex in Europe and elsewhere. In the USA the two systems amalgamated in 1970. The network was, of course, set up to cater for signals transmitted at the information-handling speeds of people rather than computers. By the early 1960s it was possible to transmit at the rate of 100 words per minute, advancing on the previous 75 word limit. It has been estimated that in 1969 there were 200,000 Telex subscribers in 154 countries. [7] In addition to exchange services, private wire systems were established, connecting, for example, newspapers to their press associations or the US Military to its district offices. (The Military network was the largest in the world in 1968 and it used hired facilities. It had 9 computer-controlled centres, 2700 outstations and 10 further centres serving 1600 overseas stations.) In the UK these data communication services were grouped together under the title 'Datel', and graded by tariff according to the facilities and capacities on offer. The public inland telegram service, which delivered the tape message stuck to a telegram form at the point of receipt, was suspended by the Post Office in 1983, when it was superceded by the Telemessage service offering overnight delivery. This reflected the decline in usage of the public service except for sending money or or special greetings messages.

Demand for the telex service has remained strong although this is changing now that competition from facsimile and electronic mail is growing. Nevertheless, it is now a much improved service, linked into the modern telecommunictions network worldwide, although its transmission rates remain comparatively slow. Today, in the EC countries alone there are about 650,000 telex terminals operating, the trend being to replace aging teleprinter equipment with word processors and through-connecting telex with the more sophisticated formats and higher speeds of teletex and facsimile transmission within the digital network.[10] For this reason it is predicted that telex will continue to feature prominently in its own right in the Single Market in Europe after 1992. Common standards are already in place for the telex service, while the fixing of standards for other messaging services remain to be negotiated. British Telecom is investing £100 million for the purpose of modernising the UK telex network, and in 1989 opened the world's largest digital telex exchange in the City of London.

By way of contrast with what was possible just a few years ago, compare today the communications arranged by British Telecom to support the 1989/90 Whitbread Round the World Yacht Race, which departed from Southampton in September 1989 – the fifth such race since the first one in 1973/74.[11] In those days navigation was manual using sextants, and the yachts would disappear from contact for long stretches during the 144 days at sea and the 33,000 nautical miles of the race. For the 1989/90 race, which was watched by an estimated 600 million people worldwide, British Telecom installed a powerful computer, connected to a private communications network at race headquarters in Portsmouth, to monitor the progress of each competitor. Live pictures were obtainable from the yachts in mid-ocean, following the development by British Telecom of a method of translating still colour video pictures into a digital format which could be compressed, stored in an on-board personal computer, and transmitted across the airwaves using high frequency radio. Upon receipt of the signal at the Portsmouth race headquarters, the signals were decoded and the pictures transmitted to TV stations around the world. The process took seven minutes to complete.

On board, the competitors navigated by satellite, obtaining digitised weather maps from shore-based meteorological services which the ships' computers used for routing predictions, and each operator at sea could pre-set the time he required this information to be sent. (The yacht, 'British

Satquote Defender,' the combined-services contender in the race, was described beforehand as having the navigation facilities of a modern warship.) An additional facility supporting the race was the provision of a dedicated telephone satellite link connecting the Portsmouth headquarters with the other ports of call in the race. These were at Punta del Este (Uruguay); Freemantle (Australia); Auckland (New Zealand); and Fort Lauderdale (United States). Race information, including the relative position and the track of each yacht, could be transmitted from data plotted automatically by satellite. In addition screen-based data was available daily through the Dialcom network to all those with computer links to it. Available through the network was text, positions and tables listing fleet and handicap placings, as well as estimates of speed and distance to finish. All the data was updated daily throughout the race.

The question to be answered is how such a temendous expansion in the capacity of the telecommunications network to deliver this kind of information has taken place. By comparison with the past twenty years or so, the prior history of telecommunication has been eventful and evolutionary, but not revolutionary to the extent depicted by the yachting illustration above. Prior to the 1970s, society was used to the identifiable and independent services provided by the telegraph, and thereafter by telephone, radio telegraphy, and television. Data and voice transmission by telegraph and telephone meant two-way narrow-band communications compared with the one-way broadband requirements of television broadcasting. (The sound of the human voice is produced by waves that can vary from 20 to 20000 Hz (cycles per second) with best reception from 100–4000Hz; radio operates between 1 million and 100 million Hz (1–100 MHz); and '625 line' television operates at 0–5.5 MHz.) An infrastructure and consumer market built up to support these services, which retained their functional independence in the public mind. While there were continual advances in the range, scope, efficiency and quality of these services, there can be no comparison with the subsequent development, in recent times, of a general purpose digital network, able to carry a vast range of audio, video and data material at speeds never anticipated before.

The expansion of the telephone network into every country in the world, connecting together 600 million telephones, is rightly regarded as one of man's great achievements in communication, despite the work still to be done to increase the volume of telephone access in the developing countries.[14] The success of radio and television, as independent broadcasting media, has been no less spectacular. However, contrasting the sheer pace of technological development now taking place, these early successes are likely to be judged as no more than than precursory to the global communications revolution currently underway. The capacity to translate information in the form of sound, text or pictures into electrical energy that can be communicated at high speed to its intended destination, and the convergence of this technology with that of the digital computer, has created major opportunities for society, both economically and socially. This section examines the development in communication techniques that has produced the network, while identifying the new services that have grown up out of these changes.

THE EVOLUTION OF THE DIGITAL NETWORK   The history of digitisation, that is, the encoding, transformation and transmission in bit form, of information, whether voice, data or visual, encompasses the development of transmission facilities, switching techniques and terminal receivers.[15] In the case of transmission, the task has been twofold; first, to replace the aging analogue system, which served the telephone network until the onset of digitisation, and second, to enhance the scope of transmission media, by cable, satellite and radio, in order to accommodate the increased demand upon the network brought about by the integration of existing services with new ones. With switching technology, the objective has been to introduce microelectronics in place of the electro-mechanical control system for the routing of calls. Invented by Almon Strowger, the original switch led to the development of 'Strowger Exchanges', the last of which have been phased out 100 years after the original invention of the switch in 1889. Computer-based stored program control techniques now establish and release connections in a fully digital environment. Advances in terminal equipment have involved the introduction of computer-based terminal facilities supporting a range of voice and data services in place of conventional telephone and telex connections. These advances have created the opportunity to develop the ISDN network, the object being to produce a means by which all forms of communication could be carried via a single connection using common equipment. In Europe the implementation of this network is now fully underway, the objective being to bring 80% of subscribers within reach of an ISDN exchange by the commencement of the open market in Europe after 1992.

THE DEVELOPMENT OF TRANSMISSION SYSTEMS   The telephone network was built around the principle of analogue signal transmission. Analogue

263

signals are those that are 'analogous' to the characteristics of the information to be transmitted, in the sense that the signal monitors and emulates the variation of sound energy produced by the information, for example, the human voice. A difficulty, however, was finding a satisfactory method of boosting the signal to enable comunication by phone at longer distances. Analogue signals distort easily, particularly as distance builds up.[16] Initially the partial solution was to use thick 5 mm. copper wires, weighing up to 600 lbs per mile of wire.[17] The weight of these wires caused major problems in bad weather and an alternative method of establishing long-distance circuits was sought. A further contribution was the development of loading coils, inserted at intervals along the telephone cable and designed to reduce the loss of higher frequency signals which caused distortion to the sound of the human voice.[18] This technique was used in the United States in the first transcontinental line connecting New York with San Francisco which came into service in 1915.[19]

The key development, however, which hastened the opening of the coast-to-coast link, was the vacuum tube amplifier called the thermionic triode valve, which not only boosted analogue signals rendering loading coils redundant, but also provided the basis for long-distance radio, and potentially television, communications.[20] The invention was made by an American named Lee De Forest who obtained his doctorate in mechanical engineering at Yale in 1899. The triode valve was as revolutionary in its time as the transistor was to become 40 years later. A patent was obtained in 1907, one of 300 that the great inventor was ultimately to possess. The key to the valve was the insertion of a third element in the tube that could amplify faint signals. This discovery was incorporated in repeaters, which amplified the signal at regular intervals enabling the problem of signal attenuation (the variation of signal strength over time) to be partially overcome.[21] However, despite improvements produced in the performance of repeaters,[22] an underlying problem remained, in that the amplifiction of signals through an electrical circuit always carried with it interfering signals which marked or distorted the transmission. This could be caused by the interruption of the channel by other equipment spilling over in the form of unwanted electrical impulses, the consequential effect of processing the signal, electron interference in the receiving equipment, or possibly atmospheric disturbance.[23] The interference manifested itself in a crackling sound otherwise known as 'noise'. On long distance calls the amplification of the signal also enhanced the magnitude of the noise.[24] The problem was closely connected with the nature of the analogue signal itself

– constantly changing and easily distorted. An entirely new transmission method was required if this problem was to be overcome.

The theory of digital transmission developed as a direct consequence of attempts to find ways of resolving the problems of noise, distortion and cross-talk. In 1937 an Englishman named Alec Reeves, who had qualified as an engineer and worked on radio communications with the International Western Electric Company (now part of Standard Telephones and Cable), proposed a transmission system in which analogue speech signals could be electronically coded into a string of electrical pulses. These would then be transmitted and converted back into speech signals at the point of destination. The underlying concept was very simple and involved sampling the strength of the analogue signal – that is the height of the wave – at regular intervals. With cinema pictures the sampling rate necessary to create the deception of movement to the eye is 24 frames per second. For speech, however, it was necessary to sample at the rate of 8000 times per second in order to reproduce a reasonable voice quality. The sampling results thus produced would be measured on a scale of 0–256 and converted to 8-bit binary code, to develop a pulse waveform unique to each binary number. (Each binary-coded sample level can be transmitted in a few microseconds (millionths of a second) so there is considerable unoccupied time in each slot which can be used for other transmissions.) The pulses would either be 'on' or 'off' according to the 1s or 0s of the binary representation. With 8000 samples, each represented by 8-bit code, this meant that 64,000 bits (64K) were produced each second (64kbit/s bit rate). These would then be transmitted down the cable for decoding at the point of destination back to analogue form and, thereafter, electronically re-constituted into the sound of the caller's voice.[25]

The idea was revolutionary, and unfortunately ahead of its time, since the equipment had not been developed to exploit its potential. Electronic circuits in thermionic valve form were incapable of providing the processing speeds necessary for handling the digital transmission. The theory became a practical proposition with the invention of 'solid-state' means of performing binary operations, that began in the 1950s with the launch of the transistor and continued with the shift into micro-electronics and the silicon chip. Digital switching carried with it other advantages over that of analogue communication.

One advantage was the opportunity to increase transmission capacity. Since samples of a signal, rather than the whole signal itself, would be transmitted, the same line could be used simultaneously for more than one call. Individuals would require sole use of the line connecting their telephone to the network, but not the lines between the exchanges themselves. Using this technique, known as 'multi-plexing', multiple use of existing trunk lines was possible, producing capacity to carry up to 30 conversations at one time. The method was equally adaptable to the high-density, high-traffic links subsequently developed for transmission purposes.[26] The idea was originally known as 'carrier telephony', and was developed in response to the crowded conditions above ground, in which telegraph poles became laced with wires. An early technique was a method of transmitting telegraph signals over telephone lines without interfering with telephone conversations. The concept was called 'superposing', where a phantom circuit was derived by using the mid-point of transformer wires. It was first operational in 1918, twenty years before Alec Reeves developed the theory of digital transmission which was to lend itself so well to the notion of carrying numerous communication channels over a single transmission line.[27]

The multi-plexing methods subsequently applied were of two types: by 'time division' in which the signal was sampled for a period of two to three microseconds every 125 micro-seconds (the speed required for voice transmission), leaving spaces between the pulses which could be used for other signals; and 'frequency division', in which each speech channel was allocated a unique portion of the bandwith, enjoying exclusive use of that section of the frequency band for each signal transmission.[28] When these techniques were used in the USA on the trunk network, which deployed the common twisted-pair copper wires, it increased capacity to between 12 and 24 voice channels using frequency division multiplexing, and 24 and 96 channels by time division.[29] A further potential advantage of digital transmission techniques, compared with analogue, was the universal character of the signal definition. In the case of analogue channels, the signal varied continuously according to the information in transmission, which meant in practice a different channel for each type of signal – for example telephone or radio broadcast. With digital channels, the only difference to be considered was the binary transmission speed necessary to transmit the information, whether it took the form of data, image or the human voice. It has already been established that voice transmission requires a bit transmission rate of 64kbit/s. To transmit a television picture, however, requires a bit rate of approximately 70Mbit/s (70 million bit/s), reflecting the increased complexity of the signal information. Thus the convergence of transmission services through a single channel, transparent to the signals to be carried, became possible with the onset of digitization.[30] It is now coming into operation, with the advent of the integrated services digital network.

Cable   The veins of the telephone network in the UK at the turn of the century were the thick copper wires necessary to preserve the strength of the signal. This represented the biggest capital cost in investment in the network. The introduction of loading coils and later repeaters enabled significantly thinner wires to be introduced by the 1920s. The twisted-pair cable came into use at that time, linking telephones to local exchanges and the telegraph with local offices. This arrangement reduced the capacitance between the wires. Sometimes groups of four might be paired together, and a number of these insulated together in the same cable to provide a number of channels. At the system's peak, cables could carry up to 2000 twisted pairs in a single sheath. At the same time efforts were being made to lay the cables underground. This eased the unsightly congestion experienced above ground and reduced the risk of storm damage and consequential interruption of the service. A major difficulty was protecting the cables from moisture, for which one proposed solution was to use lead sheaths, supplemented by layers of paper and hessian impregnated with bitumen.[31] The first satisfactory underground telephone cables were laid between London and Birmingham in 1915. In due course this transformed the appearance of big cities such as New York, and influenced the growth of a specialist electronics engineering profession, given the increased levels of skill demanded by underground cabling.

A continuing problem with the twisted-pair cable was a phenomenon known as the 'skin effect'. It arose particularly as the frequencies of signal transmission grew to accommodate different kinds of multi-plexing.[32] This resulted in the gathering of electrons on the surface of the wire and an increase in resistance. To overcome this it was necessary to add repeaters along the wire to maintain the quality of the signal. The development of the co-axial cable was designed to tackle this difficulty. The cable contained two conductors, placed one inside the other but insulated separately, the outer consisting of a tube of braided copper. A crucial advantage of co-axial cable was its capacity to transmit at a higher frequency than that of its predecessor. This was advantageous because the larger bandwidth increased the scope of the cable link. Because more of the wire surface was exposed, resistance and loss of signal strength was reduced, as well as the amount of 'noise' interference and unwanted transfer of energy from one wire to another known as 'cross-talk'. The higher frequency, combined with multi-plexing, increased the line capacity to between 1800 and 10,800 simultaneous telephone conversations, and in the pre-digital era this was about the maximum that could be achieved in a single cable. The highest number of voice channels, however, was the 132,000 produced by AT&T using a 22-tube co-axial cable supported by repeaters placed at intervals of 1 mile.[33] Digital transmission, which involved sampling the analogue voice signal 8000 times a second and converting the sample into 8-bit code, reduced co-axial capacity to approximately 2000 channels. With the advent of fibre optics this barrier was quickly shattered.

The first co-axial telephone cable in the UK was laid by the Post Office between London and Birmingham in 1936. A submarine cable connected Britain with Holland in 1937 and to North America in 1956. Known as TAT-1 it operated for 22 years, providing initially 36 4kHz channels and later expanded to 48 3kHz channels on 2 co-axial cables.[34] There were 51 one-way repeaters in each line between Scotland and Newfoundland. In contrast to the 48 voice channels of the 1956 cable, further cables were laid providing an additional 128 channels in 1963, 845 in 1969 and 4000 in 1976 with the laying of TAT-6.[35] By the 1970s more than 140 separate submarine cable systems were in existence around the world providing upwards of 20,000 circuits for voice communication.[36]

Fibre Optics 1. Into the Digital Fast Lane. To appreciate something of the extent of the breakthrough in telecommunications represented by the discovery that it is possible to transmit information as pulses of light down a glass fibre, it is necessary, first of all, to understand a little about the information theory pioneered by Claude Shannon after World War II. Digital telecommunication is based on the idea that it is possible to transmit a digital signal derived from a sampling of the frequency of the amplitude (strength) of an electromagnetic wave produced by a sound. The frequency is the number of cycles generated each second by an electromagnetic wave. This is measured in Hertz (Hz) and varies according to the information being transmitted. The sound of the human voice, for example, can normally produce frequences within the range 100Hz to 7kHz (its theoretical range might reach up to 20kHz), whereas high-fidelity music requires a range to 20kHz.[38] The amplitude is a measure of the height of each cycle at the high point of each wave oscillation.

A vital characteristic of the signal is the bandwidth, which is a measure of the range of frequencies produced by the signal transmission. The size of the bandwith varies according to type of signal being transmitted. In the case of the human voice just described, the bandwidth required to accommodate its transmission is 6900 Hz or 20kHz for hi-fi music. Telephone speech requires a bandwidth of 3100kHz. With colour television the range of frequencies is much wider than that of speech or music. This is because the measurement that is converted into the vision signal is the amount of light energy absorbed by each small spot on the surface of the television screen. Details of colour, light and shade, as well as sound, must all be incorporated into the transmission. The bandwidth required for current UK 625-line television is up to 5.5–6mHz (million Hertz).[39]

It can be deduced, therefore, that the greater the bandwidth available, the greater is the amount of information that can potentially be transmitted. Telecommunication takes place within the electromagnetic spectrum, which comprises the complete set of frequencies available to mankind. At the low frequency end of the spectrum, alternating current provides the means of transmission through traditional wire or co-axial cable.[40] Alternatively, transmission can occur within the electromagnetic energy that surrounds the surface of the earth. Radio waves operate within a wide range of frequencies, from 10kHz to approximately 1THz (1GHz = 1 billion Hz, 1THz = 1000GHz). Other naturally occurring phenomena, such as light, extend the spectrum much further, beginning with infra-red followed by visible light, ultra-violet light, X-rays, gamma and cosmic rays, operating at phenomenally high frequencies.[41] Visible light, for example, operates in the region of 100–1000THz.

Given the importance of communications worldwide and the need to regulate use of the electomagnetic spectrum, the World Administrative Radio Conference of the International Telecommunication Union has allocated bands of frequencies for different purposes. Within this framework, governments similarly regulate the precise allocation of frequencies for different forms of broadcasting services.[42] For example, in 1988 the British Government published a consultative document about the use of the radio frequency above 30GHz (i.e. above 300 times the frequency of VHF radio). It discussed the possibility of opening this section of the radio frequency to commercial use in the 1990s. Services might include short-range television; very fast data transmission; cable-less internal telephone systems; electronic funds transfers at the point of sale; communications between buildings in line of sight; and mobile services such as route guidance for vehicles or portable telephones.[43] In August 1989, the Department of Trade and Industry announced that the Government had allocated the 40GHz band for local television. Between 25 and 30 channels will be available for entertainment, similar to that of cable systems.[44]

2. Exploiting the Light Spectrum. It is in the exploitation of the light spectrum that the real breakthrough in telecommunications has occurred – the transmission of pulses of light along strands of glass known as optical fibre. Operating at very high optical frequencies, and correspondingly short wavelengths compared with ordinary radio waves, bandwidth potential at this level provides infinitely more communications capacity than at lower levels of the spectrum. Whereas the conventional voice channel operates within a bandwidth of 3.1kHz, microwave radio communications operate at a frequency one million times greater, within a bandwidth that is 2000 times wider than that necessary for medium-wave radio transmissions within the 300kHz-3MHz range. At the lowest end of the light spectrum, the frequency of the infra-red light band is 100k times greater than microwave, or 100k million greater than voice frequency. Bandwidths of several Giga-bits per second are therefore possible.[45]

The concept of light waves as a means of carrying information was known about for some time prior to the first successful public telephone transmission by optical fibre link in 1977. The transmission took place between British Telecom Research Laboratories at Martlesham Heath in Suffolk and the town of Ipswich in 1977 – a distance of 13km.[46] There was considerable interest in overcoming the difficulties underlying communications by light which, with its phenomenally high-channel bandwidth, substantially in excess of even micro-wave proportions, offered the possibility of carrying almost unlimited volumes of information at very high speeds. Whereas the notional speed of transmission throughout the electromagnetic spectrum is the speed of light: 300 million metres per second in a vacuum, the actual speed varies with the medium through which the wave passes. With cable, for example, there was always resistence to the current flow, resulting in a weakening of the signal and despite successive enhancement to this technology in terms of improved channel capacity and quality and reliability of transmission, neither cable nor the radio or microwave frequencies could match the potential of optical fibre.

The concept of glass and light taking over from copper wire and electricity required the coming together of several technologies before success was achieved. The glass would have to be completely pure, otherwise the impurities present would scatter the light and destroy the signal in a matter of a few metres. Therefore a fibre, less than the diameter of a human hair, was perfected, surrounded by an outer cladding which reduced the scattering of the signal by reflecting the infra-red rays back along the core of the inner fibre.[47] The core and outer cladding would then be coated for protection against physical harm and placed in a protective sleeve no more than a few millimetres thick. As many fibres as necessary could be held in this way within the same cable.

Secondly, a light source was required to carry the digital signals along the glass fibre at the speed of light.[48] Infra-red laser light proved the most amenable to the process, since it operated over a narrow spectrum and found the glass to be more transparent to its rays than other alternative light sources. Alternatively a light-emitting diode emitting a wide beam of light for very high capacity transmission, such as is required for under-sea cables, provided an alternative to laser. Light pulses lasting a few thousand millionths of a second would transmit the data, which would change back into electrical pulses at the point of reception of the signal by means of a photodiode.[49]

The advantages of digital optical-fibre transmission systems are clear. Apart from the very substantial bandwidth and therefore high transmission capacity already identified, production costs are low, since the raw material for fibre production – sand – is both widely available and cheap. Moreover, the cables themselves, being smaller and lighter to handle than copper, reduce installation costs by comparison with conventional cable.[50] The quality of transmission is also superior to that available through copper wire, since no electric current is induced. This averts cross-talk from adjacent fibres as well as reducing the attenuation of the signal that is normally produced by resistance within the cable conductor. The need for repeaters to amplify the light signals over long distances is expected to extend from one every 30 kilometres to distances of 100 kilometres or more in the 1990s. This compares favourably with co-axial cable which required signal amplification every few kilometres to maintain strength.[51]

3.   First Generation Systems. The first generation of optical fibre systems was introduced in the late 1970s. The Martlesham–Ipswich link became a permanent part of the public telephone network in 1978, the first to do so in Europe, while communications during the 1980 Los Angeles Olympic Games utilised optical fibres which carried 1342 voice channels at rates of 90Mbit/s.[52] Bit rates of up to 140Mbit/s marked the transmission limits of this first level of optical fibre technology. At this speed of communication,

carrying capacity matched that of the best co-axial cable at 1920 voice channels, 256 music channels or just 2 television channels.[53] Given the sampling frequency and translation and bit-rate conversion of the original analogue signal, digital transmission required a much greater bandwidth than did analogue transmission. Currently, single, or mono-mode, fibre systems are being installed, transmitting at the rate of 565Mbit/s.[54] Two strands can carry 30,000 telephone calls simultaneously.[55]

Expectations are that second-generation transmission rates will reach 2.4 Gbit/s by 1991 (so providing 30,720 voice channels, 4096 music channels and 32 television channels).[56] Such capacity will be necessary in the 1990s if a European High Definition Television Standard (HDTV) is agreed. A 1250 line system was publicly demonstrated for the first time in 1988, following collaboration, and a £250 million investment involving some 30 European industrial companies, broadcasters and research institutes from 10 countries.[57] HDTV transmission played an important role during the Seoul Olympics in 1988, and will be used again when the Olympics take place in France and Spain in 1992. HDTV offers TV pictures of a quality comparable to 35mm film. The HDTV screen does not introduce any signal deterioration, as may be detected on conventional colour screens, and there will be no ghosting of objects or figures moving in the picture. At double the number of lines currently in use, this will also double the transmission bit-rate to approximately 140Mbit/s, and halve the number of channels capable of being broadcast by optical fibre compared with its capacity to handle conventional TV requirements.[58]

The introduction of optical fibre communications on an international scale has gathered pace since the mid-1980s. It has concentrated on the long-distance part of the network and on establishing international links. The first transatlantic optical fibre cable (TAT-8) was laid in 1988, capable of carrying 37800 voice channels simultaneously, four times that of the TAT-6 co-axial cable laid in 1976 and more than one thousand times the capacity of the first such cable (TAT-1), laid in 1956, which could handle just 36 calls at the outset.[59] Plans are now well underway to construct the first trans-Soviet fibre optic telecommunications link, which would connect Europe and Japan. The system could also extend access to south-east Asia and Australia via other cable systems. Such connections will be vitally important to the development of the international financial trading markets and other worldwide services. Other additional systems have been or are currently being laid in both the Atlantic and the Pacific.[60] Exploitation of optical fibre technology is only in its infancy and is certain to challenge satellite communication in certain sectors of the information market. Although it is becoming widely available in the long distance (trunk) part of the telecommunications network, it will take longer to penetrate the local transmission service, where copper cable still predominates. In the UK, cable franchises have been issued for cable TV, but there is no consistency in the choice of cable being used. The market seems to be preferring the cheaper copper alternative to fibre optics in bringing pay-TV into the home.[61]

It is suggested, however, that the first few years of the 1990s will mark the cost cross-over point in favour of fibre optics, though it is recognised that upgrading the 'last kilometre' of the network into the home will take a substantial time to complete. Nevertheless, when it does, domestic tele-communications services will be transformed by the terrific increases in bandwidth capacity brought about by optical means of transmission and the digital format of the signal.[62] A hint of what is to come was demon-strated as long ago as 1985, when scientists at Bell Labs in the United States combined 10 laser beams in a single glass fibre, producing a trans-mission rate of 20 Gbit/s, without amplification, over a distance of 68 Km. This was approximately equivalent to sending data equivalent to 200 volumes of an encyclopaedia in just one second.[63] Research into 'heavy metal flouride' fibre optic cables also suggest a dramatic reduction in signal loss, permitting repeater spacing to extend up to 6000km in the future. The potential of optical fibre communications, combined with its accelerating reduction in cost, will ensure that it plays a significant part in the communi-cations infrastructure that will govern into the twenty-first century.[64]

Satellite Communication – Exploiting Space Segment   The availability in the UK of satellite television, following the launch of Sky TV with 16 channels and British Satellite Broadcasting with a further 5, together with the appearance of satellite dishes on the side of peoples' homes, has done much to publicise the value to the consumer of satellite communications. From the United States, Cable News Network (CNN) has become well-known too, serving more than 90 countries via five regional satellites.[65] Clearly, broadcasting is only one of several important uses of the space segment, which include remote sensing of terrestial conditions for military or other purposes, international business and domestic communication and research and development. Compared with its terrestrial counterparts, the deployment of the technology has added significantly to the flexibility of the international telecommunications network and to the extension of services at an international and regional level.

The era of satellite communications began in 1957 when the Russians launched Sputnik 1. Since then, several thousand satellites have been launched, of which no more than ten percent provide civilian communications services. In 1988 alone, 150 satellites were launched for a variety of scientific, military and communications purposes.[66] So far as commercial communications satellites are concerned, it is estimated that approximately 2500 transponders were in orbit in 1990.[67] Transponders on a satellite receive transmissions from a high-powered Earth station and re-transmit these signals to either single or multiple receivers on the ground.[68] Of these transponders currently in space, approximately 40% are US based, 30% part of international systems operated, for example, by Intelsat (the International Telecommunications Satellite Organisation)[69], 6% European or Japanese based, 4.5% Canadian and the remaining 13.5% divided among the rest of the world.[69]

With the rapid development of the technology, satellites have increased rapidly in sophistication and power. Satellite weight has increased from under 50kg to nearly three tons, height to that of a four-storey building, and the average operational orbital lifetime from 2 to 15 years or more. At the same time, ground station equipment has evolved to include the use of very small satellite antennae.[70] Miniaturisation, increased reliability and solid-state engineering has further contributed to the capacity and transmission rates of communications satellites which emit and receive in the 6/4 GHz (C-Band) and (since 1980, with the Intelsat V and V-A satellite series) in the 14/11–12 GHz (Ku-Band) frequency bands.[71] The higher power of the Ku-Band frequencies promotes access by smaller Earth stations. Domestic satellites within the C-Band frequency routinely operate within a bandwidth of between 500 and 1000 MHz (1 GHz), although the current Intelsat VI series of communications satellites deploy an increased bandwidth of 3.3 GHz. Satellites operating in the C-Band can support up to 24 transponders with a passband of 34 MHz for each one. This allows a gap of 6 MHz between transponders, so avoiding congestion. Using signal modulation techniques this produces a 3000 voice channel capacity per transponder.[72] Already, transponder bandwidths have increased into the 50, 72 and 240 MHz levels with further developments expected in the higher Ku- and Ka-Band frequencies.

1. The Birth of Intelsat. The International Telecommunications Satellite Organisation (Intelsat) has been a major influence in this success since its establishment on 20 August 1964, when, led by the United States, 11 countries agreed to set up a global commercial telecommunication satellite system. The objective at the time was to provide services throughout the world without discrimination.[73] This was achieved by offering telecommunications operators with international transmission capacity by way of voice, data and telex circuits, telegram facilities and television channels which could then be sold on.[74] Since Intelsat's 'Early Bird' launch 25 years ago, the organisation has grown to a membership of 119 countries, with Nepal, Zimbabwe and Mozambique joining in 1989, and Romania in May 1990.[75] It currently maintains 14 satellites in synchronous orbit over the Atlantic, Pacific and Indian Ocean regions, transmitting to approximately 800 communications antennae at 638 Earth stations, through more than 2000 separate communications links in 157 countries. The first communications satellite was 'Early Bird' (Intelsat 1) which was launched on 6 April 1965. This had a capacity of 240 two-way voice channels, or one television channel, and transmitted between the United States and four European countries.[76] Though designed to function for 18 months, it operated for 3 years.[77] 'Early Bird' was also the first communications satellite to be placed in a geosynchronous orbit at 22,240 miles altitude above the Earth. At this point a satellite will circle the globe at the speed of the Earth's rotation. It will, therefore, stay in a fixed transmission position in relation to land. In this position it can broadcast a message to any point on up to one-third of the Earth's surface.[78]

The Intelsat II launched in 1966/67 provided similar capacity to the Pacific region, but thereafter performance levels increased.[79] In the 1970s improvements in design permitted the simultaneous use of the same frequencies through deployment of directional antennae for both reception and transmission. In capacity terms this produced the equivalent of nearly twice the number of transponders. During the latter part of the 1980s Digital Circuit Multiplication Equipment (DCME) was introduced, increasing capacity per satellite channel again by up to five fold.[80] This technology has been built into the current Intelsat VI series of five communications satellites, the first of which came into provisional service ahead of schedule in late 1989, assisting in the international coverage of the Bush/Gorbachev Malta Summit and subsequent top-level meetings.[81] Each Intelsat VI satellite has an average capacity of 24,000 simultaneous two-way telephone circuits (twice that of Intelsat V), plus three TV channels.

Using DCME technology this will increase the potential capacity of the satellite to 120,000 circuits. The VI series will operate into the 21st century providing enhanced voice, video and data services. Each satellite will have 48 transponders, 38 at C-Band and 10 at Ku-Band.[82] Intelsat VI has also been integrated with the organisation's new telemetry tracking command system (TTC), which is a distributed-processing communications network linking the Intelsat Satellite Control Centre with seven other TTC stations around the world. This will allow for remote computer command of all Intelsat satellites and co-ordination of all network antenna-related resources. It will also facilitate faster transmission of satellite commands.[83]

Plans are currently underway for the Intelsat VII programme which will address the special needs of users in the Pacific Ocean region, with an average capacity of 18,000 two-way telephone circuits and 3 TV channels (90,000 with DCME). Although the Intelsat VII programme is smaller than the VI series,[84] its higher spacecraft solar power,[85] at both the C- and Ku-bands, will enable high-quality digital services to be offered bringing reception within the grasp of smaller antennae without loss of capacity.[86]

2. Telephone and Broadcasting Services. Satellite means of communication are deployed for a number of purposes. First, as just discussed, they play a significant role in inter-continental telephone services, where two thirds of calls are carried by satellite. In addition to the basic international telephone service they also provide a rudimentary satellite communications service for rural and remote communities that currently possess inadequate or no telecommunications facilities. Its 'Vista' and 'Super Vista' services provide international toll-quality telephone channels which can be used also for telegraph and low-speed data applications.[87] With the future in mind, Intelsat is also planning for the adoption of the Integrated Services Digital Network (ISDN). The organisation has launched an integrated digital communications service known as IDR, designed to provide ISDN-quality Intelsat routes for connection within the public switched-telephony network as well as in dedicated private digital networks.[88] It can also be implemented with Digital Circuit Multiplication Equipment, DCME, to obtain multiple channels.

Second, satellite technology has opened the door to the expansion of broadcasting services, particularly television. Direct broadcasting by satellite (DBS) transmits directly into homes where receiving antennae exist. Currently, there is competition in the UK between Sky Television which has capacity to broadcast up to 16 channels from the Astra satellite, and the 5 channels available from British Satellite Broadcasting through its Marcopolo satellite launched in 1990. Other services include TDF 1 (France), TV-SAT 2 (E. Germany), Olympus (EBU/Italy) and Tele X (Scandinavia). Sky TV was the first to establish a niche in the UK market, reaching one million homes on November 4 1989. (Of these, 635,000 are linked to cable or SMATV (shared dish – Satellite Master Antenna Television) systems, while the other 365,000 have their own home dishes.) Competition will come from British Satellite Broadcasting which raised guarantees of £800 million in January 1990 to capitalise their operation, beginning with the launch of five new television channels in April 1990. Currently the BBC leases a television channel on the Olympus satellite to transmit programmes to Europe. This is the largest civil satellite to be launched to date. An alternative arrangement to DBS is transmission by a fixed satellite service (FSS), where the signal is transmitted to earth stations at specific points for onward transmission to the wider audience by cable.

The first live satellite transmission across the Atlantic took place on 11 July 1962. It was beamed via a steerable aerial located in Andover, Maine, to the Telstar satellite which then transmitted to the UK via the Post Office's Goonhilly station in Cornwall. The broadcast lasted no more than 20 minutes, since Telstar, launched in 1962, was not in geostationary orbit. It was, instead, in a elliptical orbit passing over the Atlantic every two and a half hours. The 20 minute broadcast matched the length of time during which both ground stations could 'see' the satellite.[89] Since then, Intelsat has dominated the transmission of intercontinental and transoceanic television services with over 90% of provision.[90] Figures for 1988 show that in that year Intelsat provided more than 68,000 television channel hours via its satellite network, compared with only 28,000 hours in 1980 and less than 8000 hours in 1975.[91] Intelsat co-ordinated the worldwide television coverage of the Live Aid Concert for famine victims in Ethopia, deploying 13 channels on 8 Intelsat satellites in all three ocean regions to provide pictures to 88 nations.[92] On 1 December 1989 Intelsat achieved a new record, when it transmitted 218 TV programmes in one day reporting on the Bush/Gorbachev Malta Summit.[93] In Europe, the European Telecommunications Satellite Organisation, Eutelsat, which provides national telecommunications administrations with satellite links, also supports the European Broadcasting Union (EBU) with TV programme exchange capacity through the Eurovision system.[94] The 1990s are likely to see the development of High Definition Television by satellite transmission, once agreement on standards are reached at European Community level and through the auspices of the International Telecommunication Union.[95] The first international HDTV transmission took place in April 1989, between the United States and Japan.

  3. Satellite Business Communications. A third application of satellite technology is in business services, particularly business communications. This use, in parallel with terrestial transmission facilities, offers tremendous opportunities for companies to streamline their activities, cut the cost of research and development, reduce production and distribution schedules, reduce stockpiles of components and finished products, and maintain better communications with employees. It is possible for several service providers to share the same transponder. This reduces costs and encourages applications. Moreover, the availability of very small satellite antennae for reception of business transmissions provides a further incentive for adoption by business subscribers.[96] Within the UK, given the present regulatory regime, terrestrial data services currently provide a cost-effective means of communication for business. On an international scale, however, satellite technology is competitive. The Intelsat Business Service (IBS), for example, offers a digital global service providing telex, voice, facsimile, data and videoconferencing facilities, distributed by satellite via aerials located on or close to end-user facilities.[97] This minimises dependence on land-based switched networks.[98] IBS also provides communications for other applications, including computer-aided design and manufacturing, electronic document distribution, electronic funds transfer and ISDN services.[99] IBS offers a wide range of data transmission rates. In the low- to medium-capacity levels, individual bit streams ranging from 64 to 768 kbit/s are available for voice communications, low- and medium-speed data transfer, facsimile and other business communications requirements. High-capacity bulk-bit stream rates vary from 1.54 to 8.45 Mbit/s for full-colour videoconferencing, high-speed data transfer, multi-plexed services and other high-capacity communications applications.[100]

  Business television services, which offer point-to-point or point-to-multipoint sound and vision transmission, have also established themselves. This occurred first in the United States, which broadcast more than 30,000 hours of live business TV in 1989.[101] These private TV services might be used by companies to maintain contact with branch offices, or to distribute marketing information or any other corporate message. British

Telecom now provides such services using satellite, microwave and cable links.[102] Six other licences have been issued in the UK, permitting satellite uplinks for one-way point-to-multipoint transmissions of 'specialised satellite services in the UK.[103] These will concentrate on video or business television provision.[104]

Concerning data transmission, one study has identified 17 possible applications, including 'database updating, mainframe use from remote locations, inquiry/response links such as for airline reservation systems, mainframe timesharing, point-of-sale record keeping, videotex distribution of periodicals and other information media, remote monitoring of equipment, computer data transfer, batch processing, electronic mail and security for voice using scrambling and digital voice encryption.'[105] Although satellite business services are in their infancy, satellite data networks are already widely used in the distribution of financial data. Reuters are major information providers in this field.[106] Intelsat also offers a data collection/distribution digital service known as Intelnet, which is accessible by antennae no bigger than 0.6 metres in diameter. This system is used typically by banks, insurance companies, government agencies, news agencies and other multi-national organisations for news distribution, financial information systems, reservation systems, point-of-sale and credit verification, oil- and gas-exploration, data collection, and electronic mail. Broadcasters have also found distinct benefits in deploying satellite technology for international news gathering for both television and sound services. The availability of small transportable equipment capable of being handled and operated by no more than two individuals, enables rapid deployment of personnel who can carry the equipment and check it through ordinary baggage channels on scheduled flights.[107]

Another area where satellite business services have developed rapidly is in videoconferencing.[108] In Europe this has been a reality since the launch of the Eutelsat 1-F2 satellite in 1984, which also facilitated an intra-European business service for data transmission. Videoconferencing is also supported by Intelsat's IDR integrated digital communications service, which operates via Earth stations with antennae 5.5 meters in diameter or larger. IDR carrier information rates vary from 64 Kbit/s to 44 Mbit/s, fulfilling a wide range of communications requirements including digital TV, audio and text transmission. Currently British Telecom supports 10 videoconferencing centres in the UK for hire on a half-hourly basis. Some companies have installed their own private facilities, and a growing number of such centres are being established abroad.[109] There is now a move to capitalise on the technology further, by providing continuing education courses and conferences via satellite links (the largest international video-conference to date took place on 13 November 1987, when 50,000 people in 79 cities in 16 countries participated in a discussion about world hunger).[110] British Telecom scientists at BT's Research Laboratories at Martlesham Heath are studying software engineering, advanced manufacturing technology, and object-oriented design within the EuroPACE programme of advanced continuing education. Initiated by the European Community in 1987, this provides training for company engineers, scientists and post-graduate students via satellite and electronic mail, drawing on advanced scientific and technological knowledge from universities, research centres and industrial laboratories.[111] The production of low cost satellite antennae on a large scale will promote these developments. One survey estimates the likely potential of videoconferencing as involving the use of between 1 in 10,000 to 1 in 1000 of all telephones in the EC. If so, there will be some 10,000 to 100,000 participants in the EC alone. It also predicts the advent of desktop videophones, via terrestrial or satellite links, operating without the additional high-quality facilities associated with videoconferencing from a dedicated studio. The survey suggests eventual penetration of between 10 and 25 million units in the EC.[112]

4. Mobile Satellite Communications. A fourth application for satellite transmission technology concerns mobile communications to ships and land-based vehicles on the move. Although fibre-optic communications may be cheaper on long-distance point-to-point links, terrestrial transmission facilities could never compete in the mobile sector. In shipping, the shift from simple morse radiotelegraphy to satellite communications, providing facsimile, teleprinters, and computer-to-computer communications, is now underway. The first satellite systems for shipping were introduced in the early 1970s, with a worldwide communications network established a decade later. In 1979 the International Maritime Satellite Organisation (Inmarsat) was established, serving in excess of 6000 ships. Inmarsat has two dedicated maritime communications satellites in operation, with further capacity available through Intelsat. A new generation of dedicated satellites is planned for the 1990s.[113]

In addition to basic telephone, telex, data and facsimile communication Inmarsat also supports distress and safety communications services to the shipping and offshore industries. Since use of Inmarsat services has been entirely optional, the International Maritime Organisation (IMO) is planning new rules to require shipping to link in to the network. In addition to the improvement this would bring for ship management[114] it would provide early warning of distress conditions and natural disasters, as well as pinpointing the position of any ship in distress and other ships in the vicinity that could assist. Distress alerts could be transmitted and received automatically over long distance, unaffected by meteorological or interference conditions.[115] The IMO is planning to introduce its Global Maritime Distress and Safety System for all ships of 300 tons or more operating within the Inmarsat umbrella. This has been achieved in part by the economies achieved in developing the new Standard-C terminal antenna which is approximately 30cm in diameter. The low-gain fixed-antenna does not need to be lined up accurately with the satellite and it can send and receive signals, deploying compact and inexpensive antenna-steering equipment. It could be deployed on small pleasure craft and fishing vessels, just as currently it is extending to aircraft.[116]

The first telephone call from a scheduled airliner took place in October 1987, from a Japanese Airline's 747 to a coastal Earth station at Ibraki in Japan. This was achieved via Intelsat's Pacific Ocean satellite.[117] From the technical point of view, the extension of communications to the 4000 commercial aircraft operating in the world today is feasible. The frequency bands used for ground-to-air communication are adjacent to the maritime bands, and light-weight antennae could be fitted to the outside of aircraft, similar in size to the video cameras suggested as a safety precaution following recent air crashes involving engine failure. In February 1990, trials took place in which passengers called any telephone number they wished via satellite and British Telecom's international service. Inmarsat is now extending the service rapidly, taking advantage of the four-fold increase in channel capacity of the new second generation of satellites to be launched by the organisation from 1990.[118] By the mid 1990s, spot-beam technology could increase line capacities to 32 channels per aircraft, offering voice, facsimile, telex and lap-top computer communications from an 'in-flight' office.[119] This is likely, before long, to extend to the general aviation market, which comprises 20,000 aircraft in the United States alone.

The Standard-C antenna has a further application in mobile land services, since the compact dish can readily be mounted on motor vehicles. Incompatibility of land-based facilities and the heavy exploitation of radio frequencies for commercial mobile communications has encouraged the exploitation of the space segment in this sector. The Inmarsat Standard-C system transmits both to and from the satellite at 600 bit/s. Road hauliers, too, would be able to exchange telex messages with drivers, with the future prospect of voice communications after 1992. Ultimately, a pan-European digital mobile-communications network will emerge, once technical, compatibility and frequency-band allocation problems are overcome. Eutelsat has been conducting trials of a base-to-vehicle satellite link service called 'Euteltacs'. Lorries were equipped with a circular antenna 11 inches in diameter, able to send and receive messages via a display unit with keyboard. The system also fed other data through to the lorry, including details of the vehicle's location to within 100 metres. The International Maritime service, Inmarsat, is similarly experimenting at this time with land communications to lorries.[120] In March, 1990 the European Conference of Post and Telecommunications Administrations (CEPT) decided that mobile land services be provided throughout Europe by Inmarsat's International Maritime Satellite system. This effectively makes Inmarsat the standard for European public mobile voice and data services.[121] No decision has yet been taken as to a system for private mobile voice and data services.

5. Data Processing in Space. A further important use of satellite communication is the ability to gather and process data in space. This has become known as 'remote sensing', and refers to 'the examination, study, exploration or monitoring of the Earth and its resources "remotely", or from a distance.'[122] Recent NASA space probes to Jupiter and beyond illustrate what can be achieved in the gathering of data. The major advantage of remote sensing technology is its capacity to collect data rapidly over both large and small areas through photography, multispectral scannners and radar. Apart from the obvious intelligence and military applications, and the prospects of commercial news gathering from space,[123] the technology also provides useful data in agricultural production, fisheries, forestry, metal mining, oil and gas exploration, weather forecasting and landscape planning. A good illustration of remote sensing capacity came in the aftermath of the Chernobyl nuclear reactor disaster, when on 29 April 1986, a Landsat satellite[124] was the first to produce an image of the reactor facility in which the still-burning reactor was identified by a bright pixel on the photograph. Digital evaluation techniques enabled the United States to determine the continuing status of the reactor during the incident. Further evaluation of infra-red and thermal imagery of the reactor cooling pond

confirmed the Soviet Union's statements regarding the timing of the plant's shut-down and start-up.

Another developing new market is that of microsatellites. This is indicative of the growing use of space for commercial purposes, including the processing of materials and other research and development activity that benefits from the unique environment in space of sterile conditions and no convection currents or vibrations.[125] Costing £1 million or less, these space vehicles have proved very useful in testing new technologies while in orbit, while providing a cheap alternative for some types of research that might be too risky to perform in any mainstream shuttle operation.[126] As microprocessor technology advances, the microsatellite market is expected to grow too, as the satellites become more powerful devices. Currently, in the UK, Surrey University is pioneering work in the area, with the US Department of Defense and Orbital Science Corporation active in the United States.

6. Complementary not Competing – Satellite and Fibre Optics. In assessing the future of satellite transmission against the development of fibre-optic cable, it is important to note the conceptual differences between the two forms of transmission technology. Fibre optics offer considerable potential for expansion and exploitation, with a broad bandwidth capable of carrying large volumes of traffic. Further benefits include the absence of electromagnetic interference, low error and fast data-transfer rates. Among the drawbacks are the complexity of connections, the fragility of the fibres, the cost of laying the cables and the inflexibity of the configuration once it has been mapped out. Today, by comparison, satellite performance matches that of fibre optics in data transfer and bit error rates, reliability and security. However, further breakthroughs in both fibre-optic and satellite technology can be expected, with reductions in dish size and improvements in transmission methods maintaining the competition between the two technologies. The genesis of telecommunications satellites was spurred on by the relatively low capacity of conventional cable and the high cost of provision over long distances. Distance was often cited as an appropriate criterion for comparison, because the cost of cable was directly related to its length in terms of purchase price and installation. Alternatively, the cost of satellite communications has always been determined by the cost of establishing the satellite in orbit and building the ground station facilities for transmission and reception of signals. Opinions vary as to the likely cost comparisons between the two systems in the

future. One view is that, in time, satellites will lose ground in the high-volume point-to-point domain, even over long distances.[127] Intelsat challenges this hypothesis arguing that the cost per circuit for a fully-loaded fibre-optic cable facility such as TAT-8 – the first transatlantic connection – is $1596 per circuit year, compared with $504 on Intelsat VI.[128]

Despite these comparisons, it seems likely that fibre optics will, in due course, predominate in the high-volume point-to-point long-distance communications segment. Equally, satellites will do well in the low- and medium-traffic multi-point market, where network flexibility allows for circuit expansion direct to customer premises or mobile units, avoiding expensive terrestrial connection costs to the cable head. Fibre optics will also be competitive in very short range links, for example within a company, location or town; however, satellites may challenge microwave and fibre optics in inter-city communications, as the economics of the former improve in parallel with technological advances. Most significant of all, perhaps, for the future of both forms of transmission, is the fact that each one performs well in the context of the ISDN network. This could provide the bridge between the two transmission systems ensuring interconnection, compatibility and back-up within a single worldwide telecommunications environment. Collaboration already exists, to a limited extent, as evidenced by the fact that Intelsat has been able to restore almost all of the one million circuit hours lost as a result of the suspension of the international submarine cable service during the past 10 years.[129]

The Radio Spectrum Telecommunications rely, to a great extent, on transmission through the air by means of the electromagnetic spectrum. This is a substantial but finite resource for conveying messages via radio waves. As a form of energy, similar to that of heat or light, it travels through space without physical connection. Its exploitation involves the production of waves of electromagnetic energy upon which information is carried. Those waves will oscillate in peaks and troughs to a varying degree, ranging from a few cycles per second to several hundred billion. The shorter the wave measurement from one crest to another, the higher will be the frequency of the oscillations. The waves are measured according to the number notionally passing a single point in one second, and the volume of information that can be carried by the wave is directly related to this frequency.[130] Because of this and the need to allocate spectrum capacity to appropriate applications, international co-operation has been required to police the resource and reduce the risk of interference with its use. The task of allocating the spectrum for particular objects is administered by the World Administrative Radio Conference of the International Telecommunications Union, which convenes every 20 years or so to review the position. The last such review took place in 1979. As a result, eight bands have been defined within the overall radio spectrum.[131] The 30KHz-1000MHz bands are used primarily for radio and television broadcasting; government fixed and mobile services (from low [LF] to ultra high frequency [UHF]); emergency services; and civil aviation and maritime shipping (air–ground, ship–shore). The high 1–30GHz bands supply fixed-link/government-fixed and mobile services (short-range, microwave); civil aviation (radio-navigation); government and civil radar; land mobile (civil) communications; radio astronomy; and meteorological aids.

Detailed reviews of spectrum use are a matter for governments to organise. As a result the Radiocommunications Division of the Department of Trade and Industry reported on the defence and civil uses of the spectrum in June 1988 and May 1989 respectively. On the civil side there were recommendations to move some services to higher frequencies in order to accommodate the rapid growth in mobile communications. On the defence side the committee proposed an increase in the shared use of certain bands between cellular radio operators and the Ministry of Defence. The spectrum reviews, combined with other forms of consultation, will provide data necessary for the formulation of national policy in preparation for the forthcoming World Administrative Radio Conference, provisionally arranged for 1992.[132]

In the business and commercial uses of radio communication the major distinction to be drawn is between fixed and mobile services. Microwave relay systems are the radio equivalent of cable (i.e. fixed) transmission services for the distribution of voice, television and text between the main centres of population. Microwave operates in the 1.7–1.5 GHz part of the spectrum using bands carrying eight channels each, and offering a total of 16,000 voice circuits. A US study of the telecommunications industry has suggested that microwave provision will account for 29% of inter-city capacity by 1990, representing a fall of 4% on the 1985 figure in favour of satellite and fibre optics, at 16% and 21% respectively. Copper (23%) and co-axial (11%) represent the declining part of the transmission sector.[133] Microwave communication provides a flexible third alternative to the two other flagbearers of the modern communications revolution – fibre optics and satellite. Microwave links are best suited for local rather than long-distance connections, since they depend on an uninterrupted line-of-sight link between the transmission and reception point. Performance can also be affected by adverse weather conditions. The frequency at which the service is provided determines the theoretical distance that the signal can travel. Microwave radio links have proved quite successful in the North Sea. BP, for example, chose microwave communications to provide contact between their gas platforms and their radio and control station on Humberside.[134] It is clear that the major UK network providers regard microwave as a serious transmission medium. Mercury Communications, the rival to British Telecom who has invested £1 billion in establishing its network, has 2000 kilometres of microwave links, compared with 2600 kilometres of fibre-optic cable.[135]

Development of Mobile Radio Communications Undoubtedly, though, the most significant development in radio communication since the early 1980s has been the growth of mobile services. Until recently the problem for mobile communications has been the lack of available frequencies. The radio spectrum is a finite resource and the allocation made favoured fixed links through private networks rather than mobile uses. More than 30 years ago, research at Bell Laboratories was being done to find ways of compressing channels into a smaller band space, so as to increase the number within a given frequency band. The answer that the Laboratory came up with was cellular radio.[136] Cellular telecommunications operates by dividing a region up into 'cells', each of which has a radio base station. Subscribers are allocated an exclusive radio channel for personal use from a finite set of channels awarded to each cell. Users communicate with the base station by radio signal, which can connect the caller to other cellular phones or out to the fixed telephone network. One innovation of cellular radio is that channels can be re-used. The base station monitors all traffic and directs the strongest signal by computer control throughout the honeycomb of the network. The change of channel along the route to the call's destination can be accomplished in less than 300 milli-seconds (3/10ths of a second) and is unnoticeable to the caller.[137] The main advantage of the system, however, is the re-usability of the channels by prompt reassignment of previously occupied frequencies as the signal fades on 'hand off' between cells. The system allows for cluster formations to develop, in groups typically of 7, 12, 21 and 24 cells, the density of the cell structure depending on population density and likely demand.[138]

Scope for the development of cellular radio communications began with the decision to allow private networks to relocate on the higher microwave frequencies. This left room for cellular services to occupy a segment of the UHF frequency in a band around 900MHz. The Secretary of State for Trade and Industry decided in 1985 to licence two operators – Telecom Securicor Cellular Radio Ltd (Cellnet) and Racal Vodaphone Ltd. Under the terms of the licences both companies were obliged to develop a national system and to complete 90% coverage of the country by the end of the 1980s.[139] By January 1990 the target was already well towards 100% coverage of the population. Congestion of the system, particularly around the M25 region of southern England, persuaded the Government, in January 1989, to release a further 400 of the ETACS band extra radio channels for cellular use, that had been in the hands of the Ministry of Defence until the spectrum review. Subsequently 120 of these were allocated to other regions of the country.[140] It is estimated that today 14 people out of every 1000 has a cellular telephone. This represents about 800,000 of the population and shows how rapidly the use of mobile phones has grown since the first recorded figure, of 60,000 on the two networks combined in April 1986.[141] There arc about 2.2 million users of cellular radio in Europe and this figure is growing at the rate of 66,000 per month.[141] A pan-European digital service is expected to get underway in late 1991, initially connecting major European cities, and with prospects of extension to Eastern Europe.[142,143]

The changes to the London telephone codes in May 1990 were brought about because of the need to provide more numbers, in part, to cope with the predicted future expansion of mobile services.[144] It can be argued, however, that increased demand may not arise. This would be true if the equipment allows a person to carry one number with him instead of having separate numbers allocated for the home, the office, the car or use on other forms of transport. This scenario foresees a decline in the necessity of wiring a building for voice communications. Instead those lines will concentrate upon providing value-added services such as data communications.[145]

In the United States, cellular communication has grown dramatically, as well. It is reported to have outstripped any other commodity in consumer sales. US cellular services began in 1984 and subscribers reached 1.23 million by January 1988 and 2.07 million by the year end. The number in mid-1990 is around 3.5 million – as much as 2% of the population in city areas on the east and west coasts.[146] The licensing system is different in the US, with a preference towards granting permission for cellular services in metropolitan areas at the expense of the rural communities. However, the extent of the cellular bonanza has led to a change in attitudes, with up to 700 potential operators now competing for each of the licences in the 428 rural territories defined by the Federal Communications Commission.[147] (The consumer boom in cellular radio does have its drawbacks. One cell was set up in the main valley of the picturesque Yosemite National Park. Campers began to complain when the tranquillity was rudely interrupted by the frequent ringing of the phones in adjacent tents.)[148]

With the rapid expansion of cellular telephony one might have expected to see a decline in support for conventional mobile radio and particularly the private mobile radio operations (pmr) traditionally used by the public services and others. This has not been the case, and in 1984 opportunities to expand mobile radio arose when the Government decided to release two blocks of the spectrum – Bands I and III – previously occupied by the old 405-line black-and-white TV standard. Accordingly, Band I (41–68MHz) was mainly given to mobile radio with a small saving for amateur radio and on-site paging, Band III (174–225MHz) also being given substantially over to mobile radio.[149] This widened user choice by making it economically viable to operate a trunking scheme, by which the user could develop a network through a central operator who could allocate channels from the lines available. Prior to this the only choice was a fully fledged 'pmr' scheme, equivalent to the sharing of community systems or a party line.[150] Initially two companies – National One (originally backed by GEC) and Band 3 Radio (Philips, Digital Mobile Communications, Racal and Securicor) were each given 100 channels to develop a national network, linking radio to regional exchanges which themselves link to a leased wire network available through British Telecom or Mercury. Predictions are that the new trunked system could double its subscriber base to 1 million users by 1995. This is based on the assumption that the cheaper cost of operating within Band III compared with cellular telephony will encourage uptake, especially from commercial users who want to make a number of short calls to staff on a regular and frequent basis.[151] In due course mobile radio systems may standardise on a European formula.

It is clear from the above that the current direction of mobile communications is in the provision of telephony. In addition to the cellular network, the UK paging market has enjoyed a boom, with sales approaching 800,000 – growing at 30% per year.[152] Text messages of up to 15 words accompanying these systems are now common.[153] Another more recent application is the 'Telepoint' cordless telephone (CT2 – 'Cordless Telephone 2'). Ordinary cordless telephones can only be used in the perimeter of the home. The new system, which can fit into a pocket, extends the perimeter to within 200 metres of a 'base station' serving the particular make of phone unit. The latter is connected to the British Telecom or Mercury network. A mid-range portable market has therefore been introduced and four companies have been licensed to operate.[154] A move for a common standard between the four providers is now underway. Known as the 'Common Air Interface', it nevertheless remains out of step with the rest of Europe, who have chosen DECT – 'Digital European Cordless Telephone' – for their standard.[155] This has been established by a new body, the European Telecommunications Standards Institute, set up to agree upon and ratify such standards on a pan-European level. Currently, Telepoint operates at 900MHz whereas DECT has chosen 1.8 GHz. In due course both frequencies may be adopted, since together, they provide for a product with basic and add-on feature product transmitting in the UHF band.

These products are embryonic of what is to come in the personal communications sector. Public mobile communications will expand as sophisticated portable and handheld terminals are developed. It seems likely that the 1–3GHz UHF band, chosen by the Japanese, for cordless services, will develop into the frequency for the personal communications network (PCN). An initiative to define a PCN was launched by the UK Department of Trade and Industry in June 1989, to be based on one of the European standards for cellular or cordless services.[156] In December of that year the Government announced that it had issued three licences to operate a PCN in the UK within the 1.7–1.9 GHz band. These were awarded to Mercury Personal Communications Network Ltd., a British Aerospace consortium and Unitel Ltd. The licences of the two cellular radio operators, Cellnet and Racal Vodaphone, already allow them to operate with the smaller cells of the PCM.[157]

Currently, under the European Commission's RACE program (Research on Advanced Communications in Europe) work is underway to develop a pan-European network, to allow the majority of telephone subscribers to have access to voice, data and video from a pocket-sized transceiver. The proposed transfer rate would be 2 million bit/s, supporting mobile office services to vehicles and field locations. The network would need to serve up to 100 million users and would replace the proliferation of segmented services currently available. It is anticipated that the cellular radio approach might be used, with smaller micro-clusters in inner cities and satellite-supported links in the larger rural areas.[158] Analysts predict that by the year 2000 these services will be challenging broadcasters for greater access to the radio spectrum, with broadcasters moving increasingly over to cable.[159]

THE ADVANCE TOWARDS AN 'INTELLIGENT' DIGITAL NETWORK

CONVERGENCE OF COMPUTERS AND COMMUNICATIONS When Almon Strowger patented his idea for automatic switching of telephone calls he could not have realised that the system, albeit developed and refined, would continue for a century in telephone exchanges around the world. He could not have contemplated either the digital aftermath, in which speech, data, pictures, graphics, sound and imagery would all be transmitted along the same paths in an integrated digital network. The telephone network was originally designed for speech transmission, but as early as the 1950s individuals were beginning to consider the possibility of incorporating additional services within the network.[160] Initially it was telex, the automatic dial-up teletypewriter switching service that established itelf on the network, followed by facsimile the transmission of images over communications links – which in the mid-1960s took about one minute per page (data transmission rates at that time were 100 words per minute).[161] Already by the 1960s, convergence of telecommunication and computer technologies had begun with the establishment of networks to allow remote access to computer systems. The concept was of simple terminals connected to a mainframe computer in a central location. Users would operate either leased lines or ordinary dial-up connections through a modem. Direct computer-to-computer communication was also introduced, facilitating automatic data transfer. Applications were very simple, usually involving transmission of customer orders or stock information to a central source.[162] Immediately, however, there was a problem of standards as different makes of computer were incompatible in communication.[163] The problem was tackled with the development of packet switching and local area networks.

Packet switching is the system whereby messages are divided in discrete packages and transmitted, each with a source and destination marker and an error checking element. The message enters the system through a 'PAD' – package assembler-disassembler – and is routed through the network in the least disruptive way. At its destination the PAD checks the arrival of all the packets prior to reconstitution. Following this development, national network providers (PTTs[164]) introduced packet switching networks. These comprised a grid of lines within the network dedicated to data transfer. PTTs had appreciated the resource benefit of such a grid, which ensured maximum use of each line. This contrasted well with the circuit switching of conventional telephony, which meant that once a connection was made between two points only they could utilise that connection while the call was being made. In the UK British Telecom's service was called 'Packet Switchstream' (PSS) and this was linked to the International PSS service (IPSS). To achieve compatibility between computers using PSS it was necessary to agree standards for the service, including the size of each packet, the transfer rate and other protocols. The latter define the procedures and rules specifying how data can be transferred within the network.[165] This was achieved through the International Telecommunications Union CCITT committee (the International Telephone and Telegraph Consultative Committee) when it introduced the 'X Series' of CCITT Standards. The most significant of these has been X.25, for data terminal equipment, which specifies the standard for connection to the network.[166] This was published in 1976 and has been widely adopted throughout the world since then. Other standards have since been introduced including X3, X28, and X29, (terminal links with PAD); X.75 (gateways to networks); X.21 (network numbering); and more recently X.31 (defining procedures for packet mode terminals accessing the ISDN).[166] A third way of routing data, apart from circuit and packet switching is 'message' switching, designed for longer data messages. This is a store-and-forward system in which no direct interaction occurs between originator and recipient, unlike the X.25 protocol. The CCITT issued the X.400 series of Recommendations for Message handling in 1984, making further changes in 1988. X.400 is today extremely important as it is ideally suited for Electronic Data Interchange applications (EDI) – the computer-to-computer paperless exchange system for business documents.[167]

The problem of computer communications was tackled in a second way by the development of local area networks (LANs). LANs developed as a means of computer-to-computer communication within a building or group of buildings such as offices, hospitals or college campuses. The pressure for communication between computers grew as the technology advanced through the development of minis and micros in all corners of the workplace. Instead of simple terminal connections, the idea was to join 'intelligent' devices to share data, processing power and special services such as large disk-storage media. Conventionally a LAN involved the connection of machines by co-axial cable using high-speed packet switching techniques. Inevitably, standards for the network topology had to be found, and this again brought IBM into competition with other suppliers within the industry. Digital Equipment Corporation and micro-processor manufacturer Intel collaborated to support 'Ethernet', an access protocol for a 'ring' network topology. This was developed in 1975 by Xerox Corporation. The scheme was that devices connected to the ring would detect packets of data in circulation and copy them according to destination as defined by the address.[168] With 20 manufacturers adopting Ethernet standards in their machines, it has become a strong contender as the office LAN to adopt; the more so since it offers gateway connections to the public switched network as well as X.25 packet switched networks. By contrast IBM has introduced its own 'Token Ring' LAN protocol, based on message transmission controlled by a token which travels round the ring.[169] Many users have adopted both systems for different applications. In 1987 the LAN industry was worth $2.6 billion and this rose to $4.2 billion in 1988. Estimates suggest that, by 1992, 55–60% of computers purchased by the Fortune 1000 companies in the US will connect to LANs.[170]

What has been described as one of the computer world's rare 'demand-driven' technical initiatives is Open Systems Interconnection (OSI). This is a standard architecture and protocol for international data communication being produced by CCITT and the International Standards Organisation (ISO). It is a complex seven-layer reference model designed to set standards at all levels of the communication process necessary for interconnection. (Establishing a standard can take between four and five years to agree.) The lowest three layers of the OSI model, the 'physical', 'Datalink' and 'Network' layers define practical network issues such as bit stream levels, error detection codes, routing and switching functions, etc. The fourth 'Transport' layer maps out messages into the appropriate format for transmission, hiding the details from the 'Session' layer above, which starts, controls and ends dialogue between users. The sixth 'Presentation' layer deals with format and syntax of messages providing the links necessary for incompatible 'intelligent' terminals to converse. The seventh and final segment – the 'Application' layer – interfaces directly with the user and is determined by him according to network use. For example, the X.400 message-handling standard is located here and would be appropriate for EDI applications.[171] OSI has been strongly backed by the US and UK governments and the European Commission. UK involvement dates back to 1983 when the DTI launched its 'Intercept Strategy' to identify and promote draft European standards.[172] Today, OSI standards compliance is beginning to feature in official procurement,[173] and conformance testing procedures have been established to see that OSI standards are met by products claiming to do so.[174]

Work is now continuing at the ISO on security and network management procedures, text structures, computer graphics, and database and operating system functions. However, problems with OSI still remain, as too many options remain within the standards. This means that two products could both pass conformance tests yet not be inter-operable. There is pressure, therefore, to develop tests that can confirm inter-operability between products for particular purposes. Another difficulty relates to the alternative Internet Transmission Control Protocol (TCP/IP) developed originally for US Government use. This has extended into commercial use as a high performance network protocol, with trunk line speeds of 2Mbit/s compared with the X.25 speed of 64Kbit/s. Migration from TCP/IP to OSI will not be easy since the former does not comply with OSI layers three to seven. Users of TCP/IP are expected to retain their investment in the standard for the time being.[175] It is anticipated, however, that the development of the ISDN network and the challenge of combining OSI with it, will eventually overtake the issue.

IMPLEMENTING THE ISDN   While twenty-five years or so have now passed since the idea was first mooted of a universal communication network for voice, text, data and imagery, [176] ever since the discovery by Samuel Morse that the alphabet could be represented by a series of dots and dashes, digital transmission was destined to culminate in an integrated digital network – the ISDN. The concept of digital integration relies upon the implementation of a single digital switching and transmission path for the distribution of all forms of information. Distribution must take place in binary form and without differentiation. Moreover, the network must be capable of transmitting at the speeds and volumes necessary for heavy consumption demands such as High Definition Television (HDTV) and large data sets.

The first key component for the new network technology was completed with the arrival of powerful microprocessors necessary for the digital replacement of Strowger exchanges. These are necessary to replace, with a digital alternative, the public switched analogue network, upon which the older forms of telecommunication have been based ie., voice, telegraphy and telex. Work began seriously on developing the technologies necessary for ISDN in the 1970s, once the first computer controlled switching systems were in use. The first digital exchange in the UK was opened at Glenkindie, near Aberdeen, in 1979 and this was followed in 1981 with the first System X exchange at Woodbridge in Suffolk. System X was the result of a Joint Post Office/industry study group that began work in 1969. It led to the appointment, in 1977, of a consortium of British Telecom, GEC, Plessey and STC to build System X for the UK network. More than £350 million was spent in development work on System X and currently each System X trunk exchange handles up to 1.5 million calls per hour. However, doubts about the system and competitive alternatives led to a lack of success in the export market. However, work is now underway to produce a second generation System X Exchange that will be UNIX compatible using RISC-based standard components,[177] while work in modernising the network has continued in earnest since 1984. The closure of the last old-style electro-mechanical exchange – at Thurso in Scotland – took place in June 1990. As a result Britain became the first major country in the world to complete a long-distance network that is entirely digital. The digital trunk network, carrying an average of 40 million calls per day, has been introduced as an overlay to the existing analogue trunk network which dates back to the start of subscriber trunk dialling in 1957. Since 1988 British Telecom has accelerated phasing out the analogue trunk exchanges and transferring the calls they handle to the digital network, with electronic switching at computer-controlled exchanges.

However, the connections to homes and businesses remain analogue and it will be some time before the position changes. This might have delayed implementation of ISDN for some considerable period worldwide. But methods were discovered, through the addition of software and electronic equipment, of converting copper wire to digital operation, and British Telecom now has nearly 10 million customers connected to digital exchanges. Since up to one third of the asset value of the telecommunications network is sunk into local links to the subscriber, the ability to deliver ISDN standard services, end to end, throughout the network at only 20–30% of the cost of wire replacement has proved attractive. However, since digitisation of existing subscriber lines can only double transmission capacity, full-scale development of broadband ISDN will have to wait until fibre optics are operational throughout the network; at that point the subscriber will have a full-scale ISDN interface in the home for total digital connection.[178]

Currently all PTTs in Europe are investing substantially in the digitisation of their telephone networks. By the time the single market comes into force at the end of 1992, the European Community aim to have 80% of subscribers in reach of an ISDN exchange, although only 5% of the 118 million subscriber lines will have been converted. Pressure to convert to fibre optic cable will remain, for the latter has kept pace, if not exceeded, the advance in switching techniques responsible for digital exchanges.[179] Since 1983 all new cable ordered by British Telecom for the trunk network has been optical fibre. Consequently, about 75% of the trunk network – about 400,000 kilometres – now consists of fibre-optic cable (the remainder is divided about equally between co-axial cable and micro-wave radio). Fibre optics provide the perfect transmission medium for digital communication. The capacity to exploit its almost limitless transmission capability is doubling annually, and this is expected to continue to the end of the century. Commercial systems capable of 2.0GBit/s transmission speed on a single pair of glass fibres are now available, equivalent to more than 28,000 simultaneous telephone calls.[180] With laser systems and wave division multiplexing, 20Gbit/s has been achieved and the prospects suggest much higher speeds lie ahead. This broadband capability of fibre optic communications means that the band can be split into numerous channels for all types of digital transmission. Such a network would serve all possible communications services doing away with independent systems for voice, data and imagery as exist today. Developments in switching technology, in particular fast packet switching, will also make data transmission faster. The latter can transmit 'hundreds of thousands or millions of packets per second', while conventional systems run at the rate of only a few thousand packets per second.[181] As a result, PTTs are investing heavily in fibre-optic cable and packet switching systems. In parallel with European trends, up to $10 billion had been spent in the US on fibre-optic networks by the major telecommunications companies by 1988. AT&T has already completed 25,000 miles of its optical fibre cable network, including a coast-to-coast link.[182]

Given the importance of ISDN economically and politically, there seems now to be no viable economic alternative to its full implementation as a broadband network (B-ISDN). However, although progress has been good, such a network is still essentially in its planning stage, and work at the international level to agree standards still has some way to go.[183] Some

B-ISDN systems could be operational by 1991–92, although development of the latter will continue into the early part of the next century.[184] Already research is going on that looks beyond electronic concepts of network communications towards optical switches and photonic computers that could deliver capacities 1000 times more than today.[185] In the meantime, most PTTs are moving ahead to complete the narrowband version, based on existing line conversion linked to the fibre-optic trunk network. In April 1990 British Telecom outlined its plans for narrowband development with 'ISDN2'. This service will become progressively available throughout the country, serving business communities and high streets via local digital exchanges. British Telecom is encouraging manufacturers with business applications to work together with customers to test equipment.[186] British Telecom is also testing two distinctly different fibre-optic network systems as part of its planning for an advanced commercial communications network for the next century. 400 homes and businesses have been fed with voice, entertainment and other services at speeds of 20 Mbit/s.[187]

Progress towards European implementation of ISDN services was made in 1989 when the European Conference of Posts and Telecommunications approved a 'Memorandum of Understanding' to provide public ISDN services to common standards across Europe by 1992. This deals with development of a common range of services, common standards for customer equipment and agreed arrangements for interconnecting national systems for international services.[188] The world's first global service across three continents, based on CCITT recommendations, began service in the summer of 1989, linking British Telecom's ISDN network with similar networks in the US (AT&T) and Japan (KDD – Kokusai Denshin Denwa). The service began offering 64kbit/s communications paths between customers connected to it. The network can carry pictures, data, and high-speed facsimile as well as speech.[189] Meanwhile, with the future in mind, after four years of discussion work is well in hand towards the completion of a Fibre Distributed Data Interface Standard (FDDI) based on network communications at speeds of 100 Mbit/s. Agreement is expected by the end of 1990 which will have some bearing on the early development of products, including chip sets and equipment, capable of networking within a fibre-optic B-ISDN environment.[190]

ADDING VALUE – CONSUMER USE OF THE NETWORK   We have seen already many examples of the growth in consumer use of the telecommunications network. The key to the growth of that use has been the link-up between micro-electronics and digital transmission. Software has also played a major role in bringing computer technology and telecommunications together. Improving and developing the quality of software throughout the network will be of equal importance to the more widely publicised changes. CASE tools and new programming techniques offer the chance for software to keep pace with the advances elsewhere, current evidence suggesting that advances in hardware have not been matched by those in software.[191] From the consumer's point of view some radical developments in services lie ahead. In telephony the trend will be in the continued expansion of personal communications combined with the integration of non-voice facilities including imagery. Messaging services, including telex, facsimile, electronic mail and teletex, will all continue to integrate and advance within the digital network. British Telecom, for example, is spending £100 million to produce a wholly digital telex network by 1991. Its alternative, facsimile, has grown extensively in popularity, initially for business use, but increasingly as a consumer product for home use. Higher transmission speeds, up from one minute per page, can be expected with digital transmission via the ISDN (at 64 Kbit/s), producing output of a few seconds per page together with the prospect of colour.[192]

Electronic mail (E-Mail) has been around for many years. It involves the use of a third-party host computer to receive and hold messages in the customer's 'mailbox'.[193] E-Mail has never been particularly successful, as it has always been a stand-in for direct point-to-point communications between computers. That did not establish itself until Teletex because of incompatibility between machines and a lack of standards for communication. Currently, with the support of the European Commission, E-Mail is moving towards becoming an integrated pan-European system.[194] Its success and value will depend, perhaps, on how far and how quickly electronic data interchange (EDI) standards for business communication get established. Teletex has developed into an international CCITT standard for direct E-Mail communication. It will form part of any integrated office worksatation environment, interfacing with telex and facsimile within the network.

Videotex is another service available through the network that has developed a market of its own in the supply of data on TV-type screens and other terminals. Users can communicate interactively with databases incorporating text and graphics. The first such service was the British Post Office's 'Viewdata' service which commenced operation in 1973. Known as 'Prestel', it offers a variety of business, commercial and leisure data supplied by more than 1000 organisations including banks, building socie-ties, public authorities, travel and news organisations.[195] Videotex services are interactive allowing users to purchase goods, transfer funds and make reservations.[196] Some specialised information sources are also available, such as legal information for solicitors on Prestel.[197] Videotex is more advanced in Europe than the United States as a public service, but its use is almost equal in business sectors either side of the Atlantic, with a market estimated to be worth $1.6 and $1.5 billion respectively in 1990.[198] It is estimated that approximately 10.75 million videotex business terminals were operating in Europe in 1990, with 90% of these in France. This is way ahead of the rest of Europe and reflects French policy to distribute the 'Minitel' terminal to every home that wants one.[199] Videotex will continue to develop, subject to the continuing uncertainty about the use of the service for public as opposed to commercial purposes. It may be through systems like Minitel that a broader range of value-added domestic services develop through the network, as the general public become more aware of their potential.[200]

In addition to Videotex there are other sectoral value-added service providers for defined groups of users. They include Reuters in the financial information market, with approximately 150,000 terminals connected worldwide, and SWIFT – the Society for Worldwide Interbank Financial Telecommunications – which handles worldwide electronic funds transfer transactions for banks and their clients. Another is Electronic Data Systems (EDS), the company owned by General Motors, which provides facilities management services, ie. the day-to-day management of the whole or part of a client's data-processing and telecommunications oper-ations. There are also a host of database services of one kind or another, many of which are accessible through a data transmission network. The biggest in Europe is 'Euronet', providing specialised, scientific, technical and economic data to users within the EC.[201] It is anticipated that these types of service will extend in the 1990s, particularly into the industrial sector of the economy.[202]

Another emerging feature of telecommunications in the 1990s will be the growing number of 'intelligent' aids provided by the network. This is already apparent in small ways, for example, itemised billing and the 'bleeper' warning if the handset is not put back on the telephone. The new digital exchanges offer the customer a number of optional services too, including automatic call diversion to another number and three-way con-ferencing facilities for business or family discussions. Computerised systems are also now in service to speed up repairs to the network. These will assist engineers to trace faults and test customer equipment remotely. Private automatic branch exchanges (PABXs) on customers' premises provide for increasing integration of network functions within the organisation – word processing, E-Mail and other data communications facilities – as well as a range of features on top of basic telephony.[203] These include call transfer to another extension, ring-back when free, and trunk call restrictions on selected units. An electronic directory is now available too. This records staff movements and other changes, and can be linked the company PABX to re-route the call once the correct extension is identified.[204]

SUMMARY   It is going to take two decades or so for the world community to come to terms with the immense potential of the ISDN and the increasingly powerful technology linked to it. It will take this time for the public to grasp that digital technology has created an entire new way of doing things. Traditional human skills of communication and craftsmanship have always benefitted from the technological advances achieved throughout history. Paper, the steam engine and the telephone were all aids to assist humanity in its progress. Digitisation brings with it an entirely new environment – an automated, simulated reality that produces real products and services from it. All media become immediately translatable into one another, capable of instant recall and transmission to any point within the network. Perhaps the greatest problem posed by the technology is a perceptual one, in recognising that digital representation is now the universal medium and machine of our culture. Orchestrated by software, it is as much the engine-room of production as it is the keeper of information. If it becomes the keeper of knowledge, the question arises whether humanity is ready to pass that role over. That day, if it ever comes, is some way away. For the time being we are left to come to terms with a new multi-layered existence – 'an electronic version of the noosphere'[205] – full of technological excitement but with inherent risks built in.

NOTES

1. U.S. Congress Office of Technology Assessment, *Critical Connections: Communication for the Future*, OTA-CIT-407 (Washington, DC: U.S. Government Printing Office, January 1990, pp. 3–23.

2. John Howkins, 'The Management of the Spectrum', *Inter Media* 7(5), pp. 12–16.

3. Ithiel de Sola Pool, *Technologies of Freedom (1986)*, comments: 'Machines that think, that bring great libraries into anybody's study, that allow discourse among persons a half-world apart, are expanders of human culture'.

4. See for example, Ian Miles, *Home Informatics – Information Technology and the Transformation of Everyday Life*, (Pinter Publishers, London, 1988).

5. 18 *Encyclopaedia Britannica* 15th Edition, 1979, p. 66. The Morse Code is a system of communication in which letters of the alphabet and numbers are represented by patterns of short and long signals, which may be conveyed as sounds, flashes of light, flags, electrical pulses, etc.

6. When teleprinters were introduced for transmission and reception of messages it was necessary to standardise the signal and transmission elements for individual characters. This was agreed in 1932 and designated International Alphabet No. 2 (IA2), based on the work of Murray, Baudot and others. Quoted in Smale, *Introduction to Telecommunications Systems* (1986) pp. 104–5.

7. Smale, *Introduction to Telecommunications Systems* (1986) pp. 77, 113.

8. Ibid., p. 76, n. 1.

9. Ibid., p. 114.

10. Herbert Ungerer (with the collaboration of Nicholas Costello) *Telecommunications in Europe* (1989, Commission of the European Communities).

11. The concept of the race sprang from the success of British sailors Francis Chichester, Alec Rose and later Robin Knox-Johnston in the pioneering days of offshore yachting in the 1960s. Races took place in 1973–74 (144 days); 1977–78 (134 days); 1981–82 (120 days); and 1985–86 (117 days). The 1989–90 race was won by the New Zealand ketch 'Steinlager II' in record time.

12. Meadow and Tedesco, *Telecommunications For Management* (1985) Ch. 2.

13. Communication by these methods has been described thus: Telegraph – writing at a distance; Telephone – speaking at a distance; Television – seeing at a distance and telecommunication – communicating at a distance. See Smale, op. cit., note ante, p. 1. The expression 'Telecommunication' derives from the Greek 'Tele' meaning 'far off'.

14. More than half the world's population inhabit countries in which fewer than 10 million telephones exist altogether. Tokyo has more telephones than the whole of Africa. In *The Missing Link*, Report of the Independent Commission for Worldwide Telecommunications Development (International Telecommunication Union, 1984) p. 13.

15. Ungerer, op. cit., pp. 38–9.

16. The strength of the signal is known as its amplitude and its alteration over distance is its attenuation.

17. Eryl Davies, *Telecommunications – A Technology For Change* (1983) p. 25.

18. Ibid., p. 30.

19. Williams, *A History of Technology* (1978) p. 1230.

20. British Telecom, *Pioneers in Telecommunications* (1985) p. 22.
21. Nicholl and Selfe, eds., *Understanding Communications – Poles, Pulses And The Network* (1986) p. 18.
22. In 1927 Harold Black improved the performance of repeaters with the negative feedback amplifier which improved voice quality and prevented interference between channels.
23. Carne, *Modern Telecommunication* (1984) p. 63.
24. Nicholl and Selfe, op. cit., p. 19.
25. Nicholl and Selfe, op. cit., pp. 20–21.
26. British Telecom, *Beyong The Intelligent Network* (1985).
27. Robert Techo, *Data Communications – An Introduction to Concepts And Design* (1980) pp. 95–6.
28. A third technique, known as statistical multi-plexing, has also been developed, originally for submarine telephone cables but also now for land and space links. It takes advantage of silent periods in speech to transmit other signals. See E. Bryan Carne, *Modern Telecommunication* (1984) p. 87.
29. Meadow and Tedesco, *Telecommunications For Management* (1985) p. 102.
30. OECD, *Major R&D Programmes For Information Technology* (1989) Information Computer Communications Policy Series No. 20, pp. 70–71.
31. Nicholl and Selfe, op. cit., p. 14.
32. Meadow and Tedesco, op. cit., p. 78.
33. Techo, op. cit., p. 111.
34. Carne, op. cit., p. 162.
35. Techo, op. cit., p. 115.
36. Williams, *A History of Technology* (1978) pp. 1251–2.
37. Amplitude portrays pressure, as in a sound wave which produces tiny variations in the voltage of an electric current from which the sound is reproduced following transmission.
38. Carne, op. cit., p. 68; Meadow and Tedesco, op. cit., p. 16.
39. That is 6 million Hertz. See Smale, op. cit., ch. 4, especially p. 33.
40. Alternating current is so-called since it comprises an electric current that reverses direction in a circuit at regular intervals.
41. The exact scales vary according to author. See, for example, Carne, op. cit., p. 88; Smale, op. cit., p. 9; Techo, op. cit., p. 56; Meadow and Tedesco, op. cit., p. 23; and Davies, op. cit., p. 39.
42. The frequency bands are: very low frequency below 30kHz (long distance telephony); low freq. 30kHz–300kHz (broadcasting, radio navigation); medium freq. 300kHz–3MHz (AM broadcasting, co-axial cable transmission); high freq. 3MHz–30MHz (radio telephony, short-wave radio); very high freq. 30MHz–300MHz (FM broadcasting, television, mobile radio); ultra high freq. 300MHz–3GHz (television, air-air, air-ground services); super high freq. 3GHz–30GHz (microwave, radar, multi-channel telephony); and extremely high freq. above 30GHz (waveguide). Source: Smale, op. cit., pp. 8–9; Techo, op. cit., p. 57.
43. Department of Trade and Industry, *The Use of the Radio Frequency Spectrum above 30GHz* (1988).

44. 'DTI Announces Choice of Frequency For Microwave Television Channels', Press Notice 89/614, 23 August 1989. The band 40.5–42.5 GHz will be assigned to the new Independent Television Commission for the local delivery of programme services by multipoint video distribution systems.

45. Thomas L. McPhail and Brenda M. Mcphail, *2001: A Strategist Forecast*, (1989, Graduate Program in Communication Studies, University of Calgary, Alberta, Canada) p. 20.

46. British Telecom, *Beyond the Intelligent Network* (1985) p. 16.

47. The inner core might be less than 0.01 of a millimetre.

48. Light travels at the rate of 300 million metres per second.

49. For a description of how fibre optic cable is constructed, see British Telecom, *Beyond The Intelligent Network*, pp. 16–19 and British Telecom, *Pioneers In Telecommunications*, pp. 30–31.

50. Today it is common for new office or commercial premises to have optical fibres installed throughout the building in ducts, so that telecommunications facilities are available as soon as the user's requirements are known. It is cheaper to wire the building in advance than to wait for the occupier to specify his needs.

51. Ungerer and Costello, op. cit., p. 64.

52. Meadow and Tedesco, op. cit., p. 80.

53. Intelligible speech requires 3.5kHz. With an allocated bandwidth of 4kHz, sampling the signal at 8000 times per second and converted to 8-bit code produces a speech transmission rate of 64kbits per second. Music requires higher frequency for full appreciation, with a 16kHz bandwidth, 32k sampling and 16-bit conversion code producing a 512kbit/s transmission requirement. Television flickers 25 times per second on screen. In the UK, each screen contains 625 lines and each line divides into 600 phosphor dots. This produces approximately 9 million samples per second ($25 \times 625 \times 600$). Each point has 64 brightness levels replicated in 6-digit code or 54 million bits/s for black and white TV or 70Mbit/s with colour/synchronisation added. Source: Nicholl and Selfe, op. cit., pp. 4.12–13.

54. This offers 7680 voice; 1024 music; and 8 TV channels.

55. Peter Large, 'Hi-Tech Failure: The Moral in the Fibre', The *Guardian*, 15 June 1990, p. 17.

56. Source: OECD, *Satellites and Fibre Optics – Competition And Complementarity* (1988, Information Computer Communications Policy Study No. 15) p. 15, quoting Terry Yake, Vice President for engineering of US Telecom Inc.

57. A typical HDTV screen has around 700,000 pixels or information points distributed over more than 1000 lines. Current standards deploy only 525 or 625 lines and a mere 120,000–180,000 pixels.

58. Work on HDTV has been pursued as a pan-European EUREKA project. The EUREKA initiative was launched in July 1985 to encourage collaboration and increase European competitiveness in the exploitation of technologies.

59. Ungerer and Costello, op. cit., p. 64. The figures for TAT-8 increased from

7560 to 37,800 using circuit multiplying technology (DCMS). For TAT-9, due to become operational in 1992, the figure increases to 15,120 voice circuits, rising to 80,000 with DCMS. Source: OECD, *Satellites and Fibre Optics*, (Information Computer Communications Policy Series No. 15, 1988) p. 33, quoting Euroconsult 'Ecospace' database.

60. There is the trans-pacific link (California-Hawaii) 1988; Hawaii-Japan TPC3 1990; Guam-HongKong 1990; plus private fibre optic links by Tel Optic and Cable & Wireless between New York-London in both 1989 and 1992. Source: OECD, *Satellites and Fibre Optics*, op. cit., p. 17.

61. Peter Large, op. cit.

62. For further details, see Miles, *Home Informatics* (1988, Pinter Publishers, London).

63. OECD, *Satellites and Fibre Optics*, op. cit., p. 15.

64. Costs of optical fibres have declined rapidly, for example from 3 European Currency Units/metre in 1977 to 0.3 ECU/m in 1988. Source: ibid.

65. Jonathan Alter, 'CNN's Global Village', *Newsweek*, 18 June 1990, pp. 45–50.

66. See Table of Artificial Satellites Launched in 1988, in *Telecommunication Journal* Vol 56, 1989.

67. OECD ICCP No. 15, op. cit., p. 7. In communications, a transponder is a device that receives and retransmits signals. The satellite will amplify the signal and retransmit to Earth at a different frequency. Most transponders operate at bandwidths of 36, 54 or 72 MHz.

68. Ungerer, *Telecommunications in Europe*, op. cit., p. 69. Satellite communications consist of three distinct elements: 'Uplink' – which transmits to the satellite; 'space segment' – comprising the orbiting transponders on satellites; and 'downlink' – which are the transmissions back to earth comprising the services available by satellite.

69. Based on 1986 estimates excluding military systems, the Soviet Union and China. Source: World Space Industry Survey, Ten Year Outlook. *Euroconsult* (1986) p. 155. Quoted in OECD ICCP No. 15, op. cit., p. 7.

70. For reference, see Ungerer, Berben and Costello, eds, *Telecommunications for Europe 1991 – The CEC Sources* (1989, Amsterdam/Springfield, VA/Tokyo).

71. To avoid signal interference, frequency diversity between reception and transmission of signals is deployed. At the higher Ku and Ka bands operating at 14/12 and 30/18 GHz the problem eases as terrestrial facilities such as microwave do not operate at that level.

72. Carne, op. cit., p. 156. In communications, a 'passband' is the range of signal frequencies that can be satisfactorily transmitted on a given channel (eg. the passband on a single voice-grade channel is 300–3000 Hz). Source: Longley and Shain, *Data & Computer Security* (1989) p. 246.

73. Heather E. Hudson, ed., *New Directions in Satellite Communications* (1985, Dedham, US) p. 1.

74. In Ungerer, Berben and Costello, eds., op. cit., p. 223.

75. *Intelsat News*, 6 (1), January 1990, p. 1.

76. OECD, *The Space Industry – Trade Related Issues* (1985, Paris) p. 68.
77. *Intelsat Report*, 1985–86, p. 3.
78. Carne, *Modern Telecommunication* (1984) p. 155.
79. Intelsat III (1968) 1500 and 4 TV; Intelsat IV (1971) 4000 and 2 TV; Intelsat IV-A (1975) 6000 and 2 TV; Intelsat V (1980) 12000 and 2 TV; Intelsat V-A (1985) 15000 and 2 TV.
80. The specification for DCME was agreed in August 1987.
81. The May 1990 Summit in Washington deployed a total of eight satellites – five Atlantic ocean and three Pacific satellites. A total of 12,000 transmit minutes were booked by broadcasters to cover the event.
82. Intelsat VI, *Factsheet* 1989.
83. James F. Chen, Birth of the INTELSAT VI TTC Operating System, *Intelsat News* 6 (1), January 1990, pp. 7–10. The system consists of 24 Hewlett-Packard minicomputers, 14 of which are connected through two Ethernet buses. The other 10 computers are located at seven centres around the world, linked through Intelsat's Satellite Control Centre. 750,000 lines of code in the Fortran, Pascal and C languages are necessary to operate the system.
84. Intelsat VII will have 36 transponders, 26 at C-band and 10 at Ku-band, as compared to 48 on Intelsat VI.
85. The solar array of the satellite will provide 4000 watts of power compared with 2600 watts on Intelsat VI. Source: Intelsat VII, *Factsheet* 1989.
86. Intelsat VII, *Factsheet* 1989. The solar array of Intelsat VII will provide 4000 watts of power compared with 2600 watts in Intelsat VI.
87. Intelsat Vista, *Factsheet* 1989. The Vista concept is based on consolidation of individual requirements and sharing of satellite capacity. Super-Vista takes this a stage further by employing new Demand Assigned Multiple Access equipment (DAMA), which targets transmission where it is most needed.
88. Intelsat IDR Service, *Factsheet* 1989.
89. *Telecommunications – A Technology for Change*, op. cit., p. 44.
90. Intelsat, *Overview of Major Challenges facing Intelsat* (1986) p. 3.
91. *Intelsat Report* 1988–89.
92. *Intelsat Report* 1985–1986, p. 5.
93. A.W. Meyers, 'And the Walls Come Tumbling Down – Record Breaking Coverage of Historical Events', *Intelsat News* (1), January 1990, p. 18.
94. Ungerer and Costello, op. cit., p. 71. The European Broadcasting Union is a professional association of broadcasting organisations founded after World War II to promote cooperation between its members and with worldwide broadcasting organisations. 32 countries are represented in the European Broadcasting area and a further 42 countries retain associate membership. See Stephen de B. Bate, *Television by Satellite – Legal Aspects* (1987, Oxford) p. 13 *et seq.*
95. A meeting of world HDTV experts took place in March 1990 and agreed on additional parameters for HDTV standards to be presented at the World Conference on frequency allocation in 1992, where the question of the radio spectrum for the satellite broadcasting of HDTV and sound will be con-

sidered. Source: ITU/90-7 Press Release.

96. Small antennae are called 'VSATs' – 'very small aperture terminals' – and comprise a dish measuring no more than 0.6 metres in diameter for reception of signals.
97. Global coverage is provided at both C- and Ku-Band frequencies.
98. Ungerer, Berben and Costello, op. cit., p. 223.
99. ISDN – Integrated Services Digital Network.
100. Intelsat Business Service, *Factsheet*, 1989.
101. Della Bradshaw, 'Broadcasting Bug Spreads its Wings', *Financial Times*, 1 September 1989, p. 14.
102. British Telecom, *International Communications in Manufacturing*, 1989, p. 15.
103. The six are BSB Datavision (subsidiary of British Satellite Broadcasting); Electronic Data Systems (EDS – subsidiary of General Motors); Maxwell Satellite Communications (subsidiary of Maxwell Communications Corp.); Satellite Information Service (SIS – Consortium including United Cable Television and Swedtel (subsidiary of Swedish PTO, Televerket).
104. Annabel Smyth, 'Satellite Business Services: Lift-Off at Last?', *Computer Bulletin*, December 1989, pp. 11–13.
105. 'Demand for Satellite-Provided Domestic Communications Services to the Year 2000', (1985, Lewis Research Center NASA). Quoted in OECD ICCP No. 15, op. cit., p. 8.
106. For example, compared with the terrestrial market for value-added services within the EC, which was worth ECU five billion in 1987, the value-added component of satellite business services that year was ECU 25 million. Source: Annabel Smythe, *Computer Bulletin*, op. cit., p. 11.
107. Press Release of the ITU/89-31, 23 October 1989. Such equipment has been used extensively to cover important events such as the Geneva and Reykjavik Heads of State Summits, Hurricane Hugo, the San Francisco earthquake and events from remote locations such as the Paris-Dakar car rally.
108. For an early study of this facility see Wood, Coates, Chartrand and Ericson, *Videoconferencing by Satellite: Opening Congress to the People* (1979, The George Washington University Final Report).
109. In Belgium, Canada, France, Finland, Japan, the Netherlands, Norway, Switzerland, West Germany and the USA. See *The British Telecom Business Catalogue* (1989) pp. 60–61.
110. Intelsat, *25th Anniversary Historical Chronology*.
111. British Telecom, News Release, January 27 1989.
112. Quoted in Ungerer and Costello, op. cit., p. 67. Source: Group for Analysis and Forecasting survey.
113. Ungerer, op. cit., p. 72.
114. For example, by exchange of current information, data concerning the state of supplies, fuel consumption, technical data, etc. Computer communications within a shipping organisation can treat a ship like any other branch office.

115. International Telecommunications Union Features, 'Transport and Telecommunications – Major Changes Under Way', October 1987, p. 4.

116. 'Europe: Green Light for Land Mobile Services by Satellite', *Telecommunications Journal* 56(XI), 1989, p. 685.

117. Kevin Townsend, 'Moving Targets Can Still Yield Rich Pickings', *Financial Times*, September 12 1988, p. VIII.

118. H. Nagata and D. Wright, 'A Short History of Maritime Communications', *Telecommunications Journal*, February 1990, pp. 117–25 at p. 123.

119. Rachel Johnson, 'Up above the Clouds, the Workaholic's Dream', *Financial Times*, 25 August 1989, p. 10.

120. Della Bradshaw, 'So Many Ways to get the Message through to the Truck', *Financial Times*, 22 February 1990, p. 12.

121. CEPT Press Release (NR23), 8 March 1990.

122. United Nations Centre on Transnational Corporations, *Transborder Data Flows: Transnational Corporations and Remote-Sensing Data* (1984, New York) p. 4.

123 See Office of Technology Assessment, *Commercial Newsgathering from Space – A Technical Memorandum* (May 1987, Washington DC, Ref OTA-TM-ISC-40).

124. Landsat spacecrafts carry scanners and high definition thematic mappers. The National Oceanographic and Atmospheric Administration of the US Department of Commerce are responsible for the Landsat Programme.

125. Patrick Dubarle, 'The Commercialisation of Space', *OECD Observer*, 153, August–September 1988, pp. 4–9.

126. Jeffrey W. Wsard, 'Microcomputers and Microsatellites', *Computer Bulletin* 2(5), June 1990, pp. 16–18.

127. OECD ICCP, Series No. 15, op. cit., p. 21.

128. Intelsat, *Overview of Major Challenges facing Intelsat*(1986, Washington DC) p. 11.

129. J.N. Pelton, 'ISDN Services Via Satellite and Terrestrial Means', *Telecommunciation Journal* 56(VI), 1989, pp. 390–94.

130. This is discussed in a report of the International Institute of Communications, Telecommunications – National Policy and International Agreement: A Briefing Paper in preparation for the World Administrative Radio Conference of 1979 (1977), pp. 3–4.

131 These are very low frequency (VLF); low frequency (LF); medium frequency (MF); high frequency (HF); very high frequency (VHF); ultra high frequency (UHF); super high frequency (SHF); and extra high frequency (EHF).

132. Department of Trade and Industry, Radiocommunications Division, Annual Report, 1988/89, pp. 4–5. The ongoing consultation began with a seminar in September 1988 at the Institute of Electrical Engineers in London when 200 people from industry and government met to discuss the reviews and to express opinions.

133. Arthur Andersen & Co., *New Directions in Telecommunications*, (Chicago, Illinois 1984). The comparative figures for 1985 were copper – 38%; microwave – 33%; Co-axial – 13%; Satellite – 10%; and Fibre Optics – 6%.

134. British Telecom, *News Review*, December 1986.
135. Mary Fagan 'Mercury Bites but not at Local Network Level', The *Independent*, 20 February 1990.
136. Geoffrey Charlish, 'Channelling the Way Out of Tight Bands', *Financial Times*, 27 March 1985, p. V.
137. Smale, op. cit., p. 152.
138. Dennis Longley and Michael Shain, op. cit., pp. 86–87.
139. Colin Long, *Telecommunications Law and Practice*, (1988, Sweet and Maxwell, London) p. 116. Licences were required under the Wireless Telegraphy Act 1949 and the Telecommunications Act 1984.
140. DTI Radiocommunications Division, *Annual Report 1988/89*, p. 12.
141. Mary Fagan, 'Mobile Phones Give Cell-Out Performance', The *Independent*, 20 February 1990. A figure of 15 million has been calculated as being the likely uptake of mobile units in the UK by the year 2000. Source: Hugo Dixon, 'When the Call is too Close', *Financial Times*, 5 August 1989, p. 6.
142. In May 1990 British Telecom became part of a group bidding for a licence to build and run a cellular service in Poland. The consortium is led by Swedish Telecom International, part of Televerket, the Swedish PTT, and includes Fintelcom as well as British Telecom. Source: British Telecom *News Release* (NR57) 23 May 1990.
143. The European service has been named the 'GSM Service' after the group responsible for creating the standard. This was the 'Groupe Special Mobile' set up by the European Conference of Postal and Telecommunications Administrations (CEPT). See Council Directive 87/372/EEC: *Developing Pan-European Mobile Communications*.
144. The numbers changed to '071' for inner London and '081' for outer London. The old '01' code for the whole of the Metropolis was abolished.
145. Hugo Dixon,'How Cordless Telephony Could Revolutionise People's Lives', *Financial Times*, 12 September 1988, p. VII.
146. Roderick Oram, 'Breathtaking Expansion', *Financial Times*, 19 September 1989, p. 40.
147. Ibid. Each territory will have two licensed operators. The average population covered by each territory will be 150,000 people, representing 22% of the population currently without the service. All the territories will have operational services in place by the end of 1991.
148. Ibid.
149. Five 1MHz blocks were given over to the business use of cordless telephones, including wireless private branch exchanges. Source: DTI Radio Regulatory Division, *Annual Report 1985/86*, p. 8.
150. Terry Dodsworth, 'Prospect of 1m Subscribers Woos Car Radio Networks', *Financial Times*, 12 September 1988, p. V.
151. Ibid. The cost is expected to be no more than 60% of the connection price for cellular. This is due to the larger cells of Band III which reduces the requirement on equipment.
152. Trevor Harvey, 'Paging – The Forgotten Story', Mobile

Telecommunications News 7(9), June 1989, pp. 24–7.

153. Suppliers include British Telecom, Mercury, Aircall and Racal Vodopage.
154. Della Bradshaw, 'The Need to Read Between the Pocket Telephone Lines', *Financial Times*, 24 August 1989, p. 14. The licenced companies are Phonepoint (British Telecom-led consortium); Ferranti Creditphone; Mercury Callpoint; and Byps (Barclays, Philips and Shell).
155. Terry Scott, *A4-Telecommunications Planning: Understanding the Key Issues – The Information Systems Guides*, (1989, John Wiley & Sons) para. 5.4.1.
156. That is either DECT – the Digital European Cordless Telephone Standard for cordless services, or GMS – Groupe Mobile Speciale for Cellular. See: Peter Purton, 'A Cordless Tug of War', *Financial Times*, 24 October 1989, p. 18.
157. OFTEL Press Notice (38/89), 11 December 1989.
158. Peter Purton, op. cit.
159. Malcolm Ross, Senior Analyst with Management Consultants, Arthur D. Little.
160. See H. Vaughan, 'Research Model for Time Separation Integrated Communication', *Bell System Technical Journal*, July 1959.
161. OECD, *Telecommunication Network-Based Services: Policy Implications*, Information, Computer, Communication Policy Series No. 18 (1989, Paris) pp. 17–18.
162. Ian Miles et al. *Information Horizons – The Long-Term Social Implications of New Information Technologies*, (1988, Edward Elgar, Aldershot) p. 55.
163. Most companies though produced gateways to IBM's System Network Architecture which allowed computation to be carried out at different locations. This was necessary because of IBM's 70% share of the mainframe market at the time.
164. This is the term used to describe the agencies responsible for providing national network facilities. It stands for Postal Telegraph and Telephone Authority. In the USA the regulator is the Federal Communications Commission (FCC).
165. Richard Sizer, 'Data Information and Networking', *Information Age* 10(4), October 1988, pp. 223–8.
166. X.25 Recommendation: Interface between Data Terminal Equipment and Data Circuit-Terminating Equipment for Terminals Operating in the Packet Mode on Public Data Networks and Connected to Public Data Networks by Dedicated Circuits). See Wai Sum Lai, 'Packet Mode Services: From X.25 to Frame Relaying', *Computer Communications* 12(1), February 1989, pp. 10–16.
167. EDI'88, *Proceedings of the Conference held in London in November 1988*, pp. 144–5.
168. Meadow and Tedesco, op. cit., pp. 138–40.
169. Another successful protocol is the 'Cambridge Ring' developed at Cambridge University.
170. U.S. Congress, Office of Technology Assessment, *Critical Connections: Communication for the Future*, OTA-CIT-407 (January 1990, Washington,

DC: U.S. Government Printing Office) p. 62.

171. Ian Miles et al, op. cit., pp. 57–60. See also Dennis Longley and Michael Shain, op. cit., pp. 365–7.

172. Steve Price, 'DTI Support for OSI', *Computer Communications* 9(2), April 1986, pp. 74–7.

173. Jan Wyllie, 'Linking Up Time', The *Guardian*, 19 April 1990, p. 33. It is known as 'Gosip' – Government OSI Profiles.

174. Conformance testing software has been jointly developed by the European Standards Promotion and Application Group (SPAG) and the American Corporation for Open Systems (COS). Also the Open Systems Testing Consortium (OSTC) has established to promote standard procedures in Europe among companies offering independent Spag/Cos conformance testing.

175. Jan Wyllie, 'Linking Up Time', The *Guardian*, 19 April 1990, p. 33.

176. P. Bocker and L. Schweizer, 'The ISDN: A Great Example of Synergy within CCITT', *Telecommunication Journal* 55, July 1988, pp. 448–52.

177. 'GPT Beckons UNIX Programmers', *Computing*, 15 February 1990, p. 9.

178. Ungerer and Costello, op. cit., p. 49.

179. British Telecom, News Release (NR68), 3 July 1990.

180. OTA Report (1990), op. cit., p. 48.

181. Ibid., p. 46, quoting David P. Helfrich, 'Fast Packet Switching: An Overview', *Telecommunications*, November 1988, p. 68.

182. OECD, ICCP No. 15, op. cit., p. 32.

183. OTA Report (1990), op. cit., p. 51.

184. OECD, ICCP Series No. 19, op. cit., p. 113.

185. OTA Report (1990), op. cit., p. 47. Optical switches can operate faster than electronic ones because 'beams of photons pass through each other without interfering whereas electrons get in each other's way'. This could produce new types of computer architecture hence the power increase in computers. See further, Eric E. Sumner, 'Telecommunications Technologies in the 1990's', *Telecommunications*, January 1989, p. 38; Lee Greenfeld, 'Optical Computing', *Computerworld*, 26 June 1986, pp. 83–9.

186. British Telecom, News Release (NR41), 12 April 1990.

187. British Telecom, News Release (NR20), 27 February 1990. The two systems are 'Telephony on Passive Optical Networks' (TPON) using fibre for customer local loops by means of a tree and brance configuration; and 'Broadband Integrated Distributed Star' (BIDS) which is a switched star network developed for cable TV but augmented for telephony.

188. CEPT, News Release (NR41), 10 April 1989.

189. British Telecom, News Release (PB5), 19 January 1989.

190. Barbara Darrow, 'Raising the Standard – FDDI', *PC Business World*, 6 February 1990, p. 7.

191. OTA Report (1990), op. cit., p. 48. The Report notes that a switching machine that in 1965 might have consisted of 100,000 lines of code, today requires at least 2 million. Productivity in software is therefore lagging behind hardware.

192. Peter Mitchell, 'Go-Faster Faxes and Phones on the Way', The *Independent*, 20 February 1990, p. 30.

193. Systems include Dialcom and Telecom Gold.

194. Kate Taphouse, 'Big Potential For Computerised Messaging', *Financial Times*, 24 November 1989.

195. Robert Hinton, *Information Technology and How to Use It*, (1988, ICSA Publishing Ltd., Cambridge) p. 26.

196. This distinguishes Viewdata from 'Teletext' services such as the BBC's CEEFAX and ITV's ORACLE which are one-way information providers delivered by the slower system of page reference scanned in sequence.

197. These include 'SFPS' – the Law Society's Solicitors Finance & Property Services, and the legal database – 'Lawtel'.

198. OECD, *New Telecommunications Services – Videotex Development Strategies*, Information Computer Communications Policy Series No. 16 (1988, Paris) p. 7.

199. It was originally developed as a domestic directory enquiry service, but rapidly expanded into an information service provider.

200. For a general discussion of the growth of consumer use of information technology in the home, see Ian Miles, *Home Informatics – Information Technology and the Transformation of Everyday Life*, (1988, Pinter Publishers, London).

201. Longley and Shain, op. cit., p. 198.

202. Ungerer and Costello, op. cit., p. 61. Other services include DATEV in West Germany (tax and accounting); CCMC and GSI, France (range of informational services); GEIS (part of US General Electric) and IBM.

203. Ungerer and Costello, op. cit., p. 47. This is freeing the conventional LAN to a broader role as a communications network linked to the public network.

204. Called 'Cohort 500' the system is the first of its kind in the world. It complies with the X.500 recommendation for electronic directories of the CCITT. It can also operate to X.400 message handling standards. Source: British Telecom, News Release (NR53), 16 May 1990.

205. Jan Wyllie, op. cit. The 'noosphere' was an expression coined by the Catholic Theologian, Tiellard de Chardin, to describe a new layer of the world, existing in human consciousness and outside the geographical, atmospheric and biological strata.

Bibliography

Aleksander and Burnett, *Thinking Machines – The Search for Artificial Intelligence* (1987).

Augarten, Stan, *Bit by Bit – An Illustrated History of Computers*, (1984).

Bate, Stephen de B., *Television by Satellite – Legal Aspects* (1987).

Berghaus, *The History of Railways*, (1960, English translation, 1964).

Blagden, *The Stationers' Company – A History, 1403–1959* (1960).

Brand, Stuart, *The Media Lab: Inventing the Future at MIT* (1986).

British Telecom, *Beyond The Intelligent Network* (1985).*The Microchip Revolution* (1985).*International Communications in Manufacturing* 1989.*Names and Dates for Students* (1984).

Brock, Gerald W., *The U.S. Computer Industry – A Study of Market Power* (1975).

Bronowski, *The Ascent of Man*, (1973).

Brown, P.B., *Dictionary of Electrical, Electronics, and Computer Abbreviations* (1985).

Burns and Martin, *The Economics of Information*.

Campbell, ed., *Data Processing and the Law* (1984).

Campbell Kelly, Martin, *ICL: A Business and Technical History* (1990).

Carne, *Modern Telecommunications* (1984).

Cassirer, *The Philosophy of the Enlightenment*, trans. Koelln and Pettegrove, (1955).

Close, Marten and Sutton, *The Particle Explosion* (1987).

Cranfield, *The Press and Society* (1978).*The Provincial Newspaper, 1700–1760* (1962).

Crutchley, *English Institutions – GPO* (1938).

Davies, Eryl, *Telecommunications – A Technology For Change* (1983).

de Sola Pool, Ithiel, *Technologies of Freedom* (1986).

Department of Trade and Industry, *The Use of the Radio Frequency Spectrum above 30GHz* (1988).

Derry and Williams, *A Short History of Technology* (1960).

Dickens, *All the Year Round*.

Dretske, *Knowledge and the Flow of Information* (1981).

Eardley, Marshall and Ritchie, *Information Systems in Development and Operation* (1989).

Elton, *British Railways* (1945).

Encyclopaedia Britannica, 15th Edition (1979).

Evans, *The Forging of the Modern State – Early Industrial Britain 1783–1870* (1983).

Feather, *The Provincial Book Trade in Eighteenth-Century England*, (1985).

Febvre and Martin, *The Coming of the Book – The Impact of Printing 1450–1800* (1984).

Ferguson, Marjorie, ed., *New Communication Technologies and the Public Interest* (1986).

Forester, Tom, ed., *The Information Technology Revolution* (1985).

Galileo, *Dialogue on the Great World Systems* June 1633.

George, *Machine Takeover* (1977).

Goldstine, *The Computer from Pascal to Von Neumann* (1972).

Greg, *London Publishing between 1550 and 1650* (1956).

Griffiths, ed., *Knowledge and Belief* (1967).

Guile, ed., *Information Technologies and Social Transformation* (1985).

Hankins, *Science and Enlightenment* (1985).

Hawking, Stephen W., *A Brief History of Time* (1988).

Hawking, Stephen W., 'Is the end in sight for theoretical physics?' (1980).

Hearn, *The Theory of Legal Duties and Rights* (1883).

Hinton, Robert, *Information Technology and How to Use It* (1988).

HMSO, *Telecommunications – A Technology for Change* (1983).

Hodges, *Alan Turing – The Enigma of Intelligence* (1983).

Hudson, Heather E., ed., *New Directions in Satellite Communications* (1985).

Kearney, ed., *Origins of the Scientific Revolution* (1964).

Kennedy, Noak, *The Industrialisation of Intelligence*, (1989).

Kline, 'Painting and Perspective', in Kearney, ed., *Origins of the Scientific Revolution* (1964).

Klipstein, E., *Description of a Newly Invented Calculating Machine* (1786).

Larsen and Rogers, *Silicon Valley Fever* (1984).

Lehnart, *Pre-Reformation Printed Books: A Study in Statistical and Applied Bibliography* (1935).

Leith, Philip, *Formalism in AI and Computer Science* (1990).

Longley, D., and Shain, M., *Macmillan Dictionary of Information Technology*, Third Edition (1989).

Longley, Dennis and Shain, Michael, *Data & Computer Security* (1989).

Mackie, *The Early Tudors 1485–1558* (1952).

Mackintosh, *Sunrise Europe* (1986).

Martin and Parker, *The Spanish Armada* (1988).

Mathias, *The First Industrial Nation – An Economic History of Britain 1700–1914* (1969).

Mathias, ed., *Science and Society 1600–1900* (1972).

Mayall, W.H., *The Challenge of the Chip* (1980).

McPhail, Thomas L., and McPhail, Brenda M., *2001: A Strategist Forecast* (1989).

Meadow and Tedesco, *Telecommunications For Management* (1985).

Mercer, David, *IBM: How the World's Most Successful Corporation is Managed* (1988).

Michael, *Information Law, Policy and the Public Interest*.

Miles, Ian, *Home Informatics – Information Technology and the Transformation of Everyday Life* (1988).

Miles, Ian, Rush, Howard, Turner, Kevin and Bessant, John, *Information Horizons – The Long-Term Social Implications of New Information Technology* (1988).

Moreau, *The Computer Comes of Age* (1986).

Morgan and Sayer, *Microcircuits of Capital* (1988).

Mumby, *Publishing and Bookselling* (1930).

Musson, *Science, Technology and Economic Growth in the Eighteenth Century* (1972).

Ne'eman and Kirsh, *The Particle Hunters* (1983, English translation1986).

Newton, *Opticks*.

Nicholl and Selfe, eds., *Understanding Communications – Poles, Pulses And The Network* (1986).

Nock, *British Steam Railways* (1961).

North, John, ed., *Mid-Nineteenth Century Scientists*, (1969).

Noyes, *The Institution of Property* (1936).

OECD, *Trade in Information, Computer and Communication Services* (1988).

—— *The Space Industry – Trade Related Issues* (1985).

—— *Trends of Change in Telecommunication Policy* (1987).

—— *Telecommunication Network-based Services: Policy Implications* (1989).

—— *Software – An Emerging Industry* (198).

—— *Satellites and Fibre Optics – Competition and Complementarity* (1988),

—— *Information Technology and New Growth Opportunities* (1989).

—— *The Internationalisation of Software and Computer Services* (1989).

OTA, *Intellectual Property Rights in an Age of Electronics and Innovation* (1986).*Critical Connections: Communications for the Future* (1990).

Penrose, Professor Roger, *The Emperor's New Mind* (1990).

Prum, *Information, Data and Continental Law*.

Robinson, *The British Post Office – A History* (1948).*Carrying British Mails Overseas* (1964).

Ross, *The Appeal to the Given – A Study in Epistemology* (1967).

Sherman, Barrie, *The New Revolution – The Impact of Computers on Society* (1985).

Simpson, David, Walker, Jim and Love, Jim, *The Challenge of New Technology* (1987).

Singh, *Great Ideas in Information Theory, Language and Cybernetics* (1966).

Slater, *Portraits in Silicon* (1987).

Smale, *Introduction to Telecommunications Systems* (1986).

Smith, *The Emergence of a Nation State – The Commonwealth of England 1529–1660* (1984).

Stevens, *Understanding Computers – A User Friendly Guide* (1986).

Techo, Robert, *Data Communications – An Introduction to Concepts And Design* (1980).

The *Organon*, the *Politics*, the *Ethics* and the *Poetics*.

Turkel, Sherrie, *The Second Self: Computers and the Human Spirit* (1984).

Ungerer, Herbert (with the collaboration of Nicholas Costello), *Telecommunications in Europe* (1989).

Universal Dictionary (1987).

313

Wheeler Cook, Walter, ed., *Fundamental Legal Conceptions – As Applied in Judicial Reasoning by Wesley Newcomb Hohfeld* (1966).
Wilkes, *Memoirs of a Computer Pioneer* (1985).
Williams, *A History of Technology* (1978).*The History of Technology – The Twentieth Century c.1900–c.1950.A Short History of the Twentieth Century* (1982).
Wood, Coates, Chartrand and Ericson, *Videoconferencing by Satellite: Opening*

Index

315